Clinical Metho in

SPEECH-LANGUAGE
PATHOLOGY

SEVENTH EDITION

Clinical Methods and Practicum in

SPEECH-LANGUAGE PATHOLOGY

SEVENTH EDITION

M. N. Hegde, PhD

PLURAL
PUBLISHING
INC.

9177 Aero Drive, Suite B
San Diego, CA 92123

e-mail: information@pluralpublishing.com
website: https://www.pluralpublishing.com

Typeset in 11/13 Minion Pro by Achorn International
Printed in the United States of America by Integrated Books International

For permission to use material from this text, contact us by
Telephone: (866) 758-7251
Fax: (888) 758-7255
e-mail: permissions@pluralpublishing.com

*Every attempt has been made to contact the copyright holders for material
originally printed in another source. If any have been inadvertently overlooked,
the publisher will gladly make the necessary arrangements at the first opportunity.*

Clinical methods and practicum in speech-language pathology
Library of Congress Cataloging-in-Publication Control Number: 2023037492
ISBN-13: 978-1-63550-691-4
ISBN-10: 1-63550-463-5

CONTENTS

Part II. Clinical Methods in Speech-Language Pathology

PREFACE TO THE SEVENTH EDITION

This is a text for students in speech-language pathology who are about to begin their clinical practicum. It also offers systematic information for supervisors of clinical practicums. The text describes the various structural, methodological, and ethical aspects of the student clinical practicum and its professional supervision. It enumerates clear expectations for both student clinicians and their clinical supervisors. Divided into two major parts, the book covers both the structural and functional aspects of the clinical practicum and a comprehensive review of assessment and treatment methods. It is based on the view that the clinical practicum is a learning experience for the students, and clinical supervisors are clinical teachers, mentors, and guides.

It is hoped that students who read this book prior to starting their clinical practicum will be better prepared to meet the exciting and yet often challenging task of providing ethical and effective services to children and adults with communication disorders. Readers of this book are expected to gain an understanding of the structure of different clinical practicum sites; principles of ethical practices; conduct, behavior, and competencies expected of them; justifiable expectations of their clinical supervisors; and the many fundamental principles of assessment and intervention across most disorders of communication. Clinical supervisors, too, may find the book helpful in creating a productive and exciting clinical practicum experience for their student clinicians.

The Singular Publishing Group published the first edition of this text in 1992. I am grateful to many instructors who have continuously adopted this book for the clinical practicums for well over 30 years. Throughout these three decades, instructors have offered praise and constructive criticism that have shaped each of the new editions. Instructors who have continued to adopt this text for their student clinicians have reinforced my belief that the book offers a single source of comprehensive information on clinical practicum and supervision. This revision for the seventh edition is done especially in the light of feedback from instructors.

I have kept and expanded the material the instructors have liked and have said that it should be a part of a book like this. Instructors who have adopted the book have generally found it to be a single comprehensive source on clinical methods and practicum. They have commended the easy-to-read writing style in a book that packs a great deal of information. I am grateful for their generous comments and continued adoption.

In the second part, I have revised the clinical methods sections to include new information or expand the existing information on assessment, target behaviors, and treatment strategies for all disorders of communication. The section on clinical practicums in public schools has been expanded to a significant extent to reflect current guidelines and practices. The text includes several boxed sections that refer students to specific guidelines.

Instructor-Prompted New Material in the Seventh Edition

Thank you, instructors; your thoughtful responses to the survey questionnaire that Plural had solicited from you have shaped this seventh edition of the book. I have carefully studied your concerns, comments, and suggestions. As per your suggestions for improvement, I have:

- Written a new chapter on assessment (Chapter 5) and included a sample assessment report in an attached appendix

- Infused multicultural issues into the content of the book in all relevant chapters and consequently eliminated a separate chapter on the topic

- Written a new chapter (Chapter 6) on clinical reports, treatment plans, and data documentation

- Specified ASHA's new or current requirements and guidelines for clinical practicum and certification in speech-language pathology

- Expanded and updated ASHA guidelines on telepractice, including the number of telepractice practicum hours and the simulation hours the students can count toward the total

- Summarized ASHA's latest position on the qualifications of clinical supervisors

- Described the qualifications and scope of practice of speech and language pathology assistants in various settings and speech aides in public schools

- Included in the various chapter appendices a sample each of:
  - an assessment report (Appendix, Chapter 5)

- a treatment plan (Appendix A, Chapter 6)
- an individualized education program (IEP) (Appendix B, Chapter 6)
- a progress report (Appendix C, Chapter 6)
- a SOAP note (Appendix D, Chapter 6)
- a baserate recording sheet template (Appendix A, Chapter 8)
- a baserate recording sheet example (Appendix B, Chapter 8)
- a treatment recording sheet template (Appendix C, Chapter 8)
- a treatment recording sheet example (Appendix D, Chapter 8)
- an intermixed probe recording sheet example (Appendix E, Chapter 8)
- a pure probe recording sheet example (Appendix F, Chapter 8)
- a quantitative summary of conversational skills template (Appendix G, Chapter 8)

- Uploaded the same reports and recording sheets to the companion website for the use of instructors and clinicians
- Written questions at the end of each chapter for the students to make a self-assessment of their understanding of the material
- Created a test bank and placed it on the companion website for the benefit of the instructors who wish to consider it
- Improved the scope and coverage of the PowerPoint presentation based on the book

I put significant efforts into this new edition and I hope the instructors will like the changes. I once again thank them for their suggestions and express my gratitude for their continued adoption of the text.

I would like to thank Laura Brown, Speech and Language Pathologist at the Clovis Unified School District, for her excellent help in revising and updating information related to clinical practicums in public schools, the work of speech aides, the kinds of reports SLPs write in educational settings, and the various educational codes and regulations that govern speech-language services offered to the students. Laura Brown's review of the first part of the book and her suggestions to update and improve the content have been valuable.

This revision for the seventh edition would not have been possible without the sustained support from the excellent staff at Plural Publishing. I thank Valerie Johns, Executive Editor, for her expert, friendly, and timely help at every stage of my revision for the new edition. I also thank Lori Asbury, Production Manager, and Jessica Bristow, Production Editor, for

their efficient and courteous work on getting this book beautifully produced. My thanks are also due to Kristin Banach for her diligent work on
marketing this book and to Marty Lew for his excellent sales efforts. The
quiet, competent, and supportive hand of Angie Singh, President and CEO
of Plural Publishing, has always worked behind the scenes to make it all
happen. I thank her and her exceptional team.

M. N. Hegde

COMPANION WEBSITE MATERIALS

 Look for this icon throughout the text directing you to the following materials available on the PluralPlus companion website:

- Glossary of Educational Abbreviations and Acronyms
- Glossary of Medical Abbreviations and Symbols
- Sample Clinical Interview
- Discrete Trial Baseline Procedure and Recording Sheet
- Dysfluency Types and Calculation of Dysfluency Rates
- Obtaining and Analyzing Conversational Speech Samples
- Sample Probe Recording Sheet
- Sample Treatment Plan
- Sample Lesson Plan
- Sample Diagnostic Report
- Discrete Trial Treatment Procedure and Recording Form
- Daily Progress Notes
- Sample Progress Report
- Sample Final Summary
- Sample Referral Letters

ABOUT THE AUTHOR

M. N. Hegde, PhD, is Professor Emeritus of Speech-Language Pathology at California State University–Fresno. He holds an MA in experimental psychology, a postgraduate diploma in clinical psychology, and a PhD in speech-language pathology. Dr. Hegde is a recipient of numerous awards, including the Outstanding Professor Award from the California State University, the Distinguished Alumnus Award from the Communication Sciences and Disorders Department at Southern Illinois University, and the Outstanding Contribution Award from the California Speech Hearing Association. Recently he was bestowed with the International Travel Fellowship Award from the Indian Speech and Hearing Association with an invitation to give the keynote address at the National Convention of the Association in New Delhi. A specialist in fluency disorders, child language disorders, research methods, and treatment procedures in communication disorders, Dr. Hegde enjoys world renown as a researcher, presenter, contributor of original articles to leading national and international journals, and is also the critically acclaimed author of more than two dozen highly regarded books in speech-language pathology. He has edited more than 25 books for different publishers and is on the editorial board of several scientific journals and has been a guest editor of international journals. He is also a consultant to publishing houses.

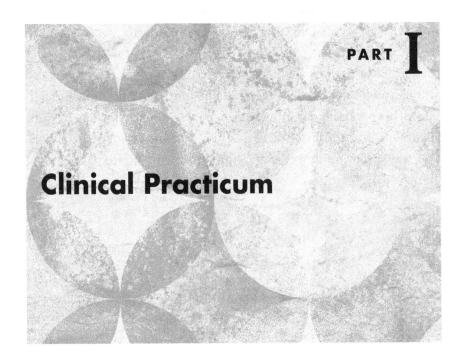

Clinical Practicum

You have completed certain graduate-level courses in your communication disorders curriculum and gained the essential knowledge about communication and its disorders. You are ready for clinical practicum and you are excited about it. And yet, not knowing the details of the practicum experience itself, you may be somewhat apprehensive. A clear understanding of what is expected of you and what kinds of support you can expect from your faculty and supervisors will help alleviate this apprehension. Therefore, this book introduces you to all important aspects of clinical practicum.

Part I of the text offers (a) descriptions of clinical practicum (Chapter 1), (b) organization of clinical practicum (Chapter 2), (c) the conduct of the student clinician (Chapter 3), and (d) the supervisor and the student clinician (Chapter 4). Read this part of the text carefully to understand what practicum is, how to interact with your supervisor, and generally, how to prepare yourself for the experience.

Part II of the text includes descriptions of clinical methods you will use while working with your clients during your clinical practicum. This part includes information on assessment, target behaviors, treatment procedures, procedures to reduce undesirable behaviors, and ways to promote generalization and maintenance of treatment gains.

CHAPTER 1

Clinical Practicum in Speech-Language Pathology: An Overview

Student Learning Outcomes

After reading this chapter, student clinicians are expected to:

- Describe what clinical practicum is and self-evaluate whether they meet their department's preclinic requirements
- Specify how the American Speech-Language-Hearing Association (ASHA), state speech-language hearing associations, state licensure boards, and departments of education affect clinical practicum
- Understand and adhere to the ASHA guidelines on practicum
- State the guidelines on telepractice in speech-language pathology
- Understand the role of, and how to interact with, speech-language pathology assistants (SLPAs)

Speech-language pathology is both an academic discipline and a clinical profession. Therefore, speech-language pathology degree programs at colleges and universities include two types of training.

The first type of training is offered through **academic coursework,** the foundation for clinical practicum. You are knowledgeable about the academic training because you have already completed all of your undergraduate program and some of the graduate program. You may take some academic courses along with your clinical practicum. Through academic training, you have gained the essential knowledge that you can expand through your own independent study. You have learned to carefully analyze the validity of new ideas and trends in the assessment and treatment of communication disorders.

The second type of training is offered through **clinical practicum,** a structured opportunity to apply and practice what you have learned in academic courses under the guidance of your clinical mentor (supervisor). You will have diverse clinical experiences that help you diagnose communication disorders, explore your clinical interests for future specialized studies, and consider a suitable employment setting for yourself. The combination of academic coursework and clinical practicum provides you with well-rounded training in speech-language pathology and prepares you to pursue a variety of career options.

This text is on clinical practicum. Therefore, if you have any questions regarding academic requirements, contact your academic advisor. Consult your advisor, clinical supervisor, or clinic director for questions regarding clinical practicum.

Clinical Practicum: An Overview

An exciting component of your education in speech-language pathology, your clinical practicum experiences are designed to prepare you for your future role as a professional speech-language pathologist (SLP). As a student clinician, you will work with a variety of professionals and clients. Your clinical practicum is a supervised experience in which you learn professional skills of assessing and treating people with communication disorders. It is also an opportunity to expand on your knowledge of communication and its disorders. Under supervision, you work individually or as a member of a team.

Enrollment in clinical practicum is a required part of the curriculum in programs accredited by the **American Speech-Language-Hearing Association (ASHA)**. Generally, students acquire most of the required 400 hours of supervised clinical practicum during their graduate study. ASHA allows only a maximum of 50 hours of clinical practicum completed at the undergraduate level. In most cases, experience at the undergraduate level may be limited to observing graduate students providing clinical services because ASHA requires 25 hours of guided observation as a part of the 400 hours of clinical practicum. Undergraduate students may assist a graduate clinician in charting responses, developing stimulus materials, and eventually working with a client for one or two sessions as the primary clinician. Your training program structures your activities to maximize your learning as well as your academic and clinical success.

Beginning student clinicians may be assigned clients with less complex disorders. Client assignment is based on the academic courses the students have completed. For example, during your first semester of graduate work, you may enroll in a course in speech sound disorders in children, and therefore, you may be assigned clients with only those disorders. As you complete coursework on other disorders of communication, your caseload will vary.

In some academic programs, student clinicians may be assigned clients with disorders on which they have not had graduate level course work. For example, as a first-semester graduate student, you may not have taken a course on fluency disorders. Nonetheless, in your clinical practicum, you may be assigned a client with a fluency disorder based on your under-graduate class in fluency and the expertise of your clinical supervisor. If you are assigned a client with a disorder for which you do not have much academic preparation, seek out guidance from your supervisor and profes-sors. It is your responsibility to garner the knowledge needed to assess and treat your clients efficiently and effectively.

The beginning student clinicians typically conduct one-on-one indi-vidual therapy sessions lasting from 30 to 50 minutes. Subsequent to the COVID-19 pandemic, ASHA guidelines on clinical practicum allow for up to 125 hours of supervised teletherapy. You may also be assigned to group therapy along with fellow student clinicians, however. University clinics may operate specialized group programs (clinics) including those for pre-schoolers, adolescents, or adults with neurologically based communication disorders. In the preschool group clinics, you may directly teach speech and language skills and conduct circle-time greeting activities, snack-time activities, and farewells. Adolescent students may master more advanced pragmatic or academic language skills in their groups. Adults with aphasia, traumatic brain injury, dysarthria, apraxia of speech, and right hemisphere disorder may practice social communication skills in the group format. You may be hand-selected by your professors to participate in the group therapy based on how you have performed in their classes or individual clinics.

Most universities require student clinicians to complete a certain mini-mum number of clinical hours at their own clinics before they are assigned to off-campus practicum sites. Such sites may include hospitals, other clin-ics, and public schools.

As you progress through your clinical and academic programs, you are given progressively greater responsibility in planning, evaluating, and treating clients. As a beginning student clinician, you will not be expected to have all the answers; your clinical supervisor will help you find those answers. Although you will be supervised throughout your clinical practicum, as you gain clinical experience, you will be expected to independently handle your clinical responsibilities. Eventually, you will be expected to conduct your clinical duties with minimal supervisory guidance.

General Preclinic Requirements

In addition to a solid academic foundation, good writing skills are necessary for success in clinical practicum. Equally important is the learning of professional speech in addressing people from all walks of life and of all ages. Finally, there are certain personal characteristics that are essential to successful clinical practicum. For example, you must be conscientious and reliable. You should be well prepared for your sessions. You should organize your schedule and allocate sufficient time to your clinical responsibilities.

Moreover, your flexibility and nonjudgmental disposition will influence your clinical success. A specific clinic assignment with which you begin a semester may be altered mid-term due to a client's schedule change, supervisor change, or other uncontrollable variables. You should accept and adapt quickly to such changes. You may be assigned a client whom you dislike—perhaps you do not approve of your client's demeanor or lifestyle. Nonetheless, you should be nonjudgmental and flexible enough to effectively work with this person. You should be committed to providing the best quality of client care possible. You are not expected to enter clinical practicum with all the necessary skills, but you should show progress in learning from your clinical experiences and the interactions with your supervisor.

Academic Requirements

You may complete the preclinic academic requirements at both the undergraduate and graduate levels. At the *undergraduate level*, your first course may be an introduction to communication sciences and disorders. Your subsequent courses may include phonetics, anatomy and physiology of speech, swallowing disorders, speech and hearing sciences, and those related to typical acquisition of speech and language. Clinical courses, especially those related to speech sound disorders, language disorders in children, voice disorders, and fluency disorders also may be taken at the undergraduate level.

Graduate courses provide you with more advanced information on all aspects of communication sciences and on assessment and treatment of speech-language disorders. Building on the bases of undergraduate courses, graduate courses offer more research-based information and emphasize specialized knowledge. For example, besides taking advanced courses in speech sound production and language, you also take courses in fluency disorders; adult language disorders, including aphasia; adult speech disorders, including dysarthria and apraxia of speech (motor speech disorders); craniofacial anomalies (especially cleft lip and palate); augmentative and alternative communication; and dysphagia.

Although *course requirements and sequences vary* to some extent from university to university, all students must meet the ASHA academic standards for certification. Discuss the specific requirements with your advisor well in advance of the time you plan to begin your clinical practicum.

General Writing Requirements

Accurately documenting and precisely reporting clinical information in writing are necessary skills in the practice of speech-language pathology. The manner of clinical documentation and the formats of reports influence several variables, including (a) insurance companies' approval of reimbursement for clinical services; (b) the assessment results that demonstrate eligibility criteria for client placement on an Individualized Education Program (IEP) in public schools; (c) reimbursement by government agencies for services rendered; and (d) decisions regarding the need for initiating, continuing, or discontinuing services. Therefore, you will learn to write reports in different formats.

Student clinicians are required to write a variety of clinical reports, including assessment reports, treatment programs, lesson plans, and progress notes. Regardless of varying writing requirements in different practicum sites, your writing skills should be acceptable at each of your assignments. Not only your supervisors, but also your clients. their families, physicians, school psychologists, teachers, and other SLPs may read your reports. Unless you have had a course on professional writing in communication disorders, you are not expected to know the specific formats for reports and some of the technical terms before clinical enrollment, but you should write clearly, concisely, and grammatically. Your writing should be well organized, coherent, free from spelling errors, avoid prejudicial and discriminatory tone and terms, and be clear and simple enough to be understood by the intended audience. With these basic writing skills, you will find it easier to adapt your writing to the different formats and styles expected at various sites. Chapter 6 has more on principles of writing and formats and contents of various clinical reports.

If you are concerned about your general writing skills and your program does not offer a course on professional writing, discuss your problem with your advisor as early in your program as possible. Your advisor can assist you in overcoming your writing problems. You may need to take a writing course, you may need additional practice in writing, and you may need to read seriously some books on good writing. A classic small book with big effect is Strunk and White's *Elements of Style* (1999), a highly recommended source for decades. Also, you may practice general, scientific, and professional writing skills in a book that is designed for self-teaching. One such book is by Hegde (2024), which gives exemplars of scientific and professional writing, along with opportunities to practice writing skills on the pages of the book itself. With these and other resources your supervisors may recommend, master good writing skills.

Oral Communication Skills

Effective oral communication skills are essential to the practice of speech-language pathology. Student clinicians communicate with clients of varied educational, socioeconomic, and cultural backgrounds. They interact with other professionals. They discuss their clients' evaluation, treatment, and progress with physical therapists, physicians, nurses, teachers, audiologists, psychologists, and other SLPs.

In all speaking situations, you must make yourself understood. With most clients, speak in simple and brief language. Use technical terms, advanced vocabulary, and complex concepts with individuals who are familiar with them. With all individuals, introduce technical terms with their simple descriptions. Use initialisms (e.g., MLUs, IEPs, AOS) sparingly, and always express the complete terms. You should develop the flexibility to speak at whatever level the communication situation requires. In all instances, you should clearly and concisely articulate information that maximizes the listener's understanding. In doing so, you will promote *health literacy,* which refers to an understanding of basic health information and services that support appropriate decisions regarding assessment and treatment (American Speech-Language-Hearing Association, n.d.a). You promote health literacy when you speak and write clearly, supplement your expressions with charts or graphs, and answer questions. For example, to help facilitate the understanding of complex information, such as standardized test scores, a student clinician or SLP may verbally explain the standard scores and percentile ranks a child has achieved on a test, supplemented by such visuals as the bell curve that plots the scores. More information on health literacy and the means to achieve it with your clients is available at https://www.asha.org/slp/healthliteracy/. Moreover, your department or one of the other departments in your university may offer a counseling course that teaches specific interpersonal communication skills. Consider taking such a course and discuss this with your academic advisor.

Personal Characteristics

Several personal characteristics are essential for successful clinical work. *Responsible behavior* is probably one of the most important characteristics.

Responsible behaviors include being prepared for treatment sessions, being on time in meeting with clients, writing timely reports, and interacting with office staff and clinical supervisors in a professional manner. You should promptly meet all deadlines for clinical assignments and scheduling of clients; complete various reporting forms the clinic administrative staff needs; and submit diagnostic reports, treatment plans, and lesson plans on time. Regardless of other academic or personal commitments, you must be well prepared for your diagnostic and treatment sessions.

To meet your many obligations efficiently, you should organize your time. You should **establish priorities** and **prepare in advance**. An examination, a new client evaluation, and a major class paper may all be due on the same day. Obviously, to accomplish all of these well, you must allow for sufficient preparation time and get started on them well in advance of the deadlines.

Student clinicians work with diverse people. Therefore, it is important for them to **maintain professional boundaries while empathizing with their clients and their families**. Neither the clients nor the clinicians should get overly involved in the personal lives of the other. However, you must combine your technical knowledge with care, concern, and regard for your clients' living situations and their personal problems that affect assessment or treatment outcomes. For example, it may not be productive to expect clients living alone in private care facilities to be able to find people with whom to practice a speech assignment. However, knowing this, you might talk with cooperative nursing assistants and ask them to help your clients practice their speech. It will be important for you to know and understand the interactions among your clients' disabilities or limitations, living situations, and support systems and how such factors affect your intervention.

Student clinicians should learn to work independently within the limits of their knowledge and the level of experience. For example, as a beginning clinician, you are expected to rely on your supervisor for assistance more than experienced clinicians do. However, you still must be prepared to research material independently and, with your supervisor's help, document and evaluate improvement in each clinical session, determine what needs to be changed or modified, and implement your supervisor's suggestions. You should demonstrate systematic progress toward working independently. See Chapter 4 for more on student clinician responsibilities.

Professional and Interprofessional Knowledge

Several agencies and professional organizations affect your training and career in SLP. Prior to enrolling in clinical practicum, you should have a basic knowledge of the various accrediting and licensing agencies that regulate the profession of speech-language pathology.

There are two agencies that affect your training and professional career the most: ASHA, the national professional organization and your state's agency (including that of the District of Columbia, DC) that issues licenses to SLPs and audiologists. The names of state licensing agencies vary. For instance, it is the Board of Examiners for Speech-Language Pathology and Audiology in California and the Department of Commerce, Community and Economic Development in Alaska. Each state and the DC have their own licensure requirements. For licensing and other professional requirements in the U.S. territories (Puerto Rico, Guam, and the U.S. Virgin Islands), visit the ASHA website and the specific territory's government website.

The American Speech-Language-Hearing Association

ASHA is the national scientific and professional organization of SLPs and audiologists. You will hear much about ASHA, which has various guidelines and requirements that affect your education and your clinical practicum. Students are encouraged to become members of ASHA's student organization, the **National Student Speech-Language-Hearing Association (NSSLHA)**.

ASHA has a long history of leadership in shaping the scientific, academic, and professional activates of communication sciences and disorders. The organization is an advocate for individuals with communication disorders and the professionals who provide services to these individuals. The association has nine purposes or goals (American Speech-Language-Hearing Association, 2017a).

ASHA works in various ways to help maintain high standards of clinical competence for SLPs and audiologists. The governing agency of ASHA, the Board of Directors, comprises 16 officers including the president, the past president, the president-elect, all vice presidents, and the national advisor to the NSSLHA. The chief executive officer of the association is

The Purposes of the American Speech-Language-Hearing Association

1. Encourage basic scientific study of the processes of individual human communication with special reference to speech, language, hearing, and related disorders

2. Promote high standards and ethics for the academic and clinical preparation of individuals entering the discipline of communication sciences and disorders

3. Help the professionals acquire new knowledge and skills

4. Promote investigation, prevention, and the diagnosis and treatment of disorders of communication and related disorders

5. Foster improvement of clinical services and intervention procedures concerning such disorders

6. Stimulate exchange of information among persons and organizations and disseminate such information

7. Inform the public about communication sciences and disorders, related disorders, and the professionals who provide services

8. Advocate on behalf of persons with communication and related disorders, and

9. Promote the individual and collective professional interests of the members of the Association

Note: Bylaws of the American Speech-Language-Hearing Association by the American Speech-Language-Hearing Association. (2017a). Available from: http://www .asha.org/policy

the only nonvoting member. This governing agency interacts with various advisory councils and committees to identify and respond to concerns and priorities of the profession.

ASHA sponsors conferences and workshops to encourage continuing professional education. It collects and disseminates data related to research, clinical service delivery, education, and career opportunities. The organization publishes scientific journals in which research is reported. The organization establishes accreditation and certification procedures that outline minimal standards of education and clinical service delivery. It specifies policies on clinical practice and academic and clinical preparation of students.

Two very important documents that stipulate the standards to which a clinician must adhere are the ASHA Code of Ethics and the ASHA Scope of Practice. As a student clinician and future professional, you must understand these documents. The documents present standards that are designed to protect consumers and the professionals who serve them (American Speech-Language-Hearing Association, 2017a). See Chapter 3 for detailed information on the Code of Ethics and other policy documents.

ASHA Accreditation

ASHA's **Council on Academic Accreditation in Audiology and Speech-Language Pathology (CAA)** accredits academic programs. The CAA develops accreditation standards for graduate programs, evaluates such programs, grants certificates to accredited programs, maintains a registry of such programs, and provides the registry to the public and other organizations. Accreditation helps prepare graduate students to enter the workforce, safeguards the public's interests, and encourages university programs to make self-evaluations to effect improvements to their programs.

The CAA comprises 18 voting members who hold a 4-year term: 11 from academic programs, five clinical practitioners, one additional audiologist, and one public member. A university must request accreditation of its program in speech-language pathology, audiology, or both. ASHA accredits only master's degree programs.

The application process includes a self-study application, peer review, site visit, final evaluation, and appeal of the accreditation decision (if needed). ASHA will send a site visit team of trained professionals to evaluate the programs seeking accreditation. The team looks at the quality and number of faculty teaching the courses, the curriculum offered by the department, physical facilities and instructional equipment, clinical facilities, research laboratories, the library, the administrative support, and such other factors that affect the education of future SLPs and audiologists.

The professionals evaluating clinical services offered by a department look at the qualifications and certification status of clinical supervisors, financial resources and management, adequacy of clinical facilities and equipment, and all other factors that affect the quality of clinical services offered to the public. The teams may schedule meetings to discuss the training program with current students as well as graduates of the program. After the site visit, the team submits a report to the ASHA board. Based on the report, a final decision on whether to accredit the program is made.

Accreditation standards are reviewed and possibly revised every 5 to 8 years. The most recent revision went into effect in January 2023. Accredited programs must continue to submit annual reports to the CAA to maintain accreditation. Currently, there are over 250 accredited master's programs in speech-language pathology (Council on Academic Accreditation in Audiology and Speech-Language Pathology, 2018). Accredited institutions may be found at: www.caa.asha.org/programs/

The CAA requirements directly influence you and your training program. First, if you are attending a program accredited by ASHA, you are assured that the department has met ASHA's standards. Second, if you obtain a master's degree from an ASHA-accredited program, you will be eligible to apply for the Certificate of Clinical Competence in either speech-language pathology or audiology.

ASHA Certification

ASHA certifies both audiologists and SLPs. The **Certificate of Clinical Competence** is more commonly referred to as the CCC (pronounced "sees"). The **Council for Clinical Certification (CFCC)** sets the standards for and awards the CCC to SLPs and audiologists who have met ASHA's academic, clinical, and ethical standards. Certification "represents a level of excellence" in the field (American Speech-Language-Hearing Association, n.d.b). Under ASHA's guidelines, individuals with their CCC may supervise student clinicians and such support personnel as SLPAs. When you complete a program of study and clinical experience approved by ASHA, you may receive certification either in audiology (CCC-A) or speech-language pathology (CCC-SLP).

Certification is voluntary; however, it demonstrates assurance that the SLP or audiologist has gone beyond the minimum requirements for state licensure, which may provide increased opportunity for employment (Council for Clinical Certification in Audiology and Speech-language Pathology of the American Speech-Language-Hearing Association, 2018). As of 2022 year's end, over 208,000 professional SLPs and audiologists held ASHA certification. Currently, ASHA evaluates CCC applicants based on the 2020 Speech-Language Pathology Standards and Implementation Procedures that were revised in September 2021 and again in March and August 2022. These revised standards went into effect on January 1, 2023. A significant element of the January 2023 standards is that up to 125 hours of graduate student supervised clinical practicum and 25% of clinical fellowship direct client contact hours may be acquired via telepractice. Those standards also allow for telesupervision of up to 3 hr of clinical fellowship experience per segment. What follows is a review of the basic requirements for certification in audiology or SLP.

Complete a Program of Study Leading to a Graduate Degree

You should earn a master's (MA or MS) or doctoral (PhD, AuD, or SLPD) degree in the area in which you are applying for certification at an accredited institution of higher education. Your graduate coursework and practicum must be initiated and completed at a program accredited by ASHA's CAA in the specialty for which the certification is sought. The education program completed must include a minimum of 36 semester coursework hours completed, which includes both academic work and clinical practicum at the graduate level. In addition to courses in speech-language pathology and audiology, you should also study the following:

- Principles of biological sciences, chemistry, physical sciences, statistics, and the social/behavioral sciences

- Basic processes and principles of human communication and swallowing

- Disorders of speech sound production, fluency, voice and resonance, language, hearing, swallowing, cognitive aspects of communication (e.g., memory, attention), social communication, and augmentative and alternative communication

- Prevention, assessment, and intervention for communication and swallowing disorders

- Knowledge of the Standards of Ethical Conduct

- Knowledge of research methods and data analysis and how they are used in evidence-based practice

Demonstrate the Required Knowledge

Your educational program will have been designed such that you acquire the knowledge and skills necessary to speak, listen, write, understand, and evaluate written clinical and research information at a level sufficient for clinical practice and professional work. The coursework you take as part of your general undergraduate requirements may fulfill some of these requirements.

You and your academic department are responsible to document on ASHA's **Knowledge and Skills Acquisition form (KASA)** that you have acquired the knowledge and skills necessary to practice the profession. Academic departments have a procedure to track and record each student's progress in acquiring the knowledge and skill. Your academic advisor and clinic supervisor (along with the department chair and clinic director) may monitor your progress and help you document how and when you have met specific requirements. This documentation should be continuous and current. Each semester, when you meet with your academic advisor, you may update your KASA form.

Pass the Praxis Examination

As you progress through your graduate program, you will be required to demonstrate your knowledge and skills in a variety of ways. Formative assessments will include oral, written, and clinical measures. You will be required to pass the summative national assessment known as the Praxis Examination in Speech-Language Pathology, which is part of the Praxis II: Subject Assessments owned and administered by ETS (Educational Testing Service, 2015). The test items are written by experts selected by ASHA.

Individuals often take the examination soon after they have completed their academic courses or after their final comprehensive examinations at the university. Studying for a comprehensive examination also helps students prepare for the Praxis. There are books available and review courses offered on studying for the Praxis in Speech-Language Pathology; one such book is by Roseberry-McKibbin et al. (2024). The Praxis

- Consists of 132 objective questions covering all primary employment settings in three context categories: Foundations and Professional Practice; Screening, Assessment, Evaluation, and Diagnosis; and Planning, Implementation, and Evaluation of Treatment
- Contains questions from the main areas of practice: speech sound production; fluency; voice, resonance, and motor speech; receptive and expressive language; social communication; cognitive aspects of communication; augmentative and alternative communication; hearing; and swallowing
- May be taken on the computer and is often administered by your university's testing office
- Stipulates a passing score of 162 for ASHA certification in speech-language pathology. ASHA must receive the score directly from ETS. ETS has a site on the web regarding the Praxis at http://www.ets.org/praxis. You can obtain information about the test; register for the test; locate score reporting codes for ASHA, your academic institution, and state boards; participate in an interactive practice test; and access a study companion among other resources (Educational Testing Service, 2015).

Complete Clinical Fellowship (SLPCF)

The Speech-Language Pathology Clinical Fellowship (SLPCF) is designed to help you transition from student clinician to independent professional.

During your SLPCF you will learn many skills specific to service delivery in your employment setting and improve and hone the skills you learned as a student clinician. The SLPCF consists of paid (or volunteer) experience mentored by a professional holding current ASHA certification in speech-language pathology. The SLPCF is not part of a university clinical training program. Your university and former professors are not typically involved in your SLPCF.

After you graduate with a master's degree, you enter the SLPCF in an employment setting. Your employer can supply SLPCF mentoring. In fact, during your preemployment interviews, it is good practice to ask if SLPCF mentoring will be provided and by whom. However, you and your mentor need not work in the same setting. You may request a qualified SLP from outside your work setting to mentor your SLPCF. The clinical fellow must verify that the mentoring SLP holds current certification. This may be done on the online ASHA website's Certification Verification System. When you start working and have an SLPCF mentor, your SLPCF also begins. You do not need permission from ASHA to begin your SLPCF.

The SLPCF year must include at least 36 weeks of full-time experience (at least 35 hr per week) or the equivalent part-time experience (at least 5 hr per week), which totals at least 1,260 hours. Eighty percent of the typical work week must include direct clinical contact hours. Your mentor will regularly assess your work based upon the Clinical Fellowship Skills Inventory (CFSI) on the SLPCF Report and Rating Form, which will be reviewed at the completion of each trimester during your SLPCF. A score of 3 or higher must be achieved in each core skill assessed on the final segment of the experience.

You may submit your application for certification to ASHA (including the Standards for Clinical Certification in Speech-Language Pathology Verification by Program Director), dues/fees, official transcripts, Praxis scores, and disclosures documents (if necessary) at any time during or along with your SLPCF Report and Rating Form at the completion of your SLPCF. Once an SLPCF experience has been initiated, the application must be completed within 48 months and submitted to ASHA, which will process it in approximately 6 weeks. Once the CCC is conferred, you may now write CCC-SLP following your name and degree.

Adhere to the Code of Ethics

The ASHA Code of Ethics is vital to the practice of speech-language pathology. It presents guidelines and standards for the protection of clients and clinicians. All student clinicians and professionals seeking ASHA certification must abide by the Code of Ethics.

Chapter 3 contains a more detailed discussion of the Code of Ethics.

Maintain Clinical Certification

ASHA certification must be renewed every 3 years by accumulating **Continuing Education Units (CEUs)**. Within any 3-year period, at least 30 hours of professional development (continuing education) hours, including one hour in ethics, and two hours in cultural competency, cultural humility, culturally responsive practice, and/or diversity, equality, and inclusion, are required to renew certification (Council for Clinical Certification in Audiology and Speech-Language Pathology of the American Speech-Language-Hearing Association, 2018). To accumulate CEUs, you may participate in workshops and conferences and other activities offered by approved providers. You may also obtain CEUs by taking certain university coursework or through appropriate employer-sponsored in-service programs. However, to renew your certification, you must obtain your CEUs within a 3-year period beginning the first January following the date certification was awarded. Therefore, the workshops you attend while preparing to become an SLP will not count toward later CEU credit.

When your 3-year interval is complete, you must submit a Certification Maintenance and Compliance Form on or before December 31 of the year the interval is completed. The Compliance Form requires that affidavits be signed that affirm that your units have been completed and that you have abided by the Code of Ethics. To maintain your CCC, you must also maintain your ASHA membership by paying annual dues by December 31 of each year. Upon renewal of your dues, you will receive your membership card.

ASHA publishes a *Certification Handbook* that contains application forms as well as detailed information regarding academic, practicum, SLPCF, fees, and membership requirements. The latest version of the *Certification Handbook* is available for download at ASHA's website.

Although the CCC does not confer any legal status, it is nationally recognized as a requisite for practice in most employment settings, excluding public schools. University instructors, for example, cannot supervise clinical practicum if they don't have the CCC in their specialty. Many state licensure requirements are based on the CCC requirements, and holding the CCC may make it easier for you to obtain a license in certain states (Council on Academic Accreditation in Audiology and Speech-Language Pathology, 2018).

The certification standards that went into effect beginning January 1, 2020 require clinical supervisors and clinical fellowship mentors to have a minimum of 9 months' experience post-certification before serving as a supervisor, as well as 2 hr of professional development in the area of supervision post-certification; applicants for certification will take coursework that covers basic physics or chemistry knowledge; knowledge and skills will be refined to include speech sound production, fluency disorders, literacy, and feeding within the current nine core content areas; applicants will be encouraged to include interprofessional education and interprofessional practice into their clinical practicum/clinical fellowship experience.

International Reciprocal Recognitions

ASHA has negotiated with the Canadian Association of Speech-Language Pathologists and Audiologists (CASLPA), the Royal College of Speech and Language Therapists (RCSLT) in the United Kingdom, and the Speech Pathology Association of Australia Limited. These agreements provide reciprocal recognition among professional organizations in the United States, Canada, the United Kingdom, and Australia.

International agreements promote common standards of clinical competence and simplify the process for mutual recognition of credentials among participating organizations. They also promote free exchange of ideas among international communities of SLPs and audiologists.

State Licensure Boards

ASHA's CCC is not sufficient to practice speech-language pathology or audiology in any of the states. Regardless of their certification, credentials, or degrees, SLPs in private practice and medical settings must be licensed by the state before they can provide clinical services. While SLPCF for ASHA certification does not require permission to begin, your license or temporary license through your state of residence may require permission prior to beginning your employment, especially for private practice and work in medical settings.

Licensure is regulated by a state government agency (e.g., Board of Examiners for Speech-Language Pathology and Audiology). All states in the United States now have licensure requirements for SLPs. With the exception of only a few states, the state licensure requirements are compatible with those of the CCC. Many states also have licensure reciprocity with the CCC. SLPs providing services in public schools or federal government agencies may be exempt from the state licensure requirement.

ASHA-accredited university programs ensure that their graduates meet the requirements of the state licensure board as well as ASHA certification requirements. However, if you are planning to move to another state after you graduate, you should contact the licensure board of that state to ensure you will have met their requirements. Access ASHA's website at http://www.asha.org for more information on each state's requirements.

Specific licensure information can be obtained from the National Council of State Licensure Boards for Speech-Language Pathology and Audiology (NCSB). Visit http://www.ncsb.info/

Departments of Education

SLPs who plan to work in public schools may need to obtain an educational **credential** or certificate from the state's department of education. A credential is a document that verifies that you have met certain requirements and have obtained certain competencies. Generally, SLPs who work in public schools are not required to have state licensure or ASHA's CCC, although many have them anyway. Most states require a master's degree and a special educational credential to practice speech-language pathology in public schools. Periodically reauthorized, the Individuals with Disabilities Education Act (IDEA), one of several amendments to Public Law 94-142, is a federal law that defines professional qualifications for individuals working in the schools. IDEA has aligned qualifications with state-approved or state-recognized certification or licensing for public school employment; the most critical of these is the special education credential issued by a state department of education. ASHA strongly endorses the requirements for SLPs to hold the highest state standards regardless of their employment setting. See Chapter 5 for more information on IDEA regulations. Educational and practicum requirements of most educational credentials are similar to those of CCC and state licensure. However, each state may have some unique requirement for the educational credential.

In addition to the coursework required for the master's degree, a student seeking a school credential may need to take courses related to public school speech, language, and hearing programs. Additional courses related to public school education also may be required. A student internship in the school setting is a typical credentialing requirement.

Several states offer more than one educational credential for SLPs. One credential may allow you to teach a special class of students with communication disorders. In these classes, you may teach academic courses, physical education, art, and music, while emphasizing intervention for each child's communication needs. Another credential may allow you to offer clinical services in individual or small group formats to children with communication disorders. Many of these services are provided in a private speech therapy room. However, as appropriate, speech and language services may be provided in the classroom itself, with emphasis on integration into the class curriculum. Each state has its own educational credential laws for SLPs.

Because of this diversity and unique educational requirements for state public school credentials, you must consult on this with your advisor early in your clinical training. As you continue your training program, you will become more familiar with the various requirements in your state. It is most beneficial for you to attain and maintain your CCCs, state license, and educational credential to maximize your employment opportunities. Your career preferences may change over time.

The National Student Speech-Language-Hearing Association

NSSLHA is a national organization affiliated with ASHA. It encourages students in speech-language pathology and audiology programs to get involved with their future profession. An excellent source of professional information in your department might be the local chapter of NSSLHA, run by students with the help of a faculty advisor.

Your local chapter is an association of supportive fellow students who organize fundraising activities, social events, professional workshops, and seminars. Therefore, it is beneficial for you to become a member of the local chapter of NSSLHA early in your undergraduate program. This membership will help you keep current with all aspects of your profession.

NSSLHA membership dues are a fraction of the ASHA dues, and yet you receive many of the same benefits offered to full dues-paying professional members of ASHA. Members of NSSLHA receive or gain online access to all ASHA journals. These journals are a valuable source of scientific and professional information you cannot do without. In addition, NSSLHA members pay a reduced ASHA convention registration fee and lower membership fees for ASHA Special Interest Groups, receive discounts on ASHA products bought through the ASHA store, and purchase affordable professional liability insurance through an affiliated company. Besides, NSSLHA gives students the opportunity to begin developing social and professional affiliations with individuals having similar interests by subscribing to the ASHA community newsletter.

ASHA Special Interest Groups (SIGs)

ASHA's SIGs are subgroups of members who specialize in specific areas. As of 2022, there were 20 SIGs. These groups range from Language Learning and Education, Fluency Disorders, Craniofacial and Velopharyngeal

Disorders, Gerontology, and Teacher to Global Issues in Communication Sciences and Related Disorders. For an additional fee, ASHA and NSSLHA members may join SIGs.

The SIG benefits include earning ASHA CEUs at minimal cost, as well as gaining access to the SIG publication called *Perspectives*. SIG affiliation also promotes participation in an online community with the aim of fostering collaboration and networking with fellow professionals. SIGs assist in the development of ASHA policy as it relates to each specific area of interest. A description of each SIG as well as additional information is available on the ASHA website at https://www.asha.org/SIG/

State Speech-Language and Hearing Associations

Many states have speech-language and hearing associations that provide local support for SLPs, audiologists, and individuals with communication disorders. The state organizations often sponsor workshops and conferences, help disseminate information, and, in conjunction with ASHA, develop professional guidelines.

Involvement at the state level allows you to be active in state legislation, organization of state and local conferences, and networking with other professionals in your vicinity. Most members of state organizations are also ASHA members.

Related Professional Organizations

Depending on their specialty and interests, members of ASHA may belong to related professional or scientific organizations. Membership in related organizations helps promote interdisciplinary collaboration and mutual learning.

Many ASHA members may join several related professional and scientific associations. For example, certain ASHA members may belong to the American Academy of Audiology, the Association for Behavior Analysis International, the American Cleft-Palate-Craniofacial Association, the International Society for Augmentative and Alternative Communication, the American Academy of Private Practice in Speech-Language Pathology and Audiology, and the Academy of Neurologic Communication Disorders and Sciences.

ASHA Guidelines on Clinical Practicum

To ensure that students receive a broad but comprehensive training program, ASHA has established guidelines on clinical practicum. You satisfy the clinical practicum and internship requirements by earning the required number of clinical clock hours under the supervision of an ASHA-certified SLP or audiologist.

ASHA mandates requirements for both students and clinical practicum supervisors. This section describes the requirements for students. Chapter 4 describes the supervisor qualifications and responsibilities.

Guided Clinical Observation

Clinical observation offers students an introduction to the clinical activities. You observe the work of more experienced clinicians. Through observation, you find out how the knowledge acquired through the academic coursework is applied in a clinic. By observing other clinicians, you begin to understand the assessment and treatment process. To maximize learning and meet ASHA's observation requirements, take note of the following:

1. **A minimum of 25 clock hours**. ASHA requires students to obtain a minimum of 25 clock hr of supervised clinical observation as part of its clinical practicum. Although the 25 hr are a minimum requirement, students often observe for a greater number of hours. Completion of the 25 observation hr is not a requisite for direct client contact; however, to enhance learning and ease your transition to active clinical involvement, you should observe as many evaluation and treatment sessions as possible.

2. **Live or video-recorded sessions.** Most students will observe live clinical sessions. However, observation of video-recorded sessions or of live sessions on closed-circuit television monitors done under the supervision of a certified SLP is also acceptable.

3. **A variety of clinical sessions.** Observation hours may be obtained for treatment and evaluation of individuals with communication or swallowing disorders. Observations may be of children or of adults. Also, observe some clients over a period of time to note the progression of treatment. Regardless of the required distribution of observation hours, the 25 hr is a minimum requirement, and additional observation hours are strongly advised.

4. **Guided observation under an ASHA-certified professional's supervision**. Your observation should not be passive. All observations must be interactive; they must be under the supervision of an ASHA-certified professional. The student clinician may discuss what is observed with the graduate clinician conducting the sessions and the clinical supervisor. You will document your observation hours on a log provided by your university clinic. Your supervisors, the clinic director, or both will examine the observation log to verify your logged observation hours.

5. **Critical evaluation of observations**. It is not sufficient to just "watch" a clinical session and expect to gain much useful knowledge. You should critically evaluate what you observe. Your supervisor will help you note the many variables that influence service delivery. To maximize the observation experience, you should take notes and describe specific components of a session. If possible, and with the supervisor's approval, you should review the client's file or discuss the session with the clinician prior to observing.

Questions a Student Should Be Able to Answer After Completing an Observation

1. What type and severity of communication disorder did the client exhibit?

2. What were the objectives of the session?

3. What were the target behaviors?

4. How did the clinician greet the client?

5. How was the session structured?

6. How did the clinician close the session and dismiss the client?

7. How was the room arranged?

8. How were the client and the clinician seated in relation to each other?

9. What types of materials and activities were used?

10. What strategies did the clinician use to teach the target behaviors?

(continues)

11. What types of response cues were used (e.g., visual, tactile, or auditory)?

12. What types of reinforcers were used and on what schedule?

13. How were undesirable behaviors decreased?

14. How were responses charted?

15. What activities seemed to be most effective?

16. What activities seemed to be least effective?

17. If you were the clinician, what changes might you make for the next session?

Responsibilities of Student Observers

Student observers should behave responsibly and ethically. On- or off-campus, you should comply with these guidelines on clinical observation:

1. **Arrive on time for observations.** Regardless of how unobtrusive you try to be, if you arrive late for a scheduled observation, you may disrupt those who are observing (e.g., the clinical supervisor and members of the client's family). You also will not have a chance to discuss the client with the clinician prior to the session. If you do not know how the sessions started, you may have trouble understanding what you observe. Arriving late for a scheduled observation is irresponsible behavior. Clinical supervisors may not allow late arrivals to observe a session. Try to arrive 5 to 10 min before the observation begins, but no earlier, as the previous session may still be in progress.

2. **Introduce yourself and request permission to observe.** Clinical supervisors are responsible for their clients' rights to privacy and for ensuring that you derive the greatest benefit from your observations. Although the observation may have been scheduled previously, there may be reasons to disallow a particular observation. For example, the client may have, for whatever reason, decided against being observed; the clinical supervisor may have determined that the observation area was too crowded; or that the observation would not be beneficial for you or the client.

3. **Observe the entire clinical session.** This is necessary to obtain the greatest benefit from your observation. Each treatment and

evaluation session contains certain sequenced events and procedures. If you arrive late or leave early, you get only a glimpse of the clinical process, and, hence, you do not get the total picture. You may observe some isolated techniques while missing out on the rationale, antecedents, or consequences of certain techniques.

4. **Always respect the client's right to confidentiality**. All client information is confidential. As a student you will discuss with or report to others on your observations. These follow-up discussions or reports, or both, will help enhance your learning. However, be careful to protect each client's privacy. Never discuss clients in public areas. If you have a report to make regarding your observation, you may refer to the person observed as "the client," "the individual," or, in some cases, you may use an alias for the client's name.

5. **Privately discuss a client with the clinician or the supervisor**. Discuss the client only when confidentiality is ensured. Do not discuss the client when there are other people who may overhear your conversation.

6. **Do not interrupt the session or waste the clinician's time**. Clinicians need time to prepare for their sessions and the few minutes they have between clients are important for them. Ask appropriate questions when the clinician has time to respond, but do not converse about unrelated topics. Arriving on time for your observations and observing entire sessions should help provide opportunities for you to talk with the clinician.

7. **Do not remove clinical files from the clinic area**. In most cases, you will be able to review a client's file to obtain background information. While reviewing the files, do not write in them or remove anything from the files. Take only notes that are helpful to your observation (e.g., medical history, therapy history). Once again, remember that all client information is confidential. Do not discuss with others any personal or clinical information you read in client files. See Chapter 3 for more specific information on client confidentiality.

8. **Increase your observation skills**. To accomplish this, phonetically transcribe utterances, chart correct and incorrect productions, and take note of test results. This practice may help sharpen your observational skills as well as increase the recording skills you will use when you begin your own clinical practice. The more you learn during your observations, the more skills and confidence you will bring to your first practicum experience.

9. **Complete an observation report or appropriate documentation form for each client**. If you are required to complete an observation report at your university, do this as soon as an observational session ends. Request that the clinical supervisor sign the observation report. Without a signature, observation hours are not valid. Observation reports should be turned in to the clinic director, clinical supervisor, or assigning faculty. These reports will be used to substantiate your observation hours before your admittance to clinical practicum. Each university requires different reports and documentation. Follow the specific guidelines of your training program.

10. **Present yourself as a professional**. There will be clients, family members of the client, and other professionals at your observation site. You need to dress and behave like a professional. Therefore, follow the clinic dress code. Professional attire is considered appropriate dress. If you have doubts as to whether something is appropriate to wear, do not wear it. Communicate appropriately with the clinician, clinical supervisor, other student observers, clients, and clients' family members. Others, especially clients and their families, may easily misinterpret careless comments. It is not appropriate to verbalize judgment regarding the performance of the graduate clinician you are observing or the client receiving treatment. Avoid judgmental remarks and unnecessary questions.

Various clinical sites may have additional rules and procedures. For example, university clinics may require students to bring their own earbuds to access receivers. It is your responsibility to know the guidelines for observers at your site and to follow ASHA's Code of Ethics, described in Chapter 3.

Supervised Clinical Practicum

After you have completed your training program's requirements, you are qualified to begin working directly with clients. Clinical practicum clock hours are earned for *screening, evaluation, and treatment* of communication and swallowing disorders. Some hours may also be earned from clinical staffings.

Throughout the course of your practicum, you will gain experience with children and adults, practice in a variety of settings, and work with clients from diverse cultural and language backgrounds. You will have some experience with audiological clients, but, of course, most of your experience will be in speech-language pathology. To ensure quality training of SLPs and audiologists, ASHA has developed minimum clinical practicum requirements and documentation of clinical clock hours. The practicum experience must be gained under appropriate supervision. What follows is a description of practicum and its requirements. Supervision, supervisor qualification, and the interaction between the student clinician and the supervisor are discussed in Chapter 4.

Number of Clinical Clock Hours Required

Students initiating their graduate study on or after January 1, 2023, should obtain a minimum of **400 clock hr** that include the following:

1. **A minimum of 25 guided (supervised) clinical observation hours.** These hours may be obtained by undergraduate students. Many of these hours will precede direct client contact; however, it is not required that all 25 hr be completed prior to working directly with clients. Observation of video-recorded clinical sessions is permitted. Time spent discussing the observed treatment or assessment procedures with the supervisor may be counted. More than 25 hr of guided observation may be desirable but cannot be included in the 400 clinical practicum hours.

2. **A minimum of 250 hr of supervised clinical practicum at the graduate level must include on-site and in-person direct client contact.** These hours must involve direct contact with the client or patient and their family members. The direct client contact hours in speech-language pathology may include working with clients with disorders of voice, fluency, speech sound production, dysphagia, or language. There is no specified maximum under this category.

3. **Up to 50 hr of on-site and in-person direct contact hours obtained at the undergraduate level may be included in the 400 required clock hours.** Obviously, the majority of clinical practicum hours must be completed only at the graduate level.

4. **Up to 20% or 75 direct contact hours may be obtained through clinical simulation (CS) methods.** These includes simulation technologies such as standardized patients, virtual patients, and computer-based interactive programs. Debriefing activities may not be counted. CS hours are optional (not required).

5. **Up to 125 clinical contact hours may be acquired through telepractice.** To count these hours, telepractice must have been approved by the practicum site and should meet all the existing state and institutional regulations. Services offered through telepractice must be commensurate with the student's skill level and should

be appropriate for the student, the clients, and their families. The supervisor should also have expertise and experience in guiding the student's telepractice. Telepractice hours are not required, as they are optional.

6. **Clinical practice with clients representing diverse demographics.** Clock hours must be earned with children and adults from culturally or linguistically diverse backgrounds. Also, the clock hours must reflect experiences with a variety of types and severities of disorders and differences. Clients served should represent ages across the life span. To obtain these diverse experiences, you may need to complete your practicum in several settings. For instance, your practicum may include assignment at an acute care hospital, a public school, and your university clinic.

7. **Adequate depth and breadth of supervised clinical experiences to enable screening, evaluation, and prevention activities.** The scope of experience should include the following:

   • **Perform screening and prevention activities**. You will learn to use standardized and non-standardized methods to screen for communication or swallowing disorders. For example, if you are completing practicum in a medical setting, you may learn to perform a bedside swallowing evaluation to determine if a client needs to be referred for a videofluoroscopy. If you are working with young children, you may screen their speech to determine whether speech sound production errors are developmentally appropriate or whether a complete evaluation is required. In the case of certain infants who are at risk for developing communication disorders, you may design a home language stimulation program to prevent or reduce the magnitude of the disorder.

   • **Obtain case history information from a variety of sources**. Much of your case history information will come from your client's family. Chapter 6 provides guidelines for interviewing and obtaining a client's history. In addition, you will obtain information from reports by other professionals. A review of records and previous evaluations is necessary, as it may dictate your selection of testing, provide a means to document progress or a lack thereof, and highlight essential information. You may request copies of written reports, or you may have information that was shared verbally. A release of records may need to be signed, depending on the setting in which you are practicing. See Chapter 3 to learn more about respecting and maintaining client confidentiality.

- **Choose and administer appropriate standardized tests or use non-standardized assessment procedures to meet a client's needs.** You may use published instruments to assess a communication disorder. In addition, there is much information that you can obtain from non-standardized measures, including speech and language sampling and analyses, behavioral observations, and alternative assessment procedures (see Chapter 6). You will learn to select and use the methods appropriate for your client and setting.

- **Make a diagnosis and recommendations.** As you gather speech, language, or swallowing data, you will form an opinion regarding your client's diagnosis and make appropriate recommendations based on your diagnosis. Integrate all the information gathered during the assessment, including the case history, informant interviews, skilled observations and analyses, informal and standardized testing, and so forth.

- **Document and report information verbally, in writing, or both.** Each of your practicum sites may have different paperwork and reporting requirements. In the clinic setting, you may write a diagnostic report as well as a treatment plan. In the school setting, you may write a diagnostic report, but your treatment plan will be in the context of an IEP. In the medical setting, you may write an initial evaluation with a plan of care. Each setting necessitates a different report style, which will be discussed in Chapter 5. Learning a variety of styles will help you adapt more quickly when you graduate and begin your independent work.

- **Refer clients if other services are needed.** You may not always recommend speech-language pathology services for each client you evaluate. You will learn to identify persons who will benefit from your services and those who require different services. Certain clients may require services in addition to (or instead of) what SLPs provide. You will learn to identify when a client needs to be referred for other services and where in your community those services can be obtained.

8. **Sufficient depth and breadth of supervised clinical experiences to develop and provide effective treatment.** You will acquire the necessary skills to perform the following activities:

    - **Develop and write appropriate intervention plans and measurable goals.** Your intervention plans will vary, depending on your clinical practicum setting. For example, in the school setting, your intervention plan will follow the format of the IEP. In the university clinic, your intervention plan may be more narrative and will align with those required at the clinic or by your clinical supervisor. In any case, your plans will reflect the specific needs of your client and contain measurable and achievable goals. Chapter 7 contains specific information for selecting and writing treatment target behaviors.

- **Provide intervention**. Your intervention may include direct service to the client or training family members and other individuals to work with the client. Generally, you will begin providing individual intervention and progress to training the client and others to assist with intervention, generalization, and maintenance. In some cases, you may begin by training family members to provide intervention. For example, when working with certain infants and toddlers, the primary interventionist may be a family member and the SLP is the consultant. Collaboration with informants such as families, teachers, nurses, and doctors should occur when devising treatment plans. Furthermore, all intervention supplied should utilize evidence-based practice procedures. See Chapter 8 for intervention procedures.

- **Use appropriate materials and equipment for intervention and prevention**. There are many and expensive products on the market designed for intervention. You should select appropriate materials and equipment, although it is unnecessary to spend a great deal of money on too many commercial intervention packages. You will learn to create your materials, purchase commercially available materials, and use items found within your clinic and the client's home. You will not be expected to purchase large, expensive items. For example, your training program or practicum site stock standardized tests and more expensive assistive technology equipment required for certain clients. However, if a client needs to use a "low-tech" communication system, such as a picture exchange system or a simple communication board, you may be involved in creating the necessary items.

- **Collect data to measure your client's performance**. You will learn to collect and record data on your client's speech, language, or swallowing behaviors and to analyze the information that you acquire. The most efficient way to collect data is to first have well-written goals that contain behaviors that can be measured. See Chapter 7 for more information on target behavior selection and measurement.

- **Modify intervention as necessary**. Rarely does intervention follow a prescribed course. Individual differences and each individual's unique response to treatment necessitate procedural modifications.

- **Document and report information in writing, verbally, or both**. Each professional site will have its own documentation and reporting requirements. You will learn to complete any of the recordkeeping and reporting requirements at each of your practicum sites.

- **Make referrals as and when necessary**. For example, in the school setting, you may initially work with a student who is receiving only speech and language services. Subsequently, you, the parent, and the teacher may see a need for such special services as reading, math, or counseling. After receiving permission from the child's responsible party, the child may be referred to the resource specialist or school psychologist.

9. **Opportunities to advance personal qualities and interaction skills**. You will acquire the necessary skills to do the following:

   - **Communicate effectively with individuals of varied cultural, verbal, educational, and socioeconomic backgrounds**. You will interact with families and clients of different backgrounds. Therefore, you should communicate effectively with a variety of individuals. Please see ASHA's practice portal articles on health literacy for additional information on this topic.

   - **Collaborate with other professionals**. You will learn to work with other professionals to provide optimal services and case management for your clients. Audiologists, neurologists, otolaryngologists, nurses, primary care physicians, occupational therapists, physical therapists, psychologists, and teachers are just a few of the professionals with whom you may interact. Chapter 2 describes professionals you may typically work with.

   - **Counsel clients, family members, and caregivers regarding communication and swallowing disorders**. In all settings, it will be necessary for you to educate others about your clients' disorders. For example, while working with an individual who has dementia, you need to discuss the individual's communication strengths and limitations with the family members and caregivers at the facility. You may suggest strategies of interactions that are more or less effective in communicating with the individual. You may suggest a schedule of regular assessment to evaluate the skill maintenance and newer strategies of communication as the disease progresses. In another case, you may work with a young child who exhibits behavior problems because of difficulty communicating basic needs. You will educate the family on how the communication deficit affects the child's behavior, teach the family strategies that facilitate communication, reinforce appropriate behaviors, and discuss available community and professional resources. In each of these examples, to achieve the most successful outcomes for your clients and their families, you will need to listen carefully and learn fully about not only the needs of the clients, but also about the needs and the dynamics of the families and other caregivers.

- **Adhere to the ASHA Code of Ethics and other professional standards of your site.** To protect client confidentiality and allow correct data reporting, you should maintain client files in a certain order and in a certain location. Always follow the ASHA Code of Ethics. Also adhere to other guidelines such as ASHA's Scope of Practice and universal health precautions (Council for Clinical Certification in Audiology and Speech-Language Pathology of the American Speech-Language-Hearing Association, 2018).

What to Count as Clinical Clock Hours

To document your clinical practicum clock hours accurately and completely, follow these guidelines:

1. **Count clock hours earned in conjunction with a class assignment and during clinical practicum.** For example, if as part of a class assignment in a course on aphasia, you evaluated a client with aphasia, you may earn diagnostic clock hours even when not enrolled in clinical practicum. However, to earn such diagnostic hours, you must be supervised by an SLP who holds the CCC in speech-language pathology and has the other qualifications described earlier.

2. **Count clock hours spent on screening and assessment of communication and swallowing disorders.** Typically, the student clinician may screen individuals at local preschools, area public and private schools, private practices, medical facilities, and the university clinic. Evaluations will likely be part of your experience at any clinical site. Assessment hours may be earned while you are enrolled in a section of the clinic designated solely for diagnostics.

Formal reevaluations may also be counted. For example, you also may acquire diagnostic hours as part of the assessment of your clients at the beginning of a treatment period. Readministering specific tests or other assessment procedures at the end of treatment to document the status of the client also may be counted as evaluation hours. However, administering probes during the treatment period should be counted as treatment hours, not evaluation hours.

3. **Count clock hours spent counseling clients or counseling or training family members**. Such counseling, of course, is closely related to the swallowing or communication disorder of a client. For example, providing treatment for a woman with a diagnosis of dysarthria might include not only direct communication intervention with her, but also sharing information with her family. You may explain to the family members what dysarthria means and how they can help her improve the impaired communication behaviors. Or your treatment for a preschool child with a speech sound disorder might include a home training program. In that case, you need to train the parents to ensure that they are able to carry out the home assignments.

4. **Count clock hours spent in obtaining or giving assessment and treatment information**. You can count the time you spend taking a case history and interviewing the client, the client's family, or both. You can also count the time you spend discussing your diagnosis and recommendations with the client or client's family.

5. **Count clock hours spent on treatment of communication and swallowing disorders**. You will work with clients of varying ages who exhibit different kinds of disorders. In your medical practicum site, you will gain much experience in treating swallowing disorders. You will also treat clients with such disorders as aphasia, dysarthria, apraxia of speech, right hemisphere disorder, and traumatic brain injury associated with neurological disorders. Working with school-age clients, you will treat disorders of fluency, speech sound production, voice, language, and literacy. You may work with infants and toddlers who have speech, language, swallowing, and feeding problems secondary to genetic syndromes or other risk factors. Each site will offer different learning opportunities, so learn as much as you can at each clinical setting and count the hours directly spent on treatment.

6. **Count time spent on certain clinically related activities**. These include activities performed to prevent communication disorders or to develop, maintain, or maximize communication skills. For

example, in certain settings, the team of professionals providing rehabilitation services for a client may meet to discuss the client's treatment, progress, prognosis for further gains, and recommendations for future treatment. Also, you may be in a setting where you will train certain staff members to communicate more effectively with your client and to assist your client in communicating more effectively with the staff.

7. **Do not count preparation time as clinical clock hours.** Although you will spend much time in gathering materials, learning about clinical strategies, writing reports and lesson plans, scoring tests, or transcribing language samples, you cannot count clock hours spent on these activities. Remember that most clinical practicum clock hours are earned for direct client contact time only. Your clinical supervisor will answer any questions you have regarding how to count, record, or report your clinical hours.

8. **Do not round up minutes.** Do not round up sessions lasting 45 or 50 min to 1 hr.

Telepractice in Speech-Language Pathology

Telepractice is delivery of clinical services through telecommunication and Internet technology to clients and families away from the clinic or the clinician. The terms *telemedicine, telehealth,* and *telepractice* may be used interchangeably, although ASHA prefers *telepractice* because unlike the other two terms, this one does not limit the practice to medical settings. Assessment and intervention may be conducted remotely by connecting with the client through various computer and Internet applications (e.g., the widely used Zoom). Telepractice may be useful in delivering instruction and clinical education to clients, their family members, and professional caregivers. Supervision, mentoring, continuing education, and any type of consultation also may use the telepractice model. Telepractice is within the ASHA's scope of practice of speech-language pathologists (https://www .asha.org/practice-portal/professional-issues/telepractice).

There are a few varieties of telepractice. In **synchronous telepractice**, the clinician and the client are in real-time audio and video contact, simulating the typical face-to-face clinical sessions. In **asynchronous telepractice**, images, advice, data, and information may be stored and viewed by the clients and others at a different and convenient time. **Hybrid telepractice** is a combination of synchronous, asynchronous, and remote monitoring (e.g., wearable sensors) telepractice methods. Some sessions may be in person and others may be virtual. Because of its limited capability, *remote monitoring* is not useful for assessment, treatment, or consultation and may not be reimbursable.

Technology may be simple or sophisticated. The telephone may be used for individual or group consultation or conferencing; interactive video or digital broadcasts may be used for visual consultations. In addition to face-to-face interaction, certain instrumentation (such as an otoscope) may be attached to the recording device. In telepractice, a client may be several thousand miles from a specialist providing the service, but they are linked by the Internet or other technology. The provider may offer information directly to the client or to another specialist who is treating the individual. Different professionals also may come together to discuss assessment or treatment options for a client. Such groups may discuss research ideas or share research data.

Telepractice Guidelines

1. **Quality of telepractice**. It should match that of in-person practice.

2. **Ethical practice**. Telepractitioners should adhere to the ASHA Code of Ethics and comply with all state and national laws and regulations that apply to the SLP clinical practice.

3. **Licensing considerations**. According to ASHA, the client's location is the site of service and the provider's location is the distant site. The client's and the provider's sites may be in different states. Technically, telepractitioners should be licensed in both states. Working with state and regional organizations, ASHA has established the Audiology & Speech-Language Pathology Interstate Compact (ASLP-IC) which allows telepractice in multiple states without having to obtain multiple state licenses. Practitioners should apply for the compact privilege to the ASLP-IC commission, which may be fully operational in late 2023 or early 2024. Visit the website aslpcompact.com for more information and updates on the states that are in the compact.

4. **Informed consent**. Clients must give written informed consent to telepractice.

(continues)

5. **Multicultural considerations.** Multicultural issues that affect in-person services (see Chapters 6 and 8) also affect telepractice.

6. **Licensure laws.** Practitioners should adhere to licensure laws affecting their delivery of services in their own state as well as that in which the clients reside.

7. **Client confidentiality.** The Health Insurance Portability and Accountability Act (HIPAA) and the Family Educational Rights and Privacy Act (FERPA), which safeguard medical and student records, must be followed. Any information provided through the Internet or other technology must be secure.

8. **Equipment selection and maintenance.** The service provider should maintain and update the hardware and software, and they must be available to both the SLP and the client. Reliable connectivity to the Internet must be available to the clients. Backup and substitute equipment should be readily available for immediate use if the equipment fails just before a scheduled remote consultation.

9. **Reimbursement.** The SLP must become familiar with reimbursement regulations for private insurance, Medicare, and Medicaid. Insurance coverage, billing codes, and other documentation requirements are regulated by state and federal laws and may differ from those that apply to in-person services.

10. **Client selection.** It is critical to select clients who will benefit from telepractice. Some clients may not benefit from it. For example, a client with sensory deficits that affect hearing or vision may not see the computer monitor or hear the SLP. Moreover, clients with behavioral or attentional deficits who frequently leave their seat are not suitable for telepractice. A trial period of telepractice may be essential to determine candidacy.

11. **Method selection.** Assessment and treatment methods selected for clients should be suitable for telepractice. Certain procedures (e.g., manual guidance to produce a speech sound) are not implementable in telepractice.

12. **Documentation.** Telepractice requirements for reliable and objective documentation of improvement under treatment are the same as those for in-person services.

13. **Support personnel training**. Only the properly trained SLPAs, instructional aids, and any other support personnel should assist the SLP in telepractice.

14. **Environmental modifications**. The SLP and the client should have access to therapy rooms that ensure quietness, provide adequate lighting, assure safety, and safeguard confidentiality. Additional modifications may include the camera placement for good eye contact, slower speech rate, and exaggerated facial and hand gestures.

15. **Modifications of service delivery**. The SLP should promptly modify assessment and treatment procedures to suit an alternative setting. Certain tests have provisions that specify the modifications required for telepractice administration. Such modifications must be specified so as to accurately interpret the data.

16. **International telepractice**. ASHA-certified SLPs who provide teleservices to persons in other countries should adhere to all ASHA practice requirements and guidelines, including the Code of Ethics, Scope of Practice, and Preferred Practice Patterns. SLPs should also adhere to any laws that regulate telepractice in the client's country of residence.

17. **Efficacy**. Some evidence supports telepractice, but much research needs to be done. Efficacy studies are few, and the evidence greatly varies across communication disorders. Telepractice holds much promise for providing services in rural communities and for enhancing communication and collaboration among professionals. SLPs who consider telepractice should visit the Evidence Map for Telepractice on the ASHA website.

SLP Clients in the Digital Age

The Internet has promoted many positive developments in speech-language pathology. Before parents or family members bring clients in for an evaluation, it is not unusual for them to have researched their concerns on the Internet. Adult clients, parents of children, and family members may have spent numerous hours on the Internet researching the problem at hand.

They may have visited the websites of the National Institutes of Health and PubMed, which give free access to journal articles and other sources. They may have communicated with support groups of parents with similar concerns. They may have seen advertisements for materials, intervention techniques, speakers, and materials that offer all the answers and "cures."

Parents, family members, and clients who have done all that research before meeting with an SLP may be quite knowledgeable about a disorder. Some people may be motivated and willing to apply their knowledge to assist with intervention. Their understanding of a particular disorder may be helpful in completing the evaluation and may decrease the amount of intervention time needed. Unfortunately, other people may be misinformed because the Internet, especially social media, is also a platform for propaganda, outright misinformation, superstition, and distortion of scientific evidence. Also, it is easy to take information out of context without understanding the background or related information.

SLPs may reeducate their clients by explaining what is known and what has been proven to be effective in treating specific disorders. You will also encounter people who resist learning the facts, however. They may insist that you provide a certain therapy that they read about on the Internet. If the therapy the client or the caretakers insist on getting is judged to be inappropriate or ineffective, your supervisor may decline to offer it to the client.

Regardless of the type of client or family member you encounter, it is important that you be well informed. Know as much as you can about the disorders your clients have. In addition, know what information and misinformation are published on the Internet. Know the latest fads and be able to explain why certain interventions are not appropriate. Always support your recommendations and evaluations with research evidence. When necessary, request your supervisor to discuss the issue with the clients or their family members. Learn from the discussion.

Speech-Language Pathology Assistants (SLPAs)

One or more of your clinical internship assignments may involve working with SLPAs. The scope of practice of SLPAs is limited compared to that of licensed, certified, and credentialed SLPs. Assistants are expected to supplement, not supplant, SLPs in all professional settings. Assistants cannot practice the profession independently; they work under the supervision of professional SLPs. By performing work permitted under their scope of practice, assistants may free the SLPs to increase the frequency and intensity of service offered or concentrate on more complex cases. Assistants, however, have a higher level of training than aides (e.g., speech aides in public schools; see Chapter 2). Several colleges and universities in the U.S. now offer SLPA training programs (American Speech-Language-Hearing Association, 2022).

Student clinicians neither supervise SLPAs nor are supervised by them; however, you may work closely with them. You should know what kind of help you can expect from them and what you should not ask them to do. Family members or other staff may question you regarding the qualifications of SLPAs. Understand that the licensed, credentialed, and certified SLP who is supervising your clinical practicum shoulders the legal, ethical, and scientific responsibilities for service delivery. The SLPA is held to the same professional standards of other employees at your practicum or internship site and can be very helpful in assisting the SLP.

To work as a certified SLPAs, individuals must (American Speech-Language-Hearing Association, 2022):

- Complete an SLPA training program at an accredited institution, get a bachelor's degree in communication disorders or another discipline, and complete ASHA's online Assistant Education Module. The module includes coursework in introduction to communication disorders, phonetics, speech sound disorders, and language development

- Complete a mandatory course or training in ethics, universal safety requirements, and patient/client/student confidentiality

- Complete a minimum of 100 hr of field work or clinical experience equivalent supervised by an ASHA certified SLP (80 hr of direct client contact and 20 hr of indirect contact; observation hours cannot be counted)

- Obtain on-the-job training specific to SLPA responsibilities

- Pass ASHA's Assistant Certification Exam in Speech-Language Pathology

- Obtain ASHA's Assistant Certification in Speech-Language Pathology (C-SLPA)

- Adhere to ASHA's Assistant Code of Conduct

- Complete a Maintenance of Certification Assessment (MOCA) at the end of their 3-year certification maintenance interval

- Meet any state or federal credentialing requirements that supersede ASHA's requirements regarding the work of speech-language pathologists

Under Supervision, SLPAs May

- perform only what the supervising SLP approves and assigns
- self-identify as an SLPA to students, clients, families, and others
- administer and score speech and language screening and assessment tools if the SLPA meets the examiner requirement specified in the test manuals, but without offering interpretation of test results
- develop and implement treatment and assessment materials and activities
- implement treatment plans, including IEPs and IFSPs developed and supervised by a qualified SLP as provided during in-person or telepractice models
- collect treatment data to document client performance
- develop low-tech AAC devices (such as a simple communication board) and provide training in using other AAC devices
- provide caregiver training
- perform clerical duties and departmental operations such as scheduling and recordkeeping
- participate in in-service training and public relations programs and offer primary prevention information to individuals and groups
- assist in research projects
- offer bilingual interpretation and translation services
- check and maintain equipment
- collect and document data for quality improvement
- offer services via telepractice to students and clients whom the SLP selects

SLPAs May Not

- claim to be an SLP
- interpret standardized or non-standardized test results to diagnose a disorder or disability
- screen or diagnose clients with feeding or swallowing disorders
- demonstrate swallowing strategies or precautions or treat medically fragile clients without 100% direct supervision
- diagnose a communication disorder
- participate in any parent or case conferences without a supervising SLP
- counsel clients or families
- develop or modify treatment plans
- assist with treatment without supervision and without a treatment plan prepared by the SLP
- select AAC devices
- sign or initial treatment plans, assessment reports, or other formal documents
- select, refer, or discharge clients
- disclose confidential information

Please note that the scope of practice guidelines summarized here is not comprehensive. Consult ASHA (2022) for the full list of approved and unapproved activities of SLPAs.

Payment for Clinical Services

ASHA guidelines permit student clinicians to be paid for their work under supervised practicum. Payment may be wages, stipends, grants, or scholarships (American Speech-Language-Hearing Association, 2017d). Only a few sites pay student clinicians; most do not.

A university may have restrictions on students receiving payment for their clinical practicum, in which case its policies supersede those of

ASHA. Regardless of whether the sites provide students monetary reimbursement, each site must adhere to ASHA's guidelines on student practicum and supervision.

Clinical Practicum as a Learning Experience

Clinical practicum is designed to give you an exceptional learning experience. It gives you an opportunity to gain experience with a wide variety of individuals and communication disorders under the supervision of qualified SLPs. You will gain experience in varied clinical settings, including acute-care hospitals, rehabilitation facilities, psychiatric hospitals, skilled nursing facilities, private practices, and public schools.

Initially, you may be somewhat apprehensive about beginning your practicum. This is a typical response, but you will discover that clinical practicum is exciting and rewarding, and, as you gain more experience and with it, greater confidence. You are encouraged to experience as many types of clients and clinical settings as you can.

You will not be expected to perform like an experienced professional, but you will be expected to act responsibly within the guidelines of ASHA and those of your training program. You should demonstrate consistent progress in each of your practicum assignments. Speech-language pathology is exciting because there is always something new to learn and what you learn helps you make a difference in the lives of persons with limited communication skills.

Now you have a general idea of the personal and academic requirements for a successful clinical practicum. You also know ASHA's requirements for types of practicum hours and clinical settings in which to acquire them. This is your chance to apply information learned in academic classes and explore some of the challenging and exciting possibilities the profession of speech-language pathology has to offer.

(?) Questions for Self-Assessment

1. What preclinic requirements should you fulfill before you may begin your clinical practicum? How do you keep track of your progress in meeting those requirements?

2. Distinguish between ASHA accreditation and ASHA certification. As an individual, which one do you eventually apply for?

3. Which one may be legally enforced: ASHA certification regulations or state licensing regulations?

4. Summarize what an SLPA can and cannot do. Can an SLPA supervise your clinical practicum? Why or why not?

5. How many clock hours of supervised clinical practicum are you required to complete? Break the total down into the following allowable categories: Observational hours: _____. The number of hours acquired at the undergraduate level: _____. Minimum hours required at the graduate level: _____. The number of telepractice hours you may count: _____. The number of simulation hours: _____.

References

American Speech-Language-Hearing Association. (n.d.a). *Health literacy.* https://www.asha.org/slp/healthliteracy/

American Speech-Language-Hearing Association. (n.d.b). *General information about certification.* https://www.asha.org/certification/AboutCertificationGenInfo/

American Speech Language-Hearing Association. (n.d.c). *Certification standards to change in 2020.* https://www.asha.org/Certification/Certification-Standards-Change-in-2020/

American Speech-Language-Hearing Association. (n.d.d) *Special interest groups.* https://www.asha.org/SIG/

American Speech-Language-Hearing Association. (2016). *Code of ethics.* http://www.asha.org/policy/

American Speech-Language-Hearing Association. (2017a). *Bylaws of the American Speech-Language-Hearing Association.* http://www.asha.org/policy/

American Speech-Language-Hearing Association. (2017b). *Issues in ethics: Ethical issues related to clinical services provided by audiology and speech-language pathology students.* https://www.asha.org/practice/ethics/ethical-issues-related-to-clinical-services-provided-by-audiology-and-speech-language-pathology-students/#sec1.1

American Speech-Language-Hearing Association. (2018). *Speech-language pathology certification handbook of the American Speech-Language Hearing Association.* http://www.asha.org/uploadedFiles/SLP-Certification-Handbook.pdf

American Speech-Language-Hearing Association. (2022). *Speech-language pathology assistant scope of practice* [Scope of practice]. http://www.asha.org/policy

Council for Clinical Certification in Audiology and Speech-Language Pathology of the American Speech-Language-Hearing Association. (2018). *2020 Standards for the Certificate of Clinical Competence in Speech-Language Pathology.* http://www.asha.org/certification/2020-SLP-CertificationStandards

Council of Academic Programs in Communication Sciences and Disorders. (2013). *White paper: Preparation of speech-language pathology clinical educators.* http://scotthall.dotster.com/capcsd/wp-content/uploads/2014/10/Preparation-of-Clinical-Educators-White-Paper.pdf

Council on Academic Accreditation in Audiology and Speech-Language Pathology. (2018). *Accreditation handbook.* http://www.caa.asha.org/wp-content/uploads/Accreditation-Handbook.pdf

Educational Testing Service. (2015). *Praxis study companion: Speech-language pathology.* http://www.ets.org/s/praxis/pdf/5331.pdf

Hegde, M. N. (2024). *A coursebook on scientific and professional writing for speech-language pathology* (6th ed.). Plural Publishing.

Roseberry-McKibbin, C., Hegde, M. N., & Tellis, G. (2024). *An advance review of speech-language pathology: Preparation for the NESPA and comprehensive examination* (6th ed.). Pro-Ed.

Strunk, W., Jr., & White, E. B. (1999). *Elements of style* (4th ed.). Pearson.

CHAPTER **2**

Organization of Clinical Practicum

<hr>

Student Learning Outcomes

After reading this chapter, student clinicians are expected to:

- Summarize the information on various clinical practicum sites available to them
- Describe the structure and function of on- and off-campus clinical practicum sites and clinical internship experiences
- Be prepared to effectively collaborate with other professionals
- Follow the general clinic administrative procedures and properly manage clinical supplies, materials, and supplies

<hr>

Clinical practicum in speech-language pathology (SLP) is organized on a hierarchy of clinical experiences and expectations. In most cases, student clinicians may begin clinical practicum after completing the required hours of supervised clinical observation, prerequisite coursework, and other departmental requirements. Initially, the student clinicians are assigned one to three clients. As student clinicians gain experience and begin to make relatively independent decisions, their client caseload is increased and varied.

After they complete one to three semesters of practicum at the university clinic, students may be assigned to off-campus clinical settings for

Commonly Available Clinical Practicum Sites

- **University clinic**. For most students, the practicum experience begins at the university speech, language, and hearing clinic. On-campus clinical practicum prepares the students for off-campus experiences

- **Public schools**. Most, if not all, students gain practicum experience in public schools to qualify for the state department of education credential. University programs in communication disorders generally require clinical practicum in an educational setting

- **Hospitals**. Clinical practicum in a medical facility is essential to gain skills in assessing and treating communication disorders associated with various medical conditions as well as swallowing disorders

- **Skilled nursing facilities**. Practicum experiences may be gained in skilled nursing facilities, where individuals requiring convalescent care may be cared for

- **Rehabilitation facilities**. These facilities offer opportunities to learn specialized methods of restoring or improving communication

- **Psychiatric hospitals or clinics**. State or privately operated psychiatric hospitals and clinics offer opportunities to learn assessment and treatment procedures for communication disorders associated with behavioral disorders

- **Early intervention agencies**. Experience in assessing and treating children in the age range of birth to 3 years may be gained in an early intervention setting

- **Preschool agencies**. Experience in assessing and treating children in the age range of 3 to 5 may be gained in preschool settings

- **Prisons**. Adult prisons and juvenile detention facilities also offer clinical practicum experiences

- **Private practice**. Expanding opportunities for clinical practicum are available in many private clinics and with privately contracted service providers

clinical practicum. The following sections describe the structure and function of several clinical practicum sites.

On-Campus Clinical Practicum

Your practicum begins at the clinic on your university campus. University clinics provide services to the community, conduct clinical research, and create opportunities for the students to master clinical skills under supervision.

Typically, the clinic is designed and equipped to facilitate both academic and clinical training. Student clinicians also may assist faculty in clinical treatment or assessment research.

University Clinic

In addition to previously mentioned coursework and guided observation, your university department may have additional requirements. These may include a health clearance, acceptance into the graduate or clinical practicum program, faculty recommendations, and so on.

Beginning student clinicians are not expected to work without guidance from a supervisor. However, they are expected to apply information learned in academic coursework, implement supervisor recommendations, ask questions, and, as the semester progresses, show systematic improvement in their clinical work. Based on your clinical performance, improvement in assessment and treatment skills, professional behavior, and acceptable oral and writing skills, your supervisor may give you a grade and judge your ability to succeed in future clinic assignments.

Schedules

Typically, a university clinic is operated on an 8 a.m. to 5 p.m. weekday schedule. Some universities also have evening hours to accommodate individuals who cannot attend the clinic during regular business hours. Other university clinics may provide services only during the academic year. This schedule is not optimal because it disrupts services offered to clients who often need sustained and continuous treatment. To provide more continuous services, some clinics operate 12 months of the year, with professional staff providing services during the intersessions. In other clinics, graduate clinicians continue to provide treatment during the summer term to prevent an extended break of service.

Clients receiving speech-language pathology services usually are scheduled for two to three sessions per week, with each session lasting 30 to 60 min. Evaluation sessions may be longer. Most clients receive individual treatment; however, some clients may be scheduled for group sessions (e.g., speech-language preschool or adult aphasia group). Generally, you will be allotted 5 to 10 min between clients to get yourself organized for the next client. It is important to be prepared for your sessions in advance; the few minutes between clients is not the time for planning assessment or treatment activities. This is the time for you to finish with one client, clean your clinic space, and greet the next client in the clinic waiting room.

At the beginning of the semester, you will receive your clinical assignment. This will include your scheduled clinic time, your clients, and your designated clinical supervisor. At most universities, student clinicians may be asked to telephone the client or the family, introduce themselves, and confirm the client's clinic appointment.

Student clinicians should routinely check with the clinic administrative assistant to verify clinic appointments and note any changes in their clinic schedule. Each university has different methods for scheduling clients and communicating the scheduling to student clinicians. To avoid confusion, missed appointments, or last-minute preparations, adhere to the procedures of your university.

Prior to meeting your client, you must review the client's clinical file, develop a plan for the first session, and discuss any evaluation plans with your supervisor.

Types of Clients

A wide range of ages and communication disorders are represented in the university clinic's caseload. The university caseload is influenced by demographic factors and the availability of other speech-language pathology services in the community. For example, if there is a large rehabilitation agency in the area, the clinic may enroll fewer clients with diagnoses of aphasia or traumatic brain injury (TBI); if there is a pediatric hospital offering speech and hearing services, the clinic may serve a limited number of children. Clients may also be referred for additional services from surrounding school districts if their school SLP recommends additional outside services to the student's parents. Finally, economic factors also affect the types of clients typically seen at the university clinic. Compared with private practices or hospitals, a university clinic often is maintained on a reduced fee scale or a donation-based system; this may attract clients with limited incomes or without insurance coverage. Clients or parents who ask questions about fees, waivers, payment plans, and so forth should be referred to the clinic office.

Other factors influencing the university client caseload are the expertise of faculty members and the department's relationship with allied health professionals. For instance, if your department has faculty members well known for their expertise in fluency disorders, the clinic may attract a large number of clients with these disorders. In addition, if your university is affiliated with a medical center, your clinic may provide outpatient or follow-up services for individuals with dysphagia, TBI, laryngectomy, and other medically involved communication disorders.

Report Writing and Recordkeeping

University clinics have varying policies and terminology regarding writing assignments. You first write an **assessment report** on a client following a diagnostic session. Subsequently, the course of the proposed treatment may be in the form of **daily lesson plans, weekly lesson plans, semester treatment plans**, or a combination of these. Typically, you submit computer-printed reports and plans. Your supervisor will review all your plans. Throughout the term, you will be required to regularly document your clients' progress in quantitative terms and general session information on an approved recording sheet such as the ones you will find in the Appendices of Chapter 8. Any changes to your treatment plans must also be documented. At the end of the term, you will be required to write a **final summary** or **progress report**. The final summary should describe the client's status at the beginning of treatment, the treatment goals, the treatment procedures, and the progress made by the client.

Your clinical supervisor will give you instructions regarding the format and timelines for all written work. See Chapter 6 for details on writing various kinds treatment plans and reports and see Hegde (2024a) for guidelines and multiple templates and exemplars.

Off-Campus Practicum Sites

Typically, you begin off-campus practicum following the completion of on-campus practicum, which may range in duration from one to three semesters. Common off-campus practicum sites include public schools, hospitals, skilled nursing facilities, rehabilitation agencies, psychiatric hospitals, preschool programs, prisons, and private speech and hearing centers. Less common clinical practicum experiences may be available through partnerships between your training program and international organizations. Check the American Speech-Language-Hearing Association (ASHA)'s website or talk with your clinic director for information on international practicum opportunities.

All off-campus sites must comply with ASHA's regulations on the frequency and type of supervision. An ASHA-certified SLP who works at an approved external site, with consultation provided by the university clinic director, usually supervises off-campus practicum. University policy and the department's criteria of acceptable performance dictate the grading. The off-campus supervisor evaluates the student's performance and suggests a grade.

Student clinicians usually are required to follow the holiday schedule of the off-campus site instead of that of the university. Student clinicians also must comply with the site's requirements regarding professional responsibility and conduct. This includes appropriate work attire, which may vary from business casual to scrubs, depending on the practicum setting.

Public Schools

SLPs who supervise your clinical practicum in a school setting typically have a **credential** (or certificate) issued by the state's department of education and ASHA Certificate of Clinical Competence in Speech-Language Pathology (CCC-SLP). The education credential authorizes SLPs to provide individual speech and language services in the schools, teach in a classroom, or both. In many states, to eventually obtain an educational credential or certificate, student clinicians must complete a practicum experience in a school setting. ASHA requires CCC-SLP for all student practicum supervisors in all settings. Clinical practicum hours completed under uncertified SLPs cannot be counted for ASHA certification.

A university seminar on legal and regulatory guidelines related to SLP and special education services offered in school settings may accompany the school clinical practicum assignment. The seminar may discuss the organization and administration of speech-language pathology programs in the public schools, offer student clinicians an opportunity to share their practicum experiences, and exchange ideas with fellow students and the university faculty.

The prerequisites to internship in a public school depend on the university and state credential requirements. Prerequisites may include completion of coursework relative to childhood speech and language disorders, experience working with children of different ages and disorders, enrollment in your university's *credential program,* and a *certificate of clearance* demonstrating that you are professionally fit to begin fieldwork in the school environment.

To issue a certificate of clearance, the credential program's personnel review your records, required test results, grade-point average, and so on. Certain states may require you to pass a competency examination. In conjunction with the credential application, individuals may be required to obtain a character and identification clearance that includes submission of Live Scan digitalized fingerprinting to the Department of Justice and the Federal Bureau of Investigation (FBI). In addition, credential applicants must show evidence of having passed a recent tuberculosis (TB) test. Review your school's prerequisites with your advisor.

Schedules

In schools, assignments are generally full-day, 3 to 5 days a week, often from 8 a.m. to 3 p.m., perhaps in conjunction with a weekly seminar on your university campus as noted. Nonetheless, you should be prepared to spend additional time on writing reports and individualized education programs (IEPs), planning sessions, billing, attending meetings (often before or after the school day), and preparing materials.

Although basic diagnostic and treatment principles do not vary from setting to setting, several scheduling and service delivery models may be unique to public schools. For example, your on-campus clinical practicum with children may have followed only the individual treatment format, whereas school-based speech-language services may combine different service delivery models. Each student receiving services for special education has an **IEP**. A continuum of services must be discussed by the team to determine the **least restrictive environment (LRE)**. The LRE is outlined in the Individuals With Disabilities Education Act (2004a, 2004b) (IDEA), which requires each public agency to ensure, to the maximum extent appropriate, that children with disabilities are educated with children without disabilities. Removal from the general education environment should only occur if the nature or severity of the disability impedes placement in the general education classes because of the need for supplementary aids and services. As a result, to align with federal law and ASHA practice policy, many students with mild to moderate disabilities may be *fully included* in regular education classes (American Speech-Language-Hearing Association, 1996). That is, they receive instruction in a regular education classroom with peers of their age. This setting is referred to as an *inclusive setting*. Typically, support is provided to fully include students by different educational specialists, who provide services in the classroom, make suggestions to the teacher, or both.

Different specialists may offer their services in different educational environments when a student's LRE requires instruction outside the regular education setting. For example, a student may receive specialized academic instruction from a resource specialist, modified curriculum in a special day class, related speech and language services in a speech room, or a combination of these. Placement decisions are made individually.

To provide a continuum of services, schools may use either a direct or an indirect service delivery method. **Direct** services entail an SLP working with a student individually or with other students to specifically work on skill mastery outlined in IEP goals. These services may be provided in the traditional clinical format in which a clinician works with individual children or children in small groups. In the **pull-out model**, students travel outside of their classroom and are served in the SLP's office or a dedicated clinical room. Students attend treatment sessions as stipulated in their IEPs (a specified number of minutes served 1 day per week, 2 days, etc.).

Speech and language goals must be aligned with the state's curriculum. For example, most states have drafted common core state standards, detailing the information children should learn at each grade level in mathematics and English language arts. Many states require that all goals on an IEP be aligned to one of the standards. In this case, IEP paperwork addresses this by requiring documentation that references what standard a certain goal is tied to (see Chapter 5 for additional information on goal writing for an IEP). It is essential for the school curriculum to be incorporated into the student's speech or language treatment. Treatment may include some stimulus material unrelated to classroom curriculum, however.

You also may provide direct speech-language services in the student's class one-to-one or in small groups. This is sometimes referred to as **push-in** services. The push-in model helps students generalize skills, identifies the varying demands of different settings, and allows for ongoing changes to be made to the service delivery throughout the school year (Dixon, 2013). In this case, you may provide treatment for one or more students in a separate area of the classroom while the rest of the class continues other activities. When classroom instruction is divided into *learning stations*, you may treat children at one of the stations. The classroom teacher and aide may be responsible for two other learning stations, and another station may be for independent study. Students rotate from one station to the next, typically spending 10 to 15 min at each station. This type of scheduling may be common in kindergarten and special day classes.

Teachers who have specialized training in educating children with different severities of disabilities work with students in **special day classes**. A student may be in the special day class for much of the day, but also may have **mainstream activities** to participate in regular education for designated times during portions of the day (e.g., recess, lunch, music, or any other appropriate learning activities).

A different model of whole class intervention is more commonly used at the secondary level. In this model, the school SLP teaches one period of the day and students attend the class as they would their regular academic classes. In some schools, this class may fulfill the students' requirements for

English language. This model is also commonly used at the preschool level as well. Speech and language services may be provided in the setting of a class while specifically working on speech and language targets. This may be referred to as a **language laboratory** or a **language and speech class**.

Direct speech-language services in the schools also may be provided within a **collaborative service delivery model** in which the SLP works as a member of a **transdisciplinary team**. In addition to students, parents, and administrators, each team member from the various disciplines (academic, nursing, psychological, etc.) meet and discuss the needs of the students. Needs are addressed in a collaborative method, not restricted to an individual discipline. The SLP, classroom teacher, and other service providers coordinate assessment procedures, devise goals, provide intervention, and document the program outcomes (American Speech-Language-Hearing Association, 1991). Collaborative models have been identified in various ways.

Collaborative Intervention Models in Schools

- **Supportive learning or supplemental teaching** allows the primary instructor to teach a lesson while the co-instructor (who may be an SLP) provides supplementary teaching or activities. The SLP may teach a lesson while the classroom teacher offers supportive activities. In another lesson, the classroom teacher may instruct the class and the SLP may provide supplementary and supportive activities. In this model, the student clinician might present language lessons to all the students in the class. During the lesson, you also work on the speech and language objectives of the students enrolled on your caseload. Occasionally, you may teach a subject, such as mathematics, to demonstrate to the teacher how adapting the language in a lesson can benefit children with language disorders.

- **Team teaching** is a model in which the teacher and SLP share in the responsibilities of planning and teaching a lesson. Typically, the lesson is divided into segments, with each professional teaching certain parts of the lesson.

(continues)

- **Complementary instruction** is similar to team teaching. The SLP and teacher instruct a lesson together. The teacher may teach content areas (e.g., science, social studies, math). The SLP may teach such language-related skills as mapping of ideas, selecting main ideas, outlining, and taking notes.

- **Station teaching** incorporates dividing the curriculum into parts and providing instruction in separate locations in the classroom, with students rotating to each.

- **Parallel teaching** also involves dividing instruction between instructors with half the class receiving instruction by each instructor. The SLP is responsible for teaching those students who may require additional modifications or progress at a slower pace (American Speech-Language-Hearing Association, n.d.).

Sufficient planning time is critical to the success of collaborative instruction. You must allow time not only for teaching a lesson, but also for planning with the teacher. The SLP and classroom teacher discuss the needs of the class as a whole and the specific needs of the students receiving speech or language services. The SLP models an appropriate language and learning environment for students with communication disorders. The teacher and SLP share effective methods of teaching and obtain new ideas by observing each other. In addition, students with communication disorders receive services in a natural communication setting that emphasizes the classroom curriculum and assists with generalization of skills.

Indirect speech-language pathology services are another service delivery option used in the public schools. Indirect services are provided under a **consultative model** in which the SLP works with the student's parents, teachers, or other professionals to address the needs of the student. In this model, the teacher receives suggestions for working with certain students who are not on the SLP's caseload. In other cases, the SLP may determine that certain students who were receiving treatment for a language disorder no longer require direct services. You discuss with teachers and parents ways to modify communication to maximize a student's performance. The students remain on your caseload for a few months as you monitor their progress using the consultative model. During this monitoring stage, you may make suggestions to the parents and teachers. In some instances, you may determine that a student requires the reimplementation of direct services.

All these models have a place in the delivery of speech-language pathology services. However, each should be viewed on a continuum of need. Some students require intensive, direct services for longer durations than others. Some may transition from intensive and direct intervention to a less intense and indirect model. Others require less direct intervention from the beginning and benefit from modification of teaching strategies provided under a consultative model. As in assessment and treatment considerations, the SLP must view each student's unique needs. Your public school practicum is an opportunity to learn when and how to effectively implement the various service delivery models while supporting the students' needs.

Scheduling sessions, as you might imagine from the variety of service delivery options, can be difficult. A new experience in a public school setting is that you also may be required to serve a large number of students. At the university speech and hearing clinic, you may be used to working with two to four clients per term. In your school practicum, it is likely that you will be asked to gradually assume a caseload of a full-time clinician. You will treat students based on the minutes allocated in the IEP. Each student served will differ in service minutes, goals, accommodations, and location of instruction.

States have differing guidelines on the caseload size for a school-based SLP. *Caseload* refers to the number of students the SLP serves. *Workload* refers to all of the activities that an SLP must accomplish in addition to treatment. Rather than the caseload determination based on the number of students served, ASHA recommends that states establish caseloads based on a *workload* analysis (American Speech-Language-Hearing Association, 2002). Caseload should vary based on the overall workload of the SLP, which includes responsibilities in direct assessment and treatment, indirect activities, and compliance with local, state, and federal laws. Therefore, ASHA does not recommend a maximum caseload number, as this will vary from site to site. At this time, some states utilize a numerical measure to guide caseloads, while others leave the decision to the district. A large caseload limits the SLP's effectiveness; however, a reduced and manageable caseload size is a goal that has yet to be realized in all of the nation's public schools (American Speech-Language-Hearing Association, 2002). For additional information, please see ASHA's practice portal at https://www.asha.org/Practice-Portal/Professional-Issues/

Group treatment sessions may be a new kind of clinical experience you may have in a public school setting. Because of the large number of students, public school SLPs typically serve students in small groups. Often, the number in each group depends on the total caseload of the clinician. The larger the caseload, the bigger the group size.

Options for Grouping Children

- **Homogeneous grouping** is the practice of grouping together students with similar disorders.

- **Heterogeneous grouping** is the practice of grouping together students who exhibit different disorders. This type of grouping may allow one student to model for another student. For example, a child with a language disorder whose speech production skills are typical may provide an excellent model for production of /r/ for a child with a speech sound disorder. The child who mispronounces /r/ may model plural morphemes for a child with language disorders.

- Other factors to consider when grouping students:

  - **Same grade/class:** Given the choice of grouping children of widely different ages (e.g., 5 to 12-year-olds) and those of different disorders, it may be better to group according to age or class to better target common speech-language and academic skills.

  - **Same track:** For year-round schools, scheduling groups from the same track will not otherwise disrupt groups throughout the year.

  - **Time constraints:** If you are at a school site for only a certain number of days each week, you may have time restrictions to consider. Also, if a kindergarten class is scheduled only during the morning, your morning availability for other students may be reduced.

  - **Severity of disorder:** Students with more severe disorders may require more individual intervention to make progress.

  - **Treatment goals:** Certain goals may necessitate individual or group treatment (e.g., individual sessions to teach a set of basic words but group treatment for social communication skills).

  - **Behavioral limitations:** A student may not work well with certain peers or in a large group, requiring the SLP to spend most of the session managing that student's problem behaviors.

In addition to scheduling specific students, you must allow extra time each day to communicate and collaborate with other professionals such as the classroom teacher, school psychologist, reading and writing (literacy) specialist, and school nurse. Also, you need specific blocks of time allocated for testing students, writing reports, making telephone calls, and meeting with parents. School placements may also require school-based duties such as recess monitoring.

Types of Clients

The caseload for student clinicians in public schools can be varied enough to satisfy almost anyone's professional interests. In addition to the different age groups (birth through 22 years), children diagnosed with a wide range of disabilities are served in public schools.

During your school internship, you also will gain experience in preventing reading and writing difficulties and in providing direct services to enhance literacy skills in children (American Speech-Language-Hearing Association, 2016). With the national emphasis on literacy, the SLP's role in helping children acquire prereading, reading, and writing skills has gained much importance. You may work as a member of a team to understand how language and learning disorders affect children's acquisition of literacy skills and, when found necessary, provide direct literacy services to children and offer strategies to teachers and parents. That said, direct literacy services are provided by academic specialists in the educational setting and supported via language targets in the speech program (see Chapter 7 for literacy intervention targets).

School-based SLPs also might work with students with multiple physical and sensory disabilities. Children who have speech or language disorders associated with autism spectrum disorder (ASD), TBI, cerebral palsy, emotional or behavioral disorders, cognitive impairment, hearing loss, or cleft palate also are served in public schools. Your school internship gives you the opportunity to work with children with varied clinical conditions exhibiting a variety of communication disorders.

A caseload at a comprehensive kindergarten through sixth grade school may consist of students with fluency, language, speech-sound, and voice disorders. A caseload at the middle or high school level may include more students with language, speech sound, fluency, or voice disorders. With older students, more advanced language skills (academic and abstract language, narration, discourse, etc.) are targeted in the context of academic goals (Nippold, 2021). Some schools specialize in serving a specific population. For example, a residential school for children with severe hearing loss may teach oral communication and another may instruct sign language for the Deaf. SLPs may assess how a communication disorder in a student affects academic performance.

Federal and State Laws

Speech-language pathology services in the public schools are mandated by federal legislation. Services are designed to address the needs of all individuals who meet eligibility requirements due to a speech or language disorder. The 1975 Education of All Handicapped Children Act (EHA), Public Law 94-142, improved the identification and education of students with disabilities, encouraged the evaluation of such services, and safeguarded the rights of students and families (https://sites.ed.gov/idea/about-idea; United States Department of Education, n.d.). In 2004, the law was renamed IDEA and was amended again in 2015 through Pub. L. 114-95, Every Student Succeeds Act. In 2020–2021, 7.5 million infants, toddlers, children, and youth with disabilities were served under the law.

IDEA mandates that students with disabilities, including those with speech or language impairment, receive a **free and appropriate public education (FAPE)** in the LRE for students with disabilities. FAPE includes special education and related services (e.g., speech and language, psychological, and occupational services). All services are free of cost; meet the standards of the state educational agency; include preschool, elementary, and secondary school; and are provided in compliance with the student's IEP (Individual with Disabilities Education Act, 2004a). IDEA Part B requires services for preschool through adult education students (ages 3– 21 years) and Part C mandates intervention services for infants and toddlers (birth through 2 years) and their families.

The *eligibility criteria* for public school students to receive speech-language pathology services differ from those used in most university clinics. IDEA stipulates that all states must meet its requirements at a minimum; however, state laws may offer more protection to individuals and their families. Therefore, state laws and regulations on special education also affect speech-language pathology services provided in the public schools. For example, federal stipulations outline eligibility, which is often further defined by states, and even further interpreted by school districts. IDEA stipulates that a child with a disability must be evaluated and meet eligibility in accordance with the *Code of Federal Regulations* (CFR) under one of the 13 categories and that the disability adversely affects a child's performance. It is often considered a two-pronged eligibility standard. CFR defines speech and language impairment as "a communication disorder, such as stuttering, impaired articulation, a language impairment, or a voice impairment, that adversely affects a child's educational performance" (Child With a

Disability, 2023). Furthermore, in many states, to meet eligibility criteria, speech or language skills must be determined to be a *significant* area of need. For example, in California, a child who only has a single speech-sound error may be ineligible to receive services through the public school until 8 years of age. Services may be offered only if it is demonstrated that an error negatively affects educational achievement. That same child might receive treatment at a much younger age at a university clinic. Your supervisor in the school will provide you with the eligibility guidelines that are specific to the educational setting (please consult the IDEA website at https://sites.ed.gov/idea/ for more information).

Case law (court judgments about particular cases) also affect the interpretation of federal and state regulations. For example, the United States Supreme Court clarified the scope of FAPE in *Endrew F. v. Douglas County School District* (2017). The court ruled that IEP goals must be "appropriately ambitious" with "challenging objectives" based on the child's unique needs. Previous case law used a *di minimis* standard of providing *some* educational benefit. This is no longer the case and will affect how IEPs are written. School SLPs must know and follow all laws and guidelines affecting their school sites. Your onsite supervisor will apprise you of mandated services in public schools.

Many states have established a **Multi-tiered System of Supports** (MTSS) to coordinate several systems of intervention (e.g., academic, behavioral, social-emotional) for all students. **Response to Intervention** (RtI) is a multi-tiered, systematic, data-driven intervention that falls within the MTSS model. Federal law does not require RtI programs; however, IDEA does permit states to determine whether a student responds to effective, research-based intervention. Typically, RtI incorporates universal screening, data-driven decision making, high-quality instruction matched to individual students' needs, and frequent progress monitoring.

There is no single RtI model. Three tiers of support progress from less intensive to more intensive intervention; tier 1 involves high-quality instruction provided within the classroom; tier 2 encompasses more specialized instruction in small groups; and tier 3 includes more intensive individualized intervention, which may or may not be provided by special education instructors (Learning Disabilities Association of America, 2006). According to ASHA, the role of SLPs in the RtI process includes program planning, collaboration, and serving students. SLPs are expected to (a) participate in the selection of screening measures and evidence-based practice regarding literacy interventions, (b) conduct speech-sound error screenings for K–3 students and offer intervention; (c) provide information to families regarding screening and progress under intervention, and (d) consult with teachers to support literacy and language needs (Ehren et al., 2006). Speech and language RtI programs (non-IEP services) may be offered at your school practicum placement (e.g., speech-sound production, fluency, or social communication skills). Your supervisor will inform you on the programs and eligibility guidelines that are specific to your district and placement.

Report Writing and Recordkeeping

School SLPs also have administrative duties of report writing and recordkeeping. You will learn to organize and maintain records for students on your caseload according to each of their IEPs or Individualized Family Service Plans (IFSPs) from birth to 3-year-olds.

The IEP is a legally binding document that outlines a child's eligibility for services, presents levels of academic and nonacademic performance, documented needs, annual goals, accommodations/modifications, services, and educational setting that will be provided. The IEP is one of the cornerstones of service delivery in the public schools and is discussed in greater detail in Chapter 5. In addition to learning more about the IEP and how to write one, you will learn other new terms in your school practicum. Visit the companion website for a Glossary of Educational Abbreviations and Acronyms.

Working With Parents and Professionals

Student interns in public schools schedule and conduct meetings with parents and other professionals. You will learn to communicate effectively and work cooperatively with them to enhance your students' learning. Some schools employ speech-language pathology assistants (SLPAs) to support the SLPs. As described in Chapter 1, ASHA has several guidelines on the scope of practice for SLPAs and their supervision (American Speech-Language-Hearing Association, 2022).

Collaboration with other professionals is an important component of school internships. You may learn to work closely with or make referrals to school nurses, physicians, audiologists, occupational therapists, assistive technology specialists, social workers, psychologists, principals, or special and regular education teachers. You may participate in staff and community in-service that your supervisor and other professionals provide. Because of the limited time you have with each student, maximize your effectiveness through collaboration.

Hospitals

Hospital speech-language pathology covers a gamut of services. In a hospital setting, you may work with individuals in the acute-care phase, subacute-care facility, inpatient rehabilitation unit, outpatient department, or at the home of the client under the home health care program. In medical settings, you will learn new skills and vocabulary and understand how associations and organizations affect services offered. For example, you will hear about the **Joint Commission on Accreditation of Healthcare Organizations (JCAHO)**. The JCAHO is a regulatory agency that sets standards for individual care and accredits hospitals that meet its standards. Similar to ASHA's accreditation activities, JCAHO periodically reviews accredited hospitals to verify that they maintain the standards. JCAHO and its regulations will influence your clinical practicum in a hospital.

Your practicum experience will depend both on the organization of the hospital and the requirements of your individual practicum assignment. The following sections are only an overview of some of the experiences you may gain in hospital settings, which offer a wide range of stimulating and challenging learning opportunities.

Generally, to begin clinical practicum at a hospital, academic courses in *aphasia, voice disorders, dysphagia* (swallowing problems), *motor speech disorders* (dysarthria and apraxia of speech), *TBI, dementia,* and *right hemisphere disorder* (RHD) may be prerequisites or highly recommended. You should review textbooks and class notes on anatomy, physiology, and neurology of speech and hearing mechanisms. Some experience in assessing and treating clients with communication disorders associated with medical conditions will be an advantage.

In the acute hospital setting, a large percentage of clients with swallowing disorders will be on the SLP's caseload. You may be dealing with barium swallow studies and tracheostomy evaluations. Therefore, you should have completed at least one course in dysphagia.

Schedules

Hospital-based SLPs typically work for 8 hr a day, 5 days a week. SLPs may be required to work a variable schedule depending on client and staffing needs. For instance, to cover swallowing treatment during the individuals' breakfast or dinner, the day may begin and end earlier or later. In addition, SLPs may travel between hospital sites to ensure that they are sufficiently productive (generate billable time). Hospital clinicians may be assigned a rotating schedule that includes home health services, alternating weekends, or both. For example, a clinician may work 4 months in the hospital, 4 months with home health, and 4 months with outpatients. The SLP may also be required to work some weekends to cover the required 6-day-per-week treatments. In addition to hospital-based clinicians, private agencies or individual SLPs contracting for these services may provide in-home speech services.

Treatment in hospital settings is typically offered in individual sessions. The clinician works with a patient in his or her hospital room, the clinician's own office, or designated treatment rooms. Bedside evaluation and treatment are sometimes provided for individuals with acute medical conditions. For example, a client just recovering from a cerebrovascular accident (CVA) or TBI may not be medically stable enough to leave his or her hospital room. It still may be necessary for you to perform an assessment to determine the individual's communication status and need for intervention. In medical settings, SLP consultation is becoming more frequent as a model of care. The client's decreased length of stay (due to decreased medical reimbursement to acute-care hospitals) may limit assessment and intervention to a client's immediate needs and safe discharge to other settings. Once you have received a doctor's order to see hospitalized individuals, speech and language services may be offered 5 or 6 days per week. Outpatients are usually seen less frequently and may be seen in the office or as part of home health services.

Clients in the hospital may be seen more frequently than those attending university clinics, but they may receive services for a shorter duration. Because of health-care costs, most hospitals discharge individuals as soon as possible, with due regard for their well-being. Consequently, just when you are beginning to know your clients or observe some progress, they may be discharged from the hospital. In fact, hospital-based speech-language pathology services are increasingly concerned with discharge planning rather than sustained treatment.

Types of Clients

In hospital settings, you will encounter individuals with *aphasia, TBI, dementia, RHD,* or *motor speech disorders* and those facing or recovering from *laryngectomy.* Mostly, SLPs serve patients with swallowing disorders. In the rehabilitation or outpatient settings, SLPs assess the need for augmentative and alternative communication and train those who need it.

In most hospitals and RFs, you may work with individuals of all ages, except for a pediatric hospital, in which you serve only children. Serving on a **multidisciplinary team,** SLPs assess and treat individuals admitted for rehabilitation services. In addition to SLPs, the teams may consist of a nurse, physician, audiologist, physical therapist, occupational therapist, family caregiver, and social worker.

Some clients are transferred to the rehabilitation department after discharge from the acute-care setting. Other clients are discharged from the hospital for convalescence and may later be readmitted when they become candidates for rehabilitation. Discharge to home is also a possibility.

In a hospital rehabilitation setting, you may have the opportunity to work with individuals over a longer period of time than you will with those in acute-care settings. You will establish both short-term and long-range communication objectives for your clients and help them to regain their independent living skills.

Individuals may be discharged from the hospital acute-care or rehabilitation setting before they have completed their speech or language treatment. These individuals may be served in the hospital outpatient setting or in their homes via home health services if they are too ill to travel. Individuals also may seek services from private or university clinics.

Home health service may be provided to individuals after they are discharged from the hospital. Home care providers travel extensively to assess and treat the individuals at their homes. Service offered in the homes helps evaluate and modify the clients' functional communication skills and the pattern of family interactions in their natural environments.

You should consider a few variables in treating individuals and their family members in their homes. You must be aware of cultural or traditional characteristics of the home. For example, members of a family may remove their shoes before entering the home; other families do not readily accept strangers into their homes. You also must be aware of safety factors, such as the type of neighborhood a home is located in (e.g., a high crime area), the presence of an aggressive dog in the home, the possibility of substance abuse in the home, and the overall safety of the home. Also, while in a client's home, there are many distractions from other family members, doorbells, and ringing telephones.

State and federal government agencies regulate all clinical services, including those of the SLP's. The sort of clients on your caseload and the frequency, duration, and type of service largely may be influenced by private insurance company policies and the federal government's Medicare programs.

Report Writing and Recordkeeping

As in all settings, you are responsible for carefully documenting and reporting assessment results, treatment plans, and progress in hospital settings. See Chapter 5 for details on report writing. In hospital settings, you will also learn to complete different insurance and Medicare forms. In many cases, accurate and appropriate documentation will determine if your hospital receives reimbursement for your services from an insurance company. You will frequently hear and read the acronym **FIM**, which means **functional independence measure**. FIMs are similar to the objectives you write in your initial clinic experiences; however, FIMs emphasize patients' functional tasks (e.g., tell when he or she is ill) with as little assistance as possible. Hospital professions may communicate with each other through Subjective, Objective, Analysis, Plan (SOAP) notes in the client's charts; consult Chapter 5 for additional information on SOAP and other kinds of progress notes.

Hospital patient charts contain many abbreviations, symbols, and acronyms with which you may be unfamiliar. Visit the companion website for a Glossary of Medical Abbreviations and Symbols.

Working With Families and Professionals

Counseling and educating individuals and their families about communication disorders in hospital settings is an SLP's responsibility. The goal is to assists them in learning to deal with the disorder during the rehabilitation process. To deliver the best care for your clients, you will work with a team of professionals, including physical therapists, nurses, audiologists, social workers, occupational therapists, and physicians (see a later section in this chapter on professional collaborations).

Similar to the school setting, many hospitals promote **transdisciplinary teams** that are composed of different professionals who may provide some services for another team member. For example, if your client's goal is to communicate when in discomfort, the nurse may work on this goal during nursing activities and the SLP may be a consultant.

Multiskilling is similar to the idea of transdisciplinary teams. Multiskilling occurs when professionals are trained to offer more than one service across related disciplines. In multiskilling, an SLP might be trained to take a client's temperature and blood pressure during management of a swallowing disorder. Generally, multiskilling is not popular with most hospital personnel but is being offered as a cost-saving alternative by some insurance and research groups. Read ASHA's position paper on the use of multiskilled personnel before you begin a medical internship (American Speech-Language-Hearing Association, 1997).

In *hospital rounds*, you and other care providers meet with the physician in charge, check the status of patients, and share information about all the patients under the care of the same team of specialists. You might ask questions about assessments and treatments.

Skilled Nursing Facilities

Skilled nursing facilities (SNFs) or **long-term care facilities (LTCs)** provide services for individuals requiring convalescent care, often following discharge from the hospital and before the client returns home. The SNF also provides long-term medical care. Generally, services in the SNF are similar to those in a hospital.

Nursing care in the SNF involves regularly monitoring of the individual's vital signs (such as temperature, pulse, blood pressure, respiration), giving medications, and offering other types of medical care. Individuals also may receive services from other professionals, such as a physical therapist, SLP, occupational therapist, recreational therapist, and social worker.

Typical individuals receiving care in an SNF are older. Therefore, in addition to courses related to medically related communication disorders (e.g., aphasia and dysarthria), a course in gerontology is highly desirable. The completion of courses addressing dementia and memory care are also beneficial.

Schedules

Individual treatment sessions are common in SNFs, although some group sessions may be held to promote social communication skills because in the SNF environment, opportunities for social interaction may be limited. Group sessions also are used to monitor clients' swallowing abilities as they progress to independent eating. In an SNF, many clients fatigue quickly, so the lengths of both the evaluation and treatment sessions may be brief.

Typically, work in the SNF is 5 days a week for 8 hr a day. For certain clients, speech-language pathology services are provided 6 days per week, including Saturdays. To manage a client's swallowing, you will often work during mealtimes. To arrive during mealtime tray distribution, SLPs sometimes begin at 6:30 a.m. or arrive later and work until 7 p.m. Follow the schedule of your clinical supervisor unless other arrangements are agreed on.

Types of Clients

As noted, older individuals are the typical clients in SNFs. In these individuals, communication disorders commonly treated are associated with *TBI, stroke, tumors of the brain, RHD, carcinomas of the head and neck, hearing loss,* and *a variety of neurodegenerative diseases* that lead to dementia (e.g., Alzheimer disease, Huntington disease, Parkinson disease).

Although persons residing in SNFs have communication disorders, the majority of them have dysphagia. However, because of liability issues and different levels of training, student clinicians may work with persons who have dysphagia only on a limited basis, and that too, under 100% supervision.

Report Writing and Recordkeeping

Reports and progress notes written in the SNF are similar to those in hospital settings. In an SNF, you may need the physician's orders to evaluate or treat an individual.

In the SNF, you also assist in billing private and federal insurance. Additionally, you may participate in the process of appealing decisions of third-party payers (e.g., insurance companies) that deny payment for services. As in all settings, your documentation and report writing should be accurate and appropriate in SNFs.

Working With Families and Professionals

In addition to direct client contact, the SLP provides *indirect services through consultation* with the SNF staff. A significant part of this indirect service is to (a) educate the staff (nurses and aides) regarding communication and swallowing disorders; (b) train the staff to help identify and refer clients who may have communication disorders; and (c) train both the staff and the families on ways to optimize communication. The family members should be invited to take part in treatment and generalization planning and execution.

For your clients who have swallowing disorders, you will work closely with the dietitian and nursing staff. If you are asked to participate in feeding the patients, you will ensure that you are properly trained and constantly supervised.

Rehabilitation Facilities

RFs provide comprehensive services to individuals disabled by an accident or illness. The goal of rehabilitation is to maximize recovery and minimize any residual dysfunction.

An RF may be a stand-alone specialty institution, housed in a hospital, or be a private agency. Members of a multidisciplinary team that includes an SLP offer both inpatient and outpatient services. To derive the greatest benefit from your practicum experience in an RF, you should have completed coursework in *aphasia, motor speech disorders, TBI, RHD, dementia,* and *dysphagia.*

Schedules

Clients served in RFs receive intensive treatment, sometimes 2 times per day, 5 to 6 days a week. The typical 8 a.m. to 5 p.m. schedule may vary depending on the needs of the client.

Student clinicians are encouraged to be flexible, as schedule changes may occur daily. As in other medical settings, your treatment may cover mealtime for patients with a swallowing disorder. Therefore, you may begin and end your workday earlier or later than is typical.

Types of Clients

Many patients in an RF may have had TBI, resulting from falls, accidents, gunshots, domestic violence, and so forth. TBI resulting in communication disorders may include dysarthria and a variety of social communication impairments (Hegde, 2024b). Individuals with TBI may also exhibit impaired attention, orientation, memory, and dysphagia.

Individuals recovering from CVA in RFs typically exhibit aphasia. Additional independent and coexisting problems may include apraxia of speech, dysarthria, and dysphagia. With patients who have had a tracheostomy, the SLP may work to improve swallowing as well as vocal qualities. A respiratory therapist may also be involved.

RFs also serve individuals with orthopedic problems, including children with cerebral palsy. All these individuals benefit from physical, speech-language, and vocational therapy.

You may assist the client with relearning daily living activities, functional communication, and memory skills. You may also teach the use of assistive communication devices to individuals with limited verbal communication skills.

Report Writing and Recordkeeping

Documentation requirements in an RF are similar to those of many hospitals. Follow the requirements of your site.

Read Chapter 5 to learn more about different kinds of report writing.

Working With Professionals and Families

The rehabilitation team often includes a physiatrist, physical therapist, SLP, occupational therapist, nurse, neuropsychologist, and social worker. A **physiatrist** is a physician trained in rehabilitative medicine and often serves as the team leader. There is close communication among team members whose services are interrelated. For example, based on information obtained during client staffing, the SLP may find that a specific client cannot reach across midline. During speech therapy, the clinician carefully places pictures the client is required to point to within his or her reach. In another instance, the physical therapist may learn from the SLP that a nonverbal client in physical therapy sessions can produce single-word utterances and begin to prompt such responses.

The rehabilitation team also works closely with the client's family members to encourage their participation in rehabilitation. A psychologist or social worker may counsel family members to help them deal with the needed emotional adjustments. The SLP also counsels the family and works with them to reestablish an individual's communication skills.

Psychiatric Hospitals

Psychiatric hospitals often are state-operated and designed to serve *individuals who are diagnosed with behavior disorders (mental illness) or intellectual disabilities.* Most of these facilities offer speech and hearing services. Although residential care is part of psychiatric hospitals, outpatient services also are available. In recent years, there has been an increased emphasis on mainstreaming those who are diagnosed with mental illness or intellectual disability. You may work closely with the client's family, teachers, or employers. You may work in more or less restrictive facilities, including state psychiatric hospitals, outpatient clinics, or schools.

Clinical practicum in a psychiatric setting offers you an opportunity to work with unique cases and interact with many professionals. You will learn to work as a member of a multidisciplinary team that helps modify behavioral problems. Your main responsibility on the team will be to evaluate and treat individuals with communication disorders associated with behavioral disorders, intellectual disabilities, or both.

In addition to a strong background in speech and language disorders, student clinicians preparing for an internship in a psychiatric hospital will need skills in behavior management. Courses in applied behavior analysis and abnormal or clinical psychology are useful. Some sites also may use assistive technology.

Schedules

The frequency and length of treatment sessions in psychiatric facilities will vary, depending on the needs of the client, the specific setting the client is seen in, and the financial resources of the client and the agency. The length of a session also is dependent on the duration for which the client can effectively participate in treatment. Some psychiatric clients benefit from a 45-min treatment session, whereas others may need a shorter session because of limited attention span.

Frequent schedule changes due to multidisciplinary scheduling conflicts may occur in psychiatric settings. When your therapy schedule conflicts with that of another professional, discuss the matter and make schedule modifications.

Types of Clients

In psychiatric facilities, the SLP provides services to both children and adults. Frequently, the SLP is requested to evaluate an individual's communication disorder, which might be contributing to his or her problem behavior.

The complex needs of the clients served in psychiatric setting necessitate working with a team of professionals, including a psychiatric nurse, psychologist, social worker, psychiatrist, as well as other professionals. Together, the team designs treatment programs for clients diagnosed with various psychiatric conditions (e.g., schizophrenia, depression).

Preschool Agencies

Preschool agencies typically serve children ages 3 to 5 years. **Early intervention centers** serve infants and toddlers from birth until the third birthday. Both private and government agencies serve children under 5 years of age. Typically, SLPs serve in such government programs as Head Start, state preschools, economic opportunity programs, regional centers, and local school districts. To be most effective, services should be provided in settings familiar to the child, including the home and school settings that simulate, to the extent possible, children's home environment.

Since the passage of Pub. L. 94-142 and its amendments, public schools have been providing preschool services for children with special needs. In many communities, SLPs providing their services to preschool children are employees of the school district. In other communities, the school districts may contract with a private practice to provide mandated services for preschool children with speech-language disorders.

A good understanding of normal and disordered speech and language development, infant speech perception and production, and techniques of early intervention is essential to work in preschools. A general knowledge of child development is helpful.

Schedules

In public schools and Head Start programs, the SLP frequently works as an itinerant clinician, daily traveling from one location to another, sometimes to multiple sites. Some districts have early intervention or preschool centers that serve the entire preschool population. In this case, SLPs may work full time at such centers.

Preschools use several service delivery models, including individual and group therapy formats. Children with speech sound, voice, or fluency disorders are usually seen individually. Those with disorders of language are seen individually or in small groups. Often, language, social, and educational activities may be embedded within the daily routine to promote more natural communication interactions. Therapy may be provided in the home, preschool, speech room, or community. Such integrated activities may promote generalization and maintenance (Wilcox & Woods, 2011).

Types of Clients

In preschool programs, you will work with a variety of children with a wide range of communication disorders. Generally, the more severe the physical and sensory disabilities of a child, the greater the communication needs. In some preschools, you may work with children using augmentative and alternative communication devices. In other preschools, you may work with children who primarily have speech-sound or language disorders. In many settings, you will assess preliteracy skills and intervene if warranted. ASHA strongly endorses the role of the SLP in developing reading and writing skills as they relate to language development (American Speech-Language-Hearing Association, 2001).

With the increasing demand for services for young children diagnosed with ASD, you are likely to be working with preschoolers with this diagnosis because of their impaired or limited communication skills. Your services may include assessment, treatment, referring to and coordinating services with other agencies, and helping families receive available support services.

Report Writing and Recordkeeping

Some children progress slowly, whereas others progress at a rapid rate. In all cases, documentation of treatment and its results are essential. Your clinical supervisor will outline the requirements of documentation and report writing at your practicum site.

The age of the preschool child dictates the formal paperwork required. If a child is in the birth to 3-year age range, you will become familiar with writing an IFSP. Once a child turns 3 years old, an IEP must be written. See Chapter 5 for more information on report writing.

Working With Families and Professionals

In preschools, you will learn to provide consultative services to the student's parents and teachers. You will learn to train preschool teachers and their assistants on ways to maximize your clients' communication and to reinforce emerging speech and language skills. You also will work closely with the parents of preschool children. A partnership between the SLP and the student's family is the cornerstone of early intervention. The aim is to foster "family-centered practice" (Blue-Banning et al., 2004). Often, it is difficult for parents to initially accept that their child has a communication disorder. In working with parents of preschoolers, you will use the skills you have acquired in previous practicum experiences and in any counseling courses you have taken.

Your work with parents of preschoolers involves training them in conducting home treatment programs when necessary. Training parents to work regularly with their child to teach target behaviors and to routinely provide language expansion activities is a major part of your work.

Prisons

Prisons are a growing industry in the United States and a large number of prisoners have communication disorders. Speech-language pathology services may be provided in adult prisons and are mandated services in juvenile facilities.

In addition to a strong background in speech and language disorders, the student preparing to work in a prison should understand criminal behavior and criminal justice. Before beginning your internship, you will be required to pass a security clearance. Also, you may be required to pass a training course that focuses on how to interact with prisoners, how to dress, and how to behave in an emergency.

Schedules

Schedules will vary depending on the facility. Typically, services will be provided between 8 a.m. and 5 p.m., Monday through Friday. In adult prisons, the frequency and duration of services will depend on the needs and availability of your client. For example, you may see a client twice a week in sessions lasting 45 min. However, there may be times when your client is unavailable because of a personal discipline or prison lockdown.

In a juvenile facility, your services will be regulated by your client's IEP. Refer to the section on public school services and Chapter 5 for more information about IEPs. Also, services will be influenced by your client's personal discipline, facility lockdown, and duration of his or her sentence.

Types of Clients

In correctional institutions, you will see clients with disorders of speech-sound production, voice, fluency, and language. Some clients may have only one disability or may have multiple disabilities. Some clients may have limited education and some may have behavioral disorders.

Behavioral contingencies are often embedded in the daily regime of prisons. Prisons have strict rules for earning certain "benefits" and consequently, prisoners may be motivated to work with you. You may use a token or points system to reinforce target communication skills.

Report Writing and Recordkeeping

Accurate and thorough report writing and recordkeeping are essential components of this setting. Your supervisor will give you complete information on the facility's requirements.

If you work in a juvenile facility, you will write IEPs. See Chapter 5 for more information.

Working With Families and Professionals

Depending on the prison you are working in, you may have little contact with your clients' family. If contact with a client's family is attained, follow the regulations on site.

Although family contact may be limited, you may work with the prison's nurse, teachers, or correctional officers. These professionals may assist you in providing effective intervention for your clients. You will find that having to work in a locked facility and relying on each other for your safety helps build a close professional community.

Private Practice

Private practitioners offer services in their own offices as well as in such contracted sites as hospitals without speech and hearing departments, RFs, home health care agencies, skilled nursing homes, psychiatric facilities, and private preschools. They also may contract to serve children in local public schools. Across the nation, private practices in speech-language pathology are rapidly growing.

Some private clinics may specialize. For example, one private practice may specialize in pediatric services, with another perhaps serving adults only. Yet another private clinic may have expertise in treating clients with laryngectomy or stuttering. There also are extensive private practices that hire large numbers of SLPs who contract to serve individuals in skilled nursing facilities and home health-care agencies.

Student practicum opportunities in private settings is somewhat limited because the clients and their families who pay for the services expect to receive them from the professional. Students planning a practicum assignment in a private practice need a broad educational background.

Clients may range from infants to older individuals. The entire range of communication disorders may be treated in private settings.

Because the private practitioner depends on favorable public relations, you will need to have, or quickly develop, good interpersonal skills. You will gain insight into the business aspects of your profession. You will learn about marketing your services to the public and getting reimbursed by insurance companies and government programs such as Medicare.

Schedules

Schedules will vary depending on the type of service delivery in which the private practice is involved. If you are working in an SNF, your schedule will resemble that already described.

If you are working with clients in the private practice office, your schedule will be influenced by the times clients are available for appointments. Although many practices operate on an 8 a.m. to 5 p.m. schedule, often certain days are reserved for appointments outside of regular business hours (e.g., 6 p.m. to 9 p.m.). Typically, treatment is scheduled for 30-min sessions two to three times per week. The duration and frequency of treatment are based on each client's needs and financial resources.

Types of Clients

Clients may range from infants through adults. Disorders can cover the gamut of communication difficulties. Severity may spread across the continuum from very mild to severe.

Of course, if you are assigned to a private practice that specializes in a certain disorder, you will mostly see clients with that disorder. For example, a private practice may specialize in communication interventions for children diagnosed with ASD.

Working With Families and Other Professionals

One advantage to working with clients in private practice is that they have sought out the services and are highly motivated. Therefore, it is sometimes easier to get the family members involved in treatment. On occasion, however, because of the cost of private speech and language services, some families expect the SLP to provide a quick cure for a client. On other occasions, it may be necessary to immediately include family members in a client's treatment because the client's finances or insurance allows only a limited number of treatment sessions.

Regardless of the situation, you will learn to communicate effectively and to work closely with various family members. Communication with other professionals may be written or verbal. You will interact with different professionals. For example, if you are working in a rehabilitation setting or SNF, you will collaborate with different members of the facility's staff (e.g., physical therapist, occupational therapist, social worker, nurse, physician) to maximize your clients' treatment.

Other Clinical Settings

There are many other clinical practicum settings that have not been discussed in this chapter. Among these are the speech-language pathology services provided at **adult day health-care centers, veterans' administration hospitals, and public clinics.**

The range of settings in which you might complete your clinical practicum may be limited by demographic factors and your university's resources. More frequently, however, the range is limited only by your own initiative. If you wish to gain practicum experience in a new setting, discuss your interest with your supervisor, clinical director, or academic advisor.

Distance Education and Online Learning

Distance education and **online learning** programs, which have grown since the 2020 coronavirus pandemic, may offer some or nearly all courses using an online learning format. Distance learning programs may be accredited by the Council on Academic Accreditation in Audiology and Speech-Language Pathology (CAA) (see Chapter 1). Students enrolled in distance education programs take academic classes via the Internet and video-recorded or televised courses. Distance learners often are not on the host campus that offers the courses. Clinical practicum requirements may be designed specifically for students in that program. In most instances, clinical practicum is completed in a more traditional on-site manner as supervised by an ASHA-certified supervisor.

Practicum experiences through an online format called telesupervision is uncommon. **Telesupervision** uses a two-way digital video conferencing system allowing an ASHA-certified SLP to supervise a student clinician's sessions from a distance. All ASHA regulations and supervision requirements must be followed. Advantages of this method include fostering clinical independence, providing more opportunities for practicum, and promoting more flexibility in scheduling. However, this method may not be appropriate, depending on the clients, settings, and skill level of the student clinician. Furthermore, it may be difficult to maintain all the state and federal confidentiality laws. Therefore, use of telesupervision is dependent on ASHA regulations, the laws of a particular state, and the policies of a university (Dudding, 2012).

Clinical Internships

Internships are a part of clinical practicum, completed at an off-campus site. They provide comprehensive, on-the-job experience for more advanced students. The qualifications of the student clinician and the requirements of the clinical site determine the type of internships available.

Clinical internships may be *part time* or *full time*. There are advantages and disadvantages to each. With help from your faculty advisor, you will select a schedule that best balances your academic and clinical workloads.

Part-Time Internships

Part-time internships can be *intermittent* or *daily*. **Intermittent part-time internships** allow clinical practicum at a given site on a periodic basis. For example, you might receive a practicum assignment at a skilled nursing facility for 2 hr per day, 2 days per week. Other intermittent internships may allow your hours to vary from week to week. In **daily part-time internships,** you are assigned a clinical site for a specified number of hours. You practice there each day of the work week.

Part-time internships allow you to schedule your work and academic classes around clinical practicum. Some part-time internships may be so limited that you will not learn much about the setting and the clients served there. However, in the early stages of clinical practicum, many student clinicians need additional time to assimilate and integrate new information and experiences. Part-time internships may serve these students well.

Full-Time Internships

Full-time internships are similar to the work schedule of the clinical-site staff. They require you to participate in a clinical practicum with the number of hours, workdays, and holidays parallel to those of the staff clinician. If you are participating in a full-time practicum assignment at an elementary school, you might be there from 8 a.m. to 3:30 p.m., Monday through Friday for a specific number of weeks or total number of hours. If you were assigned to a hospital practicum site as a full-time intern you probably would be required to arrive at 8 a.m. and work until 5 p.m., Monday through Friday for a certain number of weeks or until you earn a specific number of clinical hours.

Full-time and even daily part-time internships provide a more comprehensive practicum experience than do intermittent assignments. In full-time internships, you may experience more of the professional and interpersonal aspects of an assigned setting. In addition to direct client contact, you also may be included in rounds or staffing and be more closely involved with allied professionals. You may attend or even provide staff development (training) in-service. A full-time internship allows you to experience the daily routines and pressures associated with a particular setting and to obtain a better understanding of the personal as well as professional requirements of the work setting. Part-time internships rarely provide you with this opportunity because you are not on-site long enough.

Because full-time internships are intensive and allow minimal time for class work, they often are reserved for student clinicians in their final term of graduate work or for summer practicum assignments. However, if you wish to take up a full-time internship sooner, discuss it with your advisor.

Collaborating With Other Professionals

Fully licensed, certified, and credentialed SLPs working as independent professionals collaborate with various related professionals. The same clients may simultaneously receive services from an SLP and such other professionals as physicians, physical therapists, psychologists, or special education teachers. Professionals refer their clients to each other, exchange assessment and treatment reports, and discuss common concerns to improve interprofessional service delivery. Interprofessional relationships are mutually beneficial and effective for their clients.

Student clinicians generally do not independently interact with other professionals. A student clinician cannot directly and independently refer a client to another professional. The clinical supervisor mediates a student clinician's interactions with other professionals. If you see a need to coordinate your services with those of other professionals, you must discuss this with your clinical supervisor. Nonetheless, student practicum affords opportunities to learn about interprofessional collaboration. It is good to know how this is done and what kinds of specialists most commonly interact with SLPs.

To work effectively with other professionals, SLPs must know their expertise and the services they offer. Following is a brief summary of the services different specialists provide that may be useful to you and your clients.

Health and Allied Health Professionals

1. **Audiologist.** *The audiologist is a specialist in the identification, measurement, and rehabilitation of hearing impairments.* SLPs work

closely with audiologists in all professional settings. SLPs refer clients who do not pass their hearing screenings to audiologists, and audiologists screen speech and language and refer individuals who fail the screening to SLPs. The audiologist may recommend repair, modification, or replacement of hearing aids your client may wear. SLPs and audiologists collaboratively develop and implement speech rehabilitation programs for children with hearing loss and those with cochlear implants. The two professionals may work together to provide community access to assistive listening devices.

2. **Board-Certified Behavioral Analyst**. *The board-certified behavioral analyst* (commonly referred to as a BCBA) *is an individual who conducts behavioral assessments and designs and supervises interventions based on the principles of applied behavioral analysis (ABA).* The BCBA minimally has a master's degree, has completed a specified number of practicum hours, and has passed an examination. The BCBA has become the professional of choice to develop and oversee intervention programs for children with ASD. If you work with children diagnosed with ASD, it is likely you will collaborate with BCBAs.

3. **Neurologist**. *The neurologist is a physician with specialized training in function and disorders of the nervous system.* Within neurology, there are subspecialties such as pediatric or geriatric neurology. Neurologists treat individuals who have had strokes, head trauma, brain cancer and tumor, and various degenerative neurological diseases that are associated with communication disorders. The neurologist may request a speech and language assessment of a client with a neurological disorder. An SLP may request a neurological assessment of a person who has aphasia, TB, or dementia.

4. **Occupational Therapist**. *The registered occupational therapist (OT) provides evaluation and treatment of individuals with disabilities who need help with their daily living activities* that include assessing and retraining in dressing, cooking, and bathing. The OT also may train the individuals in the use of adaptive living devices (e.g., modified eating utensils and cooking equipment) that help individuals live more independently. Depending on the setting, either the OT or the SLP heads the dysphagia team.

5. **Orthodontist**. *The orthodontist is a specialist in dental occlusion.* SLPs work closely with the orthodontist, who provides services for

a client with cleft palate, other craniofacial anomaly, or myofunctional disorder. The orthodontist may request an SLP for a speech evaluation.

6. **Otorhinolaryngologist.** *The otorhinolaryngologist* (commonly called an ENT) *is a physician specializing in evaluation and treatment of disorders of the ear, nose, and throat.* SLPs often collaborate with ENTs in treating individuals with voice disorders, those who have undergone laryngeal surgeries, and children with otitis media.

7. **Pediatrician.** *The pediatrician is a physician specializing in the medical care of children.* SLPs may refer children to their pediatricians because of suspected chronic health problems (allergies, colds, and so on). A pediatrician may refer a child to an SLP because of speech and language delay or disorders.

8. **Physiatrist.** *The physiatrist is a physician with specialized training in rehabilitative medicine.* The physiatrist directs the rehabilitation of an individual diagnosed with a disability. When your client's disabilities are caused by CVA or head trauma, you may work closely with a physiatrist. The specialist may request a speech and language assessment and treatment progress report. You may offer suggestions to assist in the client's reentry into school, work, or home environments.

9. **Physical therapist.** *The registered physical therapist (RPT or PT) or doctor of physical therapy (DPT) provides assessment and treatment for disorders related to physical and musculoskeletal injuries.* In the hospital and rehabilitation setting, the SLP and PT often provide services for many of the same clients who have motor disabilities, positioning and postural problems, and swallowing disorders. Both SLP and PT may be members of a team developing augmentative and alternative communication for minimally verbal or nonverbal individuals.

10. **Prosthodontist.** *The prosthodontist is a dentist with specialized training in the development and use of prosthetic appliances.* The SLP and prosthodontist may consult regarding a client with insufficient velopharyngeal closure. You may refer a client with velopharyngeal incompetence (VPI) to a prosthodontist. A prosthodontist may ask you to help assess velopharyngeal adequacy in a client before and after a prosthetic appliance is used. You also may be asked for suggestions regarding choice of appliances.

11. **Registered Nurse.** *The registered nurse (RN) is responsible for most medical care the physician prescribes for patients.* RNs can provide information on daily communication skills of individuals with strokes, TBI, right hemisphere syndrome, laryngectomy, and other individuals under their care. SLPs may train the nursing staff in effective communication with individuals whose skills are impaired.

12. **Social Worker.** *The social worker is a professional who investigates and finds social, economic, health, and other resources and support for individuals in need.* Social workers are members of the hospital's rehabilitation team working with the patient's family. Social workers help find needed community services for your clients along with available social or financial support. For example, while serving older clients in their homes, an SLP may observe that neither the spouse nor the client can prepare meals for themselves. The social worker may be able to obtain part-time help for the couple or arrange for delivery of prepared meals through social service.

Educational Specialists

1. **Adaptive Physical Education Specialist.** *The adaptive physical education (APE) specialist is an expert in physical education of individuals with disabilities.* Adaptive physical education specialists often are members of the IEP team.

2. **Educational Audiologist.** *The educational audiologist specializes in the assessment and management of hearing disorders in school children.* School-based SLPs may work with children with hearing loss and those who have had cochlear implants.

3. **School Nurse.** *The school nurse is a registered nurse with additional training in laws related to public schools.* The school nurse often screens students' hearing and vision, maintains a health history for each student, and acts as a liaison between the educational staff and other health professionals. Licensed vocational nurses (LVNs) may also work with students in the educational setting. For example, if a student with severe medical needs requires a nurse assigned to him or her throughout the day to manage health needs, an LVN may be assigned as a one-to-one nurse.

4. **School Psychologist.** *The school psychologist is trained and credentialed to offer psychological services in the public school setting.* School psychologists test students to determine their educational strengths and

weaknesses and help determine appropriate educational placement. They recommend intervention techniques and offer counseling to students and their families. School psychologists may request speech and language assessments on students they work with. SLPs may seek help from the school psychologist on managing a child's behavior problems that interfere with treatment. Psychologists and SLPs may administer certain assessments together and make team decisions.

5. **Special Education Teacher or Resource Specialist.** *The special education teacher or professional in a resource specialist program (RSP) is a credentialed teacher with additional training in teaching children with specific disabilities or disorders.* Many students receiving services from a special education teacher also need the services of the SLP. Special education specialists work with students (a) who are Deaf or hard of hearing (DHH), (b) who have various levels of disabilities, (c) with severe emotional disturbance, (d) with severe orthopedic disabilities, and (e) with visual impairments.

6. **Teacher.** *The regular education teacher is an important professional with whom school-based SLPs work.* Many children with disabilities are in inclusive general education classrooms with accommodations and modifications. Special education teachers and other specialists, including SLPs, collaborate and support the teacher to maximize learning opportunities for the student. SLPs may incorporate the curriculum into their treatment plans. To promote generalization and maintenance of speech-language skills, SLPs may provide services in the classroom or request the teacher to reinforce and support the clinically established communication skills.

7. **Instructional Aides (IAs).** *Instructional aides are support staff who may be trained to work with students.* IAs may be employed in the general education classroom, special education classroom, and speech room to support the professionals. Undergraduate students in their SLP training program may apply for IA positions, even though their work hours cannot be counted as clinical practicum hours. They may do so to improve their chances of admission to graduate programs in speech-language pathology and to gain some real-world knowledge in a school setting. Under the supervision of an SLP, IAs may conduct therapy for speech and language disorders and offer clerical support. Requirements may include some coursework on special education, speech and language disorders, and child development. Passing a state's basic education skills test may be an additional requirement.

Guidelines on Effective Collaboration

Effective collaboration requires clear communication among the professionals. Mutual respect and appreciation of services each provides are equally important. Following guidelines and learning from your supervisor can help you master interprofessional collaborative skills.

1. **Provide high-quality service.** This will help develop a reputation for excellence. Be well prepared for each clinical session and meeting.

2. **Communicate effectively.** Provide clear, concise, and relevant information in a timely manner. Share results of assessment or treatment progress to facilitate efficient decision making. Report the effects of your services in direct and measurable terms and minimize the use of jargon. Supplement your narrative with graphs and tables that show the clinical progress of your clients.

3. **Be courteous.** Regardless of your feelings, be courteous. If you offer an inappropriate or unexpected response, that is how you will be remembered. You can disagree and present your viewpoint in a gracious manner.

4. **Understand and respect the services provided by other professionals.** Know what other professionals do and how it affects your services. Appreciate their services and their value to your client.

5. **Respond promptly.** Reply readily and accurately to inquiries from clients and professionals. Send your reports promptly because clinical services may need urgent attention.

6. **Acknowledge referrals.** Send a thank-you letter to professionals who refer clients to you. You may receive additional helpful information or more referrals. Visit the companion website for sample Referral Letters.

7. **Educate other professionals about speech-language pathology services.** Do not miss an opportunity to educate other professionals about speech-language pathology. Offer accurate information about your services and the needs of particular clients.

8. **Respect professional boundaries.** Give information only about speech-language pathology. Do not give information, advice, or treatment that is not within the scope of speech-language pathology. Expect other professionals to respect the SLP's autonomy and expertise.

9. **Get your supervisor's approval before you contact another professional**. Always get the supervisor's approval and advice before contacting another professional.

General Administrative Procedures

Any clinical facility, in addition to offering high-quality clinical services, has to have administrative procedures in place. Student clinicians need to learn some of the skills necessary to run a clinical facility.

The university department will maintain its academic and clinical facilities. The department makes sure that its equipment is properly calibrated and functional. Other administrative procedures may include the determination of placements as well as the maintenance of student clinician records.

Facilities and Equipment

The university ensures that both on-site and off-site facilities are adequate and appropriate for clinical practicum. The university speech and hearing clinic maintains a current inventory of evaluation instruments and supplies, provides a professional and safe environment in which to provide clinical services, and offers adequate supervision and guidance to students through qualified supervisors.

The clinic also should have a method to review and improve the quality of the clinical services it offers the public. It is important to have measurable clinical goals and objective outcome indicators. The quality review and improvement process might include such activities as surveys of client satisfaction, review of calibration logs, and review of clinic documentation.

Off-site practicum locations are also evaluated for the appropriateness of facilities. The university clinic director may visit the facilities to ensure they are safe and adequately maintained. If you have any concerns about on-campus or off-campus facilities, discuss them with your clinic director, faculty advisor, or both.

Scheduling Practicum Assignments

Several variables affect scheduling and assignment of practicum experiences. The student's experience, the student's clinical clock hour needs, the student's specific area of interest, availability of practicum sites, the number of clients seeking services, and the availability of clinical supervisors all affect scheduling.

Because of these and other variables, you may not always get the kind of assignments you desire. Some universities allow for requests regarding placement. The better the communication between you and the clinic director, the greater the likelihood of your having a successful practicum experience. Therefore, follow the format your university uses in registering for practicum each term and for expressing your practicum preferences ahead of time.

Student Records

Prior to being admitted into clinical practicum, students' records are reviewed to find out if they meet the academic requirements for clinical practicum. Although ASHA provides minimum guidelines for student performance, individual universities may have additional requirements the students must meet.

The clinic staff maintains records of student clinicians. These records are reviewed periodically to ensure that they meet both the university and ASHA guidelines for clinical practicum, including the types of clients served and the number of clinical hours earned. It is important that you accurately communicate, through the forms your department uses, the clock hours you have earned, and the clinical experiences you have completed. ASHA requires you to maintain a record of your academic and clinic experiences. Your university department is likely to use ASHA's Knowledge and Skills Acquisition Form (KASA) for this purpose. Get the KASA form from your department office. Find out if your university requires additional documentation.

The clinic director (or the department chair) ensures that an evaluation of your performance is written at the end of each clinical assignment. The supervisor discusses your evaluation with you and places a copy of the evaluation in your file. The evaluation of your clinical skills and the corresponding grade will influence your future practicum assignments. If your clinical skills are weak, your continued participation in clinical practicum may be a matter for discussion. If you disagree with an evaluation of your practicum, you should discuss your concerns with your supervisor. If necessary, follow established procedures students must use to protest evaluations.

Clinical Supplies, Materials, and Equipment

The university clinic and many off-campus sites provide a variety of supplies, materials, and equipment for your use. However, you also will be required to purchase some materials, equipment, and supplies. You should begin building your own inventory of materials and supplies throughout your clinical practicum, regardless of what is available to you.

Clinic *supplies* are consumable items. These include tongue depressors, gauze, cotton swabs, gloves, finger cots, tissue, and disinfectant. Carefully follow your clinic's protocol regarding disposal of items that have come in contact with saliva or blood during evaluation or treatment sessions.

Clinical *materials* also are consumable or expendable items and include test response forms and such treatment materials as articulation cards, language programs, and books. Your clinic library or media center may have a wide variety of tests for the evaluation of communication disorders. Test response forms are expensive, especially when they must be supplied to 20 to 40 student clinicians per semester. Use the response forms judiciously. It is not appropriate to photocopy response forms for clinical use unless the publisher specifically gives permission to reproduce them. Follow the checkout procedures outlined at your university or clinical site.

As you progress in your clinical practicum, you may be required to use varied assessment instruments. Instead of continually administering the same test across clients, experiment. Learn and administer new tests. Find out which tests evaluate what they purport to evaluate, which tests are standardized for specific populations, and which speech and language behaviors might be better evaluated through analysis of speech and language samples. After you graduate, you will select your own tests. Therefore, take time to learn to objectively evaluate most of the published tests made available to you at a practicum site.

In addition to numerous tests, your clinic will have a supply of treatment materials. The type and quantity of materials differ across campuses and clinical sites. Generally available are a selection of articulation cards depicting pictures designed to evoke corresponding phonemes in a variety of word positions. Also, you frequently will have access to picture or photo decks representing many vocabulary and language concepts. Comprehensive language programs and books also may be available. Your clinic may supply different types of toys for use with younger clients. There is an abundance of commercial items available, although often faculty and clinic staff preferences influence the types of materials made available to the student clinician.

Treatment materials are the most individual or personalized of items used in clinical practicum. Therefore, most student clinicians develop their own materials. Many websites have downloadable materials that are inexpensive and time-efficient. Student clinicians also may use tablet applications that are readily available and appealing to young clients.

Student clinicians find it functional, as well as beneficial, to allow their clients to create some of their treatment materials. With the assistance of a parent, a child might be asked to cut pictures out of a magazine and bring them to the treatment session to put into a speech book. Another client might be asked to bring in newspaper articles to discuss during a treatment session. You may ask clients with good drawing skills to draw picture cards for use in their treatment sessions and home practice assignments.

In the school setting, curriculum materials may be used along with other treatment materials. Clinicians in other settings may emphasize naturally occurring activities or events to evoke speech and language behaviors. Using functional and naturally occurring treatment materials can help you in promoting generalization and maintenance of target behaviors. Personalized materials the student clinician creates usually meet a specific need and are, consequently, functional; best of all, they are never checked out by another clinician. Possibly, some parents may bring their child's favorite toys and storybooks that you can use as treatment material.

Clinical **equipment** is *nonexpendable*. It is something that is used, one would hope, over a long period of time. Clinical equipment is much more expensive than supplies and materials. Examples of clinical equipment include audiometers, computerized equipment with specialty software to assess speech and voice, audio and video recorders, sound level meters, auditory trainers, and augmentative and alternative communication devices. Less expensive items like flashlights, stethoscopes, dental mirrors, and therapy mirrors are also in this category. Handle the clinic equipment carefully. If you have questions about the appropriate way to use an instrument, ask your supervisor for assistance. Notify the clinic secretary or your supervisor of missing or broken equipment.

The supplies, materials, and equipment that you need often are dependent on your clinical practicum site. It is to your advantage to work with a variety of materials and equipment in different clinical settings.

Now that you know some of the different clinical sites and practicum experiences available, you can begin planning your clinical program with your advisor. The clinical practicum portion of your training may be important in choosing the setting in which you want to work after graduation.

⑦ Questions for Self-Assessment

1. What kinds of laws govern SLP services offered in public schools? Do the same laws apply to children served in the university clinics or hospital SLP departments?

2. Give an overview of the types of clients you may work with in the university clinics, public schools, hospitals, and RFs. What kinds of clients are you most interested in working with?

3. What are the two types of clinical internships? State the advantages and disadvantages of each.

4. You wish to discuss your most and least preferred off-campus clinical practicum sites that are available to you. Rank the first three sites for yourself, compare and contrast them, and justify your ranking to your supervisor.

5. What is ASHA's KASA form? Why do you need it and what do you do with it? Search the ASHA website and download the form for your records.

References

American Speech-Language-Hearing Association. (n.d.). *School-based service delivery in speech-language pathology.* https://www.asha.org/SLP/schools/School-Based-Service-Delivery-in-Speech-Language-Pathology/

American Speech-Language-Hearing Association. (1991). *A model for collaborative service delivery for students with language-learning disorders in the public schools: Relevant paper.* Available fro https://www.asha.org/policy/rp1991-00123/

American Speech-Language-Hearing Association. (1996). *Inclusive practices for children and youths with communication disorders: Technical report.* https://www.asha.org/policy/tr1996-00245/

American Speech-Language-Hearing Association. (1997). *Multiskilled personnel: Technical report.* https://www.asha.org/policy/tr1997-00247/

American Speech-Language-Hearing Association. (2001). *Roles and responsibilities of speech-language pathologists with respect to reading and writing in children and adolescents: Position statement.* https://www.asha.org/policy/ps2001-00104/

American Speech-Language-Hearing Association. (2002). *A workload analysis approach for establishing speech-language caseload standards in the school: Position statement.* https://www.asha.org/policy/ps2002-00122/

American Speech-Language-Hearing Association. (2016). *Scope of practice in speech-language pathology.* https://www.asha.org/policy/sp2016-00343/

American Speech-Language-Hearing Association. (2022). *Speech-language pathology assistant scope of practice.* http://www.asha.org/policy

Blue-Banning, M., Summers, J. A., Frankland, H. C., Nelson, L. L., & Beegle, G. (2004). Dimensions of family and professional partnerships: Constructive guidelines for collaborations. *Council for Exceptional Children, 70*(2), 167–184.

Child With A disability, 34 C.F.R. § 300.8(c)(11). (2023) https://sites.ed.gov/idea/regs/b/a/300.8/a

Dixon, D. (2013). SIGnatures: Push-in services: Making the 'impossible' possible. *The ASHA Leader, 18* (SIG N), 56–57. https://leader.pubs.asha.org/article.aspx?articleid=1785883

Dudding, C. C. (2012). *Focusing in on tele-supervision.* https://www.asha.org/Articles/Focusing-in-on-Tele-supervision/

Ehren, B. J., Montgomery, J., Rudebusch, J., & Whitmire, K. (2006). *Responsiveness to intervention: New roles for speech-language pathologists.* http://www.asha.org/uploadedFiles/slp/schools/prof-consult/rtiroledefinitions.pdf

Endrew F. v. Douglas County School District, 580 U.S. 15-827. (2017).

Hegde, M. N. (2024a). *A coursebook on scientific and professional writing for speech-language pathology* (6th ed.). Plural Publishing.

Hegde, M. N. (2024b). *A coursebook on aphasia and other neurogenic communication disorders* (5th ed.). Plural Publishing.

Individuals With Disabilities Education Act of 2004 Section 1412 (a)(5)(A). (2004a). https://sites.ed.gov/idea/statute-chapter-33/subchapter-II/1412

IDEA: Individuals With Disabilities Education Act 20 U.S.C. §1401(9). (2004b). https://sites.ed.gov/idea/statute-chapter-33/subchapter-I/1401

Learning Disabilities Association of America. (2006). *The role of parents/families in responsiveness to intervention.* https://www.asha.org/uploadedFiles/slp/schools/prof-consult/rtiroledefinitions.pdf

Nippold, M. A. (2021). *Language sampling with children and adults* (3rd ed.). Plural Publishing.

United States Department of Education. (2010). *Thirty-five years of progress in educating children with disabilities through IDEA.* Office of Special Education and Rehabilitative Services, Washington, DC. https://www2.ed.gov/print/about/offices/list/osers/idea35/history/index.html

Wilcox, M. J., & Woods, J. (2011). Participation as a basis for developing early intervention outcomes. *Language, Speech, and Hearing Services in Schools, 42,* 365–378.

Conduct of the Student Clinician

Student Learning Outcomes

After reading this chapter, student clinicians are expected to:

- Describe professional behaviors they should exhibit in all clinical practicum sites.
- Understand and be prepared to adhere to the ASHA Code of Ethics.
- Give an overview of several other codes and regulations that affect clinical practicum.

Ethical and professional behavior is essential to practice speech-language pathology. Education in speech-language pathology includes the acquisition of knowledge about communication and its disorders as well as certain standards of behavior considered professionally appropriate.

Professional behavior is typically shaped during clinical practicum. This chapter offers a discussion of various codes and regulations governing this behavior.

General Professional Behavior

Tradition, peer influence, and generally understood guidelines influence behaviors accepted as professional. Other behaviors are clearly defined and regulated by codes of ethics or other written rules. As a student clinician, you represent the profession of speech-language pathology, the university department and its clinic, and the university at large. You will interact with numerous clients, care providers, professionals, and related agencies in the community. Others judge the profession based on your behavior. Clinical practicum is your first and the most important step in acquiring professional and ethically justified patterns of behavior. *Honesty, integrity, respect for others, and a desire to help* are behavioral qualities admired in all people. Added to professional expertise, those qualities are especially important for the speech-language pathologist (SLP).

The American Speech-Language-Hearing Association (ASHA) clarifies your professional role, behavior, and responsibilities. Guidelines described in these documents help uphold high standards of service and protect your clients. Important documents include ASHA's Code of Ethics, Preferred Practice Patterns, Scope of Practice, Technical Reports, Guidelines, Position Statements, and the Consumer Bill of Rights.

In addition to specific rules outlined by ASHA in its Code of Ethics and various reports, general rules of professional behavior include *punctuality* in meeting clinical appointments and clinic deadlines; *working cooperatively* with office staff, supervisors, and other student clinicians; *assuming responsibility* for clinic equipment and clinic facilities; being *well prepared* for each clinical session; and *maintaining appropriate dress and demeanor. Professional demeanor* is a vague term but refers to such behaviors as appearing confident in your abilities, communicating clearly and appropriately with clients and supervisors, following prescribed rules, and using clinical time efficiently.

Confidence in your ability to help your clients is essential to developing a good working relationship with them. You may be nervous when you first talk with your clients, but you should make a good impression. You will often be the first clinic representative to contact a client. Your initial meeting with a client sets the stage for future clinical relationships and may influence the client's willingness to pursue treatment at the facility. It is important for the client to see you as self-confident, well-trained, and capable of providing quality clinical services. Also, your clients must believe they are important to you and trust that you will do all you can to help them. A large part of this trust is developed as you initially establish rapport with your clients.

There are many more or less significant factors that will influence your clients' opinion of your skills and the reputation of the clinic. The degrees you have earned are important, but there are other factors. The way you dress, wear your hair, make eye contact, and shake hands and greet are sometimes overlooked, but these behaviors influence your clients' desire to work with you.

Your professional demeanor and clinical ability will also affect other students. At off-campus practicum sites, you are a representative of the university. Administrators, supervisors, and professionals in medical and educational settings may have little knowledge of the university and its training program. Based on your exemplary professional behavior or lack of it, a practicum site may continue to offer or withdraw its offer to provide practicum experiences for other student clinicians.

Special rules and regulations of an off-campus site may be learned as you begin your work there, but you should have studied the ASHA Code of Ethics before beginning clinical practicum at any site.

ASHA Code of Ethics

The ASHA Code of Ethics (American Speech-Language-Hearing Association, 2023) *gives guidelines of professional behavior* for individuals providing clinical services in speech-language pathology or audiology. The Code of Ethics applies to (1) members of ASHA who hold the Certificate of Clinical Competence in speech language pathology or audiology, (2) noncertified members of the association, (3) nonmembers who hold a clinical certificate, (4) all applicants of ASHA certification or for ASHA membership and certification, and (5) speech, language, and hearing scientists. Persons in all these four categories must adhere to the Code of Ethics.

There is no legal basis for enforcement of the Code of Ethics, except in states that have adopted it as part of licensure requirements. However, a professional violating the Code of Ethics may lose his or her ASHA certification, membership in ASHA, or both. Loss of ASHA clinical certification may negatively affect the employability of the individual because many employers of SLPs require the ASHA certification, which in turn requires an adherence to the Code of Ethics. Without the ASHA certification, individuals cannot supervise student clinicians and clinical fellows. Consequently, many university job opportunities will be closed to them.

SLPs face many pressures and dilemmas that will demand ethical judgments. Such factors as shortages of SLPs, increased demands to show profits, and wider scopes of practice can affect your service delivery. Supervisors assist student clinicians in making appropriate decisions based on ASHA's Code of Ethics and other guidelines, including those of state licensure boards and departments of education. Throughout your professional career, you will make decisions based on your own judgment and knowledge of ethical practices. Following the Code is obligatory and its violation is disciplinary. All student clinicians are required to comply with the ASHA Code of Ethics. Student clinicians should have a full grasp of the Code of Ethics, but they should also expect their supervisors to interpret the Code and help them make ethical decisions. See other sources for more detailed discussions of ethical issues in the practice of speech-language pathology (Bupp, 2012; Hudson & DeRuiter, 2021).

An ethical issue that can pose an especially difficult situation for student clinicians is the shortfall in receiving appropriate supervision from the supervisor (Bupp, 2012). If you believe that you are not being supervised as per the ASHA guidelines, you must immediately and confidentially talk to the department chair. You may also speak to the clinic director, but in many academic departments, it is the department chair who heads the faculty. Regarding most other ethical issues and dilemmas, you may speak to both the supervisor and the clinic director.

The Board of Ethics of ASHA is responsible for formulating and amending the code; developing and distributing information about ethics; adjudicating complaints; and enforcing decisions regarding the code (American Speech-Language-Hearing Association, 2023).

The following discussion emphasizes specific principles and rules of the code. However, it is not comprehensive. Therefore, you should read and understand the complete Code of Ethics, available on the ASHA website at https://www.asha.org/siteassets/publications/code-of-ethics-2023.pdf

The revised version of the ASHA Code of Ethics, which went into effect on March 1, 2023, is aimed at protecting the consumer as well as the profession. It is composed of a *Preamble, Terminology, four Principles of Ethics*, and *Rules of Ethics*. The preamble briefly summarizes ASHA's philosophy of service delivery and introduces the components of the Code of Ethics. A section of the document provides a glossary of terms found throughout the code.

There are four main *Principles of Ethics* that outline the overall ideologies of the code. Under each principle there are specific *Rules of Ethics* that either stipulate what each SLP must minimally adhere to or what would be deemed inappropriate conduct. Obviously, ASHA cannot foresee all instances that demand an ethical decision based on its code. Therefore, the Code of Ethics is designed as a guide to minimally acceptable behavior. The four Principles of Ethics are summarized in the following sections.

Principle of Ethics I

"Individuals shall honor their responsibility to hold paramount the welfare of persons they serve professionally or who are participants in research and scholarly activities, and they shall treat animals involved in research in a humane manner" (American Speech-Language-Hearing Association, 2023, p. 3).

Principle I of the Code of Ethics is straightforward and not easily mis-interpreted. Foremost are *client welfare and the welfare of individuals or animals involved in research*. Your training program will have guidelines on protecting research participants. Your academic department will likely have an Institutional Review Board (sometimes also called the Human Subjects Protection Committee), which is responsible for reviewing all research proposals to ensure that the participants are treated according to university and federal government regulations. Also, you will adhere to any additional rules outlined by ASHA's Code of Ethics.

The difficult part for beginning student clinicians is determining what is best for the person being served. If you have a question about the legit-imacy, efficacy, or ethics of a particular clinical procedure, discuss it with your clinical supervisor. There are many unproven treatment strategies and invalid assessment instruments on the market. Review the content of the course you took on research methods to evaluate treatment procedures and assessment instruments to determine their validity, reliability, effec-tiveness, efficiency, and appropriateness for specific clients in view of their disorders and ethnocultural backgrounds.

Preparation

ASHA's Code of Ethics mandates that *services be provided competently*. This mandate applies to both the student clinician and the supervisor. To pro-vide competent service, one must be well prepared. Student clinicians should have completed coursework in a specific communication disorder before they are assigned a client with that disorder. Compliance with this policy helps ensure that student clinicians are academically prepared to work with clients with a specific disorder. To be prepared, you should spend time in advance reviewing academic information related to your clients' disorders, your clients' records, and assessment materials, including standardized tests you plan to administer. Also, you will need to gather treatment materials, forms for charting target behaviors, and other supplies and equipment. Writing lesson plans, treatment plans, and clinical reports are a part of this preparation. Ensure that you have appropriate knowledge, experience, and supervision before working with a patient with a swallowing disorder, tra-cheotomy, laryngectomy, or other serious medical conditions.

You will have a general background in a specific disorder before you are assigned a client with that disorder. However, you may be required to do additional research to effectively serve your client. During training, your supervisor will refer you to appropriate sources to help you find needed information. After your formal training and throughout your professional career, you should continue your education and research by being current in your practice and by continuously refining your skills.

ASHA also addresses client welfare and clinical competence by prohibiting service delivery by clinicians who substance abuse or have physical or mental health problems. If you are affected by any of these, seek out help. Discussions with your clinic supervisors, clinic director, department head, or other faculty will be confidential. They may be able to help you find appropriate services. Acknowledging and addressing certain problems will not necessarily preclude you from clinical practicum. However, as in the case of academic preparation, your supervisor may decide when you are physically and emotionally prepared to work with clients.

Referral

When clients need service they cannot offer, SLPs refer them to another professional. Student clinicians who wish to refer a person to another professional should discuss the matter with their supervisors. For instance, if you are assigned a client following laryngectomy and are unfamiliar with training esophageal speech, you must let your supervisor know so that the client may be referred to another student clinician or a professional SLP who specializes in treating individuals with laryngectomy. Also, some of your clients may need services in addition to those of speech-language pathology (i.e., psychological services, occupational therapy, academic support), which again require referral. Additionally, a conflict of interest necessitates referral. For example, you may not want to treat a close friend or a family member. Still other clients may be difficult to schedule because of an impacted caseload. Instead of asking them to postpone treatment, they might be referred to an equally competent SLP who might offer prompt services.

There are individuals who cannot afford to continue clinical services. Your supervisor may know of other speech-language pathology services that are available for free or at a reduced cost. It is customary to provide several names of qualified professionals when making a referral.

Discrimination

The code prohibits discrimination. In service delivery or conduct of research, individuals (SLPs and audiologists) shall not discriminate on the basis of "age; citizenship; disability; ethnicity; gender; gender expression; gender identity; genetic information; national origin, including culture, language, dialect, and accent; race; religion; sex; sexual orientation; or veteran status" (American Speech-Language-Hearing Association, 2023, p. 3). To obtain the Certificate of Clinical Competence, you must gain experience in assessing and treating a wide variety of communication disorders. However, certified and licensed SLPs may specialize in treating only a certain disorder (e.g., stuttering or aphasia). Specialists my decline services to clients whose disorders are not within their specialization. This is not discrimination, however. In fact, it is consistent with the other ethical rule: that SLPs should offer services in which they are competent and should not offer services without competency. However, discrimination exists if clinicians base service delivery decisions not on their own competency, but solely on race, ethnicity, and the other variables ASHA specifies.

In sum, clinical judgments and recommendations must be made based on expertise and clinical data and not on unrelated factors. For a research project, SLPs may select participants based on their ethnicity, race, disability, and so on because of the research question being investigated. However, researchers may not choose or exclude participants who otherwise qualify for the study simply because of discriminatory practices.

Informed Consent

The code covers several rules on providing information to clients. Basically, clients must be given enough information so they can understand all aspects of clinical services that affect them so they can make a rational decision to seek services or not. Such a decision is **informed consent**. Individuals must be given information related to possible consequences of treatment as well as no treatment.

Generally, university clinics do not ask individuals to refuse treatment in writing and declare they understand possible consequences of no treatment. Private clinics may ask clients to sign a statement to that effect. However, most clinics require clients to initial or sign a plan of treatment to confirm their knowledge of the proposed services. If clients are not required to submit a written acknowledgment of the treatment plan, you should note in the records when the plan was discussed with the client and the client's verbal approval.

Clients and their families often ask questions regarding the course and outcome of treatment. The code forbids guaranteeing treatment results. For example, you should not say, "After 6 weeks of treatment, you will no longer stutter." However, you can make an informed, reasonable, prognostic statement. You may say, "This type of treatment has been successful with many individuals who had profiles similar to yours. Based on the diagnostic information I have and what I think is your level of motivation for change, the chances of improvement in your speech fluency are good." Probabilistic prognostic statements based on experience and scientific evidence, not those of certainty, are ethically justified. Student clinicians must discuss a client's prognosis with their clinical supervisor before reporting it to the client.

Informed consent is required of research participants, who may or may not be clients seeking clinical services. In treatment research, the participants must be given a choice to receive the experimental treatment or the more traditional treatment outside the scope of research. In spite of their initial consent, participants in an experimental treatment program retain their right to withdraw from it at any time and without prejudice. Potential participants should fully realize this. The academic department's Human Subjects Protection Committee (Institutional Review Board) should approve the informed consent form.

Clients also must be fully informed about who is providing the speech-language pathology services and what his or her qualifications are. In the university clinic, as well as at off-campus sites, it is explained clearly to the client that student clinicians provide services under the supervision of a certified professional. Moreover, when working in educational, private, or medical settings, you must inform the individuals you serve if any support personnel will be working with them. For example, a school-based SLP may send out a newsletter that informs students' families that an SLP intern will be providing services throughout the semester. In many settings, you will be asked to wear a name tag or identification badge that will give your name and title. In all settings, you should check to ensure that your client has signed all consent forms. Each site will have different forms.

The delegation of tasks to support personnel and student clinicians must be appropriate to the individual's scope and supervised appropriately. All responsibility rests with the certified and supervising SLP.

Treatment Efficacy

The Code of Ethics promotes the ongoing evaluation of effectiveness of clinical services. Stimuli and products used should also be beneficial and culturally relevant to the clients. Treatment whose effects have never been evaluated in appropriate research studies should not be offered. Moreover, services should not be provided to clients who may not benefit from treatment. Student clinicians and professionals should acquire necessary knowledge in research methods, especially the experimental designs that help establish treatment efficacy (Hegde & Salvatore, 2020).

Some ethical issues may be difficult for student clinicians to resolve. Professionals and agencies sometimes disagree on how to resolve an ethical issue. For example, an SLP may judge that a client with traumatic brain injury (TBI) could benefit from speech-language services. However, the insurance company, judging that the client would not benefit from treatment, may not approve payment for the services. In this instance, the clinician, who may feel frustrated because the needed service cannot be provided, has not acted unethically in recommending treatment.

Financial factors may adversely affect the decision making of those clinicians who are unclear about their values and ethical choices. Unfortunately, economic factors are important in maintaining private practice, and the business that holds little regard for ethical practice may attempt to put an SLP in a compromising position. For example, an SLP may be instructed to provide services for a specific number of clients per day. If there are not sufficient numbers of appropriate clients, the clinician may be pressured to increase the caseload by enrolling individuals for whom the benefit of treatment is questionable (i.e., an individual in extremely poor health). Clinicians who enroll individuals unjustifiably in treatment because of such productivity pressures will have violated the Code of Ethics.

With due regard to adhering to the Code of Ethics, professionals may disagree on who benefits from treatment and for how long. For example, two SLPs may not agree on the appropriate chronological age for treatment of a specific communication disorder. Also, the progress of some individuals (for instance, a person with a severe cognitive impairment) may be extremely slow and efficacy of treatment difficult to assess. The code requires clinicians to maintain objective and accurate records of client behaviors. This allows for objective evaluation of the clients' response to treatment, not only from the clinician, but also from an independent observer or evaluator.

Is it considered unethical to not record every response of a client? No. However, failure to maintain adequate records is unethical. Adequate records should document changes or lack of changes in the target behaviors over a span of treatment sessions. Treating individuals with no measurement of progress is unethical. Continuing the same treatment when repeated measures show no change in client behaviors is also unethical. Do you necessarily have to dismiss the client? No. But you certainly should evaluate and possibly change your treatment strategy.

There is no single formula to determine which individuals can benefit from treatment or when treatment should be discontinued. Social, educational, psychological, and health factors affect your decision. You should evaluate your clients and attempt to make the appropriate determination, but you should never try to enroll or dismiss a client without first discussing the matter with your clinical supervisor.

Confidentiality

Clients' right to privacy is a paramount ethical concern. You should *maintain client confidentiality*, except when you must reveal information to protect your clients, to safeguard the community welfare, to abide by laws, or comply with a judicial order to release information.

Federal and state laws also protect client or patient confidentiality. The **Health Insurance Portability and Accountability Act (HIPAA)** of 1996 is discussed later in this chapter. All clinical service providers must follow the HIPAA guidelines on maintaining client confidentiality.

For two reasons, client confidentiality is of special concern at university clinics. First, much of the learning at the university level occurs by individuals sharing information and experiences with each other. Second, persons not directly involved with treatment may observe clients receiving services. You will observe many clinic sessions, present information about clients to students in certain courses, and be involved in student and faculty discussions about clients' evaluations, treatments, and counseling sessions. Consequently, the clinical services offered to individuals through university training programs are less confidential than those that are offered in private clinics. Nonetheless, the clients' rights to privacy must be respected. Therefore, monitor both your written and verbal communications to ensure those rights.

Release of information to individuals or agencies outside of a facility requires a written authorization or written consent. The clinic administrative assistant at your university clinic or at an off-campus practicum site can give you information on the consent form required and the procedures for completing it.

Guidelines to Help Ensure Client Confidentiality

- **Do not discuss your client by name**. On campus, you may have meetings with your supervisor and clinic staff. Off campus, you may have hospital rounds, individualized education program (IEP) team meetings, and meetings with your on-site supervisors. Obviously, in private clinic meetings with your supervisor or affiliated staff, it is acceptable and even necessary to reveal your client's name. However, when in shared public spaces, names should not be mentioned.

- **Do not discuss your client in public areas**. Avoid discussing information about your clients in hallways or waiting areas. If you need to talk about your clients or with your clients, move to a private room where confidentiality is maintained.

- **Do not mention your client's name in class presentations or discussions.** As part of class assignments, you can easily refer to your client as "the client" or by an alias.

- **Do not leave client reports, lesson plans, or other written information unattended.** Promptly file documents in your clients' folders. If you are submitting reports or lesson plans to your supervisor, do not leave them on a table or desk that is accessible to other individuals.

- **Follow all the office rules regarding checking out and returning client folders and reports.** As a general rule, client files are not to be taken from the clinic area. If files are taken to be used during a clinic session, staffing, or meeting, follow the checkout procedures.

- **Do not take client folders home or remove information from them.** If you need information from your clients' files, allow time to take notes and keep them confidential. Do not have client names in your notes.

- **Do not discuss your client with others.** Unless your client or your supervisor has approved the communication, do not discuss your client with other professionals without obtaining an official release of information.

- **Remind your observers that they should respect client confidentiality.** Inform your session observers ahead of time not to discuss your clients by name in front of others.

- **Obtain written consent to make video recordings or take photographs of clients.** Have them sign the separate consent forms your clinic administrative assistant maintains.

- **Comply with all clinic rules regarding the release of information.** Check with your clinic supervisor for forms to be signed and procedures to be followed in releasing information to an outside agency. When giving information over the telephone, you also must respect client confidentiality. For example, if you have clients who also are receiving speech-language services in the public schools, their school clinicians may phone you. If in doubt as to when you may give information over the telephone, discuss it with your clinic supervisor.

(continues)

- **Honor client confidentiality during communications on the Internet**. There are several Internet listservs and chat rooms operating that provide forums for clinical discussions. Students and professionals post questions, concerns, and comments about clients. If you participate in such a listserv or chat room, do not discuss your clients by name or use any information that could identify them. Moreover, do not post pictures or make comments on social media platforms. It is acceptable to discuss clinical issues without the clients' identities, but be cautious and use good judgment.

Several other rules related to the importance of client welfare are self-explanatory. These include not providing services if you are unfit to do so, reporting on a professional who is unfit to provide services, providing reasonable notice for a change of services, and not assessing or treating an individual solely by correspondence. The rules of ethics allow clinical practice through telepractice unless prohibited by law.

Principle of Ethics II

"Individuals shall honor their responsibility to achieve and maintain the highest level of professional competence and performance" (American Speech-Language-Hearing Association, 2023, p. 6).

Professional Competency required to offer services as well as to supervise clinical practicum is defined minimally as holding ASHA's CCC. Supervisors have to meet additional requirements as described in Chapter 4. Those in the process of getting certified may offer services that are consistent with state laws and only under certified supervision. Additional training in specific areas may be necessary to ensure competent service delivery. Master's degree offers a foundation on which to build specialized knowledge and expertise.

It is expected that all services an individual offers will be consistent with their scope and level of training. After you graduate, complete your Clinical Fellowship year, and get certified in speech-language pathology, you are required to enhance and refine your clinical skills by engaging in lifelong learning. To maintain certification, you need to earn and report to ASHA 30 hr of continuing education units (CEUs) within a 3-year period.

Your state may have additional requirements for maintaining your license or your credential.

SLPs may also seek advanced certification from ASHA in specialty areas (childhood language, fluency, neurogenic communication disorders, etc.). Visit the ASHA website for available specialty certifications, which are obtained only after you have been awarded the Certificate of Clinical Competence.

Principle of Ethics III

"In their professional role, individuals shall act with honesty and integrity when engaging with the public and shall provide accurate information involving any aspect of the professions" (American Speech-Language-Hearing Association, 2023, p. 7).

You should accurately represent your services, products, and profession. The rules under this principle emphasize that information should not be misrepresented to the general public, clients, or reimbursement agencies. SLPs must accurately portray their ability, education, credentials, and experience. Research evidence must be described accurately. Statements regarding services or products must be valid. Similarly, billing must reflect services provided. Advertising is appropriate, but only when it is not misleading and complies with contemporary professional standards. Misrepresentation of services or products is clearly unethical.

Directly related to accurate representation at the university training program is the need for clients to fully understand that students in the program provide services. This information is given to clients who contact the speech and hearing clinic to inquire about available services. The clients also are told about the clinic schedule and fees. Individuals who want to find other services are referred to qualified SLPs in the locality. Adhering to the rules of Principle III is fairly simple: be truthful.

Principle of Ethics IV

"Individuals shall uphold the dignity and autonomy of the professions, maintain collaborative and harmonious interprofessional and intraprofessional relationships, and accept the professions' self-imposed standards" (American Speech-Language-Hearing Association, 2023, p. 7).

Under this principle, the rules of ethics place specific emphasis on fostering appropriate relations with colleagues, maintaining honest professional standards, and safeguarding the code. Certification holders who are aware of another clinician's unethical behavior have an obligation to report the person to the ASHA Board of Ethics.

Professional Relationships

Effective professional relationships are important. To provide optimal care for their clients, SLPs interact with various professionals, including other SLPs or allied professionals. The dissemination of information to colleagues should be accurate. The code promotes harmonious relations with related professions while maintaining SLP's professional autonomy.

Individuals shall not make false statements to their colleagues about professional services, products, or research outcomes. Applicants for certification or membership in ASHA shall not make any false or misleading statements. All information supplied on the application forms will be complete and fully accurate.

Correct Citations

Your reports submitted for academic or clinical coursework must contain references and credit other individuals involved in the work. You should learn to paraphrase research literature in your own words; and, when quoting an author, you should know how to give credit and avoid plagiarism. Most academic departments of communication disorders use the writing style of the Publication Manual of the American Psychological Association (2020). If your department uses it, master the style and write accordingly.

In many work settings, reports may be written in conjunction with other professionals. In the university clinic setting, if you and another student collaborate in evaluating a client and writing the assessment report, both of you (and your supervisor) should sign the report. In the school setting, for example, a speech and language report may be written in collaboration with an assistive technology specialist. A multidisciplinary team in a school involving a psychologist, special education teacher, and an SLP may write an assessment report on a child with multiple disabilities. Each assessor's name and credentials should be identified on each section of such reports for which the professional was responsible. Furthermore, if you include information from a different report, the name of that clinician and the date of the report should be noted.

Professionalism

Independent clinical practice and clinical decision making is expected of professional SLPs (ASHA certified, state licensed, or educational credentialed). Student clinicians, however, learn to make independent clinical decisions under the guidance of their supervisors. Major clinical decisions, such as referral to another professional or dismissal from therapy, and parent or client counseling are done either under the guidance or at the direction of the supervisor. The eventual goal of clinical practicum is the achievement of independent judgment and autonomous professional practice upon achieving the certified and licensed status. Student clinicians practice under the supervisor's certification authority, and therefore, even if they are able to make independent judgments, they need the supervisor's approval for execution. The supervisors' goal, however, is to teach student clinicians the skills and expertise needed for independent professional practice.

The code prohibits any behavior that adversely reflects on the profession. The code calls for honesty in all components of practice. Expressly prohibited are sexual and other kinds of harassment because the supervisor is in a position of authority. The code prohibits sexual activities between clinician and client or supervisor and student. Be conscious of what words you use and how you use them.

Discrimination against clients because of their personal qualities (such as age, sex, ethnicity, gender identity, sexual orientation, disability) is also expressly prohibited. To learn to speak and write without bias, consult sources other than the code of ethics (American Psychological Association, 2016; Hegde, 2024).

Safeguarding the Code

Individuals must comply freely with the standards of the profession specified in the Code of Ethics and other guidelines. In addition to individually upholding the code, supervisors must monitor that student clinicians follow the principles and rules of ethics. The code also calls for professional clinicians to make official reports on those who have violated the code to the *Board of Ethics*. Student clinicians who learn of potential code violation by another clinician is expected to report the matter to their supervisors. It is the supervisors, clinic directors, and chairs of academic departments who evaluate the allegation and decide whether to report the clinician to the Board of Ethics (Bupp, 2012). Notifications of noncompliance must never be in retaliation or due to dislike of another student clinician or professional.

All laws relating to professional practice at the local, state, and federal level must be followed. When applying for the Certificate of Clinical Competence (CCC) or renewing certification, the applicant will be required to make honest and accurate disclosures of criminal convictions. In addition, ASHA Standards and Ethics must be notified of a misdemeanor or felony conviction within 30 days of incidence. Similarly, a denial of a license or credential by a professional organization or licensing agency (i.e., a state licensing board) must also be reported within 30 days (American Speech-Language-Hearing Association, 2023).

The main sections of the Code of Ethics have been highlighted so far. But the code contains additional rules. Visit ASHA's website at https://www.asha.org/siteassets/publications/code-of-ethics-2023.pdf

After a review, determine which of the following situations would involve a violation of the Code of Ethics:

What Would Be an Ethical Way to Handle Each Situation?

1. You were busy studying for midterm exams and "just didn't have enough time" to completely prepare for your clinical session. What would you do?

2. You are beginning your second year of graduate school. An SLP in private practice telephones and asks you to work as an aide. How would you reply? Are there any specific requirements you would need to comply with to be employed as a speech aide? Could you earn clinical clock hours? Could you perform other clinical services?

3. The mother of one of your clients contacts you and asks if you would be available to tutor her child. How would you respond?

4. A clinical supervisor allows students who were continually ill-prepared for their clinical assignments to continue in clinical practicum. Is the supervisor acting unethically?

5. You are working with a client who also is receiving speech-language services at another facility. You do not agree with the type of treatment being provided by the SLP. What would you do?

6. Your supervisor suggested that you use certain treatment procedures with one of your clients. You were unsure of how to implement the procedures but could not get to school during your supervisor's office hours to discuss the procedures. You decided to work with your client anyway, because if you do something wrong, your supervisor will see it and come to help you. Is this an ethical violation or a commonsense solution?

7. A man you have been working with for 2 months tells you that he just tested positive for human immunodeficiency virus (HIV) infection. He wants to continue treatment but does not want anyone to know about his medical history except you. Do you need to add this information into your report or do you need to maintain the client's right to privacy?

8. You have the opportunity to participate in a research project related to adult dysarthria. You have not yet had coursework in this area but have observed various clinic sessions for clients with dysarthria. What factors would determine if you could work these into this research project?

9. You feel overwhelmed by your coursework and it is almost time for you to take your comprehensive exams. You have 4 more weeks at your medical internship but feel that you have pretty much learned everything you need to know to work in that setting. At the last minute you call in sick. Later you ask your supervisor if you can miss a few days so you can catch up on your studying. Is this unethical behavior or just a reflection of the stress of being a graduate student?

10. You are completing your school internship. Your supervisor seems to have much confidence in your skills and tells you to "just go and work with the students." The supervisor is always available to answer questions but no longer observes you or the students with whom you work. What, if anything, would you do?

Other Codes and Regulations

Client confidentiality, privacy, and welfare are extensively discussed in ASHA's Code of Ethics as well as in other ASHA documents. In addition, the federal government's Department of Health and Human Services (HHS) developed standards intended to protect client privacy and to improve the efficiency and effectiveness of the health care system.

These standards were adopted under HIPAA. HIPAA, too, has implications for clinical practice.

Health Insurance Portability and Accountability Act (HIPAA)

The act requires that all health care providers, including SLPs and audiologists, who engage in electronic transactions involving health information comply with the standards. Modifications to the original law (passed in 1996) include specifications for violations and potential monetary penalties for noncompliance.

In your medical internship, you will hear much about HIPAA, and your information reporting will be guided by its standards. Even in such nonmedical settings as public schools, your practice will be influenced by HIPAA standards as well as standards regulated by the Family Educational Rights and Privacy Act (FERPA). For example, you may have to request a hospital report that was done for one of your students. To obtain this information, the hospital will require you to adhere to its HIPAA standards for disclosure of patient information. FERPA is a federal law that protects the confidentiality of educational records. Many school districts use a release of records document that requires the signature of a student's parent or educational rights holder. Therefore, it is important that you have a general understanding of certain HIPAA and FERPA regulations. Familiarity with state laws will be necessary as well because such laws also govern health information privacy.

> **Protected health information (PHI)** is any health information that is created or received by the health care provider; relates to the past, present, or future physical or mental health diagnosis, treatment, or payment; and can or does identify the individual. *Individually Identifiable Health Information (IIHI)* is what is protected. Both PHI and IIHI refer to such communications as e-mail, stored information (i.e., on flash drives), telephone conversations, exchange of insurance information, and other written and oral communications.

Before a professional can disclose any PHI for treatment, payment, or health care operations, the concerned client must give his or her consent. In addition, individuals have the right to see their medical records and make corrections to the records. Clients have the right to receive advance notice of disclosure policies and to obtain a history of who, if anyone, has had access to their records (Office for Civil Rights, 2013a).

To maintain patient privacy, comply with the rules outlined earlier in this chapter. Also, adhere to specific rules at your internship site. Your site will provide specific guidelines regarding any required client notice and consent forms, accessing and storing client charts, and disposal of any confidential information.

Updates to HIPAA have also provided guidelines regarding **electronic protected health information** (e-PHI), electronic exchange of that information, and the security of information housed electronically. The Security Standards for the Protection of Electronic Protected Health Information is known as the Security Rule. This component of HIPAA preserves confidentiality of the client's health information stored electronically (Office for Civil Rights, 2013b). For additional information, consult the HHS website regarding HIPAA at https://www.hhs.gov/

ASHA's Scope of Practice in Speech-Language Pathology

ASHA's scope of practice in speech-language pathology is an official policy statement that outlines the range of practice for the profession. The most recent revision was made in 2016. The purposes of the policy document are to outline areas of professional practice; inform others about the roles of SLPs; support evidence-based practice and research; and promote educational preparation and professional development (American Speech-Language-Hearing Association, 2016).

Essentially, the paramount objective of practice in speech-language pathology is to improve individuals' communication skills and swallow safely. Two fundamental principles help achieve these goals. First is the cultural and linguistic diversity of individuals SLPs serve. Based on cultural and linguistic differences across individuals, clinicians should distinguish speech and language disorders from speech and language differences. Second is evidence-based practice, defined as "an approach in which current, high quality research evidence is integrated with practitioner expertise and client preferences and values into the process of making clinical decisions" (American Speech-Language-Hearing Association, 2005). Consult ASHA's practice portal for resources on evidence-based practice.

The statement details the following service delivery domains: collaboration; counseling; prevention and wellness; screening; assessment; treatment; modalities, technology, and instrumentation; and population and systems. You should expect to attain experiences in each domain throughout your clinical practicum experiences. The statement reinforces that the SLP must practice only in those areas that are within the SLP's *scope of competence*, which includes the individual's experience, education, practice, mentorship, and continuing education endeavors. The scope of an SLP's practice may include communication disorders in speech production, resonance, voice, fluency, language, cognition, feeding/swallowing, and auditory habilitation/rehabilitation. Take note that the SLP *scope of practice* includes the entire range of communication disorders and swallowing problems, but the *scope of competence* is a narrower concept: It is the individual's competence in specific areas of speech-language pathology. Most SLPs are not competent to offer effective service to all kinds of communication disorders and swallowing.

The scope of practice should be interpreted in relation to other ASHA documents, such as the Code of Ethics and specific practice policy documents. Furthermore, the document does not displace state licensure laws. Recall that you must adhere to the scope of practice defined under your state's license or credentialing law. You cannot legally offer a service that ASHA's scope of practice permits but your state licensure law or the education laws that apply to schools prohibit. Visit ASHA's website for the official scope of practice at https://www.asha.org/policy/sp2016-00343/ (American Speech-Language-Hearing Association, 2016).

Preferred Practice Patterns and Practice Policy Documents

In addition to specifying the types of services professionals may provide, ASHA's preferred practice patterns also outline clinical processes, clinical indicators, equipment specifications, expected outcomes, safety and health precautions, documentation, and related matters. As with the Code of Ethics, one of the guiding principles of the preferred practice patterns is the importance of client welfare. Refer to the preferred practice patterns as an introduction to your research when gathering new information about each of your clients (American Speech-Language-Hearing Association, 2004).

Visit ASHA's website for practice policy information on specific topics (laryngectomy, early intervention, cochlear implants, etc.). A topic index is also available on the website.

Reporting Suspected Child Abuse

Although students should first assume that all client information is confidential, there are specific state laws governing disclosure of information to protect the well-being of a client or of the public. A clear example is a clinician's responsibility to report suspected child abuse. SLPs are *mandated reporters*. Child abuse can include physical, emotional, or sexual abuse, and may also include neglect and child endangerment. Unfortunately, diagnosis of a disability increases the chances of abuse and maltreatment (Child Welfare Information Gateway, 2018).

Based on federal laws and regulations, all states have established laws regulating the reporting of suspected child abuse. However, the definition of child abuse, the age range of victims, the reporting requirements, and the agency to which the suspected abuse is reported vary from state to state. Nevertheless, suspected child abuse must be reported. In most states, the individual suspecting the abuse must report it. The individual cannot leave the reporting to the agency he or she works for. Student clinicians, however, should report suspected child abuse to their clinical supervisor.

Child abuse is not always visible or easily identified. Most children are very active and consequently suffer various accidental scrapes, bruises, and broken bones. You must not jump to conclusions, but you must not disregard signs of possible child abuse. If a child arrives with a bump, bruise, bite, burn, or broken bone, you may want to ask how it happened. If you have a child who repeatedly arrives with various injuries, report it to your clinical supervisor. Again, this may not be a case of child abuse, but your supervisor can investigate it further to take action.

Signs of Possible Child Abuse

General Signs

- Shows abrupt changes in behavior or school performance
- Presents with physical or medical problems, brought to the parents' attention, with no subsequent response to seek medical care
- Demonstrates learning problems with no identifiable cause
- Appears consistently fearful of impending negative experiences
- Lacks adult supervision
- Appears overly obedient, docile, or withdrawn
- Reluctant to go home
- Avoids being in the presence of a particular individual
- Reports maltreatment

(continues)

Physical Abuse Signs

- Presents with unexplained bites, burns, bruises, broken bones, black eyes
- Presents with fading bruises or injuries following an absence from school
- Appears frightened of a parent or caregiver
- Cringes when an adult approaches
- Abuses animals
- Reports incidents of abuse

Neglect Signs

- Accumulates numerous absences from school
- Steals or begs for food and money
- Lacks medical care
- Presents as unkempt (excessively dirty or odorous)
- Lacks clothing appropriate to the weather
- Abuses substances (alcohol or drugs)
- Claims that there is no one within the home to provide care

Sexual Abuse Signs

- Appears to have difficulty walking or sitting
- Demonstrates appetite changes
- Exhibits bizarre or oversophisticated sexual knowledge or behavior
- Becomes pregnant or contracts a venereal disease
- Runs away
- Attaches abruptly to strangers or novel adults
- Refuses to change for gym or participate in physical activities
- Reports nightmares and bedwetting
- Reports abuse

Emotional Maltreatment Signs

- Presents with behavioral extremes from passivity to aggression
- Appears inappropriately adult or infantile
- Shows physical or emotional delays respective to age
- Makes attempts at suicide
- Initiates statements indicating a lack of attachment to parent

Parent or Caregiver Signs

- Makes denials or places blame regarding suspected problems
- Disciplines the child punitively
- Asks other adults to severely discipline the child
- Envisions the child as bad or worthless
- Places unattainable demands on the child
- Demonstrates a lack of concern toward the child
- Provides an inappropriate explanation for the child's injury
- Presents with a history of abuse
- Behaves in a depressed fashion, irrationally, or bizarrely
- Abuses substances
- Appears unduly protective and limits contact with others
- Appears isolated, jealous, or controlling with family members
- Berates, belittles, rejects child (Child Welfare Information Gateway, 2013)

This is not an exhaustive list of signs and symptoms. Moreover, exhibiting one or two signs on an occasion may not necessarily suggest abuse; a repeated pattern of signs is a better indicator. When you suspect child abuse, inform your supervisor immediately. Each clinical site will have a reporting procedure. You should know these procedures and follow them when necessary.

Dress Code

When people first meet you, they judge you by your appearance and demeanor. With clients, you must quickly establish a degree of trust through your professional demeanor, attire, and general appearance. A neat appearance and appropriate clothing will positively influence your clients' first impressions of you.

There is no universal dress code that you must follow in all practicum sites. However, all clinics have guidelines for what they consider appropriate professional attire. You are not expected to go out and purchase an entirely new wardrobe. Typically, shorts, jeans, sandals, and strapless dresses are not considered appropriate for professional clothing.

> If you have a question as to whether something is appropriate to wear, do not wear it.

At off-campus practicum sites, dress may be more or less formal than at the university clinic. Ask your off-campus supervisor about the dress code or guidelines at the site. Do not take literally a supervisor's causal statement, "Anything is okay to wear," while the supervisor and the rest of the staff dress very formally. In this case, it is best to dress as similarly to the staff as possible. In some medical settings, the required dress code may be scrubs. In some educational settings, there may be a spirit shirt and jeans day, which is the professional attire for that day. In all cases, dressing with a view to appearing professional is desirable, but may differ according to the setting.

Being a student during certain times of the day to being a clinician at other times of the same day can be a difficult transition. Donning professional dress helps you make that transition. It also prompts the client to regard you more as a professional and less as a student.

Professional Liability

Although you are a student in training, you still provide direct client services consistent with certain standard of care. You will be held responsible for your actions. You may be liable for any inappropriate or negligent service that results in damage or harm to a client. All student clinicians should have liability insurance before beginning their clinical practicum. You can obtain information from your clinic office regarding the procedures for obtaining liability insurance. Students may pay directly to the university for their insurance or independently purchase a policy and then provide the proof of coverage to the clinic. Insurance typically is purchased on an annual basis. A low-cost group insurance is available for students who are members of the National Student Speech-Language-Hearing Association. Get the information from your clinic or ASHA.

To avoid any suspicion of negligence or malpractice, you must closely follow the ASHA Code of Ethics, comply with all clinic procedures, and maintain appropriate communications with your supervisor. You also should be knowledgeable of current standards of care for the disorders you treat. As you know, ASHA's position statements and guidelines discuss controversial clinical or scientific issues, recommend appropriate courses of professional actions, and summarize state-of-the-art information on selected matters. You should keep yourself current on these position statements and guidelines.

Health and Safety Precautions

Because you will be working closely with people, you must follow certain health and safety precautions to protect yourself and your clients from various communicable diseases or injuries. Those who work closely with a variety of people are at a greater risk for exposure to a communicable disease than, for instance, a computer programmer might be. Also, you will work with certain individuals who are susceptible to infection, such as those in the neonatal intensive care unit (NICU), older persons, and the critically ill.

Many sites follow **universal health care precautions**, also termed **standard precautions**. Standard precautions include hand hygiene, isolation procedures, use of protective equipment, proper disposal of needles and medical waste, and sterilization of workspace and equipment. Materials that require universal precautions include blood, semen, vaginal secretions, cerebrospinal fluid, synovial fluid, pleural fluid, body fluids with visible blood, any unidentifiable body fluid, and saliva.

Each practicum site may have different health and safety regulations. You must follow the regulations of your clinical assignment. Furthermore, the Centers for Disease Control and Prevention (CDC) publishes guidelines to support infection control, including instructions for proper hand hygiene, use of equipment, and isolation precautions, among many other topics. Consult the CDC website at https://www.cdc.gov/

General Health Procedures

1. **Get vaccinations**. To participate in clinical practicum at your university clinic and subsequent internships, certain vaccinations will be required. These may include, but are not limited

(continues)

to measles, mumps, rubella (MMR), as well as hepatitis A and B vaccinations. If you do not have your immunization records, titer antibody tests may be acceptable to demonstrate immunity from previously received vaccinations.

2. **Test for tuberculosis (TB).** Testing can be completed using skin tests (most common), blood tests, chest x-ray, or sputum tests. Tuberculosis is an infectious mycobacterial disease. Generally, it has decreased in occurrence in most countries but has stabilized or increased in frequency in persons testing positive for HIV infection. Tuberculosis most often involves the lungs and, if left untreated, can result in serious complications or death. The initial infection to tuberculosis often is not recognized (Centers for Disease Control and Prevention, 2016). This is one of the reasons students, who are in close contact with a variety of individuals in their clinical experiences, are required to have a TB skin test on an annual basis. Public schools often require the skin test less frequently (every 3 years). Consult the CDC website for information regarding this and other transmittable diseases (https://www.cdc.gov/).

3. **Protect any wounds or skin lesions.** Use a waterproof dressing or gloves, or both, to protect any wounds, sores, or skin abrasions you may have.

4. **Use gloves.** Wear latex gloves when performing oral exams, during any invasive procedure of the oral cavity (such as dysphagia assessment or treatment), or during any contact with blood or bodily fluids with visible blood. To protect the client against infection, do not touch your pencil, furniture, or other unsanitized objects when wearing gloves.

5. **Wash your hands after removing latex gloves.** Your hands may become contaminated as you remove your gloves. Therefore, wash your hands after removing gloves.

6. **Wash your hands before and after working with a client.** Hand washing is one of the best ways to prevent the spread of disease. In addition, avoid touching your hands to your mouth, eyes, or nose when working with your clients.

7. **If necessary, wear eye and mouth protection.** When you expect splashing of blood, saliva, or other bodily fluid when working with a client, wear eye goggles and a mouth mask.

8. **Disinfect or sterilize equipment**. Follow your practicum site's procedures regarding sterilization and disinfection of equipment.

9. **Use disposable materials**. Whenever possible use disposable materials and dispose of them according to the established guidelines.

10. **Stay home if you are ill**. If you are ill, cancel your clinical appointments. You probably will not be very effective as a clinician anyway and may transmit your illness to your client.

11. **Treat the blood of all patients as potentially contagious**. Although it is important to be aware and assess the risk of exposure with each of your clients, you cannot determine the need for infection control based on a case history. Universal/standard health care precautions protect you and your client regardless of whether the risks are known or unknown.

12. **Be informed about communicable diseases**. There are many diseases you could be exposed to. However, knowledge about the transmission and prevention of the disease is one of the first steps in defense against the disease.

Depending on the work environment, there are other diseases of which the SLP should be aware. However, this chapter does not outline all possible diseases to which one may be exposed. Students should exercise due caution and follow the health and safety guidelines on each of their practicum sites. The clinic director and the clinical supervisor will alert you to the specific guidelines.

In addition to following health care precautions, follow the basic safety rules to help decrease the chance of injury to the client or to yourself.

Safety Fundamentals

1. **Make sure the clinic area is clean and orderly**. This will help avoid such accidents as tripping over small items left on the floor.

(continues)

2. **Do not leave children unattended in the clinic**. Children who are left without supervision may cause mischief or injury to themselves and others. They may swallow small objects, play with electrical outlets, pull furniture over, or fall.

3. **Do not let children stand on tables or chairs**. Hold the child if for some reason you want the child to stand on a table or chair.

4. **Check with the parent before giving food**. Occasionally, you may want to use food as a primary reinforcer in your treatment session. Before doing so, ascertain from the parents or caregivers that the child does not have any food allergies or swallowing difficulties and is not on a restricted diet. Also, get the parental or caregiver approval for the types of food you use as a primary reinforcer. If you are working with an adult who is under the care of a spouse or caregiver, check with that person before giving your client food. It is also appropriate to ask family members to bring a specific food or provide a written list of acceptable items. Many clinics and classrooms operate as peanut-free facilities as well. It is imperative to be cognizant of food allergies, as they may be life-threatening.

5. **Make sure clients who are in wheelchairs lock their brakes**. If they do not do so automatically, advise them to lock their brakes. If they cannot do so independently, lock their brakes for them.

6. **Before pushing individuals who are in wheelchairs, make sure their feet are in the footrests or lifted off the ground**. Clients may use their feet to propel their wheelchair with their feet resting on the ground. Do not push the wheelchair until you have secured the safety of the person in it.

7. **Do not allow smoking in the clinic area**. Typically, clinic areas are nonsmoking areas. If you see clients or accompanying persons smoking in a nonsmoking area, politely tell them of the nonsmoking policy at the clinic.

8. **Know where the fire extinguisher is**. In addition, it is important to know how the fire extinguisher works. If there is an emergency, you will not have time to read the instructions on the canister.

9. **Locate the nearest emergency telephone**. Most sites will have a telephone or intercom available for emergency communications.

10. **Adhere to safety procedures at your site**. Procedures may be variable across settings, so understand and follow the rules established at your practicum site.

Client Bill of Rights

Persons who receive clinical services in any facility have certain rights that the service providers should honor. ASHA has published a Model Bill of Rights for People Receiving Audiology or Speech-Language Pathology Services (American Speech-Language-Hearing Association, 1993). It is meant as a guideline, not a standard. The document encompasses both children and adults across all service settings in which both speech-language pathology and audiology services are offered. The statement is easily understandable to the consumers whose rights it describes. Many of the principles advocated in the Bill of Rights reflect the Code of Ethics. Before beginning your clinical practicum, read this Bill of Rights.

There are other official rights afforded to clients depending on the setting. For example, in the school setting, parents or educational rights holders will be provided with procedural safeguards that protect the rights of the child on an IEP. Each state has a specific parents' rights document that must be provided and explained to parents with school children.

In abiding by the Code of Ethics and state and federal laws, you may occasionally encounter guidelines that could be interpreted in different ways. In all such cases, you must consider the well-being of your clients as the most important basis on which to make decisions. Your supervisor or clinic director will help you make appropriate and ethical interpretations and decisions. ASHA, your state speech-language-hearing association, and your state licensure agency also are important institutions that help answer professional questions.

ASHA's Bill of Rights of Consumers (SLP and Audiology Clients)

All clients have a right to:

- Be treated with dignity and respect
- Receive treatment **without discrimination** in any form
- Know the name and qualifications of the professional offering services
- Privacy and confidentiality as provided by law
- A full disclosure of fees and other charges in advance and regardless of the method of payment
- Participate in treatment goal setting
- Explanation of evaluation results and the extent of improvement
- Accept or reject services as the laws permit
- Receive competent services promptly, including referrals
- Express concerns about the services received and to know the procedures for conflict resolution
- Accept or reject participation in activities (e.g., teaching, research studies, or promotional activities)
- Review their clinical records and correct inaccuracies
- Receive adequate notice of service termination, reasons for it, and referrals when requested

Clients, their family members, guardians, or legal representatives may exercise these rights. Students in clinical practicum, with support and guidance from their supervisors, should honor these consumer rights.

⑦ Questions for Self-Assessment

1. One of the administrators in your off-campus clinical practicum facility wants you to sign your name on a progress report on a client you had only assessed once but had never treated. You did not write the report. What would you tell the administrator? To whom

would you talk to first about this? Someone at the off-campus facility or someone in your academic department? If it is someone in the department, who? Justify your answer. To gain a perspective on such issues, read Bupp (2012).

2. What is your role in promoting evidence-based practice? How do you adhere to the principles of evidence-based practice? What kind of documentation do you have to provide your clinical supervisor to show that you are following the ASHA guidelines on evidence-based practice?

3. An 8-year-old boy you are working with in a hospital setting comes to your sessions with bruises, red spots on his arms and legs. He looks thin to you, is always tired, does not seem to get enough sleep. He shows signs of fear around a bigger person. To your knowledge, no one has done anything about it. What would you do? What are your legal responsibilities? How would you go about doing what you plan to do?

4. Your clinical supervisor asks you to make a case presentation on a client you are working with to her class on clinical methods. What would you *not* do during this presentation?

5. You are assigned a child who stutters. You expect the parents to ask you questions about (a) the efficacy of the treatment you plan on recommending, (b) whether and when their child will speak fluently, and (c) whether you will offer a different treatment about which they have read online. Write your answers down to these questions and show them to your supervisor to make sure you are on the right track.

References

American Speech-Language-Hearing Association. (1993). *Model bill of rights for people receiving audiology or speech-language pathology services.* https://www.asha.org/policy/rp1993-00197/

American Speech-Language-Hearing Association. (2004). *Preferred practice patterns for the profession of speech-language pathology.* https://www.asha.org/policy/pp2004-00191/

American Speech-Language-Hearing Association. (2005). *Evidence-based practice in communication disorders: Position statement.* https://www.asha.org/policy/ps2005-00221/

American Speech-Language-Hearing Association. (2013). *Speech-language pathology assistant scope of practice.*

American Speech-Language-Hearing Association. (2016). *Scope of practice in speech-language pathology.* https://www.asha.org/policy/sp2016-00343/

American Speech-Language-Hearing Association. (2023). *Code of ethics.* https://www.asha.org/siteassets/publications/code-of-ethics-2023.pdf

Bupp, H. (2012). 9 upsetting dilemmas. *Asha Leader, 17*(14). https://doi.org/10.1044/leader.FTR1.17142012.10

Centers for Disease Control and Prevention. (2016). *Basic TB facts.* http://www.cdc.gov/tb/topic/basics/default.htm

Child Welfare Information Gateway. (2013). *What is child abuse and neglect? Recognizing the signs and symptoms.* US Department of Health and Human Services, Children's Bureau. https://www.childwelfare.gov/pubpdfs/whatiscan.pdf

Child Welfare Information Gateway. (2018). *The risk and prevention of maltreatment of children with disabilities.* US Department of Health and Human Services, Children's Bureau. https://www.childwelfare.gov/pubPDFs/focus.pdf

Hegde, M. N., & Salvatore, A. P. (2020). *Clinical research in communicative disorders: Principles and strategies* (4th ed.). Plural Publishing.

Hudson, M. W., & DeRuiter, M. (2021). *Professional issues in speech-language pathology and audiology* (5th ed.). Plural Publishing.

Office for Civil Rights. (2013a). *Summary of the HIPAA privacy rule.* US Department of Health and Human Services. https://www.hhs.gov/hipaa/for-professionals/privacy/laws-regulations/index.html

Office for Civil Rights. (2013b). *Summary of the HIPAA security rule.* US Department of Health and Human Services. https://www.hhs.gov/hipaa/for-professionals/security/laws-regulations/index.html

CHAPTER 4

The Supervisor and the Student Clinician

Student Learning Outcomes

After reading this chapter, student clinicians are expected to:

- Understand and summarize the qualification and role of their clinical supervisors
- Describe what they can expect from their supervisors
- Summarize the differences between on-campus and off-campus supervision
- Give an overview of their own responsibilities as student clinicians and be prepared to act accordingly

Your clinical practicum in speech-language pathology is a three-way process involving you, your supervisor, and your client. A clinical mentor, your supervisor helps you acquire the knowledge and skills necessary to become an independent and competent clinician providing quality service for clients.

Depending on the university programs in speech-language pathology, clinical supervision is provided by (1) a staff of full-time supervisors who do little or no classroom teaching, (2) academic faculty members who teach regular courses and supervise clinical practicum, and (3) community-based speech-language pathologists (SLPs) who work as part-time supervisors.

You and Your Supervisor

The effectiveness of your practicum experience depends, partly, on the professional relationship you develop with your supervisor. To maximize the practicum experience, it is important that you and your clinical supervisor *establish a cooperative working relationship that ensures effective communication between the two of you.* This will enhance your clinical practicum experience and ensure the delivery of quality services. Some clinical supervisors are available before, during, and after clinic sessions to discuss clinical matters and answer your questions. Other clinical supervisors assign specific conference times. It is the responsibility of clinical supervisors to provide a forum for appropriate and effective communication between themselves and their student clinicians. However, you share in this responsibility.

You may be initially intimidated by your first clinical supervisor. To complicate matters, because of other obligations, the clinical supervisor may not always be readily available to you. Therefore, it is important to note that (1) supervisors are available to answer questions; (2) but they do have other responsibilities and cannot guess a student's needs; and therefore (3) student clinicians should clearly express their needs and concerns to their supervisors to get advice.

Read this chapter to understand the clinical supervisors' qualifications, what the supervisors are required to do for you, and what you should do to get the maximum help from them.

Qualifications and Requirements of Clinical Supervisors

Providing clinical supervision is a specialty in professional practice. The supervisors are clinical mentors who guide and monitor student practicum. Supervisors follow the guidelines of the American Speech-Language-Hearing Association (ASHA; 2008a, 2008b, 2008c, 2013). ASHA's Special Interest Group 11 is specifically concerned with administration and supervision. ASHA's Ad Hoc Committee on Supervision in Speech-Language Pathology developed a Knowledge and Skills report format to reflect the importance of effective supervision in speech-language pathology (American Speech-Language-Hearing Association, 2013).

Clinical supervisors are **clinical educators**. As such, they must have certain qualifications that ASHA stipulates (American Speech-Language-Hearing Association, 2013).

Qualifications and Requirements of Clinical Supervisors

1. **Clinical supervisors must hold a current Certificate of Clinical Competence (CCC) in speech-language pathology or audiology**. This presumes a Master's degree at the minimum. Many states require the state license, the educational credential, or both for the clinical supervisors.

2. **Supervisors must have completed a minimum of 9 months in a full-time clinical position** or its part-time equivalent.

3. **Supervisors must have completed a minimum of 2 hr of professional development in clinical instruction and supervision**. These 2 hr must be completed only after obtaining the ASHA certification.

4. **Supervisors should create a positive learning environment for their students**. A trusting relationship and reliable support for the student are essential components of this learning environment.

5. **Supervisors should clearly communicate their expectations**. Students should understand their responsibilities and obligations.

6. **Supervisors should establish student-specific goals for the practicum**. The supervisor should consider the strengths, limitations, and professional interests of their students to design an appropriate practicum experience for them.

7. **Supervisors should promote evidence-based practice**. They should guide the student in critically analyzing the research literature to select evidence-based assessment and treatment procedures.

8. **Supervisors should promote objective measurement and documentation of treatment progress**. They should educate the student clinicians in recording client responses and charting progress in treatment sessions.

9. **Supervision may be provided only in areas in which the supervisors are qualified**. SLPs may supervise all aspects of speech-language pathology service delivery, including evaluation and

(continues)

management. They also may supervise aural habilitation and audiological screenings (nondiagnostic) for the initial identification of communication disorders or as part of a speech or language evaluation. Audiologists may supervise all audiological services and aural habilitation and rehabilitation services. They also may supervise speech and language screenings for the initial identification of communication disorders. Nonetheless, a supervisor should only supervise in areas that fall within his or her *scope of competence*, which is different from the scope of practice. A supervisor with no training, gained expertise, or experience in a disorder should not supervise clients receiving services for that disorder. Under no circumstances should individuals supervise clients they believe they are not qualified or prepared to supervise.

10. **Supervise a minimum of 25% of a student's total contact with any client**. This rule must be followed regardless of a student clinician's level of experience. Additional supervision may be provided for beginning student clinicians and with more complex clients.

11. **Supervisors must be available to consult with the student**. They must be available for consultation during all service delivery.

12. **Supervisors should provide direct observation, instruction, and feedback**. Supervision also may include activities such as indirect observation via closed circuit television or recording, review of written reports, and conferences with the student clinician.

13. **Supervisors should help provide appropriate services to individuals of diverse backgrounds**. They should direct students to assessment and treatment literature that addresses multicultural issues, appropriate diagnostic procedures for clients of different language backgrounds, and selection of appropriate treatment procedures.

14. **Supervisors must abide by the ASHA Code of Ethics**. The supervisory conduct detailed in the Code includes: (a) not misrepresenting the credentials of those serving in practicum or speech-language pathology clinical fellowship (SLPCF) roles, (b) delegating job responsibilities appropriate to the level of the student or SLPCF, (c) treating the student clinician or the clinical

fellow with dignity and in a professional manner, and (d) making sure that the clinicians and fellows are abiding by the ASHA Code of Ethics (described in Chapter 3) (American Speech-Language-Hearing Association, 2023).

You should have a clear understanding of your supervisor's main responsibilities and the range of their obligations to avoid misunderstandings or inappropriate expectations. It is equally important that a clinical supervisor be aware of a student clinician's prior experience and clearly define practicum guidelines and expectations.

What to Expect From Your Clinical Supervisor

Generally, supervisors prepare you for clinical practicum and guide you throughout the semester so you acquire the necessary skills of assessment and treatment of communication disorders. They might help you understand the theoretical background of clinical procedures, direct you to published books, articles, and research databases. Obviously, supervisors consistently observe your clinical work with your clients, give feedback, and help you improve your skills. You can expect them to walk into your clinical sessions to demonstrated certain techniques or counsel the clients.

Evaluation of your work is one of their main responsibilities. Throughout the semester, their evaluations tend to be formative: designed to reinforce your strengths and suggest ways of correcting deficiencies. At the end, your supervisor will make a final evaluation and give you the grade.

It is with the help of clinical supervisors that you eventually become an independent practitioner. Read the following sections to better understand the various kinds of help you can expect from your expert supervisor.

Inform You of Practicum Requirements

Initially, your clinical supervisor will discuss the organization of your clinical practicum with you and outline expectations for your performance. You will learn more about your clinical practicum requirements. For example, your supervisor will:

- Explain how and when you will be evaluated and on what basis
- Discuss scheduling, attendance, and mandatory clinical meetings

- Explain the content requirements for written reports and submission deadlines

Your supervisor will encourage you to discuss any questions or concerns you may have at the beginning and thorough your clinical assignment. On a rare occasion when your supervisor is unavailable (perhaps on a sudden sick leave), seek advice from your clinic director or advisor.

Provide Consistent Feedback

Your clinical supervisor will provide consistent feedback on your clinical performance. Supervisors differ in their supervisory styles. One supervisor may give written feedback at the end of each session. Another supervisor may provide verbal feedback or modeling during a session and written feedback after the session. Some supervisors do not interrupt a session unless the well-being of the client is jeopardized. At the beginning of your practicum assignment, your supervisor will discuss the type and frequency of feedback you will receive.

To maximize learning, your supervisor may arrange client staffing, role playing, or other forms of clinical teaching sessions. These sessions may be held on a regular or intermittent basis and before, during, or after clinical practicum sessions. You should be an active participant in such special sessions.

Your supervisor should provide you with specific feedback. Examples are as follows:

- **Informative feedback**. This may take the form of specifying a behavior that you need to change. Just as it is not advised to always give your clients the same verbal reinforcer as "good job," it is not useful for you to hear your supervisor say, "good session," or "needs improvement."

- **Objective feedback**. This includes specific behaviors that you demonstrated or failed to demonstrate during the session. For example, beginning clinicians tend to use questions instead of statements: "Can you say /r/?" versus "Say /r/." To give objective feedback, your supervisor may count such ineffective questions you asked and model more effective questions for you. Subsequently, your supervisor may verbally reinforce you for asking more appropriate questions of your clients. If you think that you are not receiving sufficient feedback or that the feedback is unclear, discuss this with your clinical supervisor. Feedback does not necessarily imply negative criticism. It is a teaching method that you will frequently use with your own clients.

Assist in Planning Clinical Objectives

Typically, your supervisor will direct you to review your clients' charts or case histories and *develop an assessment* or *treatment plan* for your first session with your clients. Your supervisor will review these plans with you before your first session. The less clinical experience you have had, the more assistance your clinical supervisor will offer you. Your supervisor will help you develop *measurable treatment target behaviors and procedures to record the client responses in each session*. Practicum sites tend to have different ways of writing appropriate objectives:

- In the school setting, you will write goals and objectives (IEPs) related to your students' educational performance.

- In the hospital setting, you may write goals and objectives related to your clients' daily living activities such as communicating a personal need in any form possible (e.g., gesturing something to eat or going to the bathroom).

- In the university clinic setting, you may write goals and objectives that specify the target behaviors and their treatment procedures for the short- (e.g., for the semester) and the long term.

Your supervisor will help you establish priorities for treatment goals and objectives. Clinical supervisors must approve all major clinical decisions, including what to teach, how to teach, and how to measure and record the client progress. See Chapter 7 for general guidelines for selecting target behaviors and Chapter 6 for various clinical reports and guidelines on writing them.

Your supervisor also may specify or help you self-describe *personal objectives* for you to achieve. You may be asked to describe areas of professional growth and how you plan to achieve it. For example, you may identify your own weakness in augmentative and alternative communication and seek guidance in learning more about it. To supplement your knowledge, your supervisor might direct you to research on the subject and report back your findings.

Assist in Developing Assessment Skills

To help develop clinical competence in assessment and diagnosis of communication disorders, supervisors guide students in critically evaluating and selecting valid and reliable standardized assessment instruments as well as informal and naturalistic procedures. Your clinical supervisor will give you feedback on your *selection, administration, and interpretation* of tests. As a general rule, you should select the most recent revision of a test and refrain from administering tests that are not standardized on diverse populations or do not sample dialectal variations (American Speech-Language-Hearing Association, n.d.). To ensure the test is appropriate for your client, carefully read the test manual.

Learn each test administration procedure before you administer it to a client. Practice using the test by administering it to a classmate. After you have familiarized yourself with a test and practiced administering it, your supervisor will give you additional help if needed. For example, your supervisor may model both general and specific test administration procedures. Your supervisor also will advise you on how to integrate the results of standardized tests with the results of *observation* and *client-specific assessment procedures*. Your supervisor may guide you to alternative assessment procedures that are suitable to diverse clients.

Assist in Selecting and Implementing Treatment Procedures

Beginning student clinicians may be unsure of how to select an effective treatment procedure for their clients and how to implement the selected procedure. Supervisors will guide you in treatment procedure selection. However, they may ask you to read and evaluate treatment research reports and suggest a procedure or two before selecting one based on evidence.

Supervisors may enter the clinic room spontaneously or may inform you in advance if they intend to demonstrate a specific technique during a clinical session. Your supervisor may demonstrate aspects of treatment. For instance, they may show how to evoke target behaviors, give instructions, model, prompt, reinforce, and give verbal correction. When you need assistance with any aspect of treatment, do not hesitate to ask the supervisor.

Help Develop Client Management Skills

After you develop your treatment goals and treatment strategies, you should determine a progression of treatment. Your supervisor would like to know (a) your initial and subsequent treatment targets, (b) how you plan to baserate the target skills, (c) the sequence of treatment you plan to follow, (d) what performance criteria you specify for each level of training, and (e) how you plan to measure and record the client's responses in baserate and treatment sessions. Your supervisor will quiz about these to encourage you to think, plan, and implement treatment procedures.

Your supervisor may ask you to analyze not only your client's responses, but also your own clinical performance. It is your behavior that affects the client's responses. Video recording of your sessions may facilitate the supervisor's evaluation as well as your own self-evaluation. Your supervisor also may chart some of your clinical behaviors (such as your use of positive and corrective feedback, modeling, or prompting) to show how to do them more effectively.

Describe Procedures to Document Treatment Progress

Accountability and documentation are essential to good clinical practice. Some recordkeeping and documentation requirements are common across settings and others may be unique to individual sites. Supervisors will describe the requirements specific to their settings.

Appropriate recordkeeping and measurement of targeted skills during treatment sessions are necessary to document systematic improvement under treatment and to receive reimbursement from third-party payers. Your supervisor will also specify the methods to ensure confidentiality of clinical records. See the appendices in Chapter 8 for various response recording sheets you can use to document the client responses on baserate, treatment, and probe trials.

Encourage Critical Thinking and Independent Problem Solving

When you search the speech-language pathology literature, you may find many recommended assessment and treatment procedures for various disorders. Research articles may strongly suggest certain methods. Without a critical analysis of what you read, however, you may apply methods that are not based on good experimental evidence. Therefore, critical analysis of research evidence is the hallmark of evidence-based practice. Your supervisor will help you evaluate the professional literature and direct you to publications that you need to consult.

Critical reasoning is also essential for self-evaluation. Self-evaluation, in turn, is essential to understanding your own clinical strengths and limitations so you can continue to bank on your strengths and work on eliminating your deficiencies. To continue to improve your clinical skills, you should be critical of what you read as well as what you do in the clinic room. Eventually, you will learn independent problem-solving skills.

Critical reasoning and self-evaluation are essential prerequisites for learning to problem-solve independently, a significant goal of clinical practicum. You may often be challenged by a communication disorder with which you have had little or no experience or a disorder you are familiar with but is unique in a given individual. You may meet this challenge by making a critical analysis of the problem, reading new information, and generalizing from previous experiences. Your supervisor is always there to help you.

However, as you progress in your practicum, expect progressively less assistance with decision making to encourage you to perform with greater independence.

Help Develop Verbal and Written Skills

Supervisors facilitate the learning of scientific and professional verbal and written communication skills. They will model professional verbal skills for you and edit your written reports to suggest effective and grammatically accurate writing. Supervisors may suggest sources for basic good writing as well as scientific and professional writing (Hegde, 2024; Strunk & White, 1999). Also, your supervisor may provide you with well-written samples of clinical reports. In the school setting, anonymous samples or general templates of individualized education programs (IEPs) are made available to you.

Although reporting styles may vary, the need to write clear, concise, and logical reports does not (Hegde, 2024). You may revise a report more than once. Your supervisor's first editing will suggest corrections to the major and obvious problems. However, after these errors are corrected, more subtle problems may be observed, requiring you to revise your reports further. See Chapter 6 for details on report writing and its appendices for samples of clinical reports.

Professional verbal skills will be required at all practicum sites. Each site may require a specialized vocabulary, but many elements of professionally appropriate speech are common to settings. The exact type of speech will depend on the persons you speak to. You may describe your assessment results, treatment plans, and client progress to clients and their families in all settings. You should speak in simple yet scientifically and professionally accurate language to these persons. Depending on their familiarity with speech-language pathology, you speak to other professionals in more or less technical language.

Your supervisor may require you to *practice your verbal reporting skills* during client staffing, consultation with other professionals, and discussion of information with clients and their families. You may find it beneficial to write out the information you want to cover and practice presenting it out loud. It is also helpful to try to anticipate questions that might arise and prepare answers in advance. Charts and visuals may also help make your point.

Direct You to Current Resources

Your supervisor will expect you to use current information, instruments, procedures, and technology and will assist you in locating them. You will learn to research current information and use many campus resources, including the library, online databases, computer laboratories, writing clinics, and so forth. ASHA's position papers, guidelines, journal publications, and other resources are available on its website.

Your supervisor will help you learn ways of evaluating information freely available on the Internet. You may be directed to research-based scientific and scholarly information available on aggregate databases (e.g., PubMed, ScienceDirect, ERIC, or ASHA). You should search these and other research databases for effective treatment procedures. Talk to one of the university reference librarians on useful databases and on how to get free full texts of articles. ASHA website is a reliable source for research articles published in the association's journals. Blogs and wiki entries, however, may be just opinions of individuals who are not experts. You should be critical of information offered there.

Model and Demand Professional Behavior

Your supervisor will model the behavior expected of you. For example, your supervisor will be punctual, dress appropriately, be prepared for supervision, protect client confidentiality by not talking about clients in public areas, and so on. Your supervisor will treat you as a professional and expect to be treated as one.

In all clinical practicum sites, your supervisor will expect you to know and comply with ASHA's Code of Ethics. Your supervisor will outline the requirements of your clinical site, including the dress code, health regulations, and clinical practicum schedule. If you have any questions about the parameters of professional behavior at your site, ask your supervisor for clarification.

Evaluate Your Clinical Work

Your clinical supervisor will objectively and constructively evaluate your clinical work to assure that you are developing appropriate knowledge and skills that meet the requirements for ASHA's certification, state licensure, and special educational credential. Supervisors may set aside times for formal evaluations, but their regular feedback is also continuous evaluation of your work. You may receive a letter grade or grade of credit/no credit for your clinical practicum. Your supervisor will follow the university's guidelines for evaluation of student clinicians, but most evaluations include the following:

- Academic and clinical knowledge

- Diagnostic and treatment skills

- Report writing and oral expression skills

- Response to supervisory feedback
- Professionalism and ethics
- Cultural competency

Many universities use rating scales that help supervisors assess students' performance with a view to effect improvement in clinical skills. Your performance may be compared in terms of accuracy, consistency, and need for supervisory guidance from an earlier stage in your practicum to the current stage. If you have questions about your clinical practicum evaluation, discuss them with your clinical supervisor.

Help, Guide, and Support You

As a conscientious student clinician, you can expect your supervisor to be there to help, guide, and support you. Sometimes you may feel the feedback is negative, but critical feedback is essential for your continued learning and professional development.

Supervisors behave in such a way as to inspire confidence and trust in them. Your supervisor is not only your mentor, but also your advocate.

Off-Campus Clinical Supervision

Your university will have selected off-campus clinical practicum sites that meet the ASHA requirements for clinical supervision. The supervisor may be a professional employee of your practicum site. Your university training director will have provided a general background of the level of your experience to the off-campus supervisor.

The core duties of off-campus and on-campus supervisors are similar, if not the same. The off-campus supervisors also help you learn assessment and treatment techniques, professional and ethical behavior patterns, acceptable written and oral communication skills, and so forth. However, at the outset, your off-campus supervisors help you understand the variables that are unique to their setting. They may describe the client scheduling procedure, recordkeeping methods, and working hours that may be different than those at the university clinics.

You should not expect off-campus clinical supervisors to be exactly the same as the university clinical supervisors in performing their duties, however. Off-campus supervisors concurrently supervise you and maintain their own employment obligations.

Frequency of Supervision

The amount of supervision offered at off-campus sites may be more or less than what you are used to on your university clinic, although it must meet *ASHA's guidelines* for the type and frequency of supervision. At an off-campus site, you are expected to work relatively independently, but you may be supervised closely if your clients have communication disorders with which you have not had much experience. For instance, in off-campus hospital settings, you may work with critically ill patients or implement a treatment procedure which, if done incorrectly, could compromise the client's health. Also, you will be working with a full caseload of clients with a variety of diagnoses that will require greater assistance from your supervisor. The off-campus site may have additional supervisory requirements for compliance with insurance reimbursements.

Progress Toward Independence

Expect your supervisor to demand fairly independent performance from you, in spite of providing a greater amount of supervision on an off-campus facility. You take an off-campus internship placement only when you are fairly advanced in your clinical skills and are able to make some independent judgments. Because of this, your internship supervisor will expect you to act relatively independently in planning assessment and treatment sessions, problem solving, researching additional information, and in asking questions or requesting help.

You may demonstrate your clinical insight and independent judgment in many clinical activities. Some of the critical ones include the following:

- Plan and prepare your clinical sessions without the supervisor's prompts
- Select or create appropriate stimulus materials for assessment and treatment
- Evaluate standardized tests for their reliability, validity, and appropriateness for diverse clients
- Use client-specific or alternative procedures that suit diverse clients
- Evaluate treatment research and choose evidence-based intervention procedures
- Measure and record client responses in each treatment session
- Select and use such performance criteria as 80% or 90% response accuracy
- Determine when treatment may be moved to a higher level of response complexity

- Initiate training for parents, other family members, or institutional care-givers at appropriate times

- Measure and promote generalization and maintenance

Your supervisor will support you if you still need some degree of assistance with all of those listed activities. However, you should be on the right track and ask advanced questions to demonstrate your independent clinical judgment and service.

Responsibilities of the Student Clinician

Student clinicians must fulfill numerous responsibilities to ensure a successful practicum experience for themselves and to provide effective services to their clients. In all settings, however, student clinicians should (a) learn to assess, treat, counsel, and professionally work with their clients and their families; and (b) show systematic progress in their learning of those professional skills.

Throughout your clinical practicums, most of your responsibilities will remain unchanged as you progress in your internships. At all stages of internship, you will be expected to follow established procedures, abide by ethical guidelines, provide quality service, be disciplined, exhibit professional behavior, and write acceptable reports with the format accepted in different practicum sites.

The following sections enumerate student clinicians' main responsibilities. Clinicians should follow any additional and setting-specific guidelines and requirements their supervisors specify.

Adhere to ASHA's Code of Ethics

As you know from Chapter 3, ASHA's Code of Ethics describes various acceptable professional behaviors. In all clinical practicum settings, abide by ASHA's Code of Ethics.

It is your responsibility to understand the intent of the Code of Ethics and its various principles and rules. You do not want to jeopardize your career as an SLP because you have violated the Code of Ethics. When in doubt, discuss the potential ethical issues with your supervisor.

Adhere to ASHA's Scope of Practice Guidelines

ASHA's (2016) Scope of Practice guidelines specify what SLPs may and may not do. The state licensing boards do the same. At the very beginning, review the range of professional work ASHA and state licensure boards allow SLPs to perform. ASHA guidelines are not legal mandates, but licensure laws are. However, to maintain membership in ASHA and its clinical certification, SLPs should adhere to the scope of practice guidelines.

SLPs' scope of practice continuously evolves and expands. Child language disorders was one of the early inclusions in the scope of practice. Clinical management of swallowing disorders and literacy assessment and intervention are examples of the expanded scope of SLPs' traditional practice. Research advancements and expertise of SLPs justify newer areas of professional practice. Therefore, frequently consult the ASHA document on the scope of practice.

From the standpoint of clinical practicum, it is sufficient to understand that the SLP scope of practice includes eight domains of speech-language pathology service delivery: (1) collaboration; (2) counseling; (3) prevention and wellness, (4) screening; (5) assessment; (6) treatment; (7) modalities, technology, and instrumentation; and (8) population and systems. The scope of practice document specifies five domains of professional practice: (1) advocacy and outreach, (2) supervision, (3) education, (4) research, and (5) administration/leadership. The service delivery areas include communication, swallowing, and their disorders. Specifically, speech production, fluency, language, cognition, voice, resonance, feeding, swallowing, and hearing disorders may be part of service delivery. In addition, health literacy and screening, diagnosis, and treatment of autism spectrum disorders also are within the SLPs' scope of practice. Read the document for details (American Speech-Language-Hearing Association, 2016). Individual SLPs do not practice in all domains and service delivery areas. ASHA's scope of practice guidelines do not supersede state licensure laws.

Follow Clinic Policies and Procedures

The many clinic policies and procedures enable a clinic to operate effectively and efficiently. Typically, the clinic administrative assistant or your clinical supervisor will educate you on their policies and procedures. You may be offered a copy of the procedural handbook.

The following policy and procedural matters are commonly addressed at the university clinic and off-campus practicum sites:

- Enrolling in clinical practicum
- Scheduling clients
- Ensuring client confidentiality
- Reserving and checking out materials and equipment
- Maintaining and working with clients' folders

- Using the clinic telephone
- Maintaining clinic records
- Fulfilling insurance and health requirements
- Achieving quality improvement
- Taking health precautions
- Complying with the site's dress code
- Maintaining client confidentiality

If you are unsure of a specific procedure or policy at your clinical site, you must contact your clinical supervisor.

Respect Clients' Personal and Cultural Beliefs

You will work with many clients who have varied cultural and ethnic backgrounds. You are not expected to share each client's values and beliefs, or even to know every culture's traditions beforehand; however, the cultural and communication variations that affect your service delivery to particular individuals must be understood. An acceptance of your clients' diversity will maximize the effectiveness of your service delivery. Acceptance that goes beyond a nondiscriminatory disposition is essential to successfully serve clients and their families with diverse ethnocultural backgrounds.

As pointed out in Chapter 6 and other sections of this book, you should be careful in diagnosing a communication disorder in children and adults who (a) speak a specific dialect of English, or (b) speak a non-English primary language at home and speak or are learning to speak English as a second language. For example, a child may speak an African American English (AAE) at home and may attend a school in which the predominant language is Mainstream American English (MAE). Instruction is offered in MAE. In this instance, a communication disorder should not be diagnosed on the basis of the child's AAE speech or language features. For example, the production of /f/ instead of /th/ in certain words (*baf* for *bath*) or the omission of the MAE's plural morpheme in AAE are not a basis to diagnose a speech or language disorder because such productions are the typical features of AAE. Similarly, a child whose home language is Spanish may generalize speech sound or language patterns to English. Such generalizations, too, are not a basis to diagnose a communication disorder. To diagnose a communication in each of the two cases, the deviation must be a deviation in the child's primary dialect (e.g., AAE) or the primary language (e.g., Spanish or Vietnamese), not a feature that generalizes from the primary dialect or language to another form of English.

Most clients with diverse language and culture background need the alternative assessment procedures described in Chapter 6. Guidelines on serving culturally diverse clients are infused throughout the book.

Prepare for All Clinic Sessions

Review test administration and language sampling procedures before your diagnostic sessions. Inspect the tests you plan to administer before meeting with your client to make sure the tests are complete, that they contain all required materials, and that the necessary test response forms are available. Although it may be another person's job to stock the clinic rooms, it is your responsibility to have all the necessary materials before you start an assessment or treatment session. In the middle of an oral-peripheral examination, you cannot blame someone for missing tongue depressors or a flashlight.

Check any equipment that you plan to use in your clinical sessions to ensure it is working properly. Make sure you know how to operate the equipment you plan to use. Some distressing problems can occur while audiorecording on a phone or recorder. Not infrequently, student clinicians have intended to record an entire clinical session only to find that the pause button was depressed or something interrupted the recording. Needless to say, such recordings should be carefully guarded to maintain client confidentiality. Recording clients on cell phones may pose a particular risk of someone breaching that confidentiality.

Carefully review data obtained in previous sessions to determine appropriate beginning levels and possible sequences of treatment for the sessions for which you are preparing. Make sure the materials you have selected are the most appropriate for the target behaviors you plan to teach and the individual client's cultural background. The best organized and most creative materials are ineffective if the target behaviors are inappropriate or unrealistic. Treatment trials may be wasted if the selected stimulus materials are inappropriate for the target behaviors and the specific individual client's ethnocultural background.

Choose Appropriate Diagnostic Instruments

Select and use evaluation procedures and instruments that are appropriate to the client. Select procedures and instruments that are valid, reliable, nonbiased, and comprehensive. In assessing clients who speak another dialect of English (e.g., AAE) or bilinguals who speak English as a second language, it is critical to select tests that are standardized on those populations. Generally, the evaluation procedures must sample behaviors adequately and sample behaviors that are a feature of the dialect or the primary language the client speaks. Adequate behavior sampling implies that the client is given multiple opportunities to produce a single skill. Standardized tests may give a single opportunity for most skills tested (e.g., a single opportunity to produce a phoneme or a grammatic morpheme).

Comprehensive assessment may involve formal assessments (standardized and norm-referenced measures) in addition to naturalistic assessments (speech and language samples, skilled observation, informant interviews, etc.). Generally, refrain from modifying the procedures of standardized tests to suit a diverse client. If the procedures were to be modified, report in a criterion-referenced fashion by identifying skills present and absent. Make sure that detailed speech and language samples are taken to provide a more comprehensive analysis of a client's spontaneous and social communication skills.

Additional variables must be considered in assessing children and adults of diverse cultural and language backgrounds. Use an assessment approach that integrates the traditional procedures with alternative approaches (e.g., criterion-referenced, dynamic, authentic) that are more suitable to individuals of diverse ethnocultural backgrounds (Hegde & Pomaville, 2022). See Chapter 6 for such alternative approaches.

Write Measurable Treatment Objectives

Treatment objectives are often the target behaviors to be taught. These behaviors must be defined in operational (measurable) terms. You need not always develop "original" objectives. It may be appropriate or even necessary to resume work on objectives established the previous semester. See Chapter 7 for an overview of target behaviors across disorders.

In different clinical settings, goals may be written for trimester, quarter, or annual review. At the annual review in an educational setting, it is often appropriate to adjust or modify a goal that was not met. Among other variables, adjustment to the goal may be the level of prompting, the accuracy level, and the setting.

Submit Written Assignments Promptly

Your clinical supervisor will notify you of timelines and due dates for written assignments. University clinics typically require an initial written summary, daily lesson plans or a semester treatment plan, and a final summary or progress report. In the educational setting, there are initial assessment reports, triennial assessment reports, progress reports, and IEPs. Each of these has specific due dates that must be observed to remain legally compliant. Read Chapter 5 for details on various types of clinical reports. The appendix to Chapter 5 gives a sample report for you to model. To read more about clinical report writing and practice writing them before or during your clinical practicum, see Hegde (2023).

The timely submission of written assignments is important for additional reasons. First, completing assignments on time suggests that you are dependable and that your practicum assignment is a high priority to you. Second, your written work reflects your knowledge of your clients, their communication disorders, and assessment and treatment procedures you plan to implement. A promptly submitted report will help the supervisor give you timely feedback. Third, your reports may suggest to the supervisor the level of supervision you need.

Write Effective Treatment Plans

An effective treatment program may fail if it is poorly sequenced for an individual client. For example, if the initial target behavior is the correct production of a phoneme in sentences, you may never get started at all. Therefore, plan and sequence treatment using the initial and continuous assessment data (daily treatment data, probes, etc.). In addition, you should:

- Plan realistically for the time available within each session
- Design maintenance procedures early in the treatment sequence
- Include the client and the family members in the treatment process, including target behavior selection
- Use clinical procedures based on replicated research and technology (evidence-based practice)

Maintain Accurate Clinical Records

Your clients' clinical histories, assessment results, treatment plans, progress notes, and related information are placed in their permanent files. Maintain clinic files in the order established by the clinical site. Clinics may store files electronically.

Continuous measurement of target responses throughout the treatment sessions, calculating the percentages of correct responses, and charting them in the form of line or bar graphs will help facilitate the presence or absence of progress. Such quantitative measures enable you to find out quickly if treatment is appropriate or if modifications are needed. Graphs help the client, family members, and other caregivers understand the extent of progress.

Maintain an accurate and complete chronological log of clinical activity. This log should show how treatment progressed from simpler levels of training to more complex levels. See Chapter 5 for detailed information on recordkeeping procedures.

Apply Information Learned in Academic Courses

Assessment and treatment information is derived from academic courses. You may find that information learned in one class on a particular disorder can be modified and generalized to other communication disorders. The information you acquire in your academic studies is the foundation on which you build your independent professional skills and clinical experience. The more you integrate academic and clinical insights, the greater is the value of both.

Research current information to develop effective assessment and treatment plans. You may independently locate such information but consult with your supervisor before you apply it. Learn to use library resources (including current and past periodicals), the latest books, and computerized data search programs. If you are unsuccessful at resolving a particular clinical question independently, request assistance from your clinical supervisor.

As you gain more experience in working with a variety of clients in multiple settings, your repertoire of clinical skills will increase. You will continue to integrate and apply the knowledge gained from academic classes, practicum settings, research, and continuing education throughout your professional practice.

Ask Questions

Although expected to work increasingly independently, you must seek assistance when you have questions. If you are unsure of something, you should not do it. If you are uncertain about clinic policies and procedures, implementation of a specific treatment plan, or directions given by your supervisor, or you forget something that was said, ask for clarification.

Your clinical supervisor does not always immediately know when you need help. If you think you are not getting enough assistance from your supervisor, do not conclude that your supervisor "doesn't have time" or "doesn't care." Discuss your concerns with your supervisors.

Self-Evaluate Your Clinical Performance

Do not expect your clinical supervisor to evaluate everything you do in every session. As discussed before, learn to self-evaluate your clinical work. You will learn to analyze your clients' behavior and your behavior objectively. Your self-assessment skills will enable you to improve your assessment and treatment plans and will make you an independent and effective clinician.

Self-evaluation is a skill you learn from your experience and feedback from your supervisor. In helping you learn to self-evaluate, your supervisor may respond to your questions with additional questions. Your supervisor may suggest areas of research rather than giving you a ready-made answer. Your supervisor may not step in to correct your minor errors but later give a hint so you can learn to correct yourself.

Maintain Regular Attendance

Be punctual for all scheduled clinical sessions. Also, begin and end your clinical sessions on time. If client or family education is required at the end of a session, end treatment a few minutes sooner. For example, if you need to assign or review homework, ask the parent to return five min prior to the session's termination time so that you may continue your subsequent sessions promptly.

Cancel sessions only for justifiable reasons. If you are ill or have a personal emergency, *notify your clinical supervisor* and, if part of your clinic's protocol, your clients. The university or off-campus site may require documentation (physician's note) to verify absence due to illness. Studying for examinations, leaving for a vacation, or simply being unprepared is not an acceptable reason for canceling a clinical appointment. Any letter of recommendation you later seek from your supervisor or advisor for employment will be based on your clinical performance as well as your work ethic, dependability, and professionalism.

Act Professionally

Sometimes it is difficult to be a student on the one hand and a professional on the other. But even though you are in training, you are a professional helping people with communication disorders.

To learn professional behavior, model your supervisor's behaviors. Observe the behavior of senior clinicians. Do some of your fellow students generate more of an aura of professionalism than others? If you look at their behaviors, you probably will find individuals who have spent much time becoming knowledgeable about communication disorders. They will have prepared thoroughly and organized their clinical sessions. They will have researched and assimilated current information. They also will have given thought to how they speak, dress, and interact with clients and their families.

Student clinicians who present themselves as professionals also treat their clients, supervisor, clinical staff, and other professionals with respect. In turn, the student clinicians get treated as professionals.

Maintain a Clinical Clock Hour Log

You are responsible for maintaining a log of the clinical clock hours you have earned. Maintain both a daily and a semester log. If you have questions regarding where to input hours on the documentation form, ask your supervisor. A supervisor may review your hours daily, weekly, or at semester's end.

University speech and hearing clinics and ASHA have formats for recording clock hours. Carefully follow the documentation requirements of your training program because you may not get credit for incorrectly recorded clock hours. Obtain a copy of ASHA's Knowledge and Skills Acquisition (KASA) form from your department office to document your clinical and academic progress.

Maintain an Effective Relationship With Your Clinical Supervisor

You will work with many supervisors. Each may have a different supervisory style. Regardless of your practicum site or the supervisor you have, it is important to maintain contact with your supervisor. Meet with your supervisors as often as their times allow. Make use of the open office hours supervising faculty members post. If you had a great experience during a clinical session, let your supervisor know. Work cooperatively with your supervisor and do your part in maintaining an effective and interactive relationship.

The interaction between the clinical supervisor and the student clinician is the basis for learning in the practicum setting. To ensure optimal training for the student clinician and quality service for the client, the supervisor and the student clinician should diligently fulfill their respective responsibilities.

Enjoy Practicum Experience

All this work and all this responsibility and now you have to enjoy yourself? Yes! The profession you have chosen is challenging and rewarding in equal proportions. You teach your clients effective communication skills that will change their lives for the better. As you gain knowledge, skills, and professional independence, you will experience personal fulfillment. Your clients will know whether you like or dislike your job.

If you do not find joy or satisfaction in your clinical practicum, you should reevaluate your professional objectives. Burnout may come too quickly if you do not learn early on to balance your life with the responsibilities that come with this career path. But if you enjoy your work with people with communication disorders, and if their success gives you personal satisfaction, you know you have chosen the right path to a fulfilling career.

⑦ Questions for Self-Assessment

1. You understand that the clinical supervisors' job is to make your clinical practicum an effective and enjoyable learning experience for you. Write a brief essay on the most important and personally meaningful kinds of help you wish to receive from your supervisor. Consider your own academic, clinical, or personal limitations in answering this question and include any kind of special help not discussed in this chapter. If your supervisor is open to reading it, submit it.

2. Supervisors are ultimately responsible for their student clinicians' actions. And yet, they wish to promote independent and critical judgment in their clinicians. Describe the professional areas in which you can be relatively independent and the areas in which you should always defer the action to your supervisor.

3. You find yourself in a difficult ethical situation of not being properly and sufficiently supervised according to the ASHA guidelines on supervision. What would you do, and how do you go about doing it?

4. On what grounds can you justifiably cancel a scheduled assessment or treatment session? What are some of the reasons for which you never should cancel?

5. You are assigned a client whose disorder you have not studied in an academic class. You have not assessed or treated that disorder. Asking for a different client is not an option. What steps would you take to be adequately prepared to work with this client?

References

American Speech-Language-Hearing Association. (n.d.). *School-based service delivery in speech-language pathology.* https://www.asha.org/SLP/schools/School-Based-Service-Delivery-in-Speech-Language-Pathology/

American Speech-Language-Hearing Association. (2004). *Preferred practice patterns for the profession of speech-language pathology*. https://www.asha.org/policy/pp2004-00191/

American Speech-Language-Hearing Association. (2008a). *Clinical supervision in speech-language pathology: Technical report*. https://www.asha.org/policy/tr2008-00296/

American Speech-Language-Hearing Association. (2008b). *Clinical supervision in speech-language pathology: Position statement*. https://www.asha.org/policy/ps2008-00295/

American Speech-Language-Hearing Association. (2008c). *Knowledge and skills needed by speech-language pathologists providing clinical supervision*. https://www.asha.org/policy/ks2008-00294/

American Speech-Language-Hearing Association. (2023). *Code of ethics*. https://www.asha.org/siteassets/publications/code-of-ethics-2023.pdf

American Speech-Language-Hearing Association. Ad Hoc Committee on Supervision. (2013). *Final report: Knowledge, skills and training considerations for individuals serving as supervisors*. https://www.asha.org/siteassets/uploadedFiles/Supervisors-Knowledge-Skills-Report.pdf/

Hegde, M. N. (1998). *Treatment procedures in communicative disorders* (3rd ed.). Pro-Ed.

Hegde, M. N. (2018). *Hegde's pocketguide to treatment in speech-language pathology*. Plural Publishing.

Hegde, M. N. (2024). *A coursebook on scientific and professional writing for speech-language pathology* (6th ed.). Plural Publishing.

Hegde, M. N., & Pomaville, F. (2022). *Assessment of communication disorders in children: Resources and protocols* (4th ed.). Plural Publishing.

Strunk, W., Jr., & White, E. B. (1999). *The elements of style* (4th ed.). Pearson.

Clinical Methods in Speech-Language Pathology

In Part I, you learned how clinical practicum in speech-language pathology is organized. You also learned about your supervisors' qualifications, the support you will get from them, your professional conduct, and the practicum rules and guidelines you should follow.

Part II covers (a) assessment of individuals with communication disorders including those who are ethnoculturally diverse (Chapter 5); (b) writing a variety of treatment plans and progress reports (Chapter 6); (c) selecting target behaviors across all major communication disorders (Chapter 7); (d) evidence-based treatment techniques to establish the selected target behaviors (Chapter 8); (e) effective procedures to reduce the frequency of undesirable behaviors that interfere with treatment (Chapter 9); and (f) methods to promote generalization and maintenance of clinically established speech-language skills (Chapter 10).

CHAPTER 5

Assessment of Speech and Language Disorders

Student Learning Outcomes

After reading this chapter, student clinicians are expected to:

- Understand the main assessment procedures and be prepared to make comprehensive assessments of clients assigned to them
- Summarize the principles and procedures of assessing ethnoculturally diverse individuals with alternative and integrated procedures
- Describe the elements and formats of assessment reports
- Give an overview of the guidelines on working with interpreters, translators, and transliterators

Definition of Terms

In speech-language pathology (SLP), assessment, a clinical activity that precedes the treatment of a disorder, has synonyms, similar terms, and multiple meanings. *Assessment, evaluation*, and *diagnosis* are the three commonly used terms. Meanings of these terms overlap to some extent and yet vary across the clinicians and settings in which they are used (Hegde & Pomaville, 2022).

In practice, *assessment* and *evaluation* mean the same. Assessment and evaluation refer to procedural activities designed to understand a client's current level of communication and related skills, describe limitations or deficits, make a diagnosis of the disorder, suggest a prognosis, and make recommendations. Possibly, an assessment or evaluation may suggest typical communication skills that do not require clinical services.

The term *evaluation* is sometimes used to emphasize an *evaluative judgment* the clinician makes about the adequacy of skills sampled and need for intervention. Because assessments also result in such a judgment, the distinction is minor.

As applied in K through 12 educational settings, the Individuals with Disabilities Education Act (IDEA) (U.S. Department of Education, 2011) describes evaluation as a set of procedures designed to understand a child's unique strengths and limitations and to determine whether a child has a disability that qualifies for special education services (including speech, language, and hearing services).

Diagnosis is also a part of assessment (evaluation), although in many cases, a diagnosis as defined in medicine is not always possible in communication disorders. Technically, and as used in medicine, diagnosis means describing not just symptoms of a disorder or disease but pointing out its cause. Generally, in SLP, when a disorder is named (e.g., stuttering, aphasia, speech sound disorder, child language disorder, pitch disorder), a diagnosis is made.

Common Assessment Procedures

In assessing all clients, clinicians may follow certain common procedures. Assessment of communication disorders in children and adults is described in the subsequent sections. What follows is only a summative review because the student clinicians will have completed a full academic course on assessment and diagnostics. Many university training programs run a *diagnostic clinic* to teach clinical assessment skills to students.

For procedural details, the clinician may consider other sources (Hegde & Freed, 2022; Hegde & Pomaville, 2022). Both of these books have detailed protocols for conducting orofacial examinations and assessing diadochokinetic tasks.

When a client is assigned to you for assessment, develop a plan and get it approved by the supervisor. Suggest the standardized tests you may administer and briefly describe other procedures you plan to use. Let your supervisor know the scheduled assessment time. You assess your clients according to your supervisor's directions.

Case History

All clinical practicum sites will use a case history form to record the source and the reason for referral, a general description of the problem, developmental history (in case of children), medical history, family and social background, educational background, and occupational information (in the case of adults).

Aspects of information obtained may depend on the age and the disorder of the client. The case history can be extensive and include prenatal, birth, developmental, and education information in the case of children. Detailed medical, social, educational, and occupational history may be essential for adults. When you assess individuals after they have experienced a stroke or traumatic brain injury (TBI), you will also include questions about their *premorbid* skills (knowledge, skill, and performance levels before the incident resulting in communication disorders). An evaluation is scheduled following receipt of the necessary information in the clinic office.

With the help of supervisors, student clinicians learn to evaluate the reliability of information the clients or the family members provide on the case history form. Different family members of a child client may offer conflicting information on the problem or its severity. Their description of the disorder may or may not match the assessment results. Eventually, case history information is evaluated and integrated with the results of clinical observations, assessment results, and available reports from other professionals.

Clinical Interview

The interview is a means to get clarifications on the case history information, ask additional questions about the reason for referral, get details about prior services received, explore the effects the disorder has on the educational and occupational performance as well as on the quality of life of the individual. If audio-recorded, the interview may also serve as a speech-language sample.

The student clinician should practice patient, sympathetic listening skills. Professional and polite probing is acceptable when something is not clear but bombarding the client or the family members with relentless questioning is not. Practice avoiding the common mistakes in conducting clinical interviews described in the next boxed display.

Avoid Common Problems During Interviews

1. **Difficulty establishing rapport.** This problem stems from an extremely formal and stiff disposition inexperienced clinicians may exhibit. Rigid use of the case history form as an interview guide creates an unnecessarily cold format. Instead, use a warmer, conversational style to gather information.

2. **Asking too many "yes" or "no" questions.** Ask open-ended questions and create conversational interactions. For instance, instead of asking, "Does he play well with other children?" say, "Tell me about how he interacts with other children."

3. **Asking redundant questions.** Do not ask questions the family has adequately answered on the case history form. For example, "You noted on the case history that Josh was sick for several weeks as an infant. Tell me a little bit more about that." Ask redundant questions or rephrase your questions only when what the informant says is unclear.

4. **Not paraphrasing what is said.** By paraphrasing what the clients and families say, you can be certain of what they said or what they meant by certain words. You may also repeat certain words and phrases they utter to better understand what they meant.

5. **Ignoring, or bypassing, important information.** Do not overly rely on an interview "script." Instead, listen to what the informant says and ask follow-up questions. Pay attention to anecdotes the client or family members report. Such reports may be more revealing of the client and the family. It is important to direct the interview in a subtle manner, but it is equally important to listen and respond to all that is said in the interview.

6. **Entertaining preconceived ideas about clients and their families.** Avoid stereotypic notions about people, their presumed levels of cooperation, openness, and what they will or will not say. Approach the interview with an open disposition to interact naturally and professionally to get the information you need.

Hearing Screening

Speech-language pathologists (SLPs) assessing children for speech and language problems should screen hearing at 20dB HL for the frequencies of 1000; 2000; and 4000 Hz. If tested for 500 Hz, it should be at 25 dB HL. In some practicum settings, SLPs may not have access to an audiometer. In such cases, the clients are referred to an audiologist for screening. In the public school setting, the school nurse, licensed as an audiometrist, often screens children's hearing. Before evaluating children and adults wearing hearing aids, perform a hearing aid check to determine if it is functioning.

Play audiometry may be appropriate for the very young or those with intellectual disabilities. Children who fail the hearing screening should be referred to an audiologist for a hearing evaluation.

Orofacial Examination

An orofacial examination is essential to rule-out oral structural problems (such as clefts of the palates and the lips) and weakness of speech muscles as suggested by reduced range, force, and consistency of movements. The student clinician might use the standard procedure followed in the clinic in the academic department and other practicum sites.

A significant part of the orofacial examination is the administration of diadochokinetic tasks that help assess the rate, accuracy, and consistency with which a client produces rapidly alternating speech sounds. Ask the client to produce /pʌ/, /tʌ/, /kʌ/, /pʌtə/, and /pʌtəkə/ as rapidly as possible.

Integrate the Following Procedures into Your Orofacial Examination:

- *Systematically evaluate* the orofacial structures during each examination to avoid overlooking any areas. Evaluate structures in a certain sequence. For example, you may begin with general facial features, then progress to examination of lips, tongue, teeth, hard palate, and so on or you may begin with the oral cavity first and then the peripheral structures.

- *Verbally* describe your observations while audio-recording. It is helpful to orally record the evaluation. This step will allow you to continue the examination without having to stop and write notes.

(continues)

- *Observe* the speech mechanism during activities such as laughing, speaking, and eating, if the client refuses to allow invasive procedures during the orofacial examination. Tasks can be modeled and modified as necessary. Perform the examination later in the evaluation session or in a treatment session if the client is enrolled for speech services.

Speech and Language Sampling

Speech and language samples are essential to assess a client's naturalistic communication skills. Older students and adults may be engaged in a conversation for 20 min or more. The clinician may set up an interactive play situation to record a younger child's speech and language production. Parent participation in the session may be considered in sampling speech from young children.

The language samples are audio- or video-recorded and later transcribed for analysis. Accuracy of speech sound productions, speech intelligibility, and production of language features, including grammatical morphemes, and sentence structures may be assessed. Speech-language samples are crucial for an analysis of such conversational (pragmatic) skills as topic initiation and maintenance, turn taking, conversational repair, narration, discourse, and prosodic features. Disfluency frequency and voice characteristics also may be assessed through the same sample. The following guidelines help you secure an adequate and reliable language sample from your clients:

- Obtain more than one sample to ensure reliability.

- Use effective and appropriate stimuli to evoke conversational speech. With children, use pictures, toys, and books. Do not let the child get lost in play. Use storybooks with sequenced pictures to evoke narrative speech. Prompt the child to tell the story that unfolds in sequenced pictures.

- Engage children in conversation. If a child is school age, ask about most and least favorite school activities, favorite teachers, daily routines, what happens to students who get in trouble in the cafeteria, best friends, recent vacations, cartoon shows, other favorite TV shows, birthday parties, and so on. Tell the child something about yourself first to stimulate speech. For example, "I have a puppy that is so silly. Yesterday he ran through the sprinklers and then came and jumped all over me! Do you have a silly puppy or a cat?"

- Have the parent engage the child in conversation and take notes on the child's skills and the parental communication strategies.

- Direct conversation to provide clients with opportunities to produce a variety of language structures (e.g., declaratives, interrogatives, different verb tenses).

- Sample conversation in a variety of environments. With adults, use the interview to obtain at least a portion of the conversational sample. Sample conversations while the clients interact with their family members, friends, teachers in school settings, and caregivers in hospital settings. If feasible, observe conversations on the telephone, with the clinic receptionist, or with strangers.

- Avoid asking questions that are answered with "yes," "no," or one word. Ask open-ended questions (e.g., "Tell me what is happening in this picture").

- If it is difficult to obtaining a valid sample or if you need a second sample, ask parents to record a conversational speech sample at home and maintain a daily log of their children's speech for 1 week. Although the information may not be fully accurate, it will give you a better idea of the child's language performance as well as the parent's reaction to the child's communication skills.

Manually transcribing the sample and analyzing skills of interest is time-consuming. However, clinicians may save time and effort by using such computerized software programs as Sampling Utterances and Grammatic Analysis Revised (SUGAR: Pavelko & Owens, 2017), Systemic Analysis of Language Transcripts (SALT: Miller & Iglesias, 2015), and Computerized Language Analysis (CLAN: Ratner & MacWhinney, 2016). These programs are limited to language skills.

Standardized Test Administration

Standardized tests are norm-referenced. The test results are compared to the norms established during standardization. Norm-referenced standardized tests are most applicable in assessing children whose speech and language change based on age. Norms are less critical in assessing adults with neurologically based communication disorders (e.g., aphasia, dysarthria, apraxia of speech, TBI, and dementia).

Select reliable and valid tests. **Reliability** is consistency of scores upon repeated administration of the same test to the same individuals. **Validity** is the degree to which a test measures what it is designed to measure. A test of grammatical morphemes should sample grammatical morpheme productions, not some other aspect of speech or language. Unreliable tests that yield different scores upon repeated testing and tests that purport to measure one thing but measure something else cannot support meaningful assessment.

When not trained in administering and scoring a test, the student clinician should let the supervisor know and request training and guidance. Tests should be administered according to the manual. Even trained student clinicians should consult the manual before administering a test. This is part of getting prepared for an assessment session.

Standardized tests pose special challenges when the clients are ethnoculturally diverse and are bilingual or bidialectal. Read a later section for appropriate use of standardized tests with diverse individuals and alternative assessment procedures that may be more valid for them.

Analysis of Assessment Results

Pool all assessment data obtained from different sources and make an analysis that highlights the strengths and weakness of your client. Analysis may suggest a diagnosis, prognosis, and some tentative treatment targets. Consider making the following kinds of analyses:

- Analyze the client's semantic, morphologic, syntactic, and pragmatic communication skills in addition to receptive language skills.

- Analyze the production of phonemes and compute overall speech intelligibility for words, utterances, or both. Note specific speech sound errors and their types (e.g., substitutions, omissions, distortions, additions). Calculate the frequency and percentage of errors. Describe specific phonologic error patterns (e.g., syllable reduction, cluster reduction, fronting).

- Observe the quality, pitch, intensity of voice, and resonance characteristics. Note such behaviors as the number of pitch breaks in a 5-min speech sample, or the absence of adequate breath support.

- Measure the types and frequency of dysfluencies in the sample and calculate the dysfluency rate. Please visit the companion website for Dysfluency Types and Calculation of Dysfluency Rates.

- Integrate information from different sources and your assessment data.

Multidisciplinary, Interdisciplinary, and Transdisciplinary Assessment

In many settings you will be a member of a team of specialists that evaluates clients. Generally, team assessments fall within the categories of multidisciplinary, transdisciplinary, and interdisciplinary assessments.

As a member of a *multidisciplinary assessment team*, you will assess the communication skills of your client and report your findings. Other team members will perform their assessments relative to their specialty and report their findings. Typically, each member evaluates the client individually. The reports are gathered together, information is reviewed, and recommendations are made.

An *interdisciplinary team* is similar to a multidisciplinary team, with the exception of the report. Assessment is completed independently by the service providers, but the report is compiled and presented cohesively. Families are also valued as a team member in this model. Treatment may be supplied independently, coupled with consultation among the team members.

The *transdisciplinary team* may obtain similar information as the other teams but does so in a different fashion. Members of the transdisciplinary team often have prescribed roles in the assessment process but observe and assess the client together. This may be accomplished via arena assessment, when parents or other family members and professionals together assess the child (Owens, 2014).

Reassessment of Clients

Clients returning to the university clinic after a break in services should be reassessed before resuming treatment. In most cases, a brief conversational speech and language sample may be adequate. In other cases, specific tests may be administered (e.g., a phonological process test). Repeated baserates of previously taught and still missing behaviors are needed in all cases. See Chapter 8 for procedures for establishing baserates.

Reassessment is essential when interventions are prolonged and the clinician needs to find out if previously established skills have been maintained or have deteriorated. Reassessment is also an ongoing activity. In certain cases, your clients' skills will change rapidly, and, to effectively provide treatment, you should measure the client's current levels of performance.

Additional procedures and timelines for assessment and reassessment of clients are mandated by insurance companies and the public schools (i.e., a 45-day or 60-day assessment timeline in the public school setting, depending on the state). Find out about these procedures and timelines from your supervisor.

Postassessment Counseling

When you have completed the assessment and have made some preliminary analysis of results, you counsel the client, the family members, or both. This postassessment counseling requires professional skills that you will acquire and refine throughout your clinical practicum experience (Hegde & Pomaville, 2022). Your clinical supervisors in all settings will have modeled the professional manner in which the results of assessment are conveyed to and discussed with the client and the family members. Learn to conduct the postassessment counseling with the following guidelines:

1. **As a general rule, obtain your supervisor's approval before you discuss important clinical service matters with your clients or their families.** When you do not know the answer to questions they ask, tell them that you will find out from your supervisor. Then discuss the questions with your supervisor to understand how to answer them. On occasion, because of the complexity of the information to be presented, your supervisor may decide to talk with the family. In such cases, the supervisor will include you in the discussion so you will learn how to handle complex matters.

2. **Always give accurate information.** Postassessment, you may face the following kinds of questions: What caused the speech or language problem? Why does my son stutter? Why can't my youngest child talk, while two older children are doing fine? The research information may not provide a clear-cut answer that satisfies clients or their families. If there is a well-researched answer to your clients' questions, then provide that information in terms they can understand. If there is not an evidence-based answer to your clients' questions, then let them know that.

3. **Inform that the cause of a disorder may be elusive.** Our knowledge of disorders and their potential causes are applied to groups of persons, not to specific individuals. For example, you can say that we know many potential factors associated with stuttering, including hereditary predisposition, faulty learning, environmental stress, instability in the nervous system, and many others. But clinicians cannot say why a given child or adult stutters, because several factors may come together to produce a problem and most of the factors may be obscure. The etiology of a specific disorder may be apparent for such clients that have experienced a cerebrovascular accident (CVA) or TBI that has resulted in an array of problems. In these cases, with medical test results and a well-documented premorbid history of your clients' communication skills, you will be able to relate the disorders to certain specific factors. Even then, almost all potential causes are correlated events.

4. **Convey the diagnosis in terms your listeners can understand.** While "language disorders," and "speech sound disorders," are fairly

self-explanatory, "dysarthria," or "apraxia of speech" may not be. Describes the symptoms (e.g., difficulty controlling the flow of air to produce speech, problem positioning the tongue to produce sounds) but not theories behind them (e.g., *impaired neural articulatory gestures* or *difficulty realizing speech sound schema*). Although simple and direct language devoid of incomprehensible jargon is essential, do not talk down to people. For example, when the father of a child diagnosed with a language disorder is a professor of English, do not try to explain *prepositions* as target behaviors for the child. Similarly, if the mother of a child is a physician, it is unnecessary to describe the *velopharyngeal mechanism* in everyday language.

5. **Explain why a diagnosis cannot be reliably established.** Often you need more in-depth observation and data. If so, schedule a reassessment at a later time.

6. **Speak in probabilistic terms.** Neither the prognosis nor potential treatment outcomes may be guaranteed. You may tell parents that some improvements in their child's fluency may be expected after 3 months of intervention, but you may not say that "Placido will be speaking fluently in 6 months." Tell them that the effect of treatment will depend on many factors, including the motivation of the client, the amount of family support, the duration of treatment, and so forth. Recall that the ASHA Code of Ethics prohibits you from guaranteeing certain treatment outcomes.

7. **If you recommend treatment, give an overview of it.** Explain that treatment may begin at a simple level and progress gradually to more complex levels. For example, "I will begin teaching the *s* sound in single words. First, I will teach the sound at the beginning of words. After Jason masters the sound in words, we will work on using the *s* sound in phrases and sentences. Finally, we will target the sound production in conversation—here at the clinic and at home and school." Let the client and the family know that they will help select the target skills for teaching. Explain too that, although a skill may be taught relatively quickly in the clinical setting, it may take much more time to get that skill produced at home and other everyday situations. Also, let them know in advance that they may be requested to observe and take part in treatment sessions and conduct informal treatment at home after they have done sufficient observation in the clinic.

8. **Repeat important information.** Your listeners may be hearing a lot of new information at one time; therefore, repeat important

information. For example, you may describe something at the beginning of a discussion and ask if they understand your description. Later, using different words or in a different context, you may give the same information. Summarize the discussion at the end.

9. **Allow sufficient time for clients and their families to ask questions.** Any time you give technical or new information, make sure that clients and their families understand by inviting questions and comments. Answer all questions directly, accurately, fully, and objectively.

Assessment Report Writing

Write your assessment report as soon as possible. You will have written assessment (diagnostic) reports when you completed a course on assessment and diagnosis. In your clinical practicum and internship sites, you will learn to write assessment reports with varied formats, styles, lengths, and content.

A diagnostic (assessment) report is a summary of case history, assessment data, clinical impressions, conclusions, and recommendations. It provides a clear, written statement of the client's communication skills and limitations at the time of the evaluation. It also provides a forum for communicating with other professionals. Diagnostic reports may be used to help obtain payment from an insurance company for the services provided. They may also be used for research; therefore, it is important to differentiate subjective statements from objective data in an assessment report.

Each client's file must contain an assessment report. A copy of an evaluation performed at another facility may be included in a case file. When you are assigned a client who has been evaluated by another clinician, obtain a copy of the diagnostic report for the client's file.

There are several formats for writing diagnostic reports. In addition, reporting requirements vary at each practicum site. See Hegde (2024) for multiple exemplars of reports and good writing principles. To write a diagnostic report, use the following outline, or modify it to suit practicum settings. See the Appendix attached to this chapter for a sample assessment report. Also, visit the companion website for another sample of a Diagnostic Report. Generally, include the following in your assessment report:

- **Provide identifying information.** At the top of the report, specify the client's name, file number, address, phone number, date of birth, age, diagnosis, date of evaluation, name of the evaluator, and the name of the individual who referred the client. If applicable, note the client's occupation or school level and parents' names. In the school setting, include the child's grade and the teacher's name.

- **State the problem.** Briefly describe the client's presenting complaint or the reason for referral. To be explicit, write the client's comments verbatim and identify them as such in the text. For example: (1) *Mrs. Applegate stated her voice was "scratchy and old sounding."* (2) *Mr. Jarvitz reported that he stuttered. He said that his "blocked speech" occurred most frequently when he spoke on the telephone.* Use the quotation marks around the words and phrases you report verbatim. If someone other than the client was the informant, indicate it: *Mr. John Jones, an uncle of Benny accompanied him to the clinic and served as the informant during the interview.*

- **Write the report in the past tense.** You are writing about performance that you observed during the assessment. For example, write: *Final consonants were omitted in Kaylee's spontaneous speech, recorded during the assessment session.* Your observation of the client is limited to a specific time and your statements must be limited to those observations.

- **Give background information.** Obtain the client's background information from the client's case history, client or family member interview, and reports by other professionals. In the school setting, teacher report is essential. Detail only the relevant information. Include the client's developmental history, medical history, social and family history, and educational history in this section. For some clients, it will be necessary to describe in detail only certain skills; for other clients, all communication skills may need to be described. For a child with language problems, educational background must be described in detail; but for an adult with a hoarse voice, detailed educational history may be unnecessary. If the reported medical history was unremarkable for speech and language development, just say that: *The reported medical history was unremarkable.* However, document the illnesses and medications in your report.

- **Summarize prior services.** Note any previous speech-language pathology diagnoses and services the client has received. Include test scores and other kinds of results from prior reports. After summarizing information from another professional's report (another SLP, a physician, a teacher), give the professional's name, credentials, and date of report.

- **Summarize assessment information.** Describe results of the pure-tone audiometric screening (except in public school settings), orofacial examination, and speech and language assessments and observations.

- **Describe the general behavior.** Summarize your observations on the client's attending behavior and cooperativeness. For example: "*Sadie was cooperative and attended to all tasks with minimal verbal prompting throughout the 1-hour evaluation session. Results were considered representative of the client's behaviors.*" If behaviors were exhibited that may have affected the results, state those as well: "*Austin was highly distracted throughout all assessment activities. He required frequent redirection to task as well as questions posed repeatedly. He was often observed to be staring out the window and ignoring questions.*"

- **Summarize the hearing screening results.** If it was impossible to perform the screening, note this in the diagnostic report and refer the client for an audiological examination.

- **Summarize results of the orofacial examination.** If the examination was negative, just say that. Write in detail any structural or motoric deviations viewed. Please also visit the companion website for a sample of an Orofacial Examination Report.

- **Describe the speech and language assessment.** Include information about the client's articulation, voice, fluency, receptive and expressive language, and any bilingual status. Report results of standardized testing, speech and language sampling, and informal clinical observations of communication skills. Do not just list test scores, instead say what they mean. For example, the statement "*Oliver obtained a raw score of 9 on the auditory comprehension subtest of the Preschool Language Scales*" means little to your readers, unless they have memorized the meaning of test score or have the test administration booklet in front of them. Therefore, write what the test is, what it measures, what the scores are, and an analysis of the results.

- **Quantify the results of speech and language sample.** Report the total number of words or utterances in the sample. When reporting certain behaviors (e.g., correct production of plural /s/), list examples of its correct and incorrect productions as well as its absence; specify the number of times its production was evoked and give the percentages of occurrence. For example: "*Luca produced the plural /s/ correctly 75% of the 27 obligatory contexts in which it was evoked.*" This statement is more meaningful than: "*Luca produced the plural /s/ correctly in three instances.*" If the client omitted specific speech or language structures, give the total number of opportunities (or obligatory contexts) he or she had to produce them. For example: "*Luca did not produce the plural /s/ in 10 out of 12 phrases that should have contained the plural /s/.*" Please visit the companion website for a Language Sample Checklist to make sure you address all relevant language variables.

- **Present the information in a logical sequence.** Describe observations relevant to speech, language, voice, fluency, and other aspects of communication in separate paragraphs with headings (e.g., Speech Production, Fluency). Do not confuse the reader by writing about articulation performance in sections describing fluency or voice.

- **Describe each parameter of speech.** This will document that all aspects of the client's communication were evaluated, even if no disorder or deviation was noted in some areas. For example, if you made no mention of fluency in your report on a child with a speech sound disorder because you found no problem with it, the reader cannot be sure of this. Therefore, it is necessary to write such a statement as: *"Analysis of a 200-utterance speech sample revealed 97% fluent speech."*

- **Do not cross professional boundaries.** Limit yourself to speech-language skills. A common problem occurs when guessing at cognitive levels. The SLPs cannot report IQ scores. Neither can they diagnose psychological disorders (depression, cognitive impairment, etc.). However, you can report behavior that you have observed. For example, you might write: *Blake appeared withdrawn throughout the evaluation. He sat with his arms crossed through most of the evaluation and never made eye contact with the examiner.*

- **Summarize your impressions, observations, and interpretations.** Include the scores and informal measures to support your results. Report the type and severity of any communication disorder in this section. Also report if no communication disorder was exhibited. If a cause for a found disorder is known, report it in this section. You may make a statement about the prognosis here or report it in the recommendations section.

- **Write recommendations.** The work setting will influence how you state your recommendations in the assessment report. In most clinics, if a disorder is diagnosed, treatment is recommended. In the school setting, an assessment report's purpose is to document present skill levels and determine eligibility for speech-language services. Recommendations are often shared in the context of the IEP meeting to include all members in decision making. If SLP services are deemed appropriate, recommend them in this section, describe the type and amount of service needed, further assessment required, and referral to other professionals (if necessary). Although specific needs should be identified, do not report exact objectives because additional evaluation, including base-lines, may need to be performed before starting treatment. Confer with your clinical supervisor before making specific recommendations.

- **Sign the report.** Conclude the report with your name, title, and signa-ture. Your clinical supervisor also must sign the report; therefore, type his or her name and title.

See Appendix 5–A for a sample assessment report written in a university speech and hearing clinic. For a variety of sample diagnostic reports refer to Hegde (2024).

Assessment of Ethnoculturally Diverse Persons

In most practicum site, SLPs are likely to work with children and adults of ethnoculturally diverse backgrounds. Such individuals may be bidialectal or bilingual. Assessment and treatment of individuals from diverse back-grounds need some special considerations.

ASHA considers dialectal variations as social dialects, and therefore, no dialectal variation of English or any other language is a basis to diag-nose a communication disorder (American Speech-Language-Hearing Association, 1983). All languages have varied dialects. Mainstream Amer-ican English (MAE) is also a collection of different dialects, including the dialectal variations of the North, the Midland, and the South (Oetting, 2020). Each of those three geographic regions have multiple dialects. None is a standard against which the other MAE dialects are evaluated (Amer-ican Speech-Language-Hearing Association, 2003; Shriberg et al., 2019). All dialects are due to (1) regional differences in culture and language pro-duction and (2) an influence of another language and culture. Therefore, the features of a social dialect are typical and have no clinical significance.

Individuals who speak the African American English (AAE) are bidi-alectal because AAE is a variety of American English. African American Children in the elementary grades are more likely to speak AAE, especially in the Southern states where significant number of African Americans live. Older children in advanced grades may be bidialectal: they may speak AAE at home, and MAE in schools and in other broader social situations.

AAE is a language with its own cultural heritage. Its features that are different from comparable features of MAE are not a basis to diagnose speech or language disorder, just like the unique features of the Appala-chian or New England American dialect are not a basis to diagnose a disorder. Therefore, AAE's unique speech and language characteristics are not clinical targets for modification. However, parents of an African American child may request that their child be taught speech and language features of MAE because of its educational and occupational advantage. In that case, the clinician may teach the speech and language features of MAE to an African American child. Before doing this, it is an ethical necessity to emphasize to the child and the family that a different dialect (MAE) is being taught, the goal is not to eliminate the unique features of AAE, and that the child may remain bidialectal. The child may maintain both AAE and MAE and code-switch according to the communication context.

Bilingual children may come from one of several language-diverse families. The child's home language may be a variety of Spanish (e.g., Mexican, Cuban, etc.), a Native American language (Navajo, Sioux, Yupik, Hopi, etc.), an Asian language (e.g., Hindi, Thai, Chinese, Japanese, etc.), and several other non-English home languages. Children from such families may speak their home language and be in the process of acquiring English in the school and larger social contexts. In the school, the child may be an English Language Learner.

Bilingual children's English may be influenced by their home language characteristics. Therefore, bilingual children's English too is a typical dialect. As with the AAE, bilingual child's English speech and language characteristics that are a product of their first language are not a basis to diagnose a communication disorder. Those unique features are not clinical targets for modification. However, as English language learners, they may be taught MAE, but this often is the work of bilingual educators, not SLP. If there is a disorder in the child's first language, treatment may be recommended in that language. To diagnose a disorder in the child's MAE, the clinician should find evidence of deficiencies that cannot be attributed to the influence of the child's first language.

Bilingual SLPs

ASHA's Practice Portal specifies that a bilingual speech-language pathologist is one who speaks his or her own language proficiently and speaks (or signs) at least one other language with native or near-native proficiency (American Speech-Language-Hearing Association, 2017). In many geographic areas of the United States, there is an immense need for bilingual SLPs.

If you are a bilingual student, examine ASHA's definition of a bilingual SLP and your own command of language skills. People who have grown up speaking two languages may not be equally proficient in both, and hence, may not be proficient enough to provide clinical service in one of the two

ASHA-Suggested Competencies Required of Bilingual Clinicians

1. The ability to describe the development of speech and oral (or manual) and written language for both bilingual and monolingual individuals.

2. The ability to differentiate communication differences from communication disorders in oral (or manual) and written language through the use of both formal and informal evaluation.

3. The ability to provide treatment in the language most appropriate to meet the client's needs.

4. Knowledge of various cultural factors related to service delivery (American Speech-Language-Hearing Association, n.d.a).

languages. Obviously, you should know the speech and language features of both languages well enough to assess, diagnose, and treat disorders.

Student Clinicians With Diverse Backgrounds

Students from diverse cultural and linguistic backgrounds have much to offer the profession of speech-language pathology, but they may face several challenges, including subtle forms of discrimination and microaggression from faculty, practicum supervisors, and fellow students during their academic and clinical training (Abdelaziz et al., 2021; Easton & Verdon, 2021; Ellis & Kendall, 2021). If you have faced discrimination in your academic or clinical training program, talk to your advisor, the program director, or the department chair.

ASHA's Code of Ethics prohibits discrimination based on race, ethnicity, national origin, language, dialects, accents, religion, or cultural differences. In addition, ASHA's position statement on accents and nonstandard dialects states that applicants to academic programs in communication disorders cannot be rejected solely on the basis of dialectal variations or accents (American Speech-Language-Hearing Association, 1998). Student clinicians need not necessarily speak MAE. However, to succeed in clinical practicum and later in professional practice, all student clinicians should possess a certain level of knowledge and skills as described in the following box.

In general, all student clinicians should:

1. Develop a thorough knowledge of normal and disordered communication and communication development

2. Acquire effective diagnostic and intervention skills

3. Learn to effectively communicate with clients from a variety of cultural, ethnic, racial, and linguistic backgrounds

4. Develop the skill to model all target behaviors required of your clients. For example, in order to train speech sounds, you will need to be able to model each of the English phonemes or allophones.

5. Learn to write clearly and concisely, using correct grammar

Alternative and Integrated Assessment

Most of the traditional assessment procedures, including case history, hearing screening, orofacial examination, and language sampling with due consideration for cultural and language variations apply to ethnoculturally diverse individuals. However, the typical standardized test, a major assessment tool the SLPs use, may not be appropriate for diverse individuals who speak non-MAE dialects.

Two major reasons limit the usefulness of many standardized tests in assessing individuals who speak non-MAE dialects. First, the test developer may not have sampled a diverse population during standardization; a diverse individual may not have been represented in the sample. Second, the test items may sample only the MAE speech-language features. Consequently, the test cannot assess dialectal variations (e.g., AAE and first-language influenced English). Therefore, the test results cannot be used to make a valid diagnosis of a speech or language disorder.

Alternatives to the standardized test-based traditional assessment are available (Hegde & Pomaville, 2022). Consider the following alternative assessments when evaluating a diverse client who does not speak a variety of MAE.

Criterion-Referenced and Client-Specific Assessments

Criterion-referenced or *client-specific* assessment procedures do not make clinical judgments based entirely on standardized tests. A *criterion* is a performance standard. Instead of referencing a child's score on an articulation test to established norms, the clinician might adopt a criterion such as 80% accuracy to judge acceptable speech sound production. If standardized, norm-referenced tests are used, the results are not converted to standard scores, percentile ranks, and similar measures; rather, the information is used to highlight what an individual can or cannot do.

Client-specific measures also are criterion of performance; however, standardized tests are avoided altogether. Assessment materials are developed specifically for the client. Stimulus items may include toys, books, and pictures from the individual's home environment. Furthermore, client-specific procedures allow for adequate sampling of each skill being assessed. For example, the regular plural morpheme may be assessed with 20 exemplars, written specifically for the client. (A standardized morphological test may have just 1 or 2 items). Following the collection of assessment data, the clinician judges whether a client's communication levels are adequate to meet their social, academic, occupational, and personal demands. This kind of assessment data allow for effective treatment target selection (Hegde & Pomaville, 2022).

Authentic Assessment

Authentic assessment seeks to measure naturalistic and meaningful communication in real-life settings (Udvari & Thousand, 1995). Standardized tests and comparison with norms are avoided. Speech and language samples are gathered in the client's functional environments (school, home, work) during daily routines and activities. The skills assessed may be selected from the child's academic curricula (e.g., language structures, reading and writing skills required in the child's grade) as well as the home environment (words frequently used at home, language structures selected from the child's storybooks).

Skills that are useful and functional (e.g., conversational skills) are the targets of authentic assessment. Observations of a child's conversation with the teacher, a peer, or a family member may provide useful data. Interviewing the individuals who interact with the child (e.g., parents, teachers, peers) may supply additional information.

The minimal competency core (Stockman, 2008; Stockman et al., 2016) will be helpful in diagnosing a speech and language disorder in African

American children and selecting target behaviors for treatment. Stockman (2008) has reported that typical 33- to 36-month-old African American children produce the following phonemes: /m/, /n/, /p/, /b/, /t/, /d/, /k/, /g/, /f/, /s/, /h/, /w/, /y/, /l/, and /r/. In a subsequent study, Stockman et al. (2016) described core morphosyntactic skills of African American children. If the core speech and language skills are deficient, then the child has a speech and language disorder. The core skills are then selected as treatment targets.

Examples of minimal competence core for a 3-year old African American child may be found on the companion website.

Dynamic Assessment

Dynamic assessment includes brief interventions to see whether the child can learn the missing speech-language skills (Gutierrez-Clellen & Peña, 2001). The clients whose skills do not improve require treatment, whereas those who improve may not require intervention. In this method, the clinician (1) may modify the test administration (e.g., rephrase the questions and give feedback) to see if the child gives correct responses; (2) prompt correct responses, and (3) teach the skill and retest.

A problem with dynamic assessment is that modifying test procedures may invalidate the results and teaching a skill before diagnosis significantly increases the assessment time. Also, the assumption that children who improve in a brief treatment session do not need treatment may be questionable (Hegde & Pomaville, 2022). If this is the case, regular treatment also should be discontinued as soon as some improvement is evident—an unacceptable implication.

Integrated Assessment

No single alternative assessment has become a common practice because each one is incomplete. Case history, speech and language samples, orofacial examinations, hearing screening, and clinical interview cannot be dispensed with. In an *integrated assessment*, the essential elements of the traditional and the advantageous alternative methods are combined (Hegde & Pomaville, 2022). In using the integrated method, the clinician (1) interprets the results of standardized tests cautiously or avoids them altogether; (2) modifies the interview to suit the ethnocultural background of the client and family members; (3) gathers language samples in multiple environments and contexts while providing client-specific stimulus materials; (4) interprets the results of assessment in light of the client's bidialectal or bilingual status; and (5) offers postassessment counseling.

General Guidelines on Working With Diverse Individuals

Selecting appropriate assessment procedures and making diagnostic decisions in the context of the speaker's dialect and culture are the cornerstones of providing services to ethnoculturally diverse individuals. There are, however, other guidelines that the student clinician should follow. These are briefly summarized as general guidelines on working with diverse individuals.

1. Understand the client's and the family members disposition toward communication and its disorders. During the interview, explore the dispositions and practices regarding such nonverbal communication modes as making eye contact, smiling, shaking hands, and touching. Many miscommunications and misinterpretations can be avoided if you are aware of communication patterns of specific cultural groups. What is desirable or acceptable in one culture may not be in another. Understand your individual client, but do not stereotype them based on group generalizations. Also explore the beliefs and dispositions toward communication disorders, disabilities in general, presumed causes of disorders, and what the family expects from intervention.

2. Understand the first language of a bilingual client. Read about the phonological and grammatical aspects of the first (non-English) language the client speaks. Take note of the English phonemes and grammatical features that are not a part of the client's first language. Determine the dominant language for assessment.

3. Use the names and pronouns the individuals prefer. It may be Hispanic, Latinx, Latina (more specifically, Cuban American or Mexican American), Asian American (more specifically Indian or Vietnamese American), and so forth. Some Asian Americans may prefer to be addressed by kinship names (e.g., "your uncle," not "Mr. Kapoor"). Ascertain the individual's sexual identity and use only the preferred pronouns and forms of address. For guidelines on speaking and writing without bias, see Hegde (2024).

4. Understand the health statistics. It is critical to appreciate the limited access to health care and community resources, and the consequences of inequality the diverse families face. Incidence of certain diseases that affect communication (e.g., otitis media or stroke) may be higher in the client's ethnocultural background. The family

may not have health insurance or a primary care physician. They may experience many barriers to obtaining quality health care. If so, they may find it difficult to continue with speech-language services. Report these problems to your supervisor, who may help the family access resources they may not be familiar with.

5. Do not use inappropriate standardized tests. Tests that are not standardized on individuals of the same cultural and dialectal background as the client are inappropriate. Use alternative assessment methods with an emphasis on speech-language samples involving family members. Use multiple assessment tasks (e.g., conversation, narratives, discourse, criterion-referenced measures). Ask the family to suggest or supply assessment stimuli the child is familiar with. A migrant farm worker's child may not be familiar with many of the routinely used stimulus materials and toys.

6. Use an interpreter, a translator, or a transliterator. See a later section for details.

7. Explain why you will be asking questions. At the beginning of the evaluation, explain that you will be asking some questions and why. When you ask specific questions, explain why they are necessary.

8. Ask parents to compare their child's language skills to those of siblings. Instead of comparing a child's speech-language skills with questionable norms, the parents may offer information about relative skills of their children, including the one they are concerned with.

9. Study the child's academic reports. Ask the child's teacher to compare the child's performance with that of peers.

10. Take extra time. You may need to take extra time to assess some diverse clients, especially children, who may be reluctant to talk or who talk in short phases. But the child's typical language skills may be better than that. If so, do not rush to complete the assessment in the first session.

11. Diagnose a disorder only if the deficits exist within the child's dialect. In discussing the results of your evaluation and making recommendations to the client and family members, use the terms they understand; explain all technical terms in simple language. Ascertain whether they accept treatment and if so, find out if the family has sufficient resources to continue the services. If not, talk to your supervisor about getting additional help for the family.

Working With Interpreters, Translators, and Transliterators

Laws and ethics require assessment and service delivery to be provided in the language appropriate to an individual student's needs. Due to the vast number of languages spoken in the United States, SLPs and practicum students will need the services of bilingual support personnel, including interpreters, translators, and transliterators.

Roles of Bilingual Support Personnel

- *Interpreters* transform spoken or signed expressions in one language into another. The most common interpreter the SLPs know is the sing language interpreter who transforms manual signs to spoken English and spoken English to manual signs.

- *Translators* transform writing in one language to comparable writing in another language, preserving the meaning.

- *Transliterators* change the printed alphabet of one language into the alphabet of another language without giving the meaning of words; transliteration only helps pronounce the word, not understand its meaning.

There are two basic types of interpreting: *consecutive interpreting* and *simultaneous interpreting*. In consecutive interpreting, an individual talks and pauses, and then the interpreter translates. In simultaneous interpreting, the interpreter (a transliterator) "translates" as the individual talks or signs. It is more commonly used for manually coded language.

It is the licensed and credentialed SLP, not the bilingual support personnel, that is ethically and legally responsible for providing services. Trained bilingual support personnel may be an employee or a contracted person at the facility. The interpreter/translator may be a member of the client's family or a friend. Consult ASHA's Practice Portal for additional information on the use of bilingual support personnel (American Speech-Language-Hearing Association, n.d.b).

As a practicum student, you are not expected to train the support personnel. Therefore, follow the practicum site's guidelines and your clinical supervisors' suggestions on using bilingual support personnel.

1. Meet the interpreter in advance. Discuss your needs and the services the person can offer you.

2. Describe your assessment plan. Identify the areas the professional can help you with.

3. Use the same interpreter if possible. This will help develop a good working relationship.

4. Recruit an interpreter who matches the ethnocultural background of your client. The client may feel more at ease if you do that.

5. Introduce your interpreter to the client and the family. Describe what each of you will be doing and find out how each should be addressed.

6. Talk to, and look at the client, not the interpreter. You are communicating with the client, not the interpreter.

7. Speak in simpler language and at a normal rate. Give sufficient pauses between phrases and sentences to facilitate interpretation or translation.

8. Discuss first the assessment results with the interpreter. Ascertain that the assessment results and observations are accurate. You may then conduct the postassessment counseling target behaviors.

Working with interpreters, translators, and other support personnel requires some special skills. You may not get training in all practicum sites to learn those skills. If you get a chance, make good use of that.

⑦ Questions for Self-Assessment

1. What are the dos and don'ts of clinical interview? What are the effective strategies of getting detailed and valid information from the informants?

2. Distinguish between *reliability* and *validity* of standardized tests. What are the major limitations of standardized tests in assessing ethnoculturally diverse individuals?

3. Give an overview of alternative and integrated assessment approaches. Point out the advantages and disadvantages of the procedures you describe.

4. Summarize the steps you would take to obtain a reliable and valid speech and language sample from an 8-year-old boy.

5. Should an SLP academic department reject a student applicant who speaks an English dialect that is not consistent with the MAE? What are the basic expectations of students admitted to an SLP clinical program?

References

Abdelaziz, M. M., Mathews, J.-J., Compos, I., Fannin, D., Riviera Perez, J. F., Wilhite, M., & Williams, R. M. (2021). Student stories: Microaggression in communication sciences and disorders. *American Journal of Speech-Language Pathology, 30*(5), 1990–2002.

American Speech-Language-Hearing Association. (n.d.a). *Bilingual service delivery: Practice portal.* http://www.asha.org/Practice-Portal/Professional-Issues/Bilingual-Service-Delivery

American Speech-Language-Hearing Association. (n.d.b). *Collaborating with interpreters, transliterators, and translators: Practice portal.* http://www.asha.org/Practice-Portal/Professional-Issues/Collaborating-With-Interpreters/

American Speech-Language-Hearing Association. (1983). *Social dialects: Position statement.* https://www.asha.org/policy/ps1983-00115/

American Speech-Language-Hearing Association. (1998). *Students and professionals who speak English with accents and nonstandard dialects: Issues and recommendations: Position statement.* https://www.asha.org/policy/ps1998-00117/

American Speech-Language-Hearing Association. (2003). *American English dialects: Technical report.* https://www.asha.org/policy/tr2003-00044/

American Speech-Language-Hearing Association. (2017). *Issues in ethics: Cultural and linguistic competence.* https://www.asha.org/practice/ethics/cultural-and-linguistic-competence/

Easton, C., & Verdon, S. (2021). The influence of linguistic bias upon speech-language pathologists' attitudes toward clinical scenarios involving nonstandard dialects of English. *American Journal of Speech-Language Pathology, 30*(5), 1973–1989.

Ellis, C., & Kendall, D. (2021). Time to act: Confronting systemic racism in communication sciences and disorders academic programs. *American Journal of Speech-Language Pathology, 30*(5), 1916–1924.

Gutierrez-Clellen, V., & Peña, E. (2001). Dynamic assessment of diverse children: A tutorial. *Language, Speech, and Hearing Services in Schools, 32*(4), 212–224.

Hegde, M. N. (2018). *Hegde's pocketguide to assessment in speech-language pathology* (4th ed.). Plural Publishing.

Hegde, M. N. (2024). *A coursebook on scientific and professional writing for speech-language pathology* (6th ed.). Plural Publishing.

Hegde, M. N., & Freed, D. (2022). *Assessment of communication disorders in adults: Resources and protocols* (3rd ed.). Plural Publishing.

Hegde, M. N., & Pomaville, F. (2022). *Assessment of communication disorders in children: Resources and protocols* (4th ed.). Plural Publishing.

Miller, J. F., & Iglesias, A. (2015). Systematic analysis of language transcripts [Computer software]. SALT Software, LLC.

Oetting, J. B. (2020). General American English as a dialect: A call for change. *ASHA Leader Live,* November-December. https://doi.org/10.1044/leader.FMP.25112020.12

Pavelko, S. & Owens, R. (2017). Sampling utterances and grammatical analysis revised (SUGAR): New normative values for language sample analysis measures. *Language, Speech, and Hearing Services in the Schools, 48*(3), 197–215.

Ratner, N., & MacWhinney, B. (2016). Your laptop to the rescue: Using the child language data exchange system archive and CLAN utilities to improve child language sample analysis. *Seminars in Speech and Language, 37*(2), 74–84.

Schraeder, T., Quinn, M., Stockman, I., & Miller, J. (1999). Authentic assessment as an approach to preschool speech-language screening. *American Journal of Speech-Language Pathology, 8*(3), 195–200.

Shriberg, L. D., Kent, R. D., McAllister, T., & Preston, J. (2019). *Clinical phonetics* (5th ed.). Pearson.

Stockman, I. (2008). Toward validation of a minimal competence phonetic core for African American children. *Journal of Speech, Language, and Hearing Research, 51*(5), 1244–1262.

Stockman, I. J., Newkirk-Turner, B. L., Swartzlander, E., & Morris, L. R. (2016). Comparison of African American children's performances on a minimal competence core for morphosyntax and the index of productive syntax. *American Journal of Speech-Language Pathology, 25*(1), 80–95.

Udvari, A., & Thousand, J. (1995). Promising practices that foster inclusive education. In R. Villa & J. Thousand (Eds.), *Creating an inclusive school*. Association for Supervision and Curriculum Development.

U. S. Department of Education. (2011). Individuals with disabilities education act. https://sites.ed.gov/idea/IDEA-History#2000s-10s

Sample Assessment Report: Speech Sound Disorders

[Write the identifying information at the top. Include the clinic's name and address, the client's name, address, and other details according to your clinic's format.]

Diagnosis: Speech Sound Disorder

Background and Reasons for Referral

Kamala Konkan, a 6-year-old girl, was seen on [date] at the [clinic name and place] for a speech evaluation. Her pediatrician, Dr. Shenai, referred her to the clinic because of her speech problem. Saibini Konkan brought her daughter to the clinic and served as the informant.

Ms. Konkan is 38 years old. She has an engineering degree and works as a junior computer programmer. Kamala's father Nilesh is 37 years old, has a degree in food science, and owns a restaurant in town.

History

Ms. Konkan described her daughter's speech as "difficult to understand, especially for people not familiar with her." She said that Kamala omits sounds from her words. Kamala might say "top" for "stop" or "bu" for "book." Kamala also substitutes wrong sounds for the right ones, the mother reported. She tends to say, "do" for "go" and "wed" for "red."

Ms. Konkan had her daughter evaluated in another town where she had worked before. She could not take her daughter regularly to therapy sessions due to her rigid work schedule and her husband's early and late business hours. Consequently, Kamala made only minimal progress in therapy, leaving her with poor speech intelligibility.

Kamala was delivered full-term with no complications. Her social development was normal, although friends had difficulty understanding her speech. Ms. Konkan thought that her daughter's motor and language developments were typical. Kamala grew up healthy, with no major childhood diseases.

Family, Social, and Educational History

Kamala has an older brother, age 10, and a younger sister, age 3. Ms. Konkan reported no concerns about her other children's speech and language skills and no family history of communication problems on her side or her husband's side.

Kamala is a first grader in a public school and reportedly doing well in her classes. However, her teacher and classmates have reported difficulty understanding her. They say they have to ask Kamala to repeat herself. Kamala has complained about bullying from some of her classmates.

Assessment Information

Standardized tests as well as a conversational speech-language sample was used to evaluate Kamal's speech sound productions. The speech-language sample was analyzed for both speech sound production and language skills.

Orofacial Examination

An examination of the orofacial structures revealed no abnormalities in structures or functions. Lips and hard palate were symmetrical at rest. Kamala's performance on a variety of labial and lingual tasks were judged typical. The anterior and posterior faucial pillars appeared normal. Upon phonation of /a/, the vertical movement of the pharyngeal wall was observed to be typical.

Hearing Screening

Using a [specify the audiometer], the clinician screened Kamala's hearing at 25 dB hearing level (HL) for 500; 1000; 2000; and 4000 Hz. Kamala passed the hearing screening bilaterally at all frequencies.

Speech Sound Production and Speech Intelligibility

A conversational speech sample was recorded. The Goldman–Fristoe Test of Articulation (GFTA) and the Khan-Lewis Phonological Analysis [specify any other test administered] were also administered to Kamala. An analysis of the speech sample and the standardized tests revealed the following errors [list the observed client-specific errors and error patterns]:

Speech Sound Substitutions [List the errors; e.g., /w/ for /r/; /d/ for /g/; note the word positions in which the substitutions occur]

_____

_____

_____

Speech Sound Omissions or Deletions [List the errors; note the word positions in which the sounds are deleted]

_____

_____

_____

Cluster Reductions [List the errors; note whether the reduction is total or partial; e.g., "ed" for *bread* or "tov" for *stove*]

_____

_____

_____

Phonological Patterns [List the observed error patterns and give examples]
1.
2.
3.

Because of multiple speech sound errors, only 70% of Kamal's utterances without context were intelligible. However, most of her misarticulations were stimulable. Her diadochokinetic rates were within normal limits.

Language Production and Comprehension

An analysis of Kamala's conversational speech sample and observation during the interview suggested typical language skills for her age. Few grammatical morphemes (such as the plural *s*) were missing. Possibly, Kamala's omission of speech sounds accounts for some these morphological deficiencies. The mean length of utterance (MLU) of her speech sample was 7.4 morphemes, which is within normal limits for her age.

Voice and Fluency

The rhythm patterns of Kamala's speech were typical. No deviant voice characteristics were noted. A count of the frequency of disfluencies in a 5-min segment of her conversational speech revealed 4% of words spoken. This frequency is within the normal limits and the clinical judgment too ruled-out a fluency disorder.

Diagnostic Summary

Kamala Konkan exhibited a moderate speech sound disorder characterized mostly by omissions and substitutions. Untreated, her speech sound disorder is likely to have negative social and educational consequences. Because Kamala was stimulable for most of the consonants and her diadochokinetic rate was normal, the prognosis with treatment for improved speech intelligibility is good.

Recommendations

It is recommended that Kamala receive treatment for her speech sound disorder. When her speech sound production improves, her grammatical morphemic skills may be reassessed to judge whether language treatment is warranted.

Submitted by

[the name and the degree of the student clinician]
Student Clinician

Parent's Signature
Saibini Konkan, Mother

Approved by
[Name, degree, certification]
[Job title]
Clinical Supervisor

CHAPTER 6

Writing Treatment Plans and Progress Reports

Student Learning Outcomes

After reading this chapter, student clinicians are expected to:

- Describe the formats and essential elements of treatment plans, lesson plans, individualized education programs (IEPs), progress notes, subjective, objective, analysis, plan (SOAP) notes, and discharge reports
- Write different kinds of clinical reports that are acceptable to instructors or clinical supervisors
- Give an outline of the kinds of biases that should be avoided in writing clinical reports and any other kind of writing
- Understand, describe, and follow general recordkeeping procedures

Learning to write professional reports is an essential part of your clinical practicum. You learn to write (1) assessment reports, (2) treatment plans, and (3) progress notes or reports. These reports contain common elements but may differ in format and details across your practicum settings.

In your clinical practicum, you also learn general recordkeeping procedures that are essential to run and maintain clinical services. These are the topics of this chapter.

Varieties of Clinical Reports

Speech-language pathologists (SLPs) write different types of reports on their clients. Diagnostic reports provide comprehensive information on a client's pretreatment status and names the disorder (diagnosis). Treatment plans describe short-and long-term goals and the procedures used to achieve those goals. Lesson plans describe treatment planned for one or a few sessions. Description of the client performance under treatment may take the form of progress reports, final summaries, and discharge reports. See Hegde (2024) for a variety of clinical reports and opportunities to practice writing them.

In addition to generic assessment and progress reports, educational and clinical facilities have specific reporting requirements. IEPs are required in the public schools for children with disabilities, 3 through 21 years of age. Individualized family service plans (IFSPs) are required for children with disabilities, birth through 2 years of age, and their families.

In medical and rehabilitation settings, assessment of functional skills is often the main concern. SOAP notes or simple checklists, described in a later section, may be used in lieu of lengthy written reports, especially in hospitals, but in other settings as well. In most settings, an assessment report, a plan of treatment or rehabilitation, a progress report, and a discharge summary may be essential.

The following sections discuss the general format and content of various reports. Written report requirements will vary from one practicum site to another. When you first arrive at a practicum site, learn about the specific reporting formats and procedures used there. With your on-site supervisor's permission, read a few sample reports written in the setting.

General Guidelines on Report Writing

Clear and comprehensive reports are essential for several reasons. Written reports document the status of a client and thus provide a basis for future comparisons, with and without treatment. They are essential for effective communication with clients and other professionals. In clinical training programs, supervisors evaluate student clinicians' reports to judge their writing skills. Based on the adequacy of clinical reports, insurance companies and other third-party agencies authorize or deny reimbursement for clinical services. Others who read the reports and judge the writer's training and professional skills include allied health professionals, educators, clients, and the clients' family members. A poorly written report is a negative reflection on the student clinician's academic department. For all these reasons, it is essential to acquire good professional writing skills (Hegde, 2024). You write good reports in professional and yet direct, simple, and precise language. The organization of reports is uncluttered and easy to follow. Well-written reports are free from spelling, punctuation, and grammatical errors.

How to Write Good Reports

- Use the practicum site's format.

- Write in complete sentences.

- Spell all words correctly. Spell-check when you have completed the report.

- Use correct punctuation, capitalization, and numbers in numerals or words as appropriate.

- Present information in a logical sequence.

- Do not make nebulous or ambiguous statements.

- Provide as much detail as necessary to clearly describe the client's skills.

- Substantiate your statements with data or qualifying statements.

- Use necessary technical terms but define them in simpler words.

- Use only those abbreviations that are understood by the readers of your reports; visit the companion website for a Glossary of Educational Abbreviations and Acronyms and a Glossary of Medical Abbreviations and Symbols.

- Avoid the use of such qualifiers as "like," "very," "rather," and so on.

- Write in bias-free language; see the next section.

- Follow the format your supervisor specifies (i.e., correct margins, line spacing, headings).

- Proofread a printed copy of your report, correct errors, reprint it, and sign it before submitting it.

- Submit high-quality computer printouts on specified type of paper (e.g., nonerasable bond).

(continues)

- Number the pages.
- Keep a copy of your report.
- If electronic submission is required, scan and upload the report to the site.

Follow your university clinic's report-writing guidelines. In your academic training, you are likely to be introduced to the publication manual of the American Psychological Association (APA) (2020). Acceptable clinical report writing as well as scientific writing stem from good general writing skills. You should master the basic rules of American English usage, conventions of composition, precise use of scientific and clinical terms, and correct use of commonly misunderstood words (e.g., *affect* and *effect*), among others (Butterfield, 2015; Hegde, 2024; Strunk & White, 1999). A mastery of the APA writing style is a plus, even if you do not need to follow all of that style elements in your clinical reports. Your academic papers are likely to be held to APA style, as it is also the style the American Speech-Language-Hearing Association (ASHA) has adopted. Consult the cited sources on good writing. Also, take special note of one important aspect of general, scientific, and professional writing: bias-free writing. It is critical that your clinical reports are free from various kinds of biases.

Writing Without Bias

Writing without prejudicial reference to race, ethnicity, age, disability, lower socioeconomic and educational status, gender, gender identity, and sexual orientation is essential for acceptable professional and scientific writing (Hegde, 2024). Writers should set aside their personal beliefs and feelings and write in objective, nonevaluative, nonemotional terms that are acceptable to persons referred to in all reports. Negative connotations about people because of who they are should be scrupulously avoided. Written or spoken words, not intentions, matter. Critical and constant self-examination of your own views and values and a sincere effort to understand the changing perspectives about diverse people are essential to avoid unintended negative evaluations.

Terms that are generally used and those the clinicians may have used in the past may currently be inappropriate. For instance, describing someone as *heterosexual* may inappropriately suggest a norm (*heterosexism*);

cismale and *cisfemale* are preferred terms that suggest that the current sexual identity is the same as that given at birth—a nonevaluative expression. The term *transvestite* is no longer acceptable; the term *cross-dresser* is currently preferred. The term *homosexuality* currently carries negative connotations because of still-prevalent legal sanctions against it in many countries. The term *elderly, aged,* and *senior citizen* are outdated; *older person* is preferred. *Hearing loss* is preferred over *hearing impairment.* The terms *mental retardation* and *senility* have been avoided in preference for *intellectual disabilities* and *dementia* for decades, although mistakes crop up here and there. Various negative terms had their origins in sexism (women and girls are inferior to men and boys), misogyny (hatred of women and girls), transprejudice or transnegativity (discriminatory behavior toward transgender persons), heterosexism (belief that heterosexuality is normal and sets a standard), ableism (people with disabilities are inferior to those without), adultism (children are inferior to grownup persons), ageism (younger persons are superior to older people), racism (people of color are inferior to whites), and many such historically reinforced beliefs and patterns of behaviors in all societies. Even professional diagnostic categories, especially psychiatric ones, may be disputed by those to whom they are authoritatively applied. The American Psychiatric Association's (2013) *Diagnostic and Statistical Manual* (DSM-5) replaced its earlier (DSM-4) *gender identity disorder* with *gender dysphoria.* Although it may have been a step in the right direction, many Lesbian, Gay, Bisexual, Transgender, Queer/Questioning, Intersex, Asexual, and More (LGBTQIA+) community members do not believe that any of their behavior pattern is a psychiatric (or any other kind of) disorder, whatever the name—old or new (Drescher, 2014).

The pronouns used about clients and other individuals should be the ones they themselves will have selected. The issue is critical in describing persons with varied gender identity and sexual orientation as well as people of ethnic and racial diversity. In case of transgender or persons with varied sexual orientation and identity, the best practice is to ask the person for self-selected pronouns. Persons with severe hearing loss may describe themselves as Deaf, with a capital D. Regardless of appearance and dress, persons may have preferred pronouns for themselves. Persons may describe themselves as *gay* or *lesbian*, but not homosexual.

In clinical reports, the preferred usage is person-first description of individuals with communication disorders. For instance, do not write, *I assessed two stuttering men;* write instead, *I assessed two men who stuttered.* The simple rule is to start the sentence with *a person, a woman, a man, a girl, a boy* and then add the diagnostic category preceded by the preposition with: *A person with aphasia, a woman with voice disorders, a man with stuttering, a girl with hearing loss, a boy with intellectual disabilities,* and so forth.

Another mistake to avoid is to imply that persons *suffer* from their disability or disorder. *The man had a stroke* is acceptable but not that *the man suffered from a stroke.* A child has autism spectrum disorder, not that *the child suffers from it.* This does not mean that clinical reports may not describe emotional reactions. Reports may describe emotional reactions of persons with disorders and may contain a client's verbatim statements that include such terms as "I suffer from my paralysis," "I'm frustrated," "I feel bad about my stuttering," and so forth. Such statements are helpful in understanding the difficulties the clients face in their everyday living. They may be addressed in clinical sessions.

Descriptions of race, ethnicity, religion, and socioeconomic status may be unnecessary in assessment and treatment reports, unless such personal background has a bearing on assessment or treatment. For instance, persons may state that they may not attend treatment sessions because of religious holidays; in such cases, the religion, as specified by the individuals themselves, may be mentioned in the report. If socioeconomic status makes it difficult to attend clinical sessions, and the clinic or another agency arranges for free transportation, then that status may be an appropriate mention in the report. Similarly, ethnicity or race should be mentioned only if relevant to some assessment or treatment consideration. For instance, Black English features or the influence of Spanish consonants on English consonants may be discussed in an assessment or treatment report. In no case should religious, ethnic, socioeconomic, and similar personal variables simply be the individual's identity features, however. That is, with no particular relevance, it is inappropriate to write, *I assessed a Muslim child,* a *Mexican woman attended treatment sessions,* or *a man from low* (or *high) socioeconomic status has aphasia.*

Read a few reports from the clinic folders in each practicum site to understand the approved format and writing style. Most university clinics may require detailed reports. A justification for detailed reports is that if certain information is not included in the report, the reader may conclude that the clinician did not observe or consider it. Also, clinicians who have learned to write detailed reports well can always write brief reports equally well. See Hegde (2024) for multiple exemplars of general, technical, and professional writing, including several fully written diagnostic (assessment), treatment, and progress reports commonly accepted in various clinical settings and public schools. See Chapter 5 for writing assessment reports and an exemplar in the appendix attached to that chapter. Follow the requirements on the format, style, and content of reports specified at each of your practicum sites. Practice writing the kinds of reports described in the following sections. Good writing requires writing, a lot of it.

Comprehensive Treatment Plans

After the completion of assessment and report writing (see Chapter 5), write a **treatment plan** (*care plan, plan of care*) that describes short-and long-term objectives and the procedures for achieving those objectives. A well-written treatment plan and accurate progress notes will allow another clinician to review the client's records and begin treatment based on the supplied information. Written treatment plans may be reviewed or amended as the client's needs change. After giving the identifying information, treatment plans should (a) summarize the assessment results, specify the diagnosis, and suggest prognosis; (b) describe the target behaviors and short- and long-term goals; (c) specify the treatment procedures and frequency and duration of sessions; and (d) the clinician's signature, date, degree, and credentials.

The main body of treatment plans include descriptions of target behaviors, stimuli to evoke responses, levels of response complexity, performance criteria, response consequences (reinforcers and verbal corrections), probes to measure generalization, maintenance training, dismissal criteria, and follow-up assessment (Hegde, 2018, 2024). These aspects of treatment plans are discussed in detail in the following section. See Appendix 6-A for a sample treatment plan and visit the companion website for another.

The format, content, and details of treatment plans vary across settings. Public schools, clinics, and insurance companies have their own formats. The following sections present common components of treatment plans and examples specific to certain clinical settings. You are likely to receive site-specific instructions at individual practicum sites.

A comprehensive treatment plan describes the beginning of treatment to the maintenance of trained behaviors in natural environments. It details the client's and the clinician's performances as well as the interaction between the two. The treatment plan does not have to be lengthy, but it should be comprehensive (Hegde, 2024). Do the following in writing a treatment plan:

1. **Summarize identification data**. Briefly describe background information, current performance levels, and purpose of treatment.

2. **Describe target behaviors**. Specify long-and short-term objectives that are client-specific (i.e., appropriate and useful to the client), valid, functional, and measurable. Ideally, you will have established

baselines of target behaviors before preparing a treatment plan. See Chapter 7 for guidelines on target behavior selection.

3. **Describe stimuli to evoke responses**. Determine if pictures, objects, conversation, or orthographic symbols will be used to evoke target responses. Decide if visual, auditory, or tactile stimulation will be used.

4. **Describe the treatment setting**. Treatment is initially offered in the clinical setting, and eventually in more naturalistic settings (outside the clinic, at home or in a child's classroom). It is not uncommon for training to begin at a single-word level with the presentation of pictures in the clinical setting and advance to the spontaneous speech level with conversational interaction in extra-clinical environments.

5. **Describe the different levels of response complexity**. Specify the initial training level (e.g., at the syllable, word, phrase, or sentence level) and the sequence of progression. Response complexity levels are important to consider in treating all disorders of communication. For example, a client with a voice disorder initially may sustain an appropriate pitch only during single word productions. A client with a speech sound disorder may only produce or imitate the target phoneme accurately at the syllable level. All, however, need to advance to more complex responses (e.g., words, sentences, conversational speech).

6. **Describe the treatment procedure**. Initially, you might use a discrete trial procedure to teach the skills. Eventually, the skills may be reinforced in more spontaneous naturalistic conversational speech. Please see Appendix 8-C in Chapter 8 and visit the companion website for the Discrete Trial Treatment Procedure and Recording Form.

7. **Specify performance criteria**. Describe the target response accuracy criterion (e.g., 80% correct) that will serve as the guideline for moving through the treatment hierarchy. Distinguish between modeled, prompted, cued, and evoked responses.

8. **Describe response consequences**. Describe how you increase desirable behaviors and decrease undesirable behaviors. Specify any treatment modifications in the progress report or final summary. Response consequences that increase or decrease behaviors are discussed in Chapters 8 and 9, respectively.

9. **Describe probes for generalization**. Probes measure generalized production of the behaviors taught. See Chapter 8 for details on

probe procedures and Appendices 8-E and 8-F for recording sheets. Also visit the companion website for a Probe Recording Sheet. Describe the probe procedures in the treatment plan by answering the following questions:

- When will probes be administered?
- What type of probes will be used?
- What is the performance criterion?
- What is done if the criterion is or is not met?

10. **Describe the maintenance program.** Include in the description how you plan to train other significant individuals to support the maintenance of clinically established skills in the client's environment.

11. **Describe the dismissal criteria.** The criteria typically reflect production of the target behaviors in conversational speech in both clinical and extra-clinical settings. Written dismissal criteria help ensure accountability. Dismissal criteria vary according to the clinical setting. See Chapter 8 for the recommended criteria.

12. **Describe follow-up schedule and potential booster treatment.** After clients have met the set performance criteria, they are dismissed from the regularly scheduled treatment sessions. However, dismissed clients should be followed-up to assess (a) the maintenance of treatment gains and (b) the need for booster treatment. Therefore, specify the intervals for follow-up sessions in your initial treatment plan. The first follow-up may be at three months following the dismissal. Also specify how the need for booster treatment will be determined (e.g., when the dysfluencies in a person treated for stuttering increase beyond certain level). In the educational setting, for a student on an IEP, you cannot "dismiss" the student and continue to see the student monthly for follow-up. Instead, a reduction in service minutes on the IEP will address maintenance prior to assessing for continued eligibility (i.e., 30 min 1 time monthly for 6 months).

Clinical Lesson Plans

In addition to a comprehensive treatment plan, you also may be required to write *lesson plans*, which are descriptions of session-by-session or weekly activities planned for the client. This permits the supervisor to have advanced knowledge of your proposed clinical activities for a given session. To prepare yourself better for your clinical sessions, write lesson plans for each of your clients. At the university clinic, lesson plans commonly are developed on a weekly basis and submitted to the clinical supervisor in advance for approval. Please visit the companion website for a sample Lesson Plan.

The following examples show the typical information included in lesson plans:

Examples of Lesson Plans

- **Treatment objectives**. Write the treatment objectives for your client. Examples:

  a) Correct production of /s/ in initial word position with 90% accuracy in a conversational speech probe.

  b) Naming 20 pictures of family members and friends with 95% accuracy.

  c) Disfluency frequency below 2% of words spoken in a 5-min conversational probe.

  d) Correct production of the present progressive *ing* in 15 untrained words at 95% accuracy.

- **Procedures and materials for achieving the objectives**. Describe the treatment methods and materials needed to achieve the treatment objectives. Examples:

  a) The /s/ picture cards and /s/ objects will be presented to the client in discrete trials. The client will be required to name each picture. All correct /s/ productions will be verbally reinforced. All incorrect /s/ productions will be interrupted by a verbal "No" or "Stop." Corrective procedures to facilitate accurate production will then be initiated as outlined in the treatment plan.

  b) Twenty pictures of family members and friends will each be presented in discrete trials. The clinician will model the correct names for the client to imitate. Correct naming responses will be verbally reinforced and verbal correction will be offered for incorrect naming.

c) All fluent utterances in conversational speech will be reinforced with verbal praise and a token. At the sign of a stutter, the clinician will withdraw a token.

d) In discrete trials, action pictures will be presented and a relevant question will be asked (e.g., "*What is the boy doing?* to evoke "*Walking*"). Correct responses may be modeled. Correctly imitated or spontaneously produced responses will be verbally reinforced and incorrect responses will be verbally corrected.

Lesson plans give a limited picture of the overall treatment planned for a client. The plans describe what is done in a session or two, whereas the treatment plan describes the total sequence of treatment for a given period. For additional lesson plan samples, refer to Hegde (2024).

Individualized Education Programs

Public Law 94-142 and Individuals with Disabilities Education Act (IDEA) (and its many amendments) mandate a free, appropriate public education and related services for all students who have an assessed and documented disability (IDEA, 2004). Speech and language services are *related services* under the act. A written IEP is required for each child, ages 3 through 21 years, who receives special education, related services, or both.

More than a treatment plan, the IEP is a management program that links the child's present levels and areas of need, individual services, and educational outcomes. It is also a legally binding contract between the school and the family. The IEP describes what will be taught but not the teaching procedures to be used.

Specific rules regulate the development, writing, and implementation of IEPs. The time lines for services, identification, referral, assessment, and service eligibility should be specified. Laws also protect the rights of parents and their rights for due process. The following section describes the speech-language IEP writing requirements.

Guidelines on Writing Individualized Education Programs

For students who meet eligibility criteria under one of several categories and require special education, related services, or both, IEPs must be devised.

Parents are members of the IEP team. Parents express concerns relevant to their child's educational progress. They also give input in drafting the contents of the IEP.

In a comprehensive management plan, the following information is usually included on an IEP form and completed by the IEP team:

- **Give the identifying personal information, purpose of the IEP meeting, and eligibility status of the student.** The information page of an IEP lists all the required identifying information of parents and the student. The student's name, address, phone number, grade, birth date, ethnicity, race, native language, and English language learning status are important elements. For the IEP meeting (described later), specify one or more purposes of the meeting (e.g., initial, annual, triennial, transition, interim). State clearly the eligibility category or categories on the IEP. The category of **Speech or Language Impairment (SLI)** is solely determined by SLPs. The SLPs may serve on a multidisciplinary team and offer their recommendation on other categories. A child may receive speech and language services under another related category that has been chosen by the IEP team following multidisciplinary assessment. These categories include: autism spectrum disorder, specific learning disability, intellectual disabilities, multiple disability, hearing loss, visual impairments, orthopedic impairments, and traumatic brain injury. In many cases, it is not necessary to identify speech or language impairments as the secondary category of eligibility because such impairments are a component of the primary disability.

- **Document how the disability affects the student's educational or functional performance.** Describe how the speech and language disability affects the student's participation in the general education curriculum and his or her progress. The communication statement can be written in the present levels as well (i.e., *Areas of need identified in expressive and receptive language negatively affect Riley's ability to access the general educational curriculum. It is recommended that Riley continue to receive related speech and language services to further remediate such skill deficiencies and provide her with a free and appropriate public education*). For a child in a preschool program, describe how the disability affects pre-academic performance or functional environments (e.g., *Significant speech sound production errors and a low intelligibility of speech interfere with Molly's communication with others in her classroom and home environment*).

- **Describe the student's present level of performance and the parents' concerns.** Document the parents' concerns regarding the student's educational progress that the IEP team will address. Describe the strengths and interests of the student. Highlight areas of need that should be developed as proposed IEP goals. The present levels most commonly include development of the following skills:

1. **Pre-academic, Academic, and Functional Skills.** Include information on grades, reading level, state testing scores, and academic strengths and weaknesses. For a preschooler, include pre-academic skills such as naming of uppercase and lowercase letters; producing sounds; identifying shapes, colors, and numbers; counting; and matching, among other skills.

2. **Communication Development.** Describe speech sound production, intelligibility, voice, fluency, and expressive and receptive language skills. Suggest how the disability affects the student's education (e.g., *The speech sound errors interfere with oral communication in the classroom, reading skills, and spelling*).

3. **Gross and Fine Motor Development.** Include statements on gross motor skills such as running, jumping, hopping, skipping, and kicking and such fine motor skills as handwriting, pencil grasping, producing accurate drawings, and self-feeding.

4. **Emotional and Social Behaviors.** Include such skills as interacting with children and adults on campus, regulating emotions, gaining and maintaining friendships, making appropriate use of recess, and following school rules. The teacher can supply information on these behaviors when the SLP is the case manager.

5. **Vocational Skills.** Describe such skills as remaining on task, completing and turning in classwork and homework, efficiently working individually and in groups, and being organized. Again, teacher input is essential in gathering information on these skills.

6. **Adaptive and Daily Living Skills.** Address such daily living activities as self-care (e.g., toileting, hygiene), communication (e.g., expressing wants and needs, asking for help), social skills (knowing the names of familiar adults and peers on campus), independence (navigating the educational campus), community participation (e.g., naming and counting money), and safety (e.g., following rules when outside). Ask the student's teacher for input.

7. **Health History.** Include the student's health history as well as any health updates or changes. List medical conditions, medications, and vision and hearing impairments. A health plan may be attached to

an IEP if there are significant medical needs. The school nurse would supply medical information.

8. **Completing the IEP Sections.** An SLP may complete all or only the communication development sections. If a student is receiving speech or language services with no other special education services (such as reading, writing, or math), commonly referred to as a "Speech Only" IEP, then the SLP will complete all sections of the present levels. Such a student is enrolled in general education. In this case, the SLP is the **case manager**. The SLP will seek information from the teacher or other specialists. If the child is receiving speech-language services in conjunction with other special education services, the SLP will complete sections related to speech and language skills. Such a child is in a special education classroom. Other specialists (e.g., reading or writing specialist) complete their respective sections. One of the other specialists, often a special education teacher, is likely to be the case manager.

9. **Other Information Included.** Present levels of performance may include assessment information if the IEP is initial or triennial when re-assessment is completed. You may include formal and informal measures in the assessment summary. Essentially, you should report sufficient information to develop any additional goals.

- **Special Factors.** Some students may need assistive technology and equipment. Others may need assistance with their visual impairment, hearing loss, English language learning, and behavioral problems. For example, if a student is an English language learner, the IEP team must specify whether the student requires primary language support and English language development. The professional(s) responsible for instruction may also be stated. In the case of a student whose behavior interferes with learning in the classroom, specify methods to modify the behavior.

- **Summarize Statewide Assessment Results.** For example, if a student is of age to participate in the statewide assessments, specify it on the IEP. In addition, list the needed accommodations or modifications to the assessment.

- **IEP Goals.** Typically, written goals describe the child's expected performance for a year's time (from an initial date to the same time the following year). Some districts require short-term objectives for all students, while others require short-term objectives only for students in specialized programs. Short-term objectives reflect steps necessary to obtain the long-term goal or scaffold the long-term goal by including levels of cues or prompts or a lesser criterion. They may be written for quarter or trimester time frames. In some cases, these objectives are referred to as *benchmarks*. Write measurable goals or objectives/benchmarks that have a clearly identified target, the level of complexity, a time frame (i.e., by the next annual review or by a specified date), treatment stimuli, who is measuring the goal, the number of sessions required, the response mode, level of independence (evoked responses or type and number of prompts allowed), and accuracy criteria. For example:

- **Annual Goal**. *By the next annual review and in the speech room with intervention, Dani will increase appropriate use of grade level vocabulary by independently providing two definitions for 40 multiple-meaning words in response to picture, verbal, or written stimuli across 2 speech sessions as measured by the Speech and Language Specialist.*

- **Short-Term Objective 1**. *By the first reporting period in the speech room with intervention, Dani will increase appropriate use of grade level vocabulary by independently providing two definitions for 10 multiple-meaning words in response to picture, verbal, or written stimuli across 2 speech sessions as measured by the Speech and Language Specialist.*

- **Short-Term Objective 2**. *By the second reporting period in the speech room with intervention, Dani will increase appropriate use of grade level vocabulary by independently providing two definitions for 20 multiple-meaning words in response to picture, verbal, or written stimuli across 2 speech sessions as measured by the Speech and Language Specialist.*

- **Short-Term Objective 3**. *By the third reporting period in the speech room with intervention, Dani will increase appropriate use of grade level vocabulary by independently providing two definitions for 30 multiple-meaning words in response to picture, verbal, or written stimuli across 2 speech sessions as measured by the Speech and Language Specialist.*

The present levels of performance suggest the annual goals and the short-term objectives. The goals and objectives should help meet the student's needs that were reflected in the description of the present levels of performance. Although there is no required number of goals or objectives, all needs of the student must be addressed. For example, if a student has deficits in expressive language (e.g., morphologic production), social conversational skills (e.g., topic initiation or maintenance), and receptive language skills (e.g., comprehending vocabulary), the student must have a goal reflecting each of those deficits. As much as possible, goals must be aligned to the curriculum. In many states, goals are aligned to the common core state standards. For example, in the state of California, the previous goal of targeting multiple-meaning words may now be aligned to a standard of *vocabulary acquisition and use* for any of the kindergarten through 12th-grade levels. Your supervisor in the school may help you understand your state's standards. There are also phone or tablet applications available that house the standards and provide easy access.

- **Describe the offer of Free and Appropriate Public Education (FAPE).** Recall that IDEA requires it, including needed special education services. The IEP team, including the student's parents, must discuss service options that may be appropriate to the individual student. If only the speech and language services are needed, the options for the least restrictive environment may be (a) the general education setting with no additional services, (b) the general education setting with consultation services, or (c) the general education setting with direct, related services for language and speech. Each must be noted on the IEP and discussed. The team will select the service option that will address the written goals. Also included in the offer of FAPE are the following:

- **Accommodations**. IEPs detail needed *accommodations* that the general education or special education staff must adhere to or *modifications* to be made to the curriculum. Repeating instructions, checking for understanding, using multimodality instruction, using a peer buddy to assist with following directions, and using preferential seating are among the several types of accommodations. Speech and language accommodations promote maintenance and generalization of targets. For example, once a phoneme is trained and a general education teacher has been informed of the phoneme targeted in treatment, an accommodation in the classroom may be appropriate. Possibly, the teacher may provide models, cues, or discreet correction requests to encourage the production of trained phonemes in the general education environment. Modifications may include changing assignments or class materials to help students complete them to the best of their ability. However, when the curriculum is modified, the student may not receive a diploma at the end of their high school career.

- **Services**. Because of the required annual review, the duration of services is limited to one year or less. List all services that are educationally necessary for a student to make progress. Give the names of all services (professions) and all service provider titles (not individual names) on the IEP. Specify services as group, individual, or a combination of the two. Examples of stated services and service models include the following:

1. **Direct services.** *To directly address mastery toward goals and objectives, direct therapy will be provided 120 min per month, in the speech room, with the student present.*

2. **Consultative services.** *Services will be delivered using a consultation model at 30 min per month in the general education setting to provide the following: training for the general education teacher on monitoring, correcting, and reinforcing the production of trained phonemes in the classroom; consultation with the general education teacher regarding progress and concerns; and observational opportunities within the general education setting for the SLP to monitor generalization and maintenance of trained phonemes.*

3. **Collaborative services.** *Services will be provided using a direct, collaborative service delivery model at 120 min per month in the special education setting to directly address skill development toward mastery of goals and objectives; work directly with the student and special education staff to configure naturalistic teaching opportunities that promote communication; and educate the special education staff by directly demonstrating and modeling teaching strategies that support and facilitate improved communication.*

4. **Mixed service delivery.** *Services will be provided 120 min monthly, using a combination of direct and consultative service delivery. Direct therapy services will be provided 90 min per month, in the speech room, with the student present, to directly address mastery toward goals and objectives. In addition, services will be delivered using a consultation model at 30 min per month in the special education setting to provide the following: assistance with visual and tactile supports needed in the classroom to support communication; demonstrations and models to train teachers and staff on teaching strategies that support the student; teaching opportunities to promote child-directed language learning opportunities; and consultation with teachers and staff to provide necessary modifications to special education classroom instruction, curriculum, and progress monitoring.*

- **State whether the student is eligible to attend Extended School Year (ESY).** Essentially, this is summer school for special education students. Considerations for ESY are discussed at the IEP meeting. The IEP team determines if a lengthy break would cause regression in skills learned that could not be recouped in a reasonable time frame, negatively affect the learning of critical life skills, derail progress made on interfering behaviors (e.g., aggressive, self-injurious), or limit progress the following school year due to the nature or severity of the disability. Determination of regression and recoupment is often addressed by examining the clinical data of a student following extended breaks. For example, if the student was on summer break for 8 weeks, the SLP will analyze treatment data from the end of the previous school year to the 8 weeks following the beginning of the new school year. The SLP will identify whether the student recouped lost skills within that 8-week time frame. If not, it may be necessary to consider ESY for the next school year.

- **Describe the amount of time the child will spend in the general educational setting.** On the IEP, note the child's participation in regular education. Ask your school supervisor for a conversion chart that calculates the pull-out time in relation to general education placement.

- **Describe how progress will be reported.** In addition to the annual review of the IEP, you must regularly report the child's progress to parents (usually every trimester or quarter). This will be noted on the IEP paperwork.

- **Obtain the signature of all individuals attending the IEP meeting as well as the consent of the educational rights' holder.** The names, positions, signatures, and dates of participation of all individuals attending the IEP meeting must appear on the designated signature lines within the IEP. The parents, educational rights' holders (such as a foster parent or guardian), or adult student will either give consent to the entirety of the IEP or parts of the IEP or may decline the IEP and special education placement. The child, especially at the secondary levels of junior high and high school, also may attend and be a member of the IEP team. If so, have the student sign the IEP form.

- **If required by your district, complete the IEP notes.** IEP notes document the live discussions among the team members during the meeting. One IEP member may be designated to take the notes. Consult the district policy on note-taking.

The IEP Meeting

An IEP meeting may be required for different reasons. An assessment must precede placement on an IEP. An initial IEP meeting is held to determine whether eligibility criteria are met and whether services are warranted to meet the student's needs. The written assessment report serves as documentation of the student's present levels of performance and drives the contents of the IEP. If a student is placed on an IEP following the initial meeting, an annual meeting is required. Thereafter, a new IEP is drafted to reflect the current performance levels, goals, and services.

IEP meetings may be held at any time prior to the annual meeting to review progress, make amendments to the current IEP, consider an outside agency's report, or address new concerns of parents. Every 3 years, a triennial evaluation is completed. A triennial includes a reassessment of speech and language skills and any other areas of suspected disability (i.e., cognitive, social-emotional, etc.) completed by the appropriate, designated professional (i.e., school psychologist, academic specialist, etc.). Annual IEPs do not require a complete reevaluation unless the IEP team deems it necessary. An assessment plan must be proposed to, and signed by, the parents prior to any formal evaluation. Assessment should always be conducted prior to dismissal.

If eligibility continues to be met and services are required for a student to make educational progress, an IEP may continue until an individual turns 22 years of age or receives a high school diploma. By the age of 16, transition planning is required in most states for students having an IEP. Transition planning is individualized to the student, but may include plans related to training, education, employment, and independent living skills. A student must also be notified a year prior to reaching the "age of majority" (18 years in most states), which allows for educational rights to be transferred to the student. For those students who cannot serve this function, a parent can petition for guardianship and continued educational rights. Reevaluation is not required for students who age out at 22 years. For these students, a summary of academic and functional achievement is provided. The summary should include recommendations on means to achieve postsecondary goals. It should provide information and documentation to help support access to possible postsecondary programs (National Center for Learning Disabilities, 2006).

In addition to the annual review of students' progress, periodic progress reports are required. Progress reports may be required every trimester or quarter, depending on the specific age of a student or program.

Various IEP forms are in use, but the basic content is the same. For reasons of efficiency and accessibility, many school districts electronically input and store IEPs. Computer-generated and checklist formats should be diverse enough to allow the development of an individualized program. This is not a problem with most programs. Your school site will supply you with IEP forms. If training is offered for the IEP paperwork, take it.

The IEP should be presented in a draft format to indicate that it is a working document until finalized at the completion of the IEP. Parents, teachers, specialists, and administrators can discuss the IEP and make changes as needed. Parents must be included in the IEP development. Also,

IEPs in draft form facilitate a more efficient IEP meeting. Meetings may be lengthy, often requiring additional meetings. Therefore, a prepared draft IEP may reduce time spent on paperwork.

At an IEP meeting, parents should be provided with a statement of their rights, called a notice of Procedural Safeguards or Parent's Rights, required by IDEA. This is provided when a student is referred for special education assessment, when any subsequent assessment is proposed, when a change of placement is recommended, when due process has been initiated, or when the parent(s) request a copy. Many districts will also provide the rights notice to parents prior to the IEP meeting as well as explain the rights. Procedural safeguards detail rights relating to IEP decision making, due process, and key terms.

Individualized Family Service Plans

Public Law 99-457 Part H, an amendment to Public Law 94-142, established an early intervention program for infants and toddlers and their families. This program requires that an IFSP be written for children with disabilities, ages birth through 2 years. The assessment and IFSP must be developed by an interdisciplinary team of professionals and the child's parent(s). Assessment must be completed in all developmental domains: cognitive, social and emotional, self-help, receptive and expressive language, and fine and gross motor skills. The state determines the eligibility requirements and a state regional center or similar agency usually completes an initial assessment for early intervention services.

The Contents of IFSPs

- Current levels of performance in all developmental domains
- Family needs and strengths related to assisting the child
- Intervention objectives and expected outcomes
- Descriptions on how families can work on objectives in everyday routines
- Recommended services
- Initiation and duration of services
- Progress reporting procedures and reevaluations

The IEP and IFSP are similar in that they both describe clinical and educational objectives, types of services to be provided, and the beginning and ending dates of services. The IFSP differs from the IEP because of its emphasis on family involvement. The goal of services is to increase learning opportunities and participation through daily activities and routines. The IFSP targets not only the needs of the child, but the strengths and weaknesses of the family, and how these influence the child's development.

Emphasized in the 1997 and 2004 revisions of IDEA is the *location* of services. Services should be provided in the **natural environment**. Service delivery may take place in preschool-based programs, through direct services, field trips, and home visits. The IFSP incorporates public school services and the services of other public agencies (e.g., families may need respite care services or social welfare services, as well as educational and rehabilitation services). Intervention may be coupled with workshops for siblings, parents, educators, and other members of the community; support groups for parents; and access to resource centers.

The case manager, responsible for coordinating and monitoring services, is selected based on the needs of the child and the family. The case manager may be an SLP, audiologist, special education teacher, psychologist, social worker, or other professional. The IFSP must be reviewed every 6 months, compared with the IEP's annual review. Prior to the third birthday, the team must develop a transition plan. Services may continue on an IEP or they may no longer be warranted. Eligibility criteria are specific to the state.

Varieties of Progress Reports

Progress reports document what was done (intervention) and what changes followed in the skills of persons under treatment. Documentation of services offered and the effects that followed are both a professional and scientific responsibility. ASHA states on its website that *if it wasn't documented, it wasn't done.* Progress reports summarize a client's initial skill levels (baselines), treatment procedures, current performance, progress made with intervention, and further recommendations.

Progress reports may be daily or periodic. Clinical practicum students in university clinics are typically required to document the client responses to treatment in each session. The supervisor may review the session-by-session progress reports and approve continuation of the same procedure or suggest modifications. Session-based progress reports generally report quantitative data (e.g., the child's correct production of the pronoun *she* was 68% in the session) and therefore they tend to be brief.

In the university clinic setting, if a lesson plan has been prepared in advance of each session, you may write the results of the session directly on the lesson plan. Because the lesson plan has already detailed the activities, you may just specify a percentage after an activity. For example: *Initial /s/: 90% correct at the word level. Medial /l/: 30% correct at the phrase level.*

Periodic reports include those written at the end of a semester or a quarter in a university clinic. In some university clinics, reports written at the end of an academic term may also be called *final summary.* Such reports not only summarize quantitative data, but also offer narrative descriptions, analysis of performance, and recommendations for further services.

Mostly in medical settings, SOAP notes or brief narrative notes may be written to document daily progress each time a service is rendered, when a client is referred to another facility or specialist, or when necessary to claim reimbursement from insurance companies. In all facilities, a discharge report may be written when the services are terminated. In the school setting, progress reports are usually written on a trimester or quarterly basis (as stipulated on the IEP) and at the annual review.

Please see a sample SOAP note in Appendix 6-D of this chapter. Also, visit the companion website for a sample each of a Progress Report and Daily Progress Notes.

To write acceptable progress reports of any kind and for any duration of service, you need valid, reliable, and quantitative data on your clients' performance in all clinical session. **Performance** is measured and recorded as frequency of target responses under baseline, treatment, probes for generalization, and follow-up sessions. Therefore, you should record your client's responses in each session. Documentation should include the type of service provided (e.g., baserate, treatment, and probes), objective data on the frequency of target skills in every session, and the clinician's interpretation of the data and overall impression of sessions. Other than the data interpretation and clinical impressions (which may be subjective and yet valid) compiled data should be objective, accurate, complete, timely, and verifiable by your supervisor or another clinician.

Use a recording sheet to document the frequency of target skills in each clinical session. Your practicum site may provide you with a recording form or you may develop your own. You may also consider using the appendices in Chapter 8 for modifiable templates and exemplars for recording the frequency of responses under baserate (Appendix 8-A and Appendix 8-B), treatment (Appendix 8-C and Appendix 8-D) and intermixed and pure probes (Appendix 8-E and Appendix 8-F). Data recorded on such sheets enable you and your supervisor to review the client's progress and make modifications in treatment procedures. It also provides a means of communication among professionals and gives sufficient information for another clinician to serve your client if you are unable to do so.

A session-by-session treatment recording sheet, often required of practicum students, is a daily progress note. When you use a recording sheet on which you show correct and incorrect responses observed in each session (see Chapter 8 Appendices 8-C and 8-D), you have a daily progress note that is objective and quantitative. Probe response recording sheets also serve as periodic progress reports. Percent correct response frequencies are typically shown on such treatment and probe response recording forms. Writing brief paragraphs at the bottom of the form, you may state anything unusual you observed during a session and summarize your overall impression of how the session went. SOAP notes, described in the next section, also are daily progress reports.

Guidelines on Writing Progress Reports

- **Follow good writing principles.** Write clearly and briefly. Avoid biased language and use professional and scientific terms accurately. Report objective data.

- **Avoid qualifiers.** Refrain from writing "seems to" or "appeared," unless you make it clear that they are subjective opinions.

- **Minimize the use of jargon.** When necessary to use technical terms, define them. Use only those abbreviations that others will understand. (Visit the companion website for a Glossary of Educational Abbreviations and Acronyms and a Glossary of Medical Abbreviations and Symbols.)

- **Give client identification information.** List the client's name, age, address, phone number, occupation or school status, and birth date. If applicable, give the name of the parent or spouse.

- **Describe the period covered by the report.** Note the dates that the treatment period began and ended. Also note when treatment was originally initiated, if different from the beginning period of the report.

- **List the number of sessions the client attended.** Document the number of sessions your client attended, the number your client missed, and the total number scheduled.

(continues)

- **List the length of the treatment sessions**. You may see clients in 60-min or 30-min sessions. Specify the duration.

- **Summarize the client's status at the beginning of the treatment period**. Give a brief overview of the client's communication skills at the beginning of the treatment period. For example, you might state: *An analysis of conversational speech in the clinic setting recorded at the time of the initial assessment, revealed 85% fluency. Analysis of an audio-recorded sample of the client's conversational speech at home revealed 82% fluency.*

- **Summarize the treatment plan**. Describe the treatment objectives and procedures in clear terms so that the reader can understand and another clinician can replicate them. Describe and justify any changes made to the original treatment plan.

- **Describe the client's performance**. Describe how the client's target behaviors changed during the course of the treatment. Make objective statements: *At the beginning of treatment, Tom's voice was judged hoarse on 90% of his utterances. At the end of the semester, he was judged hoarse on 10% of his utterances.* Include tables and graphs that summarize quantitative data and show changes over the course of treatment.

- **Summarize your conclusions and recommendations**. Include in this section your overall impressions of treatment effectiveness and the client's improvement. Make a prognostic statement and recommendations. Did your client make progress? Do you expect your client to continue to make progress? What type of intervention will promote continued progress? For example: *John made progress throughout this treatment period. Based on his performance over the past 3 months, prognosis for continued progress is good. It is recommended that John continue to receive treatment for his voice disorder. To be most effective, treatment should be given 2 times per week for a minimum of 30 min each session.*

- **End your report with your name, title, and signature**. Also include your supervisor's name, title, and signature. For sample progress reports written for different disorders, see Hegde (2024).

SOAP Notes

SOAP notes are a special kind of progress notes, typically written in medical settings. These notes summarize objective data, clinician's analysis and subjective impressions, and subsequent plans for intervention or other clinical services.

Appendix 6-D attached to this chapter shows a sample SOAP note that may be adapted to any clinical setting. Please visit the companion website for another sample of a SOAP note.

Guidelines on Writing SOAP Notes

- *Subjective observations*: Describe the observations you made throughout the session. Consider the client's level of participation, attention, alertness, and signs of illness. You may write, for example, "The client appeared very alert and cooperative. He said, *'I'm ready to work hard today.'*" A client's attention, alertness, motivation, and similar variables, judged subjectively, may affect the objective data calculated during the session. The frequency of recorded correct responses, for instance, may vary across sessions because of fluctuating attention.

- *Objective data*: Describe the strategies used to teach the skills, including modeling and imitation, prompting (cueing) and fading, manual guidance, positive reinforcement, verbal correction, and so forth. Include the number of trials completed, and calculated percentages of correct and incorrect response rates. For example, "*The client produced four-syllable phrases with 80% accuracy in a block of 50 trials (40/50).*"

- *Analysis and interpretation of clinical data*: Make an overall analysis of the session. Offer a comparison of data recorded over multiple sessions, data trends observed during and across sessions, and data in relation to the subjective observations recorded during the course of the session. Summarize the degree of support needed (e.g., frequent cues or models, repetition of directions).

(continues)

For example: *(a) Production of /r/ increased from 65% accuracy during the last session to 90% accuracy during today's session. (b) Withdrawal of visual models resulted in a decrease in accurate production of single syllable words from 90% to 65%.*

- *Plan the upcoming session.* This may include continuing treatment as is, changing a component of treatment (the stimuli, reinforcers, level of cues, setting, etc.), initiating probing procedures, providing homework, or proposing any other suggested component of treatment to complete during the upcoming session. You might state: *(a) Continue current treatment activities. (b) Continue to train the production of functional words at the imitative level. (c) Shift the training of speech sounds to the phrase level.*

Each employment setting will have a specific location to store the daily treatment logs. To maintain confidentiality, files with identifying information are placed in restricted areas. The medium may be paper records, medical charts, or digital documents. The duration that daily logs must be retained is also determined by the work setting and state. ASHA does not specify the length; however, records are typically retained for 5 to 7 years.

Discharge Reports

A *discharge report* is written at the time clients are dismissed from treatment. Clients are dismissed because they no longer need treatment, do not benefit from it, do not attend treatment sessions regularly, or have stopped coming to the sessions because of affordability and other variables.

The discharge report follows a format similar to a progress report written at the end of a service period (e.g., a semester in an academic setting). It covers the treatment period from the beginning of treatment to the discharge date. The report summarizes the progress and states the reason for discharge. The client may be referred to another facility or scheduled for a follow-up visit.

In an educational setting, a reassessment of speech and language skills is necessary prior to exiting a student from an IEP. The reassessment report is coupled with information obtained from progress reports written on the IEP. Progress on goals as well as the present levels as identified during the reassessment may necessitate continued eligibility or indicate that the student is no longer eligible for services. In either situation, the information gathered is presented in a report, discussed in the context of an IEP, with a decision made by the team.

General Recordkeeping Procedures

Student clinicians are responsible for maintaining client files and an accurate log of their clinical practicum hours. Therefore, you should know the general procedures of maintaining client records in each of your practicum sites. Your university department usually stipulates the procedures for documenting and maintaining your clinical practicum hours.

Maintain the Client Files

Because they are confidential, clinic files are kept in a secured area, such as a locked room or in a locked file cabinet. As noted previously, you should never leave clinic files unattended. You should never release copies of reports to other professionals or agencies without permission from your supervisor and without prior written approval from the client. You may not take clients' files home. You are responsible for maintaining your clients' files in a complete and orderly fashion. You should follow your clinic's policy for filing documents, logging phone calls, and so on.

To ensure that all necessary information is in their files and is current, review your clients' files periodically and have the clients verify their phone numbers and addresses. Make notations of all changes in the clients' folders and report them to your clinic's administrative assistant. To maintain adequate records, follow the general guidelines and the specific requirements of the clinic.

Information to Be Included in Client Records

- Client identification information, including telephone number, address, file number, and so forth
- The name of the individual or agency that referred the client
- Client history, including any related information from other agencies, such as copies of medical reports, IEPs, psychological evaluations, and so on

(continues)

- The name of the SLP (and student clinician) responsible for service delivery to the client

- A diagnostic report or reports (one may have been written at another facility)

- A current treatment plan, including specific objectives and prognosis

- The date the treatment plan was discussed with the client or the responsible member of the client's family

- Notations regarding conferences held with other professionals

- Treatment reports, daily and periodic progress reports, and final or discharge reports

- A chronological log of all services provided for the client

- A signed and dated consent for release of information

At a university clinic, client files should also contain a signed and dated consent to be observed by students and faculty. All records must be signed by an individual holding current ASHA certification.

Maintain a Record of Your Practicum Hours

Before you apply for your clinical fellowship year (CFY), ASHA certification, a state licensure, or a department of education's credential in speech-language pathology, you need to submit a record of your clinical practicum hours certified by your academic department. With the help of your supervisor, you are responsible for maintaining a log of your clinical clock hours earned in clinical practicum. Your university department may provide you with a form for reporting these hours. Such a form may be a part of your academic file and will include ASHA's knowledge and skills required of students who eventually seek clinical certification.

You should consistently follow certain rules or guidelines on counting your clinical hours. Because you will not always be seeing clients for an entire hour, you may need to report fractions of hours. Use a consistent system for recording clock hours earned. For example, do not report a 30-min session one time as ½ hr, another time as 30 min, and still another time as .5 hr. At the end of the term, totaling your hours will be much easier if your reporting is consistent and systematic. Use the following guidelines for reporting clock hours and fractions of hours.

60 min = 1.0 hr	30 min = .5
55 min = .9	25 min = .4
50 min = .8	20 min = .3
45 min = .75	15 min = .25
40 min = .7	10 min = .2
35 min = .6	5 min = .1

All clock hours must be verified by a signature of the supervising SLP. Chapter 1 describes the activities that may be counted as practicum hours.

⑦ Questions for Self-Assessment

1. What terms and phrases would you avoid in writing clinical reports? Why should you avoid them?

2. Describe a *treatment plan* and a *lesson plan*. Distinguish between the two and describe their functions.

3. What are IEPs and how do they differ from IFSPs? Why are they written in public schools? What are the legal bases for these two kinds of reports?

4. Write a SOAP note on a patient in a hospital admitted for a recent stroke.

5. What kinds of information should you include in clients' files? Make a comprehensive list.

References

American Psychological Association. (2020). *Publication manual of the American Psychological Association* (7th ed.).

American Psychiatric Association. (2013*). Diagnostic and statistical manual of mental disorders* (5th ed., DSM-5).

Drescher, J. (2014). Controversies in gender diagnoses. *LGBT Health, 1*(10), 10–14.

Hegde, M. N. (2018). *Hegde's pocketguide to assessment in speech-language pathology* (4th ed.). Plural Publishing.

Hegde, M. N. (2024). *A coursebook on scientific and professional writing for speech-language pathology* (6th ed.). Plural Publishing.

Individuals with Disabilities Education Act. (2004). Section 300.34. https:// sites.ed.gov/idea /regs/b/a/300.34

National Center for Learning Disabilities. (2006). *IDEA parent guide: A comprehensive guide to your rights and responsibilities under the Individuals with Disabilities Education Act (IDEA2004)*. https://www.ncld.org/wp-content/uploads/2014/11/IDEA-Parent-Guide1.pdf

Strunk, W., Jr., & White, E. B. (1999). *Elements of style* (4th ed.). Pearson.

APPENDIX 6 – A

Sample Treatment Plan (Stuttering)

[Write the identifying information at the top. Include the clinic's name and address, the client's name, address, and other details according to your clinic's format.]

John Jones, age 7, was assessed on [date], for a fluency problem at [clinic name]. Analysis of a conversational speech sample revealed a stuttering frequency of 11% when all types of disfluencies were counted. John typically exhibited part- and whole-word repetitions, sound prolongations, pauses, interjections, and revisions. With consistent attendance at recommended treatment, prognosis for improved fluency was judged to be good.

The response cost procedure was selected for John. A token and verbal praise were given for each fluent utterance and a token was withdrawn contingent on stuttering. Tokens were backed up by a gift John would have selected at the beginning of each session.

Final Treatment Objective: A disfluency rate that is below 5% in three consecutive conversational speech samples recorded in the clinic, outside the clinic, in his school, and in his home.

Target Behaviors. (1) Increased frequency of fluent utterances in conversational speech. To begin with, fluently produced words or phrases spoken at John's typical rate will be reinforced. In gradual steps, utterance length will be increased to sentences and conversational (connected and continuous) speech. (2). Decreased frequency of disfluencies to 2% of the spoken words or less.

Treatment Procedures. Initially, a baseline of stuttering (specific forms of disfluencies) will be established in conversational speech before starting treatment. After providing instructions on the procedure, treatment will begin at the level of words and short phrases. Each fluent utterance will be reinforced with both verbal praise and a token. If necessary, fluent productions will be modeled for John. At the instance of each disfluency, the clinician will say, "oh, that was bumpy" and withdraw a token. No change in the rate of speech or prosodic features will be accepted. The length of the utterances will be increased gradually. The criterion performance will be 98% stutter-free speech at each level of response complexity.

Maintenance Procedures. When the disfluency frequency in conversational speech remains below 2% of spoken words across three consecutive sessions with the presence of John's mother in the treatment room, maintenance procedures will be initiated. John's mother will be trained to verbally reinforce John's fluent utterances. Tokens will no longer be used. John will also be taken outside the clinic to collect informal speech samples while talking to other student clinicians or clinic staff members. The mother will be requested to submit home conversational samples. Disfluency frequency will be counted and percent disfluency rate will be calculated for each sample.

Follow-up. A schedule of follow-up for 3, 6, and 12 months postdismissal will be established. If necessary, a few booster treatment sessions will be provided to strengthen fluency and encourage maintenance.

Signed: Date:
Monica Marvelson, BA
Student Clinician

I understand the results of the evaluation and agree to the recommended treatment plan.

Signed: Date:
Leticia Jones, Mother

Sample IEP (Voice Disorder)

[Name and address of the school and the school district]

Individualized Educational Program
Treatment of Voice Disorders
Student's Name: Diagnosis: Voice disorder
Speech, Language, and Hearing Specialist:
Program Initiation Date: Date of the Report:
Overall Objective: Improved voice quality
Goal: By [specify the date], the student will complete the following objectives
with 80% accuracy.

Initiation Date	Selected Objective	Evaluation and Treatment Procedures	Target Met (Specify the date)
[Specify the date]	Pitch ✓ lower __ higher ✓ in school __ in other settings	Modeling the target voice feature, prompting, and successive approximation and verbal praise and verbal correction.	[Specify]

continues

Intensity __ lower (softer voice) ✓ higher (louder voice) ✓ in school __ in other settings Nasal resonance __ decrease __ increase Voice quality ✓ reduce hoarseness ✓ reduce harshness ✓ reduce breathiness Other voice objectives (specify):	Conversational probes to assess generalization and maintenance.	

Sample Progress Report (*Speech Sound Disorder*)

[Write the identifying information at the top. Include the clinic's name and address, the client's name, address, and other details according to your clinic's format.]

Diagnosis: Speech sound disorder

Progress Report

Period Covered: [Specify the range of dates]

Background Information

On [date] Ken Chin [substitute], an 8-year-old boy, was evaluated for a speech sound disorder at [the name of the clinic]. Final consonant omissions and initial sound substitutions were the main types of errors noted in conversational speech as well as the standardized tests [name the tests administered]. Treatment was recommended. He has received treatment at this facility for one semester. Ken's mother, Christine Chin, observed all the sessions.

The final treatment objective for Ken is to produce the misarticulated phonemes with 90% accuracy in conversational speech in extra-clinical situations.

Progress

Objective 1. Correct production of [specify the sounds] in word final positions with 90% accuracy.

Method and Results: The phonemes targeted for treatment were base-rated in word final positions. Twenty words with corresponding stimulus pictures were presented for each phoneme on a set of modeled and evoked trials. Ken's correct response rate ranged from 10% to 20%. On discrete trials, stimulus pictures were presented, a relevant question was asked (e.g., "What is this?") and the correct responses were modeled for Ken to imitate. Correct responses were reinforced and incorrect responses were verbally corrected. Silent articulatory positions were demonstrated as found necessary. The training criterion for each target sound was 10 consecutively correct responses. After training six words with a target sound to criterion, generalized production was assessed with 10 probe (untrained) words for each sound. The probe criterion was 90% correct production of each sound in untrained words.

Ken has met this probe criterion. His correct response rates of the target phonemes in word final positions varied between 95% and 98%.

Objective 2. Correct production of [specify the sounds] for which he substitutes [specify sounds] in word initial positions with 90% accuracy.

Methods and Results: The procedure used to eliminate sound substitutions was the same as that used to teach word-final consonants. The same criteria were used for training and probe. Ken has met both the criteria. His correct response rates on the target phonemes in word initial positions varied between 92% and 96% on probe (untrained) words.

Summary of Progress

Ken has met both the training and probe criteria for final consonant deletions and initial sound substitutions within the current semester of intervention. Overall, he has made excellent progress. He was attentive to the treatment task throughout all the sessions.

Recommendations

During the current semester, treatment could not be advanced to the level of phrases, sentences, and conversational speech. It is recommended that at the beginning of the next semester, a conversational speech sample be obtained and the target phonemes at the word level be baserated to establish the beginning and the eventual course of treatment. Eventually, Ken's production of target speech sounds may be evoked and reinforced in conversational speech. To promote maintenance, Ken's mother may be trained to evoke and verbally reinforce the correct production of target sounds at home.

Signed:
[Name and degree of the student clinician]

Signed:
[Name, degree, credentials, and the title of the clinical supervisor]

APPENDIX **6–D**

Sample SOAP Note (Aphasia)

[Write the identifying information at the top. Include the hospital clinic's name and address, the patient's name, address, and other details according to the hospital's format.]

[Name of the clinician]

Date and Initials   Progress Note

2-10-24   Mr. Dawson was energetic this morning. He cheerfully
KPS   greeted, "Good morning, doctor!"
He correctly answered my questions about date, time, and the breakfast eaten.
He named 6 out of 10 family pictures (60% accuracy).
Confrontational naming was the treatment target in a 45-min individual therapy session. With phonetic cueing, Mr. Dawson named 20 objects with 80% accuracy (60% during the previous session).
Mr. Dawson's naming skills have consistently improved across sessions.
Phonetic cueing will be continued in the next several sessions.

2-12-24   Mr. Dawson looked distracted this morning. He did
KPS   not respond to my "Good morning" greeting.
            Nonetheless, Mr. Dawson was attentive when I
            began therapy. He correctly named 8 out of 10 family
            photographs (80% accuracy, improved from the
            previous session).
            His correct object naming improved to 95%. He thus
            met the training criterion for confrontation naming.
            Intervention for correctly naming the family members
            will continue. Naming his caregivers in the hospital
            and conversational topic initiation will be the new
            targets next week.
            The same treatment procedure of modeling, cueing,
            and verbal reinforcement will be continued.

Note: The first paragraph entered for each date contains a *subjective* statement (clinician's impressions). The next paragraph summarizes *objective* data. The last two paragraphs are *analysis* and the *plan* for the next session.

CHAPTER **7**

Target Behaviors Across Disorders

Student Learning Outcomes

After reading this chapter, student clinicians are expected to:

- Summarize the different approaches to selecting target behaviors for treatment
- Give an overview of the guidelines on selecting target behaviors
- Understand that target behaviors across disorders share certain basic speech, language, voice, and fluency parameters
- Select appropriate speech, language, fluency, voice, and augmentative and alternative communication targets for their clients with varied disorders of communication

---

Typically, you begin treatment after you have assessed your clients, selected the target behaviors in conjunction with the client and family members, as well as other caregivers. You may also experiment with a few different targets before you finalize them.

If the clients assigned to you have received services at your clinic, you should carefully read the reports in the files. You should read the initial assessment (diagnostic) report, treatment reports, progress notes, and reports from other professionals. You should then make a rough evaluation of each client's current skill levels and deficits.

If the clients were newly referred to the clinic, you should first assess them. Assessment procedures are described in Chapter 5, with a sample assessment report attached as an appendix. For details and readily usable assessment protocols, consult Hegde and Pomaville (2022) and Hegde and Freed (2022). In this chapter, you learn about selecting target behaviors for clients of all ages for all disorders of communication.

Selection of Target Behaviors

A **target behavior** is a skill or action you teach a person in clinical or educational settings. For efficient teaching, target behaviors have to be carefully *selected*. Target behavior selection is nearly as important as selection of effective treatment procedures. There are several reasons for this.

First, most clients need to learn multiple targets. Children with a speech sound disorder or a language disorder need to have a set of targets. Multiple speech sounds and language features, including vocabulary, grammatical features, and social communication skills need to be taught to children with speech-language disorders. Similarly, adults with aphasia, people who have had a laryngectomy, persons who are dysarthric, and children with cerebral palsy or hearing loss are unable to produce many target behaviors that are essential for everyday communication.

Second, multiple targets should be sequenced. Clients cannot learn multiple targets all at once; they should be sequenced from the simpler to the more complex and taught in that order. This requires thoughtful selection of behaviors to be properly sequenced. A sequence is necessary because some behaviors best serve an immediate purpose of improving communication, while others may be deferred to a later stage in treatment. For example, it is better to teach children who are minimally verbal such words as *mommy, daddy, juice*, and *cookie* than it is to teach *red, sofa*, and *triangle*. For an adult man with aphasia, the forgotten name of his wife is a better learning target than the name of the local football team in which he never had interest.

Third, some behaviors are prerequisites for other behaviors. This, too, requires target selection. For example, single words are prerequisites for phrases and sentences. Many morphological or syntactic features are useless for a child who does not produce simple words. Nouns and verbs need to be taught before many grammatic morphemes can be taught. For example, you cannot teach the auxiliary verb suffix *ing* to a child who does not produce any main verbs (*walk, eat*). Similarly, speech sounds should be taught at the word level before they can be taught in sentences. For adults with aphasia, dysarthria, or apraxia of speech, shorter utterances are more immediate targets than longer utterances. Therefore, the clinician must choose target behaviors at all stages of treatment.

Approaches to Target Behavior Selection

The two main approaches to selecting target behaviors are *normative* and *client-specific*. In the well-established **normative approach**, you select target behaviors that are appropriate for the client in view of his or her age and the age-based norms. For example, if a 4-year-old child does not produce language behaviors appropriate for 4-year-olds, then those behaviors are the targets.

In the **client-specific approach**, the targets that make an immediate and significant difference in the client's communication are selected regardless of the norms. In this approach, you do not necessarily follow the table of norms to select target behaviors. You teach behaviors that best serve a client's communicative, educational, and social needs. A study of the client's environment and the educational and social demands made on that client is likely to suggest relevant and useful target behaviors.

As pointed out in Chapter 6, the client-specific approach is suitable for choosing targets that are *culturally and linguistically appropriate* for the individual client. Because this approach requires a careful study of each individual client, the cultural and linguistic background of the client can be assessed for the relevance of target behaviors. Choosing a culturally and linguistically appropriate service model is important in the practice of speech-language pathology.

In some cases, the normative and the client-specific approaches may suggest the same target behaviors for a given client. However, in many other cases, the targets may be different. The client-specific approach is more demanding than the normative because it requires a greater study of the individual client and his or her family and cultural background.

The two approaches contrast more for children than for adults and more in the case of speech and language targets than for other targets. More research is needed to understand the best approach to selecting target behaviors. Clinicians should not automatically assume that norms are the best targets for children. Target behaviors that are especially relevant for a client may be better generalized and maintained than those that are selected with no particular regard for the needs of the individual.

Guidelines on Selecting Target Behaviors

Use the following guidelines to select treatment targets for various disorders of communication:

1. **Let the client and the family help select the target behaviors.** Select and finalize target behaviors only after discussing them with the client, the family members, or both

2. **Select functional target behaviors.** These will make an immediate and socially significant difference in the communication skills of the client. Functional target behaviors will not only improve the client's social communication, but also academic achievement and occupational performance. Select speech sounds that when corrected will most improve intelligibility in children and adults with speech sound disorders (including apraxia of speech and dysarthria). Select words, phrases, and sentences that will improve basic and functional communication of children and adults with language disorders (including aphasia and dementia). Functional communication skills that help individuals get their basic communication needs fulfilled are likely to be produced in natural settings and maintained over time.

3. **Consider selecting complex or difficult behaviors for initial teaching.** Do not assume that you teach all skills at their simplest level. Experiment. Treatment research evidence suggests that complex speech sounds may be taught before simpler sounds, and more advanced language features, mastered later by children, may be taught before less advanced features, mastered earlier.

4. **Select culturally and linguistically appropriate targets for diverse individuals.** As you do with all clients, select and finalize target behaviors only after discussing them with the client, the family members, or both. Select speech-language targets that are at variance with the child's own dialect, not those that differ from the Mainstream American English (MAE) features. See Chapter 5 for additional information and guidelines.

The following sections describe some common target behaviors across disorders of communication. But please note that target behaviors are always client-specific, to be finalized only after consulting with the clients, their families, institutional caregivers, and so forth.

Speech Sound Disorders

The very first client you treat may be a child with a speech sound disorder. This is because, in the typical undergraduate academic sequence, courses on speech sound disorders are likely to precede courses on other communication disorders.

A thorough assessment may reveal that the child misarticulates only a few sounds or multiple sounds that form different error patterns. This information informs target speech sound selection (Pena-Brooks & Hegde, 2023).

Target Individual Sounds

Select individual sounds for training when one or more of the following conditions are met:

- The child's speech is generally intelligible.
- Only a few sounds are in error and there is no need for a pattern analysis.
- The errors are related to such organic factors as cleft palate, velopharyngeal insufficiency (VPI), and neurological involvement.

Individual Speech Sound Targets

1. Score each phoneme as produced correctly or incorrectly.
2. Classify errors as substitutions, distortions, or omissions.
3. Find out the word positions in which the sounds are misarticulated.
4. Select the initial target sounds for training and write your target behavior statements in objective and quantitative terms.
5. Select the phonemes based on a clear understanding of the sound system of a bilingual or multilingual client's language or languages. The sounds that are either missing in the primary language or are used in place of other sounds are not targets unless the child and the parents wish they were.

The following is an example of a target behavior statement for a child who substitutes /w/ for /r/ in all word positions:

The target is the correct production of /r/ at 90% accuracy in conversational speech produced at the clinic and the child's home. The correct productions should be observed in all word positions and in at least three consecutive speech samples, each containing a minimum of 20 opportunities for producing the target phoneme.

Note that the example of target behavior description specifies:

1. Quantitative criterion of performance (*90% correct*)
2. Response mode (*conversational speech*)
3. Response setting (*clinic and the child's home*)
4. Number of speech samples in which the target behavior productions are documented (*three samples*)
5. Number of opportunities for producing the target phoneme in each sample (*20*)

The suggested criteria in the exemplar may be modified to suit the individual client. A different response setting (e.g., a classroom or a work setting) may be specified. Discuss these criteria with your clinical supervisor, who may suggest alternatives.

In writing target behavior statements, avoid such phrases as: *George will increase his production of phoneme /t/ in words or the client will produce /s/ in conversational speech.* George is unlikely to do it without treatment, so it is the treatment, not George, that increases the production of any target behavior. Whether the target behavior will be learned or not will depend on many variables, and some, like chronic absence from therapy, may not be under the clinician's control. Such statements as the client will do this or that may be construed as a promise to the client or family members, which is unethical. Also, state when the client will meet the goal in probabilistic terms, not by a certain date. For example: *the phoneme or phonemes are expected to be learned in 3 months of therapy given twice weekly in 30-min sessions.*

Target Speech Sound Error Patterns

Select one of two major speech sound error patterns: Patterns based on place-manner-voice analysis or those based on phonological analysis.

Patterns Based on Place-Manner-Voice Analysis

This older and still valid method of classifying speech sounds into patterns is based on how the sounds are typically produced. In this method, you find patterns in multiple substitutions that are based on the place of articulation, manner of articulation, or the feature of voicing.

Target Patterns Based on Place-Manner-Voice Analysis

1. Find out all substitution errors of the client.

2. Group substitutions that are based on place of articulation. For instance, a child may substitute lingua-alveolars for linguadentals (e.g., d/ð); or linguavelars may be substituted for lingua-alveolars (e.g., k/t; g/d).

3. Group substitutions that are based on manner of production. Sounds produced in one manner may be substituted for sounds produced in another manner. For instance, a child may substitute stops for fricatives (e.g., b/v; t/s; p/f) and glides for liquids (e.g., w/r; w/l).

4. Group substitutions that are based on voicing features. A child, for instance, may substitute voiced sounds for voiceless sounds (e.g., b/d; g/k).

5. Teach one or more sounds from each group. Probe to find out if untrained sounds in the group are produced without training (generalization). For example, teach a few fricatives to a child who substitutes stops for fricatives; teach a few voiceless sounds to a child who uses voiced sounds instead. Probe the production of untrained fricatives or untrained voiceless sounds. If not produced, teach them as well. Generalization may or may not occur; if it does, you will save clinical training time. Still, you should extend treatment to nonclinical settings for maintenance.

6. In the case of clients who are bilingual-bicultural, make this analysis with a firm knowledge of the sound system of the clients' primary language.

The following is an example of a target behavior description for a client who substitutes voiced sounds for voiceless sounds:

The target is the correct production of voiceless sounds [specify them] in all word positions at 90% accuracy in conversational speech evoked at the clinic and at the child's home. The correct productions should be observed in at least three consecutive speech samples. Each speech sample should have at least 20 opportunities for producing the target phoneme.

When you write a target behavior statement for a pattern of misarticulation, you must list the *individual sounds* as well. Just saying that you will teach voiced sounds or fricatives will not be specific enough. All sounds in a category may not be in error. Even if they are, you do not teach a category or a pattern directly. You teach specific individual sounds that belong to a conceptual category or pattern.

Target Patterns Based on Phonological Analysis

Target sound within phonological error patterns if persons have multiple misarticulations resulting in limited speech intelligibility (Hodson, 2004; Pena-Brooks & Hegde, 2023). Phonological pattern analyses are multiple and not totally compatible with each other. During your clinical practicum, you may experiment with different approaches or follow your supervisor's suggestion.

You should know the basic phonological patterns to select the appropriate patterns for a given client. The following three main patterns are commonly targeted (Hegde & Pomaville, 2022; Pena-Brooks & Hegde, 2023):

1. **Syllable structure patterns**: Final consonant deletion, unstressed syllable deletion, reduplication, and cluster reduction.

2. **Substitution patterns**: Fronting, backing, gliding of liquids, stopping, affrication, deaffrication, vocalization, denasalization, and glottal replacement.

3. **Assimilation patterns**: Velar assimilation, nasal assimilation, labial assimilation, prevocalic voicing, and metathesis.

Target Phonological Patterns

1. Select a phonological analysis procedure and follow its guidelines.

2. Record continuous speech samples, transcribe the samples, and make a pattern analysis.

3. Select patterns and the involved target sounds for intervention. You cannot eliminate an error pattern without teaching specific sounds as in any approach without a pattern analysis.

4. In the case of a client who is bilingual, make phonological pattern analyses only with a firm knowledge of the client's language

and phonological features. Only the error patterns found in the child' primary language are treatment targets. Patterns found in the child's secondary English may be targets only when the child wishes to master the sound patterns of MAE and the parents approve them.

Your initial targets should be the elimination of phonological patterns that:

- Reduce intelligibility the most

- Include sounds from different classes

- Are outgrown the soonest by normally developing children

- Tend to persist in children with multiple misarticulations

When you have selected a pattern for remediation, write target behavior descriptions that specify what sounds will be taught. Do not simply state that the "goal of treatment is to eliminate final consonant deletion." It is both abstract and negative. Also, the reader would not know what you do to eliminate a pattern. Instead, specify the speech sounds you will teach to eliminate an error pattern. For example:

> The treatment goal is to teach the correct production of the following final consonants to eliminate the pattern of final consonant deletion: [list the phonemes]. The final criterion is at least 90% accuracy in the production of the target phonemes in three conversational speech samples recorded in nonclinical settings.

Phonological patterns are theoretical ways of grouping errors; they should not be confused with direct treatment targets or methods. Therefore, you should not write: *I will eliminate phonological processes* without specifying the sound errors. Nor should you write: *I will be using the phonological method of treatment.* There is no phonological treatment method; treatment is always the elemental procedures, described in Chapter 8. Phonology has given the clinicians specific tools of analysis by which errors are classified into patterns.

Language Disorders in Children

Limited language skills of children who are still learning their language are called **language disorders**. Children with language disorders need to learn to produce and generalize basic vocabulary, grammatic morphemes, various sentence forms, advanced and academic language features, and social communication (Hegde, 2006a, 2006b, 2018a, 2018c; Hegde & Maul, 2006; McCauley & Fey, 2016; Reed, 2018). Sequencing treatment targets is essential for teaching language disorders in children.

The initial language treatment targets depend on the baseline skill levels and the next expected levels. A careful analysis of assessment and baseline data will help select the initial target behaviors. The final target in language intervention is the same as it is for other disorders: effective communication in natural settings sustained over time. It may not be achieved in all cases, but the clinicians should target the highest level of performance in naturalistic settings that can be achieved with the best possible techniques, including parent or other caregiver training.

Language Targets I: Basic Vocabulary

Individual words constitute vocabulary. They are the initial targets for many infants and children with language delay. Although words, too, should be individualized for each child, you can use a few general guidelines to select words that give a good starting point for language treatment.

Basic Target Words

1. **Concrete words that name specific objects, actions, or persons**. For the initial targets, do not select such generic or abstract words like *toys, food, clothes, parents*. Instead teach specific words like *car, milk, sock,* and *mommy*.

2. **Names of animals and pets**. Teach these names—especially the names of the child's (or family's) pets—and later integrate them into short stories to expand the vocabulary and to teach sentence structures.

3. **Verbs**. Select commonly used verbs (*run, jump, hop, walk, push, laugh, smile, eat, drink*). Represent them by action that might help keep the child's interest in therapy. Create target phrases and sentences from the mastered nouns and verbs.

4. **Adjectives to describe objects and people**. Teach simple adjectives (*big, small, tall, short, red, green*) that can be used later to expand the client's utterances.

5. **Culturally and linguistically relevant words**. For all clients, select words that are appropriate for the cultural and linguistic background of the client (e.g., names of food items, kinship terms, and festivals that are specific to the child's family).

Language Targets II: Phrases

Phrases are combinations of two or more words that are not sentences (grammatically incomplete). Construct phrases out of the words the child can produce reliably. Initially, teach two-word phrases, but experiment. Some children may handle three-or four-word phrases. As the child learns more phrases, increase the number of words in utterances until the child is ready to learn morphological and syntactic elements of language.

Target Phrases

1. **Simple phrases**. Combine already learned words to form the initial target phrases. For example, teach two-word utterances that are a combination of adjectives and nouns the child reliably produces (*big ball, little car, red sock*).

2. **Two-word utterances**. Combine nouns and action verbs you already have taught the client. You may teach such phrases as *boy run, kitty jump, baby eat*.

3. **Three-or four-word utterances**. Form these by combining already learned and yet to be learned words. Requests or mands are excellent for this kind of target response. For example, teach such combinations as *I want milk, more apple juice, I want cookie please*, and so forth. Other targets may include nouns and verbs: *boy hit ball* and *she push car*.

Language Targets III: Grammatical Morphemes and Syntactic Elements

Grammatical morphemes are aspects of language that modulate meaning. Lack of grammatical morphemes (such as the plural *s* or the present progressive *ing*) is a diagnostic hallmark of child language disorders. Start morphological training when a child can produce words and phrases. You may continue to teach new words and multiword phrases to expand the child's verbal repertoire. Before you can teach syntactic structures, you need to teach several grammatic morphemes (Hegde, 2006a).

Morphological Treatment Targets

1. **Add morphological features to already mastered words and phrases**. For instance, for a child whom you have taught the words *cat* and *hat*, add the plural morpheme *s* and teach the plural words (*hats, cats*).

2. **The present progressive *ing***. This is an early morphological feature to teach. Add *ing* to the noun plus main verb the child has already mastered (e.g., *running, jumping*). Teach such phrases as *boy running* and *kitty jumping*.

3. **Other morphological features**. Prepositions (*car in box, book on table*), regular plurals (*two cups, my cookies, give me marbles*), possessives (*Daddy's hat, Mommy's coat, Kitty's tail*), articles (*I want a cookie, give me the ball*), regular past tense inflections (*I missed it, he jumped, she smiled*), irregular plurals (*two children, three men, many women, several fish, five deer*), and irregular past tense words (*he went, I ate, she broke*).

4. **Morphological features that help expand the multiword utterances into sentences**. Expand the previously taught phrases into longer utterances by adding additional grammatical features. For example, add the auxiliary verb *is* to teach such expanded multiword utterances as the *boy is running, the man is working, the girl is smiling*, and so forth. Copula also will help expand phrases into sentences (*the man is nice, the lady is kind, the dog is big, the cat is small*). Expand phrases used to teach prepositions into sentences (*car is in the box, book is on the table*).

5. **Pronouns**. Teach them by using other, already taught sentence structures (*she is walking, he is eating, it is coming, this is my coat, that is your shirt*).

6. **Different kinds of sentences**. Select complex forms of sentences. For example, teach questions involving *who, what, where, why, how,* and *when*. Also, teach negative sentences involving *no, not, nothing,* and so forth.

7. **Culturally relevant language structures**. For clients who are bilingual and bicultural, select grammatical morphemes and syntactic structures with a clear knowledge of the clients' primary language and cultural background. For instance, if the omission of plural *s* is apparently due to the influence of the child's primary language, treat this as a language difference. Teach it only if the child and the family want you to. Discuss this with the family members, who may want their child to master mainstream English and be bidialectal.

Language Targets IV: Functional and Social Communication

The final goal of language intervention is to promote appropriate conversational speech in natural settings. Therefore, in the more advanced stages of language treatment, you should teach broader functional or pragmatic language skills.

Functional language targets may mean simple communication skills that help meet the basic needs of an individual. Requests for food and medicine, expression of pain or discomfort, asking for help with bathroom visits are examples of functional communication needed to perform daily living activities. More advanced functional or *pragmatic* language targets may include such social communication skills as conversation, narration, and discourse. Generally, functional communication would not emphasize grammatical accuracy. Any type of communication, including gestures, signs, pointing, and the use of icons on a communication board may be functional. In the behavior analysis, language responses are grouped into *functional responses classes*. Each class has a unique antecedent (stimuli) and produces a certain effect on the listener (Hegde, 2010). The better known mands, for example are a functional response class that includes everyday requests, demands, commands, and so forth. Mands essentially ask someone to do something that benefits the speaker (e.g., "May I have a glass of water, please!").

Functional Language Treatment Targets

1. **Requests (mands).** In pragmatics, requests are subdivided into requests for action, information, objects, and so on. In the behavioral analysis, all requests, commands, demands, and similar utterances are classified into a single functional response class called *mands*. It is possible that when a client learns to make certain kinds of requests, other kinds of requests will be made without further training. As you do with any other response category, teach one or two types of requests or mands and probe to see if the client begins to produce other kinds of requests or mands.

2. **Descriptive statements or tacts.** Children and adults with limited language do not readily describe or talk about events in their environment and may not comment on things and objects. Such responses are called *tacts* in the behavioral analysis, and they are excellent teaching targets. Integrate descriptions and comments into conversational skills training.

3. **Topic initiation.** *Topic initiation* requires that the speaker be the first one to introduce a new topic for conversation. However, with most clients with language impairment, you may have to ask questions or suggest a topic and prompt the client to begin talking. Fade the suggestions and prompt to promote more spontaneous topic initiation.

4. **Topic maintenance.** Discourage topic shifting without saying much on any one of them. Repeat your request to say more on the same topic and shape and reinforce progressively longer durations of speech on targeted topics of conversation.

5. **Turn-taking in conversation.** In conversations, two or more individuals take turns speaking and listening; each person is both a speaker and a listener. Teach persons with language impairment to talk and to listen in an alternating manner. You may give hand signals to stop, you then talk, you stop talking, and request continued speech.

6. **Conversational repair.** This skill helps avoid misunderstandings in conversations. Persons with language problems fail to do something when they do not understand what is said to them. Periodically say, "Tell me more about it," "I don't understand," "Please speak louder," and so forth. Such statements may

prompt the client to simplify, change words, expand, and repeat to modify the utterance in these and many other ways. Model modifications of unclear utterances. Both the listener actions and the speaker modifications are involved in conversational repair. Therefore, make unclear statements and then teach clients to request more information, to ask for clarification, or to say, "I don't understand."

7. **Narrative skill.** A more complex language skill is to narrate events, stories, and experiences in a cohesive and chronologically correct manner. Obviously, before you target narrative skills, you must have taught many other skills, including vocabulary, morphological features, and syntactic aspects of language.

8. **Discourse.** Another complex social language skill is discourse. A discourse is a well-organized speech on a given topic, issue, or problem. It may be given to persuade others to a given viewpoint. You may teach clients to talk in a cohesive, rational, objective manner on a specific topic of general interest or of special interest to the person.

9. **Culturally appropriate social communication skills.** Conversational skills are heavily culturally determined. Therefore, select skills for training only after you have made a clear analysis of the cultural communication patterns of a multicultural client. Discuss these target behaviors with the family members. For instance, if eye contact during conversation is not a part of the child's verbal culture, find out if parents still want this taught to the child. Most parents would.

Language Targets V: Literacy Skills

Literacy skills include reading and writing. **Emergent literacy skills** include a preschooler's recognition and printing of the letters of the alphabet, sight reading of words, understanding the meaning of everyday symbols, and so forth. Such skills precede and are presumed to be prerequisites for reading and writing skills, which develop later. Because literacy skills are language-based, promoting literacy skills in children is an important area of professional practice within speech-language pathology (Culatta et al., 2013; Hegde & Pomaville, 2017).

Teaching literacy skills to bilingual children is a specialty within speech-language pathology. It is important to assess the baseline skills of a child in both the languages and select the language of literacy instruction that will help the child the most in succeeding academically (Rosa-Lugo et al., 2020).

Preschool children with oral language disorders have a high risk of developing reading and writing problems later in grade school. Therefore, to prevent later literacy problems, speech-language pathologists (SLPs) need to develop a three-pronged program:

- Develop emergent (early) literacy enrichment programs that parents implement at home.

- Offer early intervention for language disorders to prevent later language and literacy problems.

- Offer literacy intervention, either integrated with language treatment or as an independent program.

Use the following guidelines in selecting intervention targets. Note that the targets include children's skills as well as certain behaviors of the parents or caretakers.

Treatment Targets in Literacy Intervention

1. **Parental behaviors that promote literacy skills in preschoolers.** Certain actions parents take promote literacy skills in their children. Therefore, target the following parental behaviors:

   a. *Storybook reading to children.* Counsel and train parents to regularly read storybooks to preschool and school-age children, until the children are independent, regular, and proficient readers. Ask parents to jointly look at the text, point to the words as they read, and periodically ask questions about what they just read. The questions can range from the simple—"Who said they were tired?"—to the more complex—"What do you think he will do after he has rested?"

   b. *Literacy-rich home environment.* Ask parents to have books and writing materials (crayons, pens, pencils, papers, child-size desks and chairs, good lighting to read and write) freely available to their children. A home rich in literacy materials is likely to promote literacy skills in children.

   c. *Modeling literacy skills at home.* Ask parents and older siblings to model such good literacy skills as frequent reading and writing. Parents and others who engage in literate behaviors are likely to stimulate such behaviors in children.

d. *Getting children involved in literacy skill practice.* Teach parents to have their children participate in such common literacy skills as writing a letter; addressing a letter; signing or writing a birthday greeting card for another child; writing the name of a teacher on a note to the teacher; preparing a grocery list or a list of things they want to buy; looking up words in a dictionary; and reading together, or helping a child to read, instructions for putting together a puzzle, a toy train track, or a vacation route on a map, and so forth.

2. **Oral language skills.** Because language disorders affect the learning of literacy skills, effective treatment of oral language skills is an excellent method of promoting later literacy skills in children. Follow the guidelines given in the previous sections on the selection of language target behaviors for children.

3. **Integrate literacy intervention with oral language intervention.** Address early literacy skills as well as traditional reading and writing skills during language intervention. If this strategy proves insufficient to promote literacy skills, implement a devoted literacy intervention program if such a program is not being implemented by another professional (e.g., a reading and writing specialist in the schools).

4. **Reading skills.** The best strategy is to target the skills directly, instead of presumed underlying patterns or theoretically linked precursors or predictors (e.g., reading readiness, fine motor development).

   • *Integrate printed letters of the alphabet in oral speech and language training.* As you model a speech sound, show the representative letter of the alphabet; as you teach a word during language training, point out each of the letters of that word.

   • *Integrate printed word stimuli during oral speech and language training.* While modeling or evoking the target speech sounds or morphological features at the word level, show the printed word as well.

(continues)

- *Integrate printed phrases and sentences into oral speech and language training.* While training speech sounds or grammatical elements, present corresponding phrases and sentences along with your oral models or evoking questions.

- *Reading the letters of the alphabet, simple words, phrases, and sentences.* Select these from the child's family environment and academic curricula. Consult with the teachers; start with teaching the names of each letter of the alphabet.

- *Reading during advanced language training.* While training such language skills as storytelling, help the child read a short story and then narrate it.

- *Reading as independent target.* Time and resource permitting, teach reading directly; begin with name reading, especially the name of the child and those of family members; subsequently, include such advanced oral language features as different forms of sentences and short stories.

5. **Writing skills**. Target the operationally definable writing skills, not theoretical precursors or processes.

    a. *Writing the letters of the alphabet during oral speech and language training.* Manually guide the child to write the letter of the alphabet that represents the speech sound, the first and the subsequent letters of the words under training, and so forth.

    b. *Writing words during oral speech and language training.* Manually guide the child to write the target words used in speech and language training.

    c. *Writing phrases and sentences during speech and language training.* Teach the child to write the phrases and sentences used in teaching oral speech and language skills.

    d. *Writing during advanced language training.* While teaching such pragmatic language skills as narration, storytelling, and story element sequencing, teach the child to write a short story to dictation.

    e. *Writing as independent target.* Teach writing directly; begin with name writing, especially the name of the child and those of family members; subsequently, include such advanced oral language features as different forms of sentences and short stories.

Voice Disorders

Voice disorders include absence of phonation or impaired phonation. Some voice disorders are related to abnormal vocal fold actions, others to oral and nasal resonance, several to physical diseases, and many to general behaviors of the client that negatively affect the health of the vocal folds. After a medical examination and a careful voice assessment, determine the nature of the disorder and the target behaviors to be trained to eliminate that disorder (Boone et al., 2020; Hegde & Freed, 2022; Hegde & Pomaville, 2022; Sapienza & Hoffman, 2022).

Target Behaviors in Aphonia

Aphonia is lack of phonation. Therefore, the treatment target for clients with aphonia is phonation (laryngeal sound production). Aphonia may be a behavioral disorder (functional, with no organic pathology) or a neurologic or structural disorder. Bilateral vocal fold paralysis, severe laryngeal injury, or surgical removal of the larynx may cause aphonia. Both medical (e.g., Teflon injection into the paralyzed folds) and behavioral interventions (alaryngeal speech) may be considered. In the case of unilateral vocal fold paralysis, effortful closure of the folds by pushing and pulling exercises is a treatment target.

Treatment Targets in Functional Aphonia

1. **Reflexive phonation.** Shape such reflexive behaviors as coughing, laughing, and throat clearing into voluntary vocalizations.

2. **Reduced laryngeal tension.** Through relaxation and gentle laryngeal massage, reduce muscular tension.

3. **Prolonged vocalization.** Shape the brief vocalizations into prolonged vocalizations.

4. **Stronger vocalization.** Shape more intensive (louder) vocalizations from weak and faint vocalizations.

5. **Phonated speech.** Shape words, phrases, and sentences from vocalizations.

Target Behaviors in Dysphonia

Dysphonia includes all voice disorders except for aphonia. Some dysphonias are caused by such physical problems or diseases as paralysis and ankylosis, carcinoma, varieties of laryngeal tumors and lesions, infections, and papilloma. Abuse and misuse of the vocal mechanism cause other dysphonias.

Physical causes of dysphonia are first treated medically or surgically. Voice therapy to improve the functioning of the vocal mechanism follows. When surgery removes the laryngeal structures, as in laryngectomy, you should integrate new ways of phonation or new sources of phonation into the voice therapy. In treating dysphonia attributable to vocal abuse or misuse, you must change the vocal and general behaviors of the client.

Treatment Targets in Dysphonia

1. **Retraining**. This is a target for persons who do not properly use the airstream to phonate and sustain speech. Two specific targets include a deep enough inhalation to sustain utterances of typical length and sustained exhalation while prolonging certain vowels.

2. **Muscular effort**. Some persons have difficulty approximating the vocal folds because of unilateral vocal fold paralysis, general fatigue, and myasthenia. Those individuals need to exert muscular effort to achieve vocal fold approximations. A specific target is to push on the arm of the chair on which the person is sitting and phonate simultaneously. Hard glottal attacks also have been targeted for such cases.

3. **Esophageal speech**. This is a target for clients who have undergone a laryngectomy. In teaching esophageal speech, target either the injection or inhalation of air; in some cases, the two may be combined. In injecting air into the esophagus, ask the client to first impound some air in the oral cavity and then push it back. The production of plosive consonants is especially helpful in this process. In inhaling air into the esophagus, ask the client to rapidly take in air while keeping the esophagus relaxed and open. The air passing through the esophagus produces vibrating sound that is articulated into speech sounds.

4. **Phonation with artificial larynx.** An electronic device, an artificial larynx provides a mechanical source of phonation to individuals who have undergone laryngectomy. Shape the mechanical sound into articulated speech sounds.

5. **Relaxation.** When excessive muscular tension affects the voice, teach the client to systematically relax the laryngeal and throat muscles.

6. **Vocal rest.** Ask the clients with infectious or traumatic laryngitis to refrain from speaking and whispering.

7. **Altered head positions.** Changing the head position while speaking often results in better voice. Try different head positions to find the one that promotes best voice quality. Extended, flexed, or tilted head positions have all been noted to change the voice.

8. **Elimination of vocally abusive behaviors.** Find out the client-specific vocally abusive behaviors and target their reduction. Ask the client to record the frequency of vocally abusive behaviors and reinforce progressively fewer of those by shaping them down. Generally, target the reduction of the following vocally abusive behaviors:

   - Yelling and screaming
   - Smoking
   - Coughing and frequent throat clearing
   - Excessive talking, singing, crying, or laughing
   - Talking too much with allergic reactions and upper respiratory infection
   - Talking in noisy situations

9. **Elimination of vocal misuse.** Reduce:

   - Frequent use of hard glottal attack
   - Excessively loud speaking
   - Habitual speaking with inappropriate pitch levels
   - Continuous speaking or singing for extended durations

(continues)

10. **Culturally appropriate vocal behaviors**. In selecting specific vocal behaviors for your diverse voice client, consider cultural patterns that affect communication. For instance, an artificial larynx may or may not be culturally acceptable to certain clients. Discuss your treatment targets and strategies with the client, family, or both, to assure yourself that they are culturally appropriate.

Target Behaviors in Disorders of Loudness and Pitch

Disorders of loudness include both **excessive loudness** and **insufficient loudness** of voice. Disorders of pitch include **too high** or **too low a pitch** for a given person. Even though not a disorder, modification of vocal pitch to a desired level may be a target in persons who are transgender/gender diverse (Adler et al., 2019).

Treatment Targets in Disorders of Loudness and Pitch

1. **Increased loudness**. This is a target for clients who speak excessively softly. Select a client-specific level of loudness.

2. **Decreased loudness**. This is a target for those who speak with excessive loudness. Again, select a loudness level that is appropriate for the client.

3. **Higher pitch**. In the typical case of high-pitched male voice, target a client-specific lower pitch.

4. **Lower pitch**. For the low-pitched female voice, target a higher pitch. The target pitch is relative to the client's typical pretreatment pitch.

Target Behaviors in Disorders of Resonance

Disorders of resonance include hypernasality, hyponasality, and reduced oral resonance.

Treatment Targets in Resonance Disorders

1. **Reduced nasal resonance on non-nasal speech sounds**. Target this for individuals with hearing loss, velopharyngeal incompetence, cleft palate, and paralysis of the velum associated with cerebral palsy, stroke, and other neurological problems. A predominant voice problem in these individuals is hypernasality.

2. **Increased nasal resonance on nasal speech sounds**. Target this for clients with hyponasality (denasality). People with hearing loss, among others, may need this target.

3. **Increased oral resonance**. Target this if the individual's speech lacks oral resonance. Increase oral resonance by reinforcing a more widely open mouth during speech production.

Disorders of Fluency

Stuttering and **cluttering** are the two main disorders of fluency. Some individuals who clutter also stutter, requiring treatment for both.

No experimental evidence justifies targeting increased self-confidence, resolution of social role conflict, reduction of parental concern for normal non-fluencies, improved self-image, fluent stuttering, acceptance of stuttering, modification of negative attitudes, and resolution of repressed psychological conflicts. Evidence-based treatment procedures generally target fluent speech or the reduction of stuttering in conversational speech (Bloodstein et al., 2021; Hegde, 2007, 2018; Logan, 2022; Yairi & Seery, 2023). Three sets of target behaviors are associated with three effective treatment programs: fluency shaping, direct stuttering reduction, and fluency reinforcement.

Target Behaviors in Fluency Shaping

Fluency shaping technique is an indirect method of reducing stuttering by targeting skills that are essential to produce and sustain fluent speech: (1) management of airflow during speech production, (2) gentle onset of phonation, and (3 reduced speech rate (syllable prolongation).

These targeted skills, when mastered, induce an unacceptably slow and unnatural-sounding speech. Therefore, normal prosodic features are also treatment targets, along with generalized fluency in conversational speech and natural settings. The final target is the maintenance of fluency across situations and time.

Treatment Targets in Fluency Shaping

1. **Management of airflow**. Teach (1) a slightly exaggerated inhalation of air and (2) a slight exhalation of air through the mouth before starting phonation. The air should not impound in the lungs and a small amount of air must be exhaled as soon as the peak of inhalation is reached. Target for most persons who stutter, but especially for those whose stutterings are associated with mismanaged airflow.

2. **Gentle onset of phonation**. Teach the client gentle, relaxed, soft, and easy onset of phonation after the slight exhalation of air through the mouth.

3. **Reduced rate of speech through syllable prolongation**. Reduce the rate of speech to a level where speech is free from stuttering; this rate is client-specific. Reduce the speech rate by syllable (mostly vowel) prolongation without pauses between words or phrases. The client should produce words in sentences as though they were a string of prolonged syllables without word boundaries.

4. **Normal prosodic features**. In the final stages of treatment, shape normal prosodic features, including a near-normal rate, intonation, and rhythm.

5. **Maintenance of fluent conversational speech in natural settings**. Target 98% fluency in the clinic and outside at the time of dismissal. This high rate of fluency may not be maintained. A minimum of 95% fluency must be maintained over time in natural settings.

Target Behaviors in Direct Stuttering Reduction

In the **direct stuttering reduction strategy**, consequences known to reduce stuttering are directly applied to instances of stuttering (dysfluencies). No fluency skills are taught, and hence, prosodic features are unaffected.

Time-out (pause-and-talk) and response cost are the two direct stuttering reduction procedures (Hegde, 2007).

See Chapter 9 for time-out and response cost procedures. They are known to be effective in reducing stuttering. Generally, time-out works better with older children and adults and response cost is preferable with preschoolers and younger school-age children. Note, however, that the treatment targets in both the procedures are the same: (1) stuttering or dysfluencies for which reinforcers are withdrawn and (2) fluent speech for which reinforcers are given.

Treatment Targets in Direct Stuttering Reduction Strategy

1. All forms of dysfluencies or stuttering as defined by the clinician.

2. Fluently produced words, phrases, sentences, and conversational speech.

Target Behaviors in Fluency Reinforcement

Suitable especially for young children, the **fluency reinforcement technique** targets fluent utterances for positive consequences. The clinician who is disinclined to use direct stuttering reduction methods may find fluency reinforcement an attractive procedure. Evidence supports its use (Hegde, 2007).

Fluency-shaping skills should not be used in the fluency reinforcement technique. Therefore, the speech prosodic features remain unaffected.

Treatment Targets in Fluency Reinforcement

1. Fluently produced words, phrases, and sentences

2. Fluent conversational speech

Target Behaviors in Cluttering

Cluttering is another disorder of fluency, characterized by an excessively fast rate of speech, reduced speech intelligibility due to this fast rate, increased frequency of dysfluencies, possible language deficiencies, and lack of concern about the problem. Cluttering is often associated with stuttering. If so, select both stuttering and cluttering treatment targets. Maintenance of intelligible and fluent speech to people who clutter is still a major clinical challenge.

Treatment Targets in Cluttering

1. **Slower rate of speech**. Target a slower rate of speech to increase speech intelligibility.

2. **Slight syllable prolongation**. Target slightly prolonged syllable durations, also to increase speech intelligibility.

3. **Pauses between phrases and sentences**. Target deliberate pausing at appropriate junctures to control the runaway rate of speech.

4. **Deliberate stress on syllables**. Target syllables produced with deliberate stress to improve articulation, slow the rate, and enhance intelligibility.

5. **Reduced dysfluency rate**. Target dysfluencies for reduction through time-out (pause-and-talk) or response cost.

6. **Language skills**. Target language skills if the client exhibits deficiencies; use standard language treatment procedures.

7. **Increased awareness of the problem**. Increase the client's awareness of his or her speech difficulty by giving contingent feedback and video monitoring.

8. **Self-monitoring skills**. Teach self-monitoring skills to promote maintenance of treatment gains.

Aphasia

Aphasia is an impairment in understanding, formulating, and expressing language in individuals with brain damage (Hallowell, 2023; Hegde, 2024). Nonfluent and fluent are the two main categories of aphasia, each with several subvarieties exhibiting a few distinguishing impairments. There is a set of deficits all types of aphasia share. These deficits are the most common treatment targets, emphasized in this section. In any case, deficits found in individual clients are always treatment targets.

Individuals with the same type of aphasia may have differing patterns of neurological and communication deficits (Helm-Estabrooks et al., 2014; Payne, 2014). Therefore, select target behaviors based on a careful assessment of aphasia type, the individual's predominant problems, specific communication needs, and chances of immediate success at communication. Generally, everyday functional targets that enhance social communication provide more immediate success and client satisfaction than complex and less frequently used grammatical structures.

Target Behaviors in Nonfluent Aphasias

Fluency is impaired in four verities of aphasia: (1) Broca's, (2) transcortical, (3) mixed (both nonfluent and some fluent aphasic features), and (4) global. In your clinical practicum, you are more likely to encounter individuals with Broca's aphasia than other types. Global is the most severe type of nonfluent aphasia.

Treatment Targets in Nonfluent Aphasias

1. **Speech initiation**. Encourage speech initiation by modeling quick responses to such questions as: "How are you today?" "What did you have for breakfast this morning?" And so forth.

2. **Naming responses**. Select names of objects, persons, and actions that are of immediate use to a client. Besides synonyms and antonyms, rhyming words, spelling selected words, and completing sentences with target words may all be useful targets.

3. **Grammatical function words**. Note that these are not functional communication units; instead certain grammatical words, called *function words*, are missing in nonfluent aphasia. Target the production of articles, conjunctions, auxiliary verbs, copula, prepositions, and the missing grammatical morphemes. *Content words* (nouns and verbs) are generally intact.

4. **Pronouns**. Target pronouns that are misused or missing. Accusative pronouns (e.g., *her, him*) are more likely targets than

(continues)

the personal pronouns (e.g., *she, he*). Using pronoun picture cards, model and reinforce correct productions.

5. **Increased phrase lengths and sentence varieties**. Select as initial targets useful phrases and simple sentences. Subsequently expand the repertoire by adding a variety of sentence forms or functional units including mands (requests, commands, demands), tacts or declarative and descriptive statements, *wh*-questions, yes/no questions, passives, and other forms. Include specific morphological features necessary for these verbal expressions.

6. **Conversational skills**. Using models and prompts, teach turn taking, topic maintenance, conversational repair, and narration.

7. **Rate of speech**. Largely because of naming and other deficits, the speech rate may be slower than typical. Target this only after the individual's naming skills improve. Model and reinforce progressively faster rate of speech until it approximates the more typical.

8. **Prosodic features**. Improvement in speech rate and fluency in naming may reduce halting speech and thus improve prosodic features as well. If not, model and reinforce varied intonation patterns.

9. **Auditory comprehension of spoken language**. May be mild and subtle in Broca's aphasia but may be significant in the mixed transcortical variety. Target this if it affects conversation. Initially, ask clients to point to named pictures, objects, or body parts. Ask yes/no questions. Later, ask for correct responses to phrases and sentences. Ask them to follow instructions. Gradually increase the complexity of speech presented to the clients.

10. **Gestures paired with verbal expressions**. If it improves communication, pair ordinary gestures or a formal system of gestures (e.g., Amer-Ind) with words and sentences. This target may be especially useful to persons with global aphasia.

11. **Writing**. Select such writing skills as copying letters, words, and sentences; and writing from dictation and spontaneous writing. Teach them in that order.

12. **Reading skills**. First, teach reading isolated words that are useful to the individual. Next, teach silent reading (and comprehension) of materials of high interest and pragmatic value. Select reading passages from graded materials. Target more complex and longer reading passages as the client's comprehension of read information improves.

13. **Associated dysarthric or apraxic speech**. If observed, target these speech characteristics; for specific targets, see sections on dysarthria and apraxia of speech.

14. **Echolalia**. If present (likely in transcortical motor aphasia), reduce it by extinction or time-out. Note that this is a target for reduction rather than enhancement.

15. **Decreased speech dysfluencies**. If present at more than 5% of the words spoken, more likely in persons with transcortical motor aphasia, decrease the frequency of dysfluencies in conversational speech by verbally reinforcing fluent utterances or time-out for dysfluencies if the former is ineffective. Note that this is another target for reduction.

16. **Social communication**. Target the production of both the intact and clinically established speech-language skills, especially conversational skills in social settings, such as groups of people that may include other persons with aphasia as well as family members.

Target Behaviors in Fluent Aphasias

Fluent, copious, well-articulated, grammatically correct, prosodically typical, but meaningless or irrelevant speech characterizes fluent aphasias. Speech comprehension deficits, severe in some cases, is also a significant feature. Four varieties of fluent aphasias include (1) Wernicke's, (2) transcortical sensory, (3) conduction, and (4) anomic (Hegde, 2024; Helm-Estabrooks et al., 2014). Wernicke's is the prototype of fluent aphasias and more likely to be seen in clinical practice than the other types. In fluent aphasias, more target behaviors need to be *decreased* rather than increased. Articulation, grammar, prosodic features, and effortful speech are not treatment targets, as they are in nonfluent aphasias. A pervasive problem of spoken speech comprehension in persons with Wernicke's and transcortical sensory aphasias is a treatment target. Unfortunately, none of the various advocated procedures for improving speech comprehension have produced impressive evidence with experimental research (Hegde, 2024; Helm-Estabrooks et al., 2014). Treatment research on all fluent aphasias is limited. Instruct, model, prompt, shape, reinforce, and verbally correct target behaviors as described in Chapter 8.

Treatment Targets in Fluent Aphasias

1. **Incessant and irrelevant speech (hyperfluency).** Target this for reduction. Listeners often have to stop the person from talking nonstop. Ask a question, model a brief and relevant answer, ask the person to imitate, reinforce the correct imitation, and use time-out if the person continues to talk or talks irrelevantly. It is doubtful if merely ignoring will stop the flow of hyperfluent speech. Fade modeling and gradually increase the length of meaningful utterances.

2. **Rapid speech rate.** Target this for reduction. Model a slower rate of responses to questions. Reduce the rate below the base-rate. Progressively require longer responses and reinforce the target rate.

3. **Comprehension of spoken speech.** This is target for persons with Wernicke's and transcortical sensory aphasias; it may not be for persons with conduction and anomic aphasias, but consider it if individual assessment results justify it. Training attention to spoken speech may be more useful than correct pointing to named pictures and similar methods. Before saying something, the person may be alerted to it, asked to pay attention, repeat what is heard, and be reinforced for correct answers. See Helm-Estabrooks et al. (2014) for other suggestions.

4. **Naming and word finding skills.** See the list of targets for non-fluent aphasias.

5. **Neologistic productions.** To reduce the frequency of neologistic word productions, (1) stop the person from speaking when you hear a neologistic word and (2) prompt the correct word.

6. **Echolalia.** If present (likely in transcortical sensory aphasia), reduce it by extinction or time-out.

7. **Writing**. See the previous list for nonfluent aphasias. May not be a target for persons with anomic aphasia but consider possible exceptions.

8. **Reading skills**. See the previous list for nonfluent aphasias. May not be a target for persons with anomic aphasia but consider possible exceptions.

Right Hemisphere Disorder

A constellation of symptoms associated with disease or damage to the right hemisphere of the brain is known as **right hemisphere disorder** (RHD), also known as *right hemisphere syndrome* (Blake, 2018; Hegde, 2024). Persons with RHD exhibit a variety of deficits in perception, attention, emotional expression, abstract reasoning, and communication.

Two special features of RHD are left-neglect and reduced awareness of illness (deficits). The client tends to ignore stimuli in the left visual field, including people, objects, and printed material. The person may be totally or mostly unaware of deficits experienced. Unlike those with aphasia, persons with right hemisphere syndrome do not exhibit serious language deficits; nonetheless, they communicate poorly because of their inattention and other deficits.

Treatment Targets in Right Hemisphere Disorder

1. **Unawareness of illness and deficits**. Increase the client's awareness of deficits by providing contingent corrective feedback on deficit behaviors. Provide video-recorded feedback of errors. Give positive feedback for appropriate behaviors to develop discrimination between acceptable and unacceptable behaviors. Teach self-monitoring skills. Teach family members and others to give corrective as well as positive feedback.

2. **Impaired attention**. Target attending behaviors during communication training. Reinforce the client for paying attention

(continues)

to treatment stimuli and instructions given and for following directions and staying on task. Integrate attention training with pragmatic communication training.

3. **Disorientation**. Frequently orient the person to place, time, and persons by asking questions and reinforcing correct responses, and by verbally correcting incorrect responses. Reduce modeling and prompt and fade both.

4. **Visual neglect**. Target improved attention to speakers on the left; reduce left-neglect during reading, writing, and drawing. Prompt and reinforce drawing the whole physical stimulus shown to the person (such as a clock and pictures of faces and objects).

5. **Facial recognition deficits**. Have the client name the photographs of family members, friends, and caregivers. Model the names if necessary, prompt subsequently, and provide positive reinforcement and verbal correction.

6. **Abstract reasoning**. Teach correct inferences drawn from read or narrated stories, understanding proverbs and metaphors, and detection of absurdities in statements.

7. **Pragmatic communication skills**. Target topic maintenance, turn-taking, narrative and discourse skills, use of appropriate terms, maintained eye contact, and so forth. Target the reduction of such deficits as confabulation and impulsive and inappropriate responding by verbal correction, extinction, and time-out.

8. **Prosodic features of speech**. Target typical intonation, stress patterns, typically fast rate of speech, and emotional prosodic features. Model and reinforce imitations and have the client explain the emotion expressed through prosodic variations.

9. **Dysarthria**. May be a target in some individuals. See a later section on dysarthria.

Apraxia of Speech in Adults and Children

Apraxia of speech (AOS) is a motor speech disorder involving difficulty in initiating and executing movement patterns necessary to produce speech, even though there is no paralysis, weakness, or incoordination of speech muscles. It is a disorder of both articulation and prosody. The difficulty is thought to be due to impaired motor planning of speech. Edema or damage to tissue surrounding the motor programmer may also cause AOS. The disorder may be associated with aphasia and dysarthrias, and if so, target the aphasic and dysarthric speech characteristics as well (Duffy, 2019; Freed, 2020).

Childhood apraxia of speech (CAS) and AOS in adults have similar features (Hegde & Freed, 2022; Hegde & Pomaville, 2022; Strand, 2020; Terband et al., 2019). Generally, the target behaviors listed in the following box are appropriate for both adults and children with apraxic speech. Each individual, an adult or a child, may present one or more unique features that your assessment may reveal. If so, target them as well.

Treatment Targets in Apraxia of Speech

1. **Speech-related movements**. Target these for those who cannot imitate speech sounds and syllables. Select those movements that are related to speech but may not involve vocalization: tongue protrusion, biting the lower lip, pressing the two lips together, tongue tip movements, and so forth. Generally, avoid movements that are unrelated to speech sound production, as they are not found to be useful. Do not start with speech-related movements unless attempts at starting treatment with speech sound productions have failed.

2. **Misarticulated but correctly imitated speech sounds**. The initial speech sounds to be treated may be those that are imitated or correctly produced with fewer trials.

3. **Sounds that are produced with visible movements of the articulators**. Such targets may lead to initial success in treatment, so they may be good initial targets.

4. **Distorted speech sounds**. Treat distorted consonants as well as vowels.

5. **Distorted phoneme substitutions**. Substituted phoneme distortions is a double target: elimination of substitutions *and* clear production of sounds in their correct positions.

(continues)

6. **Singletons and clusters**. Generally, treat them in that order, but consider the pattern of errors of individual clients.

7. **Most and least frequently occurring sounds**. Target more frequently occurring sounds first and less frequently or rarely used sounds next; however, you may experiment by reversing the sequence.

8. **Stressed syllables**. Select these for treatment if your client's performance on them is better than that on unstressed syllables. This is true of some clients.

9. **Intrusive schwa**. Reduce these epenthetic errors which may be heard within words and at word final positions.

10. **Normal speech rate**. The slower speech rate, typical of AOS, may need to be shaped up to the more typical.

11. **Rhythm**. Use it as in the Melodic Intonation Therapy, in which speech is taught with musical intonation (see Helm-Estabrooks et al., 2014 for details).

12. **Normal prosodic features**. Teach normal-sounding intonation by systematically varying it during sentence production and continuous speech.

13. **Gesturing and writing**. These are targets, especially in the case of severe AOS.

14. **Augmentative and alternative communication**. These may be the targets for individuals with severe AOS.

Dysarthrias in Adults and Children

A group of speech disorders caused by impaired muscular control of the speech mechanism are called **dysarthrias**. This impairment, in turn, is caused by brain injury, or various neurological diseases impair the speech muscle control by both central and peripheral nervous systems. Dysarthria impairs all aspects of speech production: respiratory, phonatory, resonatory, articulatory, and prosodic aspects due to neuromuscular damage.

There are different types of dysarthrias, although they share many common characteristics. The most common dysarthric impairments are listed in this section. However, select targets depending on the pattern of difficulties that are unique to your client. The pattern may be influenced by the extent of neurological involvement and the type of dysarthria the client exhibits (Duffy, 2019; Freed, 2020; Hegde, 2018a, 2018b, 2018c).

Developmental dysarthria is observed in children who sustain brain injury in the prenatal and perinatal period with a diagnosis of **cerebral palsy**. Brain injury in children is different from that in adults mainly because of their still-developing neuromuscular system and communication skills. Even so, many common effects are seen in adults and children with neuropathologies (Hegde, 2018b; Hegde & Pomaville, 2022; Yorkston et al., 2010). Therefore, the treatment targets for dysarthria are the same or very similar for children and adults. From the following list, select the specific target for the child or an adult depending on the dominant speech impairments as per the specific individual's assessment results.

Treatment Targets in Dysarthrias

1. **Appropriate posture, tone, and improved strength of muscles.** Target relaxation when there is hypertonia. Induce postural adjustments that facilitate improved speech. Improved strength of the general musculature may be targeted by the physical therapist, but the SLP's target is improved tone of muscles involved in speech production.

2. **Improved respiratory management for speech.** Improved muscle strength and appropriate postural adjustments are interrelated with this target. Teach controlled and sustained exhalation that helps produce sustained and louder speech.

3. **Improved phonatory behaviors.** Treat hyperadduction through relaxation training and hypoadduction through increased muscular effort by such means as pushing exercises. Address breathiness and harsh vocal qualities.

4. **Improved articulatory skills.** Achieve improved intelligibility of speech through articulation training. A slower rate of syllable and word production rather than the production of specific sounds may be appropriate in individual cases.

5. **Improved resonance characteristics.** Reduce hypernasality (a feature in most types of dysarthria) and increase oral resonance.

(continues)

6. **Improved prosody**. Teach improved rhythm, appropriate patterns of stress, typical loudness, and proper intonation of speech. Reinforcing typical and stable speech rates and increased phrase length may also improve prosody.

7. **Nonverbal or augmentative means of communication**. For severely impaired persons, teach nonverbal means of communication. For others, teach augmentative means to supplement oral speech.

Dementia

Dementia is persistent or progressive deterioration in intellectual skills, including memory and general behavior, associated with such neurological diseases as Alzheimer disease, Pick disease, and Parkinson disease (Bayles et al., 2020; Hegde, 2024). Dementia is diagnosed when there is a significant cognitive decline from the previous level and may include deterioration in complex attention, executive function, learning and memory, language, perceptual-motor skills, or social cognition (American Psychiatric Association, 2013).

In the typical **remediation approach**, clinicians select **impaired skills** for intervention. Results of treatment studies targeting impaired skills have been favorable, although modest in most cases (Abraha et al., 2017). However, long-term maintenance of treatment gains has been limited because of the progressive nature of underlying neurodegenerative diseases. Therefore, in an atypical strategy called the **prophylaxis approach**, some investigators have selected **intact skills** for repeated home practice to maintain them for as long as possible. Studies on this strategy, conducted mostly with individuals who had primary progressive aphasia, have produced favorable results (Flurie et al., 2020; Jokel et al., 2014; Meyer et al., 2019). Nonetheless, there is currently no way to stop the progressive decline of skills in dementia. In the advanced stages of dementia, intervention is limited to clinical management of general behaviors, caregiver training and support, and personal safety.

In selecting treatment targets from the following list, consider skills that are intact at the time of assessment. Design a home practice program involving those unimpaired skills. Practice on smartphones, tablets, and laptops may be recommended for individuals who can be trained.

Treatment Targets in Dementia

1. **Intact communication and other skills**. Have the client practice at home, with or without electronic devices (e.g., smartphone, tablets, computers), intact naming, requesting, conversational, and other functional skills to sustain them as long as possible. Train the family members and other caregivers to remind and reinforce such practices at home.

2. **Memory skills**. Design various reminders (alarms, written instructions, staff reminders, signs that remind activities, written lists of activities or appointments, use of electronic devices that remind tasks, keeping personal belongings in a specific place, etc.) and teach the client to use such reminders. Target both intact and impaired memory skills.

3. **Orientation**. Teach the client to consult signs and directions, local area maps, calendars, digital clocks with large displays, and other environmental cues to maintain orientation.

4. **Maintenance of daily living skills**. Target such skills as cooking, eating, dressing, bathing, and so forth. Physical exercise and social involvement also are targets. Physical and occupational therapists may manage these skills. SLPs may be members of the rehabilitation team and serve as consultants for managing communication needs.

5. **Maintenance of communication skills**. Teach the client:

   - various kinds of requests (e.g., to be given written directions, repeat information, simplify messages, more time to respond)

   - gestures, facial expressions, and signs to convey messages

   - descriptions (of objects and persons when naming fails)

   - conversational skills (maintenance of such skills as long as possible)

   - reduction in inappropriate, irrelevant, and vulgar verbal and nonverbal behaviors

(continues)

- social interaction with family members and friends (telling stories, maintaining topics of discussion, taking conversational turns)

- self-cueing techniques

- effective functional communication (not necessarily linguistic accuracy)

In all cases and especially in advanced cases of dementia, the treatment targets are the behaviors of family members and other caregivers who help sustain daily living skills and communication attempts as long as practical. See the next box for details.

Treatment Targets for Family Members and Other Caregivers of Persons With Dementia

1. **Understanding dementia**. Provide systematic information to promote a better understanding of dementia, its course, and its effects.

2. **Understanding the particular individual**. Provide information on the strengths and limitations of the person with dementia and general behavioral management.

3. **Understanding community resources**. Provide information on resources available to the family members in their communities.

4. **Structuring the living environment**. Ask them to:

- reduce variability in the arrangement of living conditions and such daily routines as eating and bathing; schedule such activities at the same time of the day

- reduce sensory stimuli (noise and visual distractions)

- use different rooms for specific purposes

- limit access to hazardous material

- balance the needs of security and freedom

5. **Sustaining the individual's personal care habits.** Ask the caregivers to support and reinforce independent living skills as long as possible.

6. **Exhibiting nonprovoking behaviors.** Ask them to be calm and exhibit nonprovoking behaviors to reduce the individual's emotional outbursts.

7. **Minimizing effects of negative factors.** Ask the family members and caregivers to analyze situations that lead to disturbed behaviors in the individual and teach them to minimize or eliminate such situations.

8. **Reducing the demands made on the client.** Teach them to minimize the demands they make on the client. Ask them to provide adequate help and support when they make demands.

9. **Providing respite care.** Arrange for respite care so the family members and professional caregivers have periods during which they are free from the constant demands of care.

10. **Effective ways of communicating with the client.** Teach the family members and caregivers to:

    - use gestures, facial expressions, posture, and other cues to supplement their verbal expressions
    - establish eye contact, gain the client's attention, and address the person directly
    - ask yes or no questions instead of open-ended ones
    - speak in clear, simple, redundant speech with short sentences
    - keep all instructions simple and repeat them
    - engage the individual in conversations on familiar and simple topics
    - specify the referents of speech

Traumatic Brain Injury

Individuals who sustain traumatic brain injury (TBI) exhibit a variety of behavioral deficits that include impaired communication (Hegde, 2024; Hegde & Freed, 2022; Ostergren, 2018). **TBI** typically results from physical trauma or external force that damages the brain and excludes such other causes of brain damage as stroke and progressive neurological diseases (e.g., Alzheimer disease).

Injury with an open wound in the head, crushed or fractured skull, torn meninges, and damaged brain tissue is called *penetrating brain injury*. Injury associated with intact meninges is called *nonpenetrating brain injury*. Major symptoms in both adults and children with TBI include confusion, disorientation, memory problems, slurred speech, seizure and other neurological symptoms, attention deficits, impaired thinking and reasoning, auditory comprehension problems, initial mutism and subsequent confused language, naming problems, perseveration, reading and writing deficits, dysarthria, and pragmatic language problems.

Treatment Targets in Traumatic Brain Injury

1. **Orientation.** Target orientation to time, place, and person. Design questions that test orientation (e.g., "Where are you now?" "What time is it?"); model and reinforce correct responses.

2. **Attention.** Target and reinforce increased attentiveness to the treatment task, surroundings, people and events, and conversational partners.

3. **Use of augmentative and alternative communication devices.** Target the use of such devices as a communication board in the initial stages of rehabilitation; teach their continued use if warranted.

4. **Memory for daily routines.** Prepare lists of daily routines and design written signs, instructions, and reminders that may improve memory for daily routines.

5. **Improved naming skills.** Make a list of names of significant people in the client's life and of caregivers; repeatedly model those names if necessary and reinforce correct responses.

6. **Comprehension of spoken language.** Target increased attention to communication partners and conversational topics to improve comprehension.

7. **Reduction in inappropriate, irrelevant, or tangential responses.** Target these behaviors for reduction by using extinction (ignoring) or time-out.

8. **Improved speech production.** Target the reduction of symptoms of dysarthria (respiratory, phonatory, articulatory, resonatory, and prosodic problems).

9. **Improved conversational skills.** Target such pragmatic skills as turn-taking, topic maintenance, cohesive narration, eye contact, and so forth.

10. **Self-monitoring skills.** Teach self-monitoring skills to help maintain the treatment gains.

11. **Compensatory strategies.** Target compensatory strategies (e.g., requesting information, writing down instructions, asking others to speak slowly, using electronic devices) to reduce the negative effects of residual deficits.

12. **Family support.** Target the behaviors of family members such that they provide support and encouragement to the client.

Hearing Loss

Hearing loss is reduced auditory acuity that varies from mild to severe. The degree of effect on communication depends on various factors, including the age of onset, the type and degree of loss, the quality and the time of initial intervention, and others. Even mild hearing loss in infancy is a potential cause of speech and language problems. Severe to profound loss almost always creates significant problems of oral speech, language, resonance, prosody, and intelligibility (Montano & Spitzer, 2021; Stach & Ramachandran, 2022).

Complete audiological and otological examinations and a thorough assessment of all aspects of communication are essential before selecting target behaviors for persons with hearing loss. Take note that Deaf individuals and their families may or may not opt for oral communication skills. Oral communication skills are targeted only when it is requested by the parents of children or adults with hearing loss. Speech and language targets are part of a carefully developed program of aural rehabilitation whose major components are a communication needs assessment, the use of amplification, auditory training, counseling, and working with the family members (Tye-Murray, 2024).

Target Behaviors in Hearing Loss

1. **Oral language**. For the infant with hearing impairment, an early, home-based language stimulation is started first, and formal language training is initiated as soon as practical. Typical voice characteristics; basic vocabulary; and morphological, syntactic, and pragmatic aspects of language are all targets.

2. **Speech production and improved articulation**. For the infant, the period of language stimulation is also the period of speech stimulation. In formal speech training, teach all misarticulated target sounds. Among these, fricatives, affricates, and those that are produced at the back of the mouth are especially important to teach. Also, teach correct productions of distorted vowels.

3. **Improved voice quality**. Reduced hypernasality, improved oral resonance, improved nasal resonance on nasal sounds, reduced nasal emission, and overall improved voice quality are all appropriate intervention targets for children and adults with hearing loss.

4. **Improved prosodic features**. With or without the help of biofeedback devices, teach improved rhythm and intonation of speech. Also teach modified speech rate, smooth flow of words, and appropriate pitch and loudness.

5. **Nonoral means of communication**. For clients who cannot benefit from oral speech-language training, or for those who reject oral communication, target nonoral means of communication, including American Sign Language. Refer the client to a Deaf educator who can teach the sign language.

Persons With Complex Communication Needs

Persons with complex communication needs may also be described as minimally verbal or nonverbal children and adults. They may have extremely limited oral language skills and multiple physical and sensory disabilities. They may not master the skills of oral language needed for social communication (Light et al., 2019). These persons may be candidates for forms or systems of augmentative and alternative communication

(AAC). AAC may include nonverbal means of communication (Beukelman & Mirenda, 2013; Hegde & Pomaville, 2022).

Augmentative communication systems add and enhance available but inadequate verbal communication skills. **Alternative communication** replaces verbal communication in nearly nonverbal individuals. Very few individuals are completely nonverbal. Most candidates for alternative communication have some level of verbal communication, although inadequate to meet their communication needs. In persons with severe disabilities, nonverbal means may be the primary mode of communication.

Because the individuals' oral communication needs vary on a continuum, the distinction between augmentative and alternative communication is a matter of degree. Some forms of communication may be more augmentative than others; other forms may be more alternative.

In your university program, you may or may not receive specialized academic and clinical training in AAC. Nonetheless, AAC is gaining importance in public schools and special education programs where students with multiple and complex needs are being educated. You should be prepared to serve a child with AAC needs in your school practicum. Discuss your limitations (e.g., lack of coursework) with your school clinical supervisor. She may arrange brief workshops or orientation sessions for you. Be prepared to quickly acquire the needed knowledge on both *aided* and *unaided* AAC systems through the published sources (Beukelman & Mirenda, 2013; Dodd, 2017; Hegde & Pomaville, 2022).

Unaided AAC

Unaided communication excludes the use of equipment or external devices and is produced by the body and includes gestures, signs, mime, and facial expressions. Most children and adults who need an unaided AAC are able to communicate basic needs with vocalizations of some sorts, syllables, and maybe even certain words, even if they are not articulated correctly.

Incidentally, typical speech is also unaided communication, but our concern here is AAC. In most cases, individuals who need unaided AAC have limited verbal skills.

Targets in Unaided AAC Systems

1. **Residual verbal skills**. Target existing vocal attempts at communication. If feasible, shape them into better articulated or more elaborated utterances.

2. **Gestures, facial expressions, and gaze**. Target these for individuals without serious motoric impairments (e.g., hand paralysis) to help them get their basic needs met. Teach a set of specific gestures for basic communication (e.g., *yes, no, want, don't want*). Facial expressions, head nodding, and gaze that help communicate may also be treatment targets. Gaze is especially effective as mands (requests). Communication partners can follow an individual's gaze and give an object or a food item.

3. **Patterns of eyeblink**. Each pattern can mean something through conditioning and learning; communication partners must be taught the meaning of patterns.

4. **Pointing**. Pointing is a good target for individuals with hand mobility. Its meaning is transparent.

5. **Pantomime**. This may be an independent target or one combined with available verbal expressions.

6. **American Sign Language (ASL)**. ASL is the most sophisticated and widely used system of nonoral communication. Typically taught to Deaf persons, the signs may be taught to hearing individuals who have limited oral communication potential, including those with intellectual disabilities and autism spectrum disorder.

7. **Left-hand manual alphabet**. This target is an option for individuals whose right hand is paralyzed.

8. **Signed English**. In this system, signs stand for words and morphological features. The signs parallel the word order of spoken English.

9. **Signed exact English**. Another set of signs that closely follows the spoken and written forms of English.

10. **Amer-Ind gestural code**. Also known as American Indian Hand Talk, peoples of various North American tribal bands

have communicated with it. It has been an excellent means of intercultural communication.

11. **Fingerspelling**. In this system, words are spelled by fingers; letters are represented by various handshapes.

Aided AAC Systems

Aided communication uses external devices and objects. These may be no tech, low tech, or high tech. Systems may include pictorial, graphic, or physical symbols (icons) and equipment of various sorts, including smartphones, tablets, computers, and sophisticated electronic speech generators. Aided AAC systems require learning new responses to a greater extent than the unaided AAC systems.

Newer aided systems based on computer technology are introduced regularly. Aided AAC communicators can use specialized software for both hand-held devices (such as tablets and cell phones) and laptop or desktop computers. With the help of your supervisor, you should research recent developments and select the one that is most useful and practical for a particular client.

Targets in Aided AAC Systems

1. **Operational skills**. Regardless of devices and applications, AAC users may have to learn certain operational skills to succeed. Individuals using a communication board must be able to point to the icon, word, or picture on the board. Users of tablets and computers must learn to turn the device on, access the application, type the desired message, highlight an icon, navigate through the program, turn the device off, and so forth. Users of more sophisticated computers that generate speech need to learn more complex actions.

2. **Basic mands (requests)**. For the more severely involved AAC users, target the basic requests, demands, commands, and

(continues)

so forth. These are sometimes described as the *common core vocabulary*, may include words that are not mands, and are essential in aided (as well as unaided) systems. The list may include such sample words as *eat, drink, help, stop, go, more, what, my, you*, and so forth. A *communication book* also may be prepared for individuals who open the book, go to specific pages, and point to the printed messages. The mands also may include a request to find the missing AAC device and ask for help in operating it (Dodd, 2017).

3. **Drawing a communication partner's attention**. This is a basic skill necessary for successful communication. The individual may be taught to tap, make vocal noise, gesture, or use any other means to draw someone's attention to engage in communication with that person.

4. **Responding to prompts and models**. The individual may not imitate models or respond appropriately to prompts. Therefore, it is essential to target and reinforce imitation and correct responses to prompts.

5. **Pointing or highlighting**. Teach the client to point to words, pictures, or icons, either printed on a communication board or the same displayed on the screen of an electronic device (cell phones, tablets, laptops, or dedicated AAC units). Individuals who use a communication book may point to specific messages or point to real or miniaturized objects displayed in front.

6. **Sequential pointing or highlighting**. Teach the client to point to words, symbols, or pictures in a sequence to form phrases or sentences. For example, the individual may point to the words *I, want, juice* in that sequence to form a simple sentence. The individual also may point to the word *I* and then point to the bathroom icon to essentially say, *I want to use the bathroom*. On a computer screen, the individual may highlight words in a sequence.

7. **Arranging symbols**. Teach the individual to sequentially arrange geometric shapes that stand for words, cards on which words are printed, or action pictures to conform to a rough syntax of phrases and sentences.

8. **More complex verbal skills.** The child who forms phrases by pointing to two words or two symbols in sequence may be reinforced for pointing to a progressively greater number of words or symbols in sequence to form shorter and then longer sentences.

9. **Social communication skills.** Target initiation of communication, smooth turn taking in conversation, greeting people (using the system to say *hello* and *good bye*), inviting a peer to play, asking questions about other people's well-being (e.g., "How are you?," "Are you okay?"), commenting on the events and objects in the environment, or such conversational repair strategies as changing the message when someone fails to understand or asking communication partners to simplify or repeat their messages (Dodd, 2017).

10. **Generalized and maintained target behaviors.** The final target skill is the generalized and maintained production of clinically established AAC skills. Reinforcing the skills in a variety of settings and environments will be the main strategy; see Chapter 10 on maintenance strategies.

Target behaviors described in this chapter should help you get started with most clients. You should individualize the targets in all cases because the skills are differentially impaired across individuals with the same diagnosis. What an individual needs to master is always more important than the standard lists of target behaviors.

For all individuals, the final treatment target is effective communication in natural settings, maintained over time and across situations. Throughout the treatment phase, periodically assess your client's status to find out what additional target behaviors must be taught to enhance communication. Follow the logic of moving from simple behaviors to more complex behaviors, from clinically controlled speech to speech controlled by natural events in the client's environments.

⑦ Questions for Self-Assessment

1. What approach or approaches would you take in selecting target behaviors for your clients? Describe the approach you prefer and point out its advantages.

2. What are functional communication targets? How do they differ from other kinds of targets? For what kinds of clients are they most suitable?

3. Specify the various communication disorders (i.e., diagnostic categories) in which the correct speech sound production may be a common target behavior.

4. Specify the various communication disorders (i.e., diagnostic categories) in which aspects of language production may be a common target. What aspects of language are most likely to be the common targets across the disorders you specify?

5. Are vocal characteristics, including prosodic variations, likely to be a target in disorders not technically diagnosed as a voice disorder? What kinds of non-voice disorders are likely to include vocal treatment targets?

References

Adler, R. K., Hirsch, S., & Pickering, J. (2019). *Voice and communication therapy for the transgender/gender diverse client: A comprehensive clinical guide* (3rd ed.). Plural Publishing.

American Psychiatric Association. (2013). *Diagnostic and statistical manual of mental disorders-DSM 5* (5th ed.).

Bayles, K. A., McCullough, K., & Tomoeda, C. K. (2020). *Cognitive communication disorders of dementia* (3rd ed.). Plural Publishing.

Beukelman, D. R., & Mirenda, P. (2013). *Augmentative and alternative communication* (4th ed.). Brookes.

Blake, M. (2018). *The right hemisphere and disorders of communication: Theory and practice.* Plural Publishing.

Bloodstein, O., Ratner, N. B., & Brundage, S. B. (2021). *A handbook on stuttering* (7th ed.). Plural Publishing.

Boone, D. R., McFarlane, S. C., Von Berg, S. L., & Zraick, R. I. (2020). *The voice and voice therapy* (10th ed.). Pearson.

Brookshire, R. (2015). *An introduction to neurogenic communication disorders* (8th ed.). Mosby.

Culatta, B., Hall-Kenyon, K. M., & Black, S. (2013). *Systematic and engaging early literacy instruction and intervention.* Plural Publishing.

Dodd, J. L. (2017). *Augmentative and alternative communication intervention.* Plural Publishing.

Duffy, J. (2019). *Motor speech disorders: Substrate, differential diagnosis and management* (4th ed.). Mosby.

Flurie, M., Ungrady, M., & Reilly, J. (2020). Evaluating a maintenance-based treatment approach to preventing lexical dropout in progressive anomia. *Journal of Speech, Language, Hearing Research, 63,* 4082–4095.

Freed, D. (2020). *Motor speech disorders: Diagnosis and treatment* (3rd ed.). Plural Publishing.

Hallowell, B. (2023). *Aphasia and other acquired neurogenic language disorders* (2nd ed.). Plural Publishing.

Hegde, M. N. (1998). *Treatment procedures in communicative disorders* (3rd ed.). Pro-Ed.

Hegde, M. N. (2006a). *Treatment protocols for language disorders in children, Vol. I. Essential morphologic skills.* Plural Publishing.

Hegde, M. N. (2006b). *Treatment protocols for language disorders in children, Vol. II. Social communication.* Plural Publishing.

Hegde, M. N. (2007). *Treatment protocols for stuttering.* Plural Publishing.

Hegde, M. N. (2010). Language and grammar: A behavior analysis. *Journal of Speech-Language Pathology and Applied Behavior Analysis, 5*(2), 90–113.

Hegde, M. N. (2018a). *Hegde's pocketguide to communication disorders* (2nd ed.). Plural Publishing.

Hegde, M. N. (2018b). *Hegde's pocketguide to assessment in speech-language pathology* (4th ed.). Plural Publishing.

Hegde, M. N. (2018c). *Hegde's pocketguide to treatment in speech-language pathology* (4th ed.). Plural Publishing.

Hegde, M. N. (2024). *A coursebook on aphasia and other neurogenic language disorders* (5th ed.). Plural Publishing.

Hegde, M. N., & Freed, D. (2022). *Assessment of communication disorders in adults: Resources and protocols* (3rd ed.). Plural Publishing.

Hegde, M. N., & Maul, C. A. (2006). *Language disorders in children: An evidence-based approach to assessment and treatment.* Pearson.

Hegde, M. N., & Pomaville, F. (2022). *Assessment of communication disorders in children: Resources and protocols* (4th ed.). Plural Publishing.

Helm-Estabrooks, N., Albert, M. L., & Nicholas, M. (2014). *A manual of aphasia therapy* (4th ed.). Pro-Ed.

Hodson, B. W. (2004). *Hodson Assessment of Phonological Patterns* (3rd ed.). Pro-Ed.

Jokel, R., Graham, N. L., Rochon, E., & Leonard, C. (2014). Word retrieval therapies in primary progressive aphasia. *Aphasiology, 28*(8), 1038–1068.

Light, J., McNaughton, D., & Caron, J. (2019). New and emerging AAC technology supports for children with complex communication needs and their communication partners: State of the science and future research directions. *Augmentative and Alternative Communication, 35*(1), 26–41.

Logan, K. (2022). *Fluency disorders* (2nd ed.). Plural Publishing.

McCauley, R. J., & Fey, M. E. (2016*). Treatment of language disorders in children* (2nd ed.). Brookes.

Meyer, A. M., Tippett, D. C., Turner, R. S., & Friedman, R. B. (2019). Long-term maintenance of anomia treatment effects in primary progressive aphasia. *Neuropsychological Rehabilitation, 29*(9), 1439–1463.

Montano, J. J., & Spitzer, J. B. (2021). *Adult aural rehabilitation* (3rd ed.). Plural Publishing.

Ostergren, J. (2018). *Cognitive rehabilitation therapy for traumatic brain injury: A guide for speech-language pathologists.* Plural Publishing.

Payne, J. C. (2014). *Adult neurogenic language disorders: Assessment and treatment* (2nd ed.). Plural Publishing.

Pena-Brooks, A., & Hegde, M. N. (2023). *Assessment and treatment of speech sound disorders in children* (4th ed.). Pro-Ed.

Reed, V. (2018). *An introduction to language disorders in children* (5th ed.). Pearson.

Rosa-Lugo, L., Mihai, F., & Nutta, J. W. (2020). *Language and literacy development: English learners with communication disorders, from theory to application* (2nd ed.). Plural Publishing.

Sapienza, C., & Hoffman, B. (2022). *Voice disorders* (4th ed.). Plural Publishing.

Stach, B. A., & Ramachandran, V. (2022). *Clinical audiology: An introduction* (3rd ed.). Plural Publishing.

Strand, E. A. (2020). Dynamic tactile and temporal cueing: A treatment strategy for childhood apraxia of speech. *American Journal of Speech-Language Pathology, 29*(1), 30–48.

Terband, H., Namasivayam, A., Maas, E., van Brenk, F., Mailend, M-J., Diepveen, S., . . . & Maasen, B. (2019). Assessment of childhood apraxia of speech: A review/tutorial of objective measurement techniques. *Journal of Speech, Language, Hearing Research, 62*(8S), 2999–3032.

Tye-Murray, N. (2024). *Foundations of aural rehabilitation: Children, adults, and their family members* (6th ed.). Plural Publishing.

Yairi, E., & Seery, C. (2023). *Stuttering: Foundations and clinical applications* (3rd ed.). Plural Publishing.

Yorkston, K., Beukelman, D., Strand, E., & Hakel, M. (2010). *Management of motor speech disorders in children and adults* (3rd ed.). Pro-Ed.

CHAPTER 8

Treatment: Core Techniques and Data Documentation

Student Learning Outcomes

After reading this chapter, student clinicians are expected to:

- Describe what the term *treatment* means in speech-language pathology
- Give technical descriptions of core treatment procedures that apply to all disorders of communication
- Summarize the reasons for apparent but not real treatment diversity
- Give an overview of principles of treating diverse individuals with communication disorders
- State the procedures and formats of measuring and documenting treatment progress in evidence-based practice
- Describe how they would give instructions to their clients and use physical stimuli, modeling, prompting, cueing, and shaping
- Describe the discrete trial procedure of baserating, treating, and probing for generalization
- Summarize how they would use the reinforcement procedures to increase and strengthen the target behaviors
- Distinguish between target behaviors versus target responses
- Specify how they would sequence treatment and describe criteria for effecting movement through the sequence

In speech-language pathology (SLP), several terms are more or less synonyms for treatment. For persons with communication disorders, clinicians may offer *treatment, intervention, teaching, habilitation*, or *rehabilitation*. All terms imply efforts at improving some action and concomitantly reducing other actions.

Treatment in communication disorders takes a relatively long time because it is about **teaching** new speech and language skills or re-establishing previously learned but lost (degraded) skills. **Intervention** refers to procedures designed to stop some process and effect positive changes. **Habilitation** is improving an existing unsatisfactory condition of an individual, as in teaching speech and language skills to children with significant hearing loss or intellectual disabilities. **Rehabilitation** is restoring lost or currently impaired skills (functions) to the extent possible, as in individuals with aphasia or adult with recent onset of hearing loss. Therefore, treatment, teaching, intervention, habilitation, and rehabilitation may be used as synonyms to suggest efforts at teaching new skills or re-establishing lost or degraded skills. They may be distinguished when warranted.

What Is Treatment in Speech-Language Pathology?

Treatment in SLP is an agent of change. To effect change in individuals' communication skills is the main job of clinicians and educators. To judge whether a treatment has changed the skill level under treatment, we compare the response frequencies under baserate and treatment sessions.

In communication disorders, just changing a client by teaching new skills is not enough. Actions of people who surround the client also need to be changed. For instance, parents need to pay attention to newly learned skills to make them last at home. When individuals with aphasia correctly name their family members, the family needs to smile, affirm, and reinforce the individuals. Therefore, in SLP, **treatment** is rearranging communication relations between speakers and their listeners. The **method** by which the clinician teaches new skills or improves existing but inadequate skills is treatment. So also are the methods designed to reduce errors and other kinds of undesirable behaviors.

Core Treatment Procedures Apply to All Disorders

Student clinicians who review treatment literature in communication disorders may think that there are an endless variety of procedures. But this is not the case. There are only a few core treatment procedures that are effective across disorders of communication. A mastery of the following techniques will give the student clinician the basic tools of treatment: instructions, modeling, prompting, fading, positive reinforcement, verbal correction, and a few other procedures to decrease undesirable communication and general behaviors. These core procedures are not attached to the names of treatment researchers. They do not come in kits, mini-suitcases, or bulky cardboard boxes. A clinician who masters these core procedures can treat any disorder effectively, efficiently, and with minimum materials.

The apparent diversity of treatment procedures in SLP is a result of two variables. A brief look at them will give a different picture of treatment procedures used in SLP.

Treatment Targets Differ Across Disorders

The first variable that gives an impression of treatment diversity is a failure to distinguish treatment targets from treatment procedures. **Treatment targets** are skills to be taught, whereas **treatment procedures** are the means of teaching those skills. Treatment targets are the client's actions, and treatment procedures are the clinician's actions. Treatment targets differ across disorders, but not the methods of teaching those target skills.

Obviously, a child with a speech sound disorder needs to master speech sound production, whereas a child with a language disorder needs to learn such language skills as grammatical morphemes, sentences, and conversational skills. Individuals with a fluency disorder must learn to speak fluently and those with a hoarse voice should learn to speak without vocal hoarseness, harshness, and so forth. A person with Wernicke's aphasia needs to ramble less and talk more meaningfully, but a person with dementia needs to produce (remember) words at crucial junctures. These kinds of differences do not suggest different and unique treatment procedures that apply to different disorders, however. Unfortunately, many articles and books give the inaccurate impression that if the target skills to be taught are different, procedures to teach them also are different.

Varied Treatment Programs Contain the Same Treatment Elements

The second variable that creates an apparent diversity of treatment variables is the multiplicity of **treatment programs**. Researchers attach personal or institutional names to basic scientific techniques. Dressing up scientific treatment techniques and packaging them under personal or institutional names may give the impression that something unique has been created. When a treatment package is unpacked and stripped of its nominal identities and cosmetic costumes, basic scientific procedures emerge, assuming the package does contain scientifically researched treatment elements. The emerged teaching procedures almost always include instructions, modeling, prompting, fading, shaping, manual guidance, positive reinforcement, differential reinforcement, and verbal correction described in this and other chapters. Programs that do not include these techniques are most likely ineffective. There are, of course, many attractively costumed ineffective packages.

It is generally appreciated that child language and speech sound disorders are treated with behavioral techniques. However, such communication disorders associated with organic or neurological pathology as cleft palate, aphasia, apraxia of speech (AOS) and dysarthria in adults and children, traumatic brain injury, right hemisphere disorder, dementia, augmentative and alternative communication with or without the use of technological devices, and swallowing disorders are also treated with the same core procedures (Duffy, 2019; Durfee et al., 2021; Freed, 2020; Fridricksson & Hillis, 2021; Hegde, 2024; Meulenbroek et al., 2019; Morris et al., 2018; Wilson, 2022). Behavioral intervention is the only available technique to effect improvement in impaired brain function. Clinicians cannot change the brain to modify behaviors; behavior modification changes the working of the brain. Therefore, clinicians may treat all disorders of communication in all age groups with the core procedures described in this chapter.

Treatment of Diverse Individuals

There is very little treatment efficacy research with culturally diverse individuals. No treatment research has specified unique treatment procedures for specific ethnocultural groups. No research suggests that the principles of positive reinforcement, modeling, shaping, prompting, corrective feedback, and other procedures are ineffective with a particular ethnocultural group. Therefore, you can use procedures that are known to be effective, using a few specific guidelines as follows:

1. **Teach target behaviors the client, the family members, or both approve.** Teach speech-language features that are at variance with the child's own dialect, not those that differ from Mainstream American English (MAE). However, teach the MAE features if the child and the parents request it so as to achieve academic success. For instance, parents of an Asian American child who does not maintain eye contact with teachers may want their child to learn that new skill. Similarly, the parents of an African American child may request that their child be taught the production of MAE grammat-

ical morphemes. Do not teach skills the clients or their families rule out. Diverse adult clients, too, may opt for mainstream English features to achieve wider social participation and occupational success. Follow the guidelines given in Chapter 5 on assessing diverse individuals and Chapter 7 on selecting target behaviors across disorders.

2. **Some multicultural assessment considerations are not relevant to treatment**. For instance, if a recent immigrant child from a tropical country did not name *ski lifts* or *snowmobiles* during assessment, do not conclude that the child is deficient in some aspect of language. Terms related to ski lifts and snowmobiles, however, may be excellent language targets for a Hmong child who lives in Minnesota.

3. **Do not use unfamiliar treatment stimuli**. Children from diverse ethnocultural and language backgrounds, especially those that are relatively new in the country, may not be familiar with some of the typical treatment stimuli clinicians use. They may not be familiar with the kinds of toys used, stories read to them, and pictures in storybooks. Interview the parents and seek suggestions on stimulus selection. They may suggest objects and pictures that the child is familiar with. The family members may also be willing to bring some of the toys, dolls, and picture books from home that the clinician can use.

4. **Do not use culturally offensive stimuli**. Some stimuli may be culturally offensive to some, but not necessarily to all, diverse individuals. For a vegetarian client of Hindu background, omit stimulus pictures that show individuals eating meat. For a Muslim client, do not show pictures of pork and its consumption. Stimulus materials selected from the clients' culture or ethnic background will avoid such mistakes and promote better responses. However, do not use materials that stereotype people and their cultures. They only help reinforce prejudicial behaviors. Expand the stimulus material and target responses gradually to include events and objects present in the client's wider social milieu.

5. **Use treatment activities the client is familiar with**. For instance, as backup reinforcers for token reinforcement, select games and activities that are popular at home. Once again, expand the activities that may be found in the client's larger social milieu to increase social participation.

6. **Use well-trained interpreters, translators, and transliterators**. When working with bilingual individuals whose primary language you do not speak, get help from interpreters, translators, and transliterators that the facility might provide. Review the guidelines in Chapter 5.

Overview of Treatment

Individual treatment sessions and the general intervention program begins, proceeds, and concludes in a flexible arrangement and sequence. The following summarizes the sequence and the treatment:

1. **Select the target behaviors.** Use the guidelines offered in Chapter 7. For each speech sound and language target, develop at least 20 stimulus items. Baserate all of them, use some in treatment, and use the untrained stimuli on probes.

2. **Select and develop the stimulus materials.** These should be specific to the target behavior and may be pictures, toys and other objects, manipulable objects and materials, photographs, line drawings, and so forth. Verbal statements, questions, requests, directions, commands, and so forth also are part of the stimulus array. Prepare these materials beforehand. Use constant verbal stimuli across trials. For example, two types of questions "What do you see?" or "What are these?" may both help evoke names, nouns, plural or singular objects, and so forth. But across trials, consistently use one or the other. Write down and rehearse the delivery of verbal stimuli that accompany other kinds of stimuli.

3. **Establish the baserates of target behaviors.** Baserates (used as a noun or a verb) or baselines (used only as a noun) are extended and reliable measures of target behaviors that precede treatment. Administer evoked trials on all of the stimuli first and administer the modeled trials next. Evoke the target behaviors on multiple discrete trials or in more spontaneous speech samples. See the next section and Appendix 8–A for procedural details.

4. **Evoke the target behaviors.** In addition to physical and verbal stimuli, give instructions and model the responses to get the client started. See the details in subsequent sections.

5. **Teach the nonexistent speech and language skills.** When the baseline of target behaviors is at zero or close to it, use shaping to create them. You may need to create nonexistent functional words in a child with language disorders or naming skills in an adult with aphasia. Use instructions, models, prompts, shaping, fading, positive reinforcement, and corrective feedback to shape new skills.

6. **Increase the frequency of existing target behaviors.** In other individuals, the target behaviors are present but at a low frequency,

requiring procedures to increase them. For instance, a person who stutters does speak fluently but not often enough. Use the same core treatment elements (instructions, models, prompts, positive reinforcement, and corrective feedback).

7. **Strengthen and sustain target behaviors**. To promote generalization and maintenance, teach self-monitoring skills to the clients and teach family members tactics with which they can support the skill maintenance at home and over time. Teach the family members the same procedures (models, prompts, positive reinforcement, and corrective feedback).

8. **Control undesirable behaviors**. Use procedures that decrease uncooperative and nonattending behaviors, crying, and other actions that interfere with treatment. See Chapter 10 for the procedures.

Documenting Client Progress in Evidence-Based Practice

Routine clinical practice cannot document *treatment effects*. Researchers use an experimental design to show that a treatment is effective, that is, treatment is better than no treatment. Researchers evaluate treatment effects using control group-experimental group designs or single-subject designs that compare treatment and no-treatment conditions (Hegde & Salvatore, 2021). Clinicians routinely treating clients cannot do this. *Evidence-based clinical practice* is based on the evidence collected in experimental treatment research.

Routine clinical practice, however, should document systematic improvement in targeted communication skills of clients served. **Improvement** is positive change under treatment. To show such changes in the treated skills of clients, the clinician should measure the frequency of client responses in each baserate, treatment, and probe session. It is hoped that the improvement is due to treatment; likely it is, but one cannot be sure of that because other, extraneous variables may be partly if not wholly responsible for the positive changes. For examples, typical developmental changes that occur in children with speech-language disorders, spontaneous recovery of fluency in children who stutter, improved brain health in persons with aphasia or traumatic brain injury, a teacher's work in schools, or a family member's work at home are among many extraneous variables that may affect the skills under treatment. Treatment research rules out extraneous variables, and clinical practice does not.

Evidence-based clinical practice has two requirements the clinicians in routine practice must fulfill. First, the clinicians should **select treatment**

procedures that the treatment researchers have evaluated in experimental research and have shown to be effective (better than no treatment). In essence, clinicians should not use treatment procedures whose effects have not been experimentally evaluated. Second, the clinicians should systematically, objectively, and quantitatively measure the changes in target behaviors and thus document improvement. Global qualitative statements (e.g., *the client did very well in treatment, the client made excellent progress*) are not a substitute for quantitative measures. Such qualitative statements are fine when they supplement reliable and verifiable quantitative measures of improvement. The best method is to report improvement in terms of an increase in **percent correct responses** under treatment, compared against the same measure under baserate.

Discrete trials make it relatively easy to measure and record responses. When the treatment is elevated to conversational speech level where the discrete trial procedure is not used, measurement requires some judgment regarding such skills as topic maintenance and conversational repair. Such judgments are acceptable if they are reliable. Use Appendix 8-G to quantitatively summarize the conversational skills under different clinical conditions. There is still a need to research more reliable methods of scoring specific conversational skills.

In the subsequent sections of this chapter, references will be made to various forms on which the client's response frequencies may be recorded and the percent correct responses may be calculated. Six Appendices (8-A through 8-F) contain forms to measure and record client responses on discrete trials during baserate, treatment, and probe conditions. For each of these conditions, templates as well as filled exemplars are provided. A seventh Appendix, 8-G, is a template for quantitatively summarizing assessed conversational skills.

How to Use the Discrete Trial Procedure

A **trial** is a distinct opportunity to practice a target skill; when the trials are separated, they are called **discrete**. They are especially useful in teaching narrowly defined target skills (speech sound productions, words, grammatical morphemes, naming). The discrete trials are less useful in treating fluency and voice problems and are inappropriate in teaching conversational skills.

Discrete trials are effective in the initial stages of treatment. These structured trials are administered systematically with uniform stimulus manipulations. Correct and incorrect responses given on discrete trials are more easily counted than those evoked in unstructured formats. A glance at the recording sheet may reveal the percentage of correct responses. Such quick calculations are essential to make various clinical decisions (e.g., stop modeling, give prompts, withdraw prompts, etc.).

The client also benefits from the discrete trial procedures. Because the trials are administered relatively rapidly, the client gets more focused, becomes attentive, and gets more opportunities to practice the target skill than in the less structured approaches. Almost all children, persons with neurological impairments, and those with attention problems perform better with structured discrete trials.

The eight-step discrete trial procedure may be administered as follows:

1. **Present the treatment stimulus.** These may be pictures, drawings, small toys or objects, photographs of persons; they may be used to evoke words, names, phrases, grammatical morphemes, sentences, and other target behaviors.

2. **Ask a question to evoke the target response.** Exemplars of naturalistic questions include:

    a. "What is this?" "What are these?" (to teach speech sounds, words, grammatical morphemes)

    b. "Who is this? "What is her name?" (to teach naming skills)

    c. "What is he doing?" (to teach verbs, present progressive *ing*)

    d. "Where is it [name the object]?" (to teach prepositions *in, on, under*)

3. **Model the target response if the question fails to evoke the response.** Ask the question first and then model. Some exemplars:

    a. "What is this? Say, *cup.*"

    b. "Who is this? Say, *Jane.*"

    c. "What is he doing? Say, *running.*"

    d. "Where is the book? Say, *on the desk.*"

4. **Give a few seconds for the client to respond.**

5. **Positively reinforce or give corrective feedback.** Deliver verbal praise ("Good job!" "That was excellent!). Or make a corrective statement ("That was not correct." "It is Jane, not Joan.")

6. **Record each response on a recording sheet.** See Appendices 8-A through 8-F for the various recording sheets that you can use to record the response frequencies under baserate and treatment sessions.

7. **Pull the stimulus away to mark the end of the trial**. This action makes the trials discrete and helps measure the percentages of correct response in treatment sessions.

8. **Start the next trial after a few seconds**. A brief pause also helps distinguish the trials.

There are four kinds of discrete trials; two kinds to baserate and two more to treat: (1) evoked baseline discrete trials, (2) modeled baseline discrete trials, (3) evoked treatment discrete trials, and (4) modeled treatment discrete trials. The recording forms of each of them may be found in the appendices.

There may be a debate about more structured and more spontaneous treatment sessions. But there is no either or choice in this matter. Initial treatment sessions should be more structured and as soon as the target skills have increased to some clinically judged extent, the structure should be relaxed and the session should become progressively more naturalistic. Skill training in conversational speech should not use discrete trials. The skills will have been established through discrete trials in shorter responses in earlier stages of treatment. The clinician may adopt a flexible strategy of using the tight structure if the client needs it, but use the loose structure if the client can handle it, even in the early stages of treatment.

How to Baserate Target Behaviors

Baserates or **Baselines** are a client's pretreatment response frequencies. Deficient language skills, speech sound errors, stuttering, vocal qualities, and other treatment targets need to be baserated to assess the client's improvement with treatment. The client's progress may be judged continuously against the baselines.

Baselines are needed because the usual assessment data may be dated and inadequate. A single assessment datum raises questions of reliability. Therefore, you need to establish baselines just before starting treatment to get current, reliable, and comprehensive data on a client's status before treatment.

Baselines should be established on multiple exemplars of the same target response. For instance, the production of each phoneme targeted for treatment maybe baserated in 20 words on discrete trials, as against one or two productions sampled on a standardized test. Grammatical morphemes, naming skills, and so forth also should be baserated with multiple exemplars.

Vocal quality, stuttering or dysfluencies, prosodic problems, and such other target behaviors needs to be baserated on multiple speech samples. Three brief samples help assess target behaviors that need to be measured in continuous speech.

See Appendix 8–A for a Discrete Trial Baserate Recording Sheet. Please visit the companion website to download the same sheet for your use.

How to Baserate Target Behaviors

1. Prepare all stimulus materials, as suggested earlier.

2. Baserate only those behaviors that you plan to teach immediately. Repeat a baseline before teaching any behavior. Because target behaviors change, only a baseline taken just prior to treatment is valid.

3. Plan how you might take conversational speech samples. To sample language structures adequately, direct conversation to maximize the opportunities for producing infrequently used language structures. Ask the client or parents to supply recorded conversational speech samples from home to assess the target behavior frequency in extra-clinical situations. See Chapter 5 on language sampling and analysis procedures. Visit the companion website on guidelines on Obtaining and Analyzing Conversational Speech Samples.

4. Write at least 20 response exemplars for each speech sound and language target behavior. An exemplar may be a word, phrase, or sentence that contains a target response. For instance, the word "soup" or the phrase "hot soup" or the sentence "I like soup" contains the /s/, a target response for a child who misarticulates it. Each of those three is an *exemplar*. Similarly, in teaching the present progressive *ing*, you might have such exemplars as *walking, boy walking*, and *the boy is walking*, and so forth. You may have 20 words, phrases, or sentences, depending on the initial level of training. They are likely to be words or phrases. See Hegde (2006) for a variety of target behavior exemplars that you can use to baserate as well as to treat language targets.

(continues)

5. Present the 20 stimulus items on discrete trials. A discrete trial gives the client one opportunity to produce the target response. On evoked trials (without modeling), show the picture or object, ask a question, and wait for the response. Record the response as correct, incorrect or absent. Also, baserate imitative responses on a set of modeled trials in which you ask the predetermined question and immediately model the responses. On all baserate trials, withhold reinforcers and verbal corrections. Appendix 8–A shows a recording sheet.

6. Record each response on a recording sheet. Use the format of the Exemplar Discrete Trial Baserate Recording Sheet given in Appendix 8–A and modify it to suit different target behaviors. You may download the form from the companion website.

7. Calculate the correct percentage of speech sound and language productions separately for discrete trials and for the conversational speech samples. Also, calculate the response frequencies separately for clinical speech samples and home samples. For fluency clients, calculate the percentage of dysfluency based on the number of words spoken. For voice clients, you may calculate durations of conversational speech that are free of problems (e.g., hoarseness or nasality) and those durations that sound typical.

8. Repeat the measures if any two measures for the same response mode and situation are not comparable. For instance, if two clinic speech samples show different baselines for a phoneme or grammatical morpheme, repeat them. Similarly, if two home samples disagree widely, get additional home samples. Target responses counted in home and clinic samples may vary in case of stuttering and voice characteristics, but the variability should not be excessive. Speech sound and language measures may not vary much across samples.

9. Summarize the baseline data in quantitative terms. Use the baseline data to assess improvement under treatment.

Take note of the following examples of objective statements summarizing baseline data:

- The child's correct production of /s/ in conversational speech, measured across three samples, was 20%. Each sample contained at least 10 opportunities to produce the phoneme.

- The child's production of word-initial /r/ in 20 words administered on evoked and modeled discrete trials were as follows: evoked, 30% correct; modeled: 45% correct.

- The child's baserate production of plural morpheme *s*, measured in 20 words, was as follows: 10% on evoked trials; 23% on modeled trials.

- The client's dysfluency frequency on two home samples of at least 2,000 words each was 13% and 15%, respectively.

- The client's voice was judged hypernasal on 90% of utterances that did not contain nasal speech.

- The client was hoarse 90% of the time she spoke during two baserate sessions, each with at least 500 spoken words. (Note: another durational baserate measure.)

- The baserate of the client's naming response was 20% correct, measured with 20 stimulus items on evoked trials.

- The baserate of the client's jargon was 10% of the words spoken in a 300-word conversational speech.

- The baserate speech intelligibility, measured with 20 spoken sentences, was 47%.

How to Evoke Target Behaviors

Evoking procedures are special verbal and physical stimuli needed to have clients respond during treatment. Instructions, physical stimuli, models, and prompts are evoking procedures.

Instructions

Instructions describe the skill to be learned. The young and the old need them. You give instructions in the very beginning of treatment. All target skills (speech sounds, all features of language, voice characteristics, and fluency) need to be instructed.

Write out instructions in simple, clear, everyday words. Instruct at the client's level of education and sophistication. Do not talk down to the client. Do not *elderspeak* when talking to older individuals (too loud and exaggerated intonation).

Rehearse the instructions. Gain experience and give instructions spontaneously. Deliver instructions in a natural, conversational manner. Do not read instructions or deliver them like a lecture.

Test the client's understanding of your instructions. Ask the client to repeat your instructions and do what is asked for. If necessary, repeat your instructions, change words, add gestures, and demonstrate. Also, repeat instructions when the client makes mistakes or fails to remember. Give new instructions every time you change the target behavior or shift training to a higher level.

Instructions in Treating Speech Sound Disorder

Give instructions on how to produce speech sounds. Describe tongue positions, lip configurations, direction of airflow, and mouth opening or closing, and articulatory contacts necessary to produce the target sounds. While giving these instructions, model what you describe.

Whether your client is a child with a speech sound disorder or an adult with AOS or dysarthria, you need to instruct and demonstrate target sound productions. Consider the following sample exemplar instructions to evoke the productions of speech sounds in children and adults. Write similar instructions for other sounds. Find other examples in Pena-Brooks and Hegde (2023). Write down your instructions and practice their naturalistic delivery.

Instructions to Correct an Interdental Lisp

1. Say /ʃ/(sh). While you are saying it, smile so your lips go like this [demonstrate lip retraction]. Then, push your tongue toward your front teeth, like this [demonstrate]. Let us see if your /ʃ/ (sh) changes for an /s/.

2. Let me hear you say /i/. OK, now make a long /i/ and as you make it, raise the tip of your tongue to blow the air through the teeth.

Instructions to Teach the Correct Production of /l/

1. Put the tip of your tongue here [demonstrate the correct tongue position for /l/]. Now say /a/ as you lower the tip of your tongue. Did you hear [la]? Good. Repeat that for me.

2. Look at the mirror. Open your mouth like this [demonstrate a slight mouth opening to show the tongue placement]. Now say /l/.

Instruction to Teach the Correct Production of /f/

Bite gently on your lower lip like this [demonstrate]. Now as you do it, blow air like this [demonstrate].

Instructions in Treating Language Disorders

Various aspects of language are treatment targets for children with language disorders and adults with neurologically based communication disorders (e.g., aphasia, dementia, right hemisphere disorder, and traumatic brain injury) and children and adults with inappropriate language (e.g., those with autism spectrum disorder).

Do not do the ineffective job of describing the rules of grammar to a client with language disorders. Rules of plurality will not help a child produce plural morphemes. However, while showing a picture of two cups, it may be helpful to say, "When you see two of these, you say cups." You teach many language targets for children and adults. They include words, phrases, grammatical morphemes, syntactic structures, prosodic features, and social communication (conversation) skills. It is not possible to give examples of instructions to the entire range of language targets. Therefore, the following examples are only suggestive. You may develop similar instructions for other language targets in children and adults.

Instructions to Teach the Irregular Plural Morpheme

When you see one of these [show a picture of a woman], you say, woman. Who is this? Say, woman. Good. But when you see two like these [show a picture of two women], you say, women. Who are these? Say, women. Good.

Instructions to Teach the Regular Plural Morpheme /s/

When you see one of these [show a picture], you say, cup. What are these? Say, cup. Good. But when you see two of these [show a different picture], you say, cups. What are these? Say, cups. Good.

Instructions to Teach Greeting Responses

Look at the picture here. They are eating breakfast. When it is breakfast time, you say, good morning. What do you say at breakfast time? Say, good morning. Good. And look at this picture here. They are going to bed. When it is time to go to bed, you say, good night. It is bedtime. What do you say? Say, good night. Excellent.

Instructions to Teach Correct Recall of Names to a Person with Aphasia

This is a picture of your daughter. When I ask you who this is, you say, Nina. Who is this? Say, Nina. Very good. But when I show this picture of your son, and ask who this is, you say, Tom. Who is this? Say, Tom. That was correct!

Instructions to Teach Prosodic Variations to Persons with Neurogenic Communication Disorders

Usually, depending on what we are saying, our speech may be softer or louder. Like this. [Demonstrate.] Our speech may vary in pitch as well. Sometimes we speak with lower pitch and sometimes with higher pitch. Like this. [Demonstrate.] I noticed that your speech is a bit flat. You can practice variations in loudness and pitch. I will model them for you.

Instructions in Treating Voice Disorders

Treatment targets in voice therapy include changes in vocal quality, pitch, loudness, or resonance. In all cases, first you instruct your clients about the particular target and how to achieve it. After selecting a target vocal behavior, find out how that behavior may be facilitated (see Boone et al., 2020 for voice facilitation techniques).

Instructions to Treat Vocal Hyperfunction with Altered Head Position

The position of your head while talking affects your voice. A change in the head position may improve your voice. Let us try. [Experiment with different head positions while the client produces prolonged vowels to see if a desirable change occurs.] Now it sounds like your voice improves when you flex your neck downward so that your chin almost touches your chest. Keep your head in that position and say /i/. Does your voice sound better? Good.

Instructions to Increase Oral Resonance with Greater Mouth Opening

When you talk with nearly closed mouth, your voice sounds muffled. It sounds better if you keep your mouth open while talking. Let us try. Say /a/ while you open your mouth widely. Drop your jaw and make the sound. Now close your jaw and make the same sound. Do you hear a difference? Good. Let us now practice making sounds and saying words while keeping the mouth open.

To reduce a child's *vocally abusive behaviors*, first you establish their baserate. For example, while frequently playing with toy guns, a child may produce tensed and loud phonation.

Instructions to Baserate Vocal Abuse

[*Addressing a parent*] During the next week, I would like you to chart how often your son plays with the toy guns making the loud sounds you have described to me. Also, chart how long he played each time. Record the date and the beginning and ending time of each episode. Once we know how often he engages in this behavior, we can design a plan to reduce it.

Instructions to Treat Fluency Disorders

In treating stuttering and cluttering, instructions and demonstrations play a major role. Experimentally supported treatment procedures include fluency shaping, pause-and-talk (time-out), response cost, and fluency reinforcement. Fluency shaping includes airflow management, gentle phonatory onset, and speech rate reduction through syllable stretching. Response cost and fluency reinforcement are especially effective with children. Pause-and-talk may be equally effective with older children and adults (Hegde, 2007).

Instructions to Teach Airflow Management

I would like you to breathe in a bit more air than usual. Like this. [Demonstrate a deeper than usual inhalation.] Then, immediately let a little bit of air through your mouth. Like this. [Demonstrate a slight exhalation through open mouth.] You try it. Make sure you do not hold the air in your lungs. As soon as you breathe in, breathe out a little bit of air.

Instructions to Teach Gentle Phonatory Onset

Sometimes you start your sound abruptly and harshly. Your vocal folds work too hard when you do this. You experience too much muscular tension and effort when you start sounds abruptly and harshly. Instead, you should start your sound softly, easily, and with less effort and tension. Let us practice that.

Instructions to Teach Speech Rate Reduction Through Syllable Stretching

You may have noticed that when you speak slowly, your fluency improves. Practicing a slower rate of speech is part of our treatment program. You don't want to slow down your speech by pausing between words. [Demonstrate this.] Instead, I would like you to speak slowly by stretching the syllables of words. I want you to stretch most syllables, but the first syllable of the first few words in a sentence must be stretched more than the other syllables. Like this. [Demonstrate syllable stretching.]

Instructions for Pause-and-Talk

In this procedure we call pause-and-talk, I want you to stop talking for 5 seconds when you stutter. Anytime you stutter, I am going to say "stop." You should immediately stop talking. I will be looking at my watch and after 5 seconds, I will look at you and you can then talk.

Instructions for Response Cost

In this procedure, I will give you a token for fluent speech. [Substitute *smooth speech, easy speech*, or some other term.] Every time you stutter, I will take a token back from you. You will earn a token for smooth speech and lose one for stuttering. At the end, you can exchange your tokens for this gift you have selected.

Instructions for Fluency Reinforcement

In this procedure, I will be paying close attention to your fluent [smooth] speech. Even though you stutter [have bumpy speech] you still have lots of fluent [smooth] speech. I will praise you for your fluent [smooth, easy] speech. Keep that high praise coming your way! [Add additional instructions if you also give some tangible reinforcers along with verbal praise.]

A reduced speech rate also improves the fluency and intelligibility of a speaker with cluttering. In general, instructions to persons who clutter are similar to those who stutter.

Physical Stimuli

Physical stimuli are used in treating both children and adults. Such stimuli may be pictures, objects, and demonstrated events (e.g., movements of a toy car). Physical stimuli help evoke speech sound productions in the beginning stages of teaching speech sound productions. Reluctant children may begin to talk when you show them pictures in storybooks, objects that can be manipulated, and events that can be created to arouse interest.

You should reduce or eliminate the use of physical stimuli in the final stages where you stabilize the target behaviors in conversational speech. Review an earlier section on treatment of diverse individuals for selecting appropriate treatment stimuli for them.

How to Effectively Use Physical Stimuli

1. Select pictures that are three-dimensional, colorful, and realistic; find them in popular magazines.

2. Prefer objects to pictures. Ask parents to bring the child's favorite toys and books. Ask the family members of adult clients to bring the client's preferred objects (e.g., the individual's favorite pen, mug, family photographs).

3. Use pictures in children's storybooks. Read the story to the child and ask to retell the story while looking at the pictures.

4. Fade the physical stimuli as soon as possible. Maintain verbal responses to your verbal stimuli.

Models

Models are the clinician's productions of a client's target responses. The client's reproduction of a model is **imitation**. When the client does not respond correctly with instructions and physical stimuli, model the target response. Because modeling is needed and effective in establishing new skills, it is widely used in treating both children and adults (Hegde, 1998, 2018). Modeling works across disorders. Modeling is a treatment procedure because it is the clinician's action. *Imitation* that follows modeling is *not* a treatment procedure because it is the client's response.

Technically, the modeled stimulus and the imitated response should be identical, but in initial treatment sessions, they may be slightly different, or may only be an approximation. Eventually, the client's imitation may match or come very close to the clinician's model.

Require imitated responses soon after you model. Promptly reinforce all imitated responses, or correct an approximation of your model. Require progressively better approximation and eventual correct reproduction of your model.

Modeling is most needed on discrete trial training when the skill is being established. In training target skills in conversational speech, model infrequently, if at all.

In the following sections, because of space limitation, boxed examples on how to model are not offered for every disorder and every target behavior. Instead, examples are given for four basic parameters of communication: speech, language, fluency, and voice. But if you know how to model speech sound productions, language features, fluency, and vocal characteristics, you can model for almost all disorders of communication, including aphasia, dementia, AOS, dysarthria, right hemisphere disorder, and traumatic brain injury. In treating all of these disorders, the targets are speech, language, fluency (too little or too much), and vocal characteristics.

Modeling in Treating Speech Sound Disorders

Modeling is essential to teach sounds produced in isolation or in context. Most models are live; the clinician models in front of the client. However, audio-recorded models of speech sounds provide standardized stimuli and may be just as effective as live models.

The suggestions given in the box that follows may be used in treating speech sound disorders in children and adults, including AOS and dysarthria.

How to Model Speech Sound Targets

1. Give instructions on how to produce the target sound.

2. Model the target sound production, showing the articulatory movements or positions while giving instructions (e.g., lip closure for bilabial sounds, tongue tip position for /t/).

3. Ask the client to imitate the sound you modeled. Prepare a collection of audio-recorded models and use whenever necessary.

Modeling in Treating Language Disorders

You may need to model the words, grammatical morphemes, phrases, sentences, and various conversational skills targeted for a client. A special feature of modeling language targets is that you should first ask a relevant question and then model the target (Hegde, 1998, 2018; Hegde & Maul, 2006). For example, in teaching the regular plural morpheme with the help of pictures, you should not just show the picture of two books and model "books" for the client to imitate. You should ask a question and then model the correct response. In the same example, you should ask "What do you see?" or "What are these?" and immediately model the response: "Say, books." Similarly, in teaching words, you should show a picture or an object, ask a question, and immediately model the response (e.g., "What is this? Say, cat").

How to Model Language Targets

1. Give instruction on the target response and ask the client to immediately imitate your model.

2. Show a picture or object.

3. Ask a relevant question (e.g., "What do you see?" "What is the boy doing?").

4. Model the target response immediately (e.g., "Say, I see two books;" "Say, the boy is running").

5. Fade or withdraw modeling (but not the relevant question) when the imitative response is reliably produced.

When a question precedes modeling, the correct response may be maintained later when modeling is withdrawn and only the question is asked. For example, a child who consistently imitates "books" when you say "What are these? Say, *books*" is likely to give the correct response ("books") when you stop modeling and simply ask, "What are these?" If the question did not precede modeling and was introduced only later, it may fail to evoke the response because the question is a new stimulus to which the child previously has not responded.

Modeling in Treating Voice Disorders

In treating individuals with voice disorders, the clinician may model the desired pitch, loudness, vocal quality, and resonance characteristics. In some cases, the clinician may be unable to model a desired voice characteristic. For example, an adult male clinician, typically with a low-pitched voice, may not be able to model a higher vocal pitch for a child or a woman being treated. In such cases, the voice model may be audio-recorded from another child or woman and played for the client to imitate. Also, clients themselves may provide voice models. A client with too high a pitch may produce on occasion a lower pitch with some help from the clinician. This desired pitch may be audio-recorded and used as a model for the client to imitate. With appropriate software and such instruments as Visi-Pitch, many voice characteristics may be displayed on computer monitors.

How to Model Voice Targets

1. Instruct the client in the modeling-imitation sequence.

2. Model the target vocal behavior.

3. Use recorded models when necessary.

(*continues*)

4. Audio-record the client's correct imitations.

5. Use the client's productions as models.

6. Fade and stop modeling.

Modeling in Treating Fluency Disorders

In teaching such fluency skills as management of airflow, reduced rate of speech, and gentle phonatory onset to persons who stutter, you should first model each skill separately and then in combination. For example, you may start with inhalation and a slight exhalation before saying a word or two. Therefore, model as you describe inhalation and exhalation. You then add rate reduction (prolonged speech) by describing and modeling it. Model each of the subsequent targets that were described in Chapter 7.

Note that the need to model the target responses in pause-and-talk, response cost, and fluency reinforcement is minimal. These are preferred to fluency-shaping technique.

How to Model Fluency Targets

1. Instruct the client in the modeling-imitation sequence.

2. Model each of the specific fluency skills separately, especially in the beginning stages.

3. Model a new skill when the earlier skill is correctly imitated on a few trials.

4. Model the combined skills in the sequence they are taught (e.g., airflow management and gentle phonatory onset).

5. Model the entire fluency skills in words, phrases, and sentences.

6. Fade modeling by asking the client to produce the target behavior; do not model.

Modeling in Treating Adult Speech and Language Disorders

Communication disorders in adults, especially those resulting from neurological impairments, tend to have an array of disabilities, including, speech production problems, such language deficits as naming and prosodic impairments, voice problems, limited or excessive fluency, limited conversational skills, irrelevant or rambling speech, impaired attention, poor communication despite mostly intact speech-language skills, and several other deficits.

Adults with aphasia, right hemisphere disorder, AOS, dysarthria, traumatic brain injury, and various forms of dementia need both speech and language models during treatment. Generally, modeling examples given for speech and language skills in the previous sections should work with adults with neurologically based communication disorders.

How to Model Treatment Targets in Neurologically Based Communication Disorders

1. Instruct the client in the modeling-imitation sequence.

2. Model each of the specific speech sound production skills for individuals with AOS and dysarthria as you would in treating speech sound disorders described earlier.

3. Model prosodic variations in phrases and sentences for individuals with AOS and dysarthria.

4. Model language skills (e.g., naming) for individuals with aphasia and dementia as you would for clients who have language disorders described earlier.

5. Model speech, language, attention, and other skills for clients with traumatic brain injury and right hemisphere disorder as you would for clients with speech sound and language disorders as described.

6. Fade and stop modeling.

Fade and Stop Modeling

When imitative responses are consistent (e.g., five consecutively imitated responses), ask the question, but do not model. If the response is correct (unimitated, more spontaneous), continue without modeling, so you do not overuse it. On the other hand, if the child fails to respond or responds incorrectly on two or three trials without modeling, do not continue to evoke error responses. Bring back modeling and fade it again.

To **fade** modeling, progressively withdraw parts of it while maintaining the correct response. For example, in teaching the preposition *on*, you may have asked the question "Where is the ball?" and modeled "Say the ball is on the table." Note that the modeled stimulus is a long sentence that includes other syntactic elements. A fading hierarchy for this model may look like the following. If correct response at each step is not observed, reinstate full modeling for a few trials and then begin to fade again:

- Drop the last word. "Where is the ball?" Say the ball is on the . . ." and wait for the correct response. Prompt the child to "start with the ball" because the more likely response is just "table."

- Drop another word on the next trial if the response is correct. "Say the ball is on . . ." The child should repeat the whole sentence.

- Drop one additional word on each of the subsequent trials.

- Drop modeling altogether, ask only the question "Where is the ball?"

Prompts

Prompts and models are similar in one important respect. Both are special stimuli that precede the target response. In all other respects, models and prompts are different.

A **verbal prompt is a partial stimulus**, whereas a verbal model is full-fledged. For example, when you model, you might say "Jimmy, say *the cat is jumping*;" but to prompt the same response, you might say, "Jimmy, the cat is . . ." and wait for the response. Models display the full response; prompts do not.

Nonverbal prompts are indirect stimuli; they suggest a verbal response through a nonverbal gesture. For instance, to prompt a slower rate of speech for a person who stutters, you may give a hand signal to suggest a slower rate. Some prompts may contain parts of the target response, while others may contain no part of it. For instance, your prompt "Jimmy, the cat is . . ." contains some parts of the target response. But a hand gesture to slow down the rate of speech contains no part of the target response. Actions also can work like prompts. When you teach verbs, you can demonstrate action to prompt the correct word response. For example, a hopping motion you demonstrate with your hand may prompt the word *jump*. You may prompt the correct production of a phoneme by showing the articulatory posture without saying the sound or the word.

Some prompts are a special feature of modeled responses. For example, you might place an extra vocal emphasis on the target preposition *on* when you model: Say, *the ball is **on** the table.* This vocal emphasis is a prompt within a modeled stimulus. Such an emphasis makes the target response more distinct than without the emphasis. Other ways of making a target response distinct by embedding it in a string of responses include increased vocal intensity, varied pitch, slower delivery than the rest of the words in the string, and injecting a pause just before its production.

How to Prompt Speech and Language Responses in Children and Adults

- **Start with stronger prompts and gradually make them more subtle**. Prompts should be just sufficient to evoke the desired response, not unnecessarily strong, loud, or long. Most clients find subtle prompts more acceptable than boisterous prompts. For instance, instead of lengthy verbal prompts or exaggerated nonverbal prompts, give hand gestures to prompt a slower rate of speech in a person who stutterers and a different gesture to increase the rate in a person with AOS.

- **Give your prompts promptly**. Prompt at the earliest sign of a hesitation or a wrong response.

- **Reduce the number of prompts gradually and eventually fade them**. Prompt more frequently initially and less frequently later as the client's response accuracy and speed improve. For example, make a particular hand gesture progressively smaller until it is completely faded out. A lengthy verbal prompt (e.g., "What do you say for this?") may be reduced to fewer words or word substitutions (e.g., You say . . . , This is . . .).

- **Teach the family members to prompt**. Prompts given in natural settings must be especially subtle because the clients are likely to find loud and lengthy prompts at home and other settings unpleasant or embarrassing because such clues are obvious to other persons.

Prompts, Cues, Hints, and Similar Terms

Some clinicians may wonder if *cues* that aphasiologists use are different from *prompts* that other clinicians use. There are many terms in everyday usage with the same or similar meanings.

- *Prompt, cue, gesture, hint, clue, tip, pointer, cajole, coax, sign, signal, lead, suggest, prod, allude, glimmer, glimpse,* and several other terms have similar meaning in everyday language, but not all are technical terms. They all indirectly suggest (stimulate) a correct response that is not easily forthcoming.

- **Prompts are special (contrived) stimuli**. They help evoke a clinical target response that has been learned to some extent. A totally unlearned response cannot be prompted. Prompts help fade modeling used to teach target skills to children and adults.

- **Models are different from prompts**. Modeling displays full correct response to be *imitated*. For example, "Say, *two cups*" is a *model*; the child imitates, "two cups." However, "When you see two of these, what do you say?" is a prompt. Note that modeling displayed the complete correct response but the prompt did not. Models are imitated, but prompts, except for the sentence completion variety, are not imitated.

- **Sentence completion is partial modeling and a prompt**. It does include an *element* of the target response that is imitated. For example, following a question, the clinician may prompt by saying, "This is a baa . . ." (for *ball*). The initial syllable was a prompt, and the imitated response included it.

- **Cues are prompts**. In teaching naming skills to persons with aphasia, aphasiologists describe *cueing hierarchies*. For example, following a question ("What is this?"), the clinician may say, "It starts with a *p*" (for *pen*) or "It is something you bounce" (for *ball*). Such cues are nothing but prompts. Note that like prompts, cues are not imitated. In essence, the special stimuli used to evoke mostly but not completely learned response is described as *prompts* in treating child speech-language disorders and as *cues* in treating adult neurologically based communication disorders. They are the same.

How to Prompt in Treating Speech Sound Disorders in Children and Adults

1. Prompt verbally (e.g., name the sound, "This word starts with an *es*").

2. Prompt with an emphasis on the target sound within a word.

3. Prompt with only the silent articulatory movements or fixed postures.

4. Prompt slower speech rate nonverbally (e.g., a hand gesture).

5. Fade and stop the prompts.

How to Prompt in Treating Language Disorders in Children and Adults

1. Prompt sentence completion (e.g., show two objects, and say, "These are two . . ." to evoke plural morphemes in words.

2. Prompt by asking questions (e.g., "What do you say for this?" "What do you say when someone gives you a gift?").

3. Prompt nonverbally (e.g., movements and gestures that suggest verbs and other language targets).

4. Prompt naming with the first sound of the word, use of an object ("You write with it"), what is done with an object ("You bounce it"), the personal significance of an object (e.g., "It was your 70th birthday gift"), and so forth.

5. Prompt prosodic variations by a partial model (variable intonation).

6. Prompt prosodic variables by hand gestures (e.g., higher or lower intonation).

7. Prompt the attending behavior verbally ("Look here" or "Listen carefully).

8. Prompt nonverbally to stop hyperfluent and meaningless speech (e.g., touch your sealed lips to suggest "stop talking").

9. Fade and stop the prompts.

How to Prompt in Treating Voice Disorders

1. Prompt verbally to change vocal quality (e.g., "smoother," or "softer").

2. Prompt nonverbally a higher or lower pitch (e.g., various hand gestures).

3. Prompt increased or decreased vocal intensity (e.g., hand gestures to suggest "louder" or "softer").

(continues)

4. Prompt nasal resonance (e.g., touch your nose).

5. Prompt oral resonance nonverbally (e.g., show wider mouth opening).

6. Fade and stop the prompts.

How to Prompt in Treating Fluency Disorders

1. Give prompts for each of the specific skills separately.

2. Prompt nonverbally to slow down the speech (e.g., a hand gesture to suggest slow down).

3. Prompt airflow management (e.g., touching your nose or the chest).

4. Prompt gentle phonatory onset (e.g., touching your laryngeal area).

5. Fade and stop the prompts.

How to Shape New Responses

Modeling may be ineffective, at least initially, with individuals who have severe physical disabilities and associated communicative impairments. Neurological problems may limit movement of the articulators. Children who are mostly nonverbal are unlikely to imitate verbal responses. A response that is not imitated is nonexistent in the client's repertoire. You need procedures to create new responses that do not exist.

Shaping is a technique to teach new skills through successive approximations of a model. It is a well-researched method of creating new responses from simple responses that do exist in the client's repertoire (Hegde, 1998, 2018; Vargas, 2020). In each of several successive stages of treatment, teach a simpler response that takes the client one step closer to the final, more complex target response. Each simple response the client learns is a building block of the more complex target.

Breaking a target response into its simpler components is the key to shaping it. Even the most severely involved client may make some movement that is remotely related to the target response. You then start with this movement and shape something more complex out of it by adding other components. You teach what the client can learn in each step of shaping. But you do not just evoke random responses that the client happens to produce. You teach responses that are systematically related to the final target behavior. Each new response the client masters should be a move in the right direction.

A complex skill may be simplified in several ways. Experiment with your client to find the response that can be imitated, not necessarily the simplest. If a more complex response related to the final target can be imitated, do not select a simpler response. Simplify a response only to the extent needed, not to the extent possible. Generally, the more complex the initial level, the faster the treatment progresses.

Use instructions, modeling, and manual guidance at each step of training. Reinforce imitated responses. To begin with, accept approximations of modeled responses. Subsequently, reinforce more accurate productions. Do not reinforce the initial and intermediate responses excessively. If you do, you will have difficulty moving the client to higher levels of training. You will then report to your supervisor that your client is "stuck"—your own making. Stabilize only the final target response.

Manual guidance is physical assistance in shaping a response in individuals whose movements are extremely limited. Manually, gently, but firmly make a movement happen. Immediately reinforce the client for success, even if limited. For example, a boy with a severe speech sound disorder may not move his tongue tip for an articulatory position. But the movement is possible, it is only not probable. Therefore, you may take a tongue depressor and move the tongue tip in the desired direction. A woman with aphasia may have great difficulty in moving her hand to point to a message on an electronic display, but the movement can be assisted by taking her hand and pointing to the message. When a boy with intellectual disabilities does not open his mouth to produce a vowel, you apply a downward pressure on the chin to make the jaw drop so the mouth is opened. Other examples are in the following sections.

Shaping Correct Speech Sound Production

To shape target phonemes, analyze them to identify their simpler components. Then find out if the client can perform any of the components that may be used to shape the target phoneme. For example, a boy with a severe speech sound disorder may not produce a phoneme in words. Find out if he can produce it in syllables. If not in syllables, perhaps in isolation. If not in isolation, maybe he moves the tongue tip in the right direction. If not, can he open his mouth? If not, can you make him open his mouth with manual guidance? Can you make his tongue or lips move with manual guidance? Investigate these and other similar possibilities to shape responses.

Any possible movement related to the final target (e.g., movement of tongue or lips, with or without manual guidance) is the **initial shaping response**. The production of the phoneme (in syllables or words) is the **terminal shaping response**. All other responses help bridge the gap between the initial and final response are the **intermediate shaping responses**.

It may be difficult to be specific about intermediate responses, as individuals vary greatly. Some need more intermediate responses than others. Your observations during shaping may suggest new intermediate responses. You should have a general idea of at least some intermediate responses.

How to Shape Correct Speech Sound Production

1. Define the final or the terminal target sound or syllable production.

2. Find the initial response the client can perform that is related to the terminal response.

3. Specify intermediate responses that should be shaped.

4. Shape the simplest response first by modeling and manual guidance if necessary.

5. Add intermediate responses in successive stages as the earlier responses are learned.

6. Continue to shape until the final target sound or syllable production is achieved.

Shaping Basic Language Skills

Children who are nonverbal or minimally verbal and those with severe movement problems need shaping. Syllables or simple single-word utterances are the most likely initial targets for these children. The need for shaping is the greatest in this initial stage of establishing a set of basic words. It will also be the most difficult.

In teaching word productions to children who are minimally verbal and thus do not imitate words or syllables, first you should find an articulatory movement that can be made. For example, a girl who is nonverbal may open her mouth with manual guidance of gentle, downward pressure exerted on her chin. Next, as the mouth opens, you may ask her to expel some air through the mouth. Model this and give some manual assistance; a slight push on the abdomen as the mouth opens will result in some audible expulsion of air. This audible airflow may be a basis to shape an /h/. In the successive stages, you can shape the articulatory movement for /l/ and /o/. Gradually shape these responses into a *hello*.

How to Shape Basic Language Skills

1. Define the final or the terminal language response (such as the production of a word).

2. Find a simple response that the client can perform and that is related to the final target sound or syllable production.

3. Specify intermediate responses that should be shaped.

4. Shape the simplest response first by modeling and imitation.

5. Add intermediate responses.

6. Model all intermediate responses.

7. Add additional language elements to shape phrases and sentences.

8. Reinforce all approximate productions.

Shaping Voice Characteristics

Shaping is a primary technique of voice therapy, and for the same reason: some individuals may not imitate modeled vocal behaviors. In effecting changes in fundamental frequency (pitch), vocal intensity (loudness), oral or nasal resonance, hard glottal attacks, hoarseness, and harshness, you may have to use shaping in the initial stages of treatment.

In voice therapy, manual guidance is *digital manipulation* in which you apply a slight finger pressure on the thyroid cartilage as the client produces a prolonged vowel. The pressure lowers the pitch (Boone et al., 2020; Sapienza & Hoffman, 2022). The digital pressure pushes the thyroid in the backward direction, increases the mass of the vocal folds, and lowers the pitch. Once the client achieves a lower pitch on a vowel, shape the pitch in producing words and phrases. Have the individual practice the shaped pitch in successively longer utterances until it is sustained in conversational speech.

Manual guidance also helps experiment with different head positions that might facilitate a more normal sounding voice. You might manually help the client change the head position to change a certain characteristic of voice. With manual guidance, the person may keep the head straight, tilt it toward the left or right side, or flex the neck in a downward direction to change vocal characteristics.

Do not overuse manual guidance. A male speaker may lower his pitch on a syllable or a single word with instructions and modeling. You reinforce even a slight reduction. In subsequent steps, reinforce speaking with progressively lower pitch on increasingly longer utterances. Continue the process until the most desirable pitch is established in sentences and conversational speech. A sequence similar to this may be effective in shaping other voice targets.

In shaping various target voice characteristics, you might use computerized mechanical devices that give automatic feedback to the client. For example, you may use the Visi-Pitch IV by Kay Elemetrics Corp. or the Computerized Speech Lab from KayPENTAX to modify a variety of voice qualities. In addition, the Nasometer II by KayPENTAX helps modify unwanted nasal resonance. These and other devices work on the principle of shaping. In each successive step of treatment, the client achieves a progressively higher or lower pitch, decreased or increased nasal resonance, and so forth (Boone et al., 2020; Hegde & Pomaville, 2017; Sapienza & Hoffman, 2022).

How to Shape Voice Characteristics

1. Define the final or the terminal voice quality or characteristic (such as a specified vocal pitch or loudness).

2. Select a simple response level at which the desired vocal target may be imitated (such as in producing a sound, syllable, or word).

3. Specify intermediate responses that may be shaped (words, phrases, sentences).

4. Reinforce the simplest response first.

5. Add intermediate responses.

6. Model and reinforce all intermediate response productions, including approximations.

7. Shape the desired vocal target in conversational speech.

Shaping Fluency

Shaping is a part of the *fluency-shaping technique*. As noted before, shaping is not needed in pause-and-talk, response cost, or fluency reinforcement because no particular skills are taught. You teach skills of fluent speech in sequenced steps only in the fluency-shaping procedure. Management of airflow, gentle phonatory onset, and reduced rate of speech are all interrelated, but shape one skill at a time. Then you put them together and have the client practice the skills starting at the single two-word level. As the client maintains fluency, you introduce more complex responses until the client practices fluent speech in conversation outside the clinic.

You may start with inhalation and slight exhalation before phonatory onset. Let the client practice this skill without phonation. Then add gentle phonatory onset. Ask the client to produce a syllable or a word. When the airflow management and gentle onset are established, add speech rate reduction by syllable stretching. Target single words at this stage. Before saying the word, teach the client to inhale, exhale slightly, achieve smooth onset, and speak with prolonged syllables. Teach the client to especially stretch the initial syllables and vowels.

When single-word utterances are free from stuttering, ask the client to produce two-word phrases. Monitor all the skills taught so far. When the phrases are stutter-free, have the client practice fluency skills in sentences and conversational speech.

Slowing down the speech through syllable stretching induces monotonous speech that is unacceptable in the natural environment, hence unlikely to be maintained. To strengthen fluency at a near-normal rate of speech, fade the excessively slow speech and shape normal prosodic features.

You may ask the person to slightly increase the rate, ensuring that fluency is maintained while shaping normal prosody. Increase the speech rate in carefully planned steps while maintaining fluent speech. Typically, increased speech rate brings back normal prosodic features. If necessary, you may shape intonation (pitch variations) and typical vocal loudness because excessively slow speech tends to be too soft.

How to Shape Fluency Skills

1. Define the final or the terminal target level of fluency behavior (such as less than 5% dysfluency in conversational speech).

2. Select a simple response level at which the client can practice the skills of fluency (words or phrases).

3. Select the first fluency skill to be shaped (airflow management).

4. Shape the skill at the simplest response level.

5. Specify intermediate skills that should be shaped (slower speech, gentle phonatory onset, maintenance of airflow throughout an utterance).

6. Shape the intermediate skills by modeling and positive reinforcement.

7. Shape the skills of fluency in conversational speech.

How to Increase the Frequency of Target Responses

No teaching is possible without proper feedback on the correctness or incorrectness of responses. All behaviors are learned, maintained, or diminished by their consequences (Vargas, 2020; Walker & Barry, 2022). The author once had a student clinician who objected to reinforce or give corrective feedback to her clients, saying that it is bribing, against her personal beliefs. I let her conduct a single session to teach speech sounds to a 6-year-old girl with no consequences for responses. The student modeled the correct productions. The girl responded correctly or incorrectly but did not receive any feedback. After about 10 to 15 trials, the obviously frustrated girl client said, "If you don't tell me when I'm doing it right and when I'm not, then I can't learn anything here." She was ready to walk out. Nothing would have taught the clinician better. I went in and modeled verbal praise and corrective feedback.

In this section, you will learn about procedures to increase the frequency of new responses or those at low natural frequency. In the next section, you will learn about procedures to strengthen and sustain responses.

Positive Reinforcement

Typically, what the listener does when a speaker says something is the consequence for the speaker's speech. One person (a speaker) may say "Hi!" and the other (listener) may either say "Hi!" or ignore the speaker. A baby might say "Mommy!" and the mother may pick up the child. Therefore, in everyday conversations, one person's speech is followed by another person's speech or nonspeech behavior. These listener behaviors are the consequences of speech, and they will determine if the speaker says the same thing next time.

In treatment, especially in the initial stages, the communicative behaviors and what follow them are not as naturalistic as they typically are. The communicative behaviors may be either absent or not effective—that is why the client is seeking help from the clinician. A child who is nonverbal, a woman with aphasia, a man with a laryngectomy, and a person who stutters all need to do something different in their attempts at communication. Therefore, clinicians set up target behaviors for them and arrange consequences, often unnatural (contrived).

There are two kinds of consequences. One kind, when it follows a response, makes the response more likely under similar circumstances. The other kind makes the response less likely in the future. Consequences that decrease undesirable behaviors are described in Chapter 9.

Those consequences that follow a response and increase its frequency are called **positive reinforcers**. The *procedure* of increasing responses by making positive reinforcers follow them is called **positive reinforcement**. To increase the frequency of new target responses, you must reinforce them positively.

Because no event will reinforce a response all the time, you should constantly evaluate the effects of any applied consequence to see if it continues to reinforce, keeping in perspective that *to reinforce always means to increase a skill*. Initially, you should select a potential reinforcer, arrange it as an immediate consequence for a response, and count the number of responses. If the response frequency increases, then you call that consequence a reinforcer. If the frequency did not increase, your potential reinforcer was not an actual reinforcer for that client on that occasion. Note that reinforcers always are defined *after* they are demonstrated to increase the frequency of a response. There are no a priori (before the fact) reinforcers.

There are many types of potential positive reinforcers (Hegde, 1998, 2018; Vargas, 2020; Walker & Barry, 2022). Most of them will work with clients on certain occasions. However, what worked with a client during one treatment session may not work in another session. One client's reinforcer may not be another client's. Some consequences are more powerful than others. No consequence will work with every client every time.

Primary Reinforcers

Events that increase a response frequency because of their biological (survival) value are called **primary reinforcers**. Potential primary reinforcers include food and drink, whose survival value is obvious.

In some cases, a response followed by food may be learned faster. It is often pointed out that food is an unnatural reinforcer for communicative behaviors. When a little girl correctly names the family dog the first time, no one puts some applesauce in her mouth. However, some communicative behaviors are reinforced *only with primary reinforcers*; no other type of reinforcer will do. When you walk into a fast-food place and ask for a hamburger, the person there cannot praise you for your good speech and send you out. Therefore, it is not correct to say that speech and language behaviors are never primarily reinforced. It is correct to say that some speech and language behaviors are reinforced *primarily* and *most* are reinforced *socially*. Typically, socially reinforced speech and language skills may be clinically reinforced with primary reinforcers, but those that are naturally reinforced with primary reinforcers cannot be reinforced socially.

During treatment, clinicians use primary reinforcers for clinical reasons, not because they are natural. Food and drink need to be used when other, more natural events do not have an effect.

How to Use Primary Reinforcers

1. Use food and drink to reinforce responses that are requests for food and drink (called *mands* in behavior analysis).

2. For responses that are naturally reinforced socially, use food only when social reinforcers (e.g., approval, smile, verbal praise) do not work. Expect to use them with infants, persons who are nearly nonverbal, individuals with severe autistic spectrum disorder, and those with intellectual disability.

3. Use primary reinforcers only with parental or guardian permission. Select primary reinforcers only after discussing them with the client and the family members. Consider their objections or recommendations about the kinds of food to use. Select healthy

food items. Avoid foods that are not recommended for medical reasons.

4. Ask parents to withhold the reinforcers before the session. But stay within limits and do not overly deprive the client. Better yet, arrange treatment sessions around snack time or lunch time so that the infant or child is motivated for your primary reinforcer.

5. Pair primary reinforcers with social reinforcers. For instance, praise a child for the correct response as you offer a sip of juice.

6. Fade the primary reinforcer eventually and keep only the social reinforcers.

Social Reinforcers

Reinforcing effects of some events depend on past experiences. These events reinforce because of their association with other kinds of reinforcers. Events that reinforce because of past experiences are called **social**, or **conditioned**, **reinforcers**.

In everyday communication, social responses of listeners are the typical reinforcers. Attention to a speaker, a smile, a nod, a touch, a pat on the shoulder, verbal approval (e.g., "I agree," "I like your viewpoint"), verbal praise (e.g., "you put it nicely"), and other kinds of verbal and nonverbal responses from the listener can be potential reinforcers during conversations. Therefore, they are preferable in treatment sessions. Even when you use primary reinforcers, also use social reinforcers to eventually fade out the former. This means that social reinforcers are used in all stages of treatment.

How to Use Social Reinforcers

1. Use smile and touch along with primary reinforcers, especially with infants and clients with intellectual disabilities. (Always request permission to touch.) Add praise and other verbal stimuli as they seem to gain reinforcing value for the client.

2. Use social reinforcers naturally. When you say, "Good boy!" or "Excellent job!" or "I like that!," smile and show proper

(continues)

emotional expressions that go with such statements. You should sound and look happy when a correct response is produced. Use appropriate patterns of intonation so you do not sound like a robot when praising the client.

3. Maintain the social reinforcers as you fade the primary reinforcers.

Conditioned Generalized Reinforcers

Conditioned generalized reinforcers have a more pervasive effect on behavior because they give access to other reinforcers; they are not effective by themselves. For example, a token, which is a conditioned generalized reinforcer, may be effective because it can be exchanged for a variety of other reinforcers. A token is not just a token. It can be a key to anything else you might offer your clients because it can be exchanged for many other reinforcers; therefore, it may be effective on most occasions. But verbal praise is only verbal praise. On a given occasion, it is either effective or it is not.

You can use plastic chips for tokens that may be exchanged for other reinforcers the child chooses in a session. Similarly, check marks entered in a booklet or stars and stickers pasted on a sheet of paper, points accumulated, marbles given, and coins earned may be exchanged for chosen reinforcers. You can use anything as a token, provided it is dispensed easily for correct responses and exchanged later for a reinforcer. To be effective, you should always have backup reinforcers. If you cannot afford to do that, do not use tokens. A clinician who is simply giving tokens or stickers that are not exchanged for a "real" reinforcer is not using conditioned generalized reinforcers.

Tokens are the most flexible of the reinforcers. In case of a child who does not respond to verbal praise for example, you can offer an opportunity to play if a certain number of tokens are earned. If this does not work, you can offer to read a brief story for the tokens accumulated. You may offer still other choices for the child: a small toy, a piece of gum, or an inexpensive gift. But tokens may be exchanged for reinforcers that cost little or nothing: a walk through the clinic or the campus with you, a visit to the campus bookstore or library, or a chance to draw on the blackboard.

Backup Reinforcers for Diverse Individuals

Because the backups are a collection of potential reinforcers, their selection should consider the child and the family in all cases, but even more importantly if the child is of diverse background and is relatively new in the country. What reinforces children in general may or may not reinforce a child from an ethnoculturally diverse family.

To build a collection of backup reinforcers, interview the parents, siblings, and other caretakers. Shorter activities the child enjoys that can be parceled out in the treatment sessions and longer activities they can administer at home for a larger collection of tokens are excellent choices.

How to Use Conditioned Generalized Reinforcers

1. Consider the cost of a backup reinforcement system before you design a token system. Your clinic may not have any funds to purchase backup reinforcers. Do not promise a child that the parents will back up your tokens unless the parents previously have agreed to it and supply you the backups before the treatment sessions; tokens should be exchanged for a backup reinforcer at the end of each session; not later at home.

2. Maintain a supply of backup tangible reinforcers or backup activities.

3. Ask the child to choose the backup reinforcer at the beginning of the session.

4. Tell the child how many tokens are needed to receive the backup reinforcer.

5. Set a realistic number of tokens so that the child will have enough of them to get the chosen backup reinforcer. If not, all the correct responses given in the session may be technically unreinforced. Therefore, set a number the child is likely to achieve.

6. Immediately reinforce each correct response with a token.

7. Use various activities that do not cost anything as backup reinforcers. Such activities as reading a story aloud to the child, working on a puzzle, listening to music, working on an art project, or having a brief opportunity to play outside may be just as effective.

Feedback on Performance

Both adults and children wish to know how well they are doing in therapy. When that information is systematically given to them, their performance tends to improve. Such **informative feedback** given to persons about how they have been doing may reinforce target responses.

Feedback became a powerful tool in changing behavior with the invention of mechanical feedback devices. These devices are especially helpful in giving information about neurophysiological activities that cannot be readily observed. For example, without the help of a mechanical device, you cannot give feedback to a person about the electrical activity of muscles. Such information given back to a person about his or her neurophysiological activities through a mechanical device is called **biofeedback**.

Biofeedback is used in treating stuttering and voice disorders. Several mechanical devices are available to monitor phonatory onset, continuous phonation, and muscle tension. Several kinds of electronic units help reduce the rate of speech in those who stutter by giving delayed auditory feedback (DAF) of their speech. Newer instruments give feedback on phonatory onset and airflow management. Electromyographic instruments help reduce a speaker's muscle tension. As noted before, biofeedback has been successful especially in treating voice disorders.

Increased use of computers in treatment has made mechanical feedback more common in therapy. Yet, feedback given to clients in treatment need not be mechanical. You may tell a man who stutters that his dysfluency in the previous 5 min of conversation in the current session was 15% compared with 17% in the previous session. You may inform a woman that her hoarseness has been reduced some 50% over the past three sessions. A boy in speech sound teaching session may learn that his correct production of /s/ has increased from 30% to 90%. Such information about performance levels is feedback, and when used systematically, it can increase the frequency of responses.

How to Use Feedback to Increase Target Skills

1. Give informational feedback in a comparative manner. Say where the client was and how close the performance is to reaching the final target or some intermediate criterion of performance.

2. Show progress graphically that most clients, including children, can appreciate. Use colors whenever practical. If available, use computers that provide colorful displays on progress and movement toward the target.

3. Give feedback throughout the session so you can make it contingent on responses.

4. Combine mechanical feedback with verbal praise.

5. Give positive feedback on performance. Any negative feedback given should be minimal; too much of it suggests that the client is making little or no progress. Something is not working right. Perhaps you should change the treatment procedure or further simplify the target response.

High-Probability Behaviors

An interesting fact about behavior is that one action of a person can reinforce (increase) another action of the same person. A behavior that reinforces another behavior is of *high probability*, exhibited frequently. The behavior that is reinforced (increased) is of *low probability*, of lower infrequency. The unique aspect of **high-probability behaviors** as reinforcers is that both the reinforcer and the reinforced are the behaviors of the same person.

In using this procedure, the clinician does not give anything except an opportunity to perform that highly desired behavior. But that opportunity is given only when the client performs what he or she is not likely to perform. Thus, the clinician increases the frequency of an unlikely behavior. Everyday examples abound (e.g., *eat your veggies before you touch that meat; first finish your homework and then watch TV; I will go to the movies only after I finish my term paper; you can have a beer if you mow the lawn*).

The goal of treatment is to increase the communicative behaviors of low frequency. To do this, first you must find a behavior that the client exhibits frequently. Does the client frequently paint, sing, read, listen to music, ski, go to movies, watch TV, use a tablet, or talk to friends on the phone? Can any of these actions be used to reinforce target communicative behaviors under treatment?

Some high-probability activities can be allowed in the treatment session itself. For instance, every time the child gives a certain number of correct responses (e.g., earns 20 tokens), you may allow the child to complete a part of a larger puzzle in exchange for the tokens. Opportunities to draw or paint and play with a favorite toy for a brief duration are among other high-probability activities that can reinforce target responses in the clinic.

Opportunities for other high-probability behaviors cannot be provided in the clinic. The child or an adult client cannot ski or see a movie in the treatment room. Often, these are the behaviors of highest probability with the greatest reinforcement potential. These behaviors may occur days or weeks after the treatment sessions in which the target responses are produced. High-probability behaviors in such cases are at best delayed reinforcers.

To bridge the gap between the eventual high-probability behavior and the target responses, use a token system. Reinforce each correct response with a token. Require a certain number of tokens to engage in that cherished behavior. In case of children, you should have the approval of parents who will make such opportunities available. For example, the parents of an adolescent boy receiving language treatment may take him to a ski resort after accumulating a certain number of tokens in the treatment sessions. In the case of adults, you should have some system to verify the client's compliance with the arrangement. Perhaps a spouse or a friend may help monitor access to the high-probability behavior. Unauthorized access to high-probability behaviors will make them ineffective reinforcers. You do not have a reinforcer if the client gets to ski every weekend regardless of the number of tokens earned in treatment.

Instructions, modeling, shaping, and reinforcing consequences discussed so far help you create new responses and increase the frequency of new and existing responses. But to strengthen and sustain those responses, you need to use reinforcers in certain ways. Those procedures are discussed next.

How to Strengthen and Sustain Target Behaviors

To promote maintenance of target responses, use reinforcers differently in different stages of treatment. A pattern of reinforcement arranged for a pattern of responses is called a **schedule of reinforcement** (Hegde, 2018). One kind of schedule must be used to create and increase responses and another kind to strengthen and make them last.

In the early stage of treatment, when you teach new responses or increase the frequency of existing response, you use a **continuous schedule**, in which you reinforce every response. This schedule is good to establish target skills but not for sustaining them. After dismissal, the client may not maintain the target responses because of infrequent reinforcement or lack of it in the natural environment.

A paradoxical effect of reinforcement is that intermittently reinforced responses are stronger than those that are reinforced continuously. On an **intermittent schedule**, some responses are reinforced, and others are not. There are many patterns of reinforcement and nonreinforcement, resulting in several intermittent schedules.

In a **fixed-ratio schedule**, a response is reinforced after a fixed number of unreinforced responses have been made. A fixed ratio of 10, abbreviated FR10, means that you reinforce every tenth response. This schedule creates a pattern of nine unreinforced responses and a 10th reinforced response. Obviously, an FR1 means that every correct response is reinforced.

A fixed-ratio schedule is easy to arrange and is used frequently in clinical and educational work. You should gradually stretch the ratio. For example, you may initially reinforce a child continuously for naming a set of pictured stimuli. When the child's correct responses increase substantially, say from 10% at the baseline to more than 50%, you may shift to an intermittent schedule. Your first intermittent schedule may be an FR2 (reinforce every second response). When the responses increase further, you may switch the schedule again, perhaps to an FR5. A fixed ratio allows you to progressively reduce the amount of reinforcement given for correct responses.

In a **variable-ratio (VR) schedule**, the number of responses required before giving a reinforcer varies around an average. Compared with a fixed ratio of 5, in which every fifth response is reinforced, in a variable ratio of 5 (VR5), an average of five responses are required before a reinforcer is given. Because the schedule is based on an average, the actual number of responses required on any given occasion will vary. You may reinforce the seventh response on one occasion and the third on the next. The variable ratio is not a random method of reinforcement; the ratio is determined beforehand, and reinforcers are given so as to conform to an average number of unreinforced responses.

A variable ratio produces strong responses that can withstand lack of reinforcement for an extended time. Use this schedule in the later stages of treatment, especially when you monitor the target behaviors in conversational speech. It might be an *informal* (not precisely calculated) variable schedule, but that should be fine. The schedule is also more natural than continuous reinforcement. In typical interactions, listeners do not respond reinforcingly for every response or every *nth* response.

How to Effectively Use Reinforcement Schedules to Strengthen Target Behaviors

1. Begin with continuous reinforcement. During response shaping and modeling, reinforce every correct response.

2. Switch to a fixed-ratio schedule when non-imitated (spontaneous) responses increase over baselines.

3. Start with a small ratio, perhaps an FR2.

4. Increase the ratio in small steps as the correct response continue to increase.

5. Use a large ratio during conversational speech (e.g., an FR5 or higher)

6. Lower the schedule (increase reinforcement) if a switch to a thinner schedule causes a decline in the correct responses.

Number of Target Behaviors to Be Trained in a Session

You may wonder whether you should teach only one or several target behaviors in a single session. Much depends on the disorder and its severity, the rate of learning, age, education, general health condition, associated disabilities, and other client characteristics. But equally important are the clinician's expertise, efficacy of the treatment procedure, the frequency and duration of sessions, and whether the client is treated individually or in a group.

Follow your supervisor's recommendations on the number of target behaviors to train in a session. Consider also the following recommendations; if they do not work, analyze the data to find out what went wrong:

- Initiate training on three to five phonemes in syllables or words in a session with a child or adult client (speech sound disorders, childhood and adult AOS, developmental or adult dysarthria, cerebral palsy). Scale back if necessary.

- Train two to four grammatical morphemes, syntactic structures, and other language features while working with a child who has language disorders or individuals with agrammatic aphasia.

- If you selected the fluency-shaping procedure for a person who stutters, instruct and model all the basic skills of fluency (e.g., airflow management, syllable prolongation, and gentle phonatory onset) in the first full session of treatment. In a 45-min session, you should instruct and initiate practice on all of them. In most cases, you can move from the single-word level to two-word phrases or even to short sentences in one or two sessions.

- Instruct and model the target behaviors and initiate training on voice targets in the first treatment session. Demonstrate the selected feedback instrument and start training the client on it. You may move from words to phrases and sentences in the first session or two.

- Experiment with two to four target behaviors while treating clients with neurologically based communication disorders. The rate of learning in these clients depends on their general health status.

Target Behaviors Versus Target Responses

To understand how to sequence treatment and move the client through the sequence, it is necessary to make a distinction between a *target behavior* and *target responses*. A **target behavior** is a global and conceptual skill. *Correct production of phoneme /s/, correct naming of common objects,* and *production of the regular plural morphemes* are descriptions of target behaviors. The treatment goal statements you write specify global and conceptual speech-language skills. **Target responses** are concrete exemplars of a target behavior. *Soup, sock,* and *see* are concrete and individual responses (exemplars) of the target behavior you might describe as the *correct production of /s/.* To teach a target behavior, you teach its multiple exemplars. Practice writing target behavior descriptions and corresponding response exemplars.

Recall that you use some 20 words in teaching a phoneme, a grammatical morpheme, or the naming skill. Each of those 20 words (phrase, sentences) is an exemplar of the target behavior. The production of each word (phrase or sentences) that contains the target phoneme, grammatical morpheme, or a specific name is a target response or an exemplar; the correct production of the phoneme, the morpheme, or names in varied contexts and in conversational speech is the target behavior.

An exemplar is a specific response that exemplifies a target behavior. A target behavior is a group or class of exemplars (responses). The word *soup* is an exemplar of /s/ (or another phoneme in it). The word *walking* is an exemplar of the present progressive. The word *pen* is an exemplar of naming. By teaching multiple exemplars, you teach the target behavior. By mastering multiple exemplars, a client masters a target behavior.

How to Sequence Treatment

Treatment requires a series of sequenced steps. As you move through the treatment sequence, you will be making multiple decisions, because there are choices. You follow certain guidelines in structuring the initial, the intermediate, and the final stage of treatment. New target behaviors may be introduced in a certain order, response complexity will increase, reinforcement will become less dense and more natural, frequency of modeling will decrease, the structure of treatment sessions will loosen up, the learning criteria may change, and generalization and maintenance procedures may be introduced.

You may follow the guidelines offered in this section to structure the treatment sessions and move the client through the various stages and sequences. Because individuals differ greatly in their response to treatment, base all clinical decisions on your client's performance data.

Criteria for Advancing Treatment Through the Sequence

A systematic increase in a client's target responses tells you the treatment is working. As this happens, you begin to make important clinical decisions. You move from one stage of treatment to the next, from the simpler to the more complex skill levels, and from more to less dense reinforcement.

Each movement is progress as well as a juncture that requires a clinical decision. A wrong decision made at a juncture might retard the client's progress. The client's performance data help you answer the following questions so as to move treatment from one stage to the next:

- When do I stop modeling and when do I reinstate it?
- When is a *target response* tentatively trained?
- When is a *target behavior* tentatively trained?
- When and how do I administer the probe trials?
- When and how do I increase response complexity?
- What do I do when the probe criterion is not met?
- When is a target behavior fully trained?

The following guidelines help you answer those questions and make clinical decisions at each juncture of training sequence.

When to Stop or Reinstate Modeling

1. Stop modeling when the client imitates the initial target response on at least five consecutive trials.

2. Reinstate modeling when you observe incorrect responses on three to four trials with no modeling. Again, stop modeling after five correctly imitated responses. If you have to stop and reinstate modeling repeatedly, continue modeling until the client gives 10 or more correctly imitated responses and then stop modeling.

When Is a Target Response Tentatively Trained?

A target response is a single exemplar. It is tentatively trained when the client gives at least 10 consecutively correct, non-imitated responses; it only means that a particular exemplar is mastered. For example, while teaching a child the present progressive *ing* in words, 10 correct responses in a row on an exemplar such as *walking*, would suggest that the exemplar response (not the target behavior) has been tentatively learned. A clinician's tentative criterion may be higher (15 or 20 correct responses), but fewer than 10 is a weak criterion. These criteria are *tentative* because there is still much work to be done. The client at that point has not mastered the target behavior you described as *mastery of the present progressive ing*. Also, you need to teach the feature in phrases, sentences, and conversational speech.

Extend this logic to (1) a child under speech sound training, (2) an adult with AOS whose speech production skills are being worked on, (3) a man under voice therapy who is being trained to say individual words without nasal resonance, (4) a woman with aphasia who is receiving treatment for naming problems, and (5) a man with dysarthria being treated for speech intelligibility.

When Is a Target Behavior Tentatively Trained?

A target behavior is tentatively trained when the client meets a tentative probe criterion of at least 90% correct responses on probe items.

The tentative training criterion for a target behavior is based on an external procedure. That is, you cannot decide that a behavior (e.g., the /s/, the present progressive, oral resonance, normal voice quality, naming) is tentatively trained because the responses on selected training exemplars have been correct. To consider a target behavior tentatively trained, the trained exemplars should generalize to untrained exemplars. To assess generalization, you conduct a *probe*.

When and How are Probes Administered?

A **probe** is a measure of generalized production of a target behavior. Behaviors that generalize do not need additional training at the level of training just completed. For example, a phoneme trained in a few exemplar words may be correctly produced in other, *untrained* words. A grammatical morpheme trained in a few sentences may be produced in other, *untrained* and varied sentences. A person with aphasia who has learned to name a few objects may name other untrained objects. A person with traumatic brain injury may produce typical prosodic features when trained on a set of everyday sentences. To conclude that a behavior is tentatively trained, you must document this *generalized production* by administering probes.

There are two kinds of probes. The first kind, called the **intermixed probe**, is administered when four to six exemplars have met the tentative training criterion (10 consecutively correct responses on a block of trials). Intermixed probes are so called because both trained and untrained items are administered on alternating trials. Assume that you have baserated the production of /s/ in 20 words and have trained six of those 20 to the training criterion of 10 consecutively correct responses each; you then administer an intermixed probe with six trained words and 14 untrained words presented on alternating trials:

1. On the first probe trial, present the first trained word, ask the question used during training, but *do not* model, but *do offer* reinforcers or verbal correction as done during training; record the response.

2. On the second trial, present one of the 14 untrained words; ask the question; *do not* model and *do not* offer reinforcers or verbal correction; record the response.

3. On the third trial, present a second trained word and do the same as on trial 1.

4. On the fourth trial, present an untrained word and do the same as on trial 2.

5. Reuse the trained words until all the 14 untrained words have been alternated with them.

6. Count only the correct responses given to the probe stimuli to calculate the correct probe (generalized) response rate. For instance, if the client gave seven correct responses out of the 14 untrained stimuli presented, the probe (generalized) response is 50% correct. If this is at least 90%, you may assume that the *target behavior* (not just an exemplar) has been tentatively trained.

Correctly generalized responses on probe stimuli show that the new learning may be sustained without modeling and contrived reinforcement and verbal correction. Because this probe is done relatively early in the training program, alternating trained stimuli and reinforcing responses to them will help mitigate the danger of extinguishing the trained responses.

Please see Appendix 8-E for an Intermixed Probe Recording Sheet (Example). Modify it to suit the target responses and probe stimuli.

You may also probe through brief speech samples to document generalization to a more naturalistic speech. Audio-record a brief conversational speech sample, making sure that at least 20 opportunities were available for producing the target behavior. Count the number of correctly produced responses to calculate the percentage of correct probe responses for the conversational speech to see if it meets the criterion. Use the same probe criterion at the level of words, phrases, or sentences.

You can use the same procedure to probe various language targets. For clients who stutter or for those who have voice problems, probes should be conducted at the level of response topography on which the training was just completed (phrases, sentences, conversational speech). Calculate the percentage of probe responses (e.g., percentage of dysfluency or the percentage of utterances without hoarseness) and compare them against the percentages recorded during baserate sessions.

The second kind of probe you administer is called the pure probe. When a client meets the 90% or better correct intermixed probe criterion, administer a **pure probe** on which you present only the untrained items (hence the name, *pure probe*). See Appendix 8-F for Pure Probe Recording Sheet (Example) that you can modify to suit the target responses. Responses given on pure probes are a better measure of generalization of treated targets.

What to Do When a Probe Criterion Is Not Met

Provide additional training using new exemplars when clients fail to meet a probe criterion. A probe criterion may be failed at any level of training (words, phrases, sentences). If so, give additional training at the failed level. For example, if the child fails the tentative probe criterion at the word level of phoneme /s/ training, train the same phoneme in untrained word exemplars.

Teach two to four new exemplars before you probe again. In some cases, a few additional training trials on all of the trained exemplars may be sufficient to have the client meet the probe criterion, especially when the percentage of probe responses are close to the 90% criterion (say, 85%). Give additional training on new exemplars or additional trials on already-trained exemplars after an intermixes probe or a pure probe that shows fewer than 90% generalized responses.

When Is a Target Behavior Fully Trained?

A **target behavior** is fully trained when its production in conversational speech in natural settings is acceptable. This is an ideal criterion most clinicians may neither meet nor measure for. But all clinicians, including student clinicians, should strive to meet this criterion. It is the most meaningful criterion for people who receive SLP services.

Different criteria may apply to different communicative behaviors, however. Phonemes and language structures may be considered finally trained when they are produced in conversational speech at a minimum of 90% accuracy. On the other hand, fluency is trained when the client's dysfluencies in conversational speech in extra-clinical situations do not exceed 3% or 4%. Generally, 90% fluency is too low, as most people who stutter do so only on 10% of the words they speak. A probe criterion of 98% or better fluency is desirable. Normal voice characteristics are trained when they are sustained in at least 90% or 95% of utterances or of speaking time. You dismiss the client from services only when the communicative behaviors are produced under natural conditions at some defined mastery level.

The criteria described have worked in clinical research. Use them as guidelines but do not be too rigid. Clients' performance data determine criteria. Each client's response frequency you record in treatment sessions are your data. They are your ultimate guiding principles.

The final goal of treatment is generalization of clinically established skills across natural settings and their maintenance over time. See Chapter 10 for strategies to promote generalization and maintenance.

How to Increase Response Complexity

All target behaviors are on a hierarchy of complexity. Words, phrases, isolated sentences, connected sentences, and continuous (conversational) speech are the typical levels of complexity. Initial treatment for speech sounds and language features across diagnostic categories (e.g., speech sound disorders, language disorders, AOS, dysarthria, aphasia, traumatic brain injury) typically start at the word level. Fluency and voice characteristics may be started at the phrase or sentence levels.

Follow a simple rule in moving the client through the hierarchy of response complexity:

- Move to a higher level of response complexity when a 90% correct probe response at a lower level is met. Apply this guideline and shift training from:

  - Words to phrases

  - Phrases to controlled sentences (modeled, shorter)

  - Controlled to more spontaneous sentences

  - Conversational speech (connected sentences) in the clinic

  - Conversational speech outside the clinic

Recording the frequency of specific conversational skills in baserate, treatment, and probe conditions involves some judgment, as noted before. You may use the form given in Appendix 8-G to quantitatively summarize the most frequently taught conversational skills.

Note that when you teach multiple target skills (e.g., speech sounds or grammatical morphemes) in each session, different targets may reach the probe criterion at different times. For instance, after baserating several grammatical morphemes, you may have started training on four of them: plural /s/, plural /z/, possessive /s/, and possessive /z/. Of these four, plural /s/, as an example, may first reaches the probe criterion. You have then two choices:

- Shift training on plural /s/ to phrase or sentence (e.g., *two cups, I see two cups*)

- Add a new morpheme (e.g., *walked*, past tense /ed/); assuming it was baserated

Design a similar or modified sequence to train language features, fluency, and voice characteristics. End treatment for a client only when a maintenance program, as described in Chapter 10, is completed.

⑦ Questions for Self-Assessment

1. Distinguish between a target behavior and a target response. State precisely the relation between the two. Give examples from speech sound production and language features.

2. What are the essential (elemental) treatment procedures that apply across disorders? Succinctly summarize the procedures.

3. Complete the sentences:

   a. I will stop modeling when the client _____

   _____ .

b. I will consider a target response tentatively trained when the client _____

_____

c. I will consider a target behavior tentatively trained when the client _____

_____

4. Specify the steps you would take to strengthen the target behaviors so they are more readily generalized to and maintained in natural settings.

5. How do you teach your clients skills that are nonexistent (zero baserate) and the clients do not imitate them? Be specific about the steps and the sequence.

6. A child in your treatment session frequently leaves the chair, goes to the blackboard in the room, and begins to draw a face. Your frequent admonitions have not been effective. How do you capitalize on the interfering behavior to make the child sit and work for you?

7. State the guidelines you would follow in treating language disorders in a child who speaks African American English.

8. Why are tokens especially effective? Describe how a token system may be used in treating stuttering in children.

References

Boone, D. R., McFarlane, S. C., Von Berg, S. L., & Zraick, R. I. (2020). *Voice and voice therapy* (10th ed.). Pearson Education.

Duffy, J. R. (2019). *Motor speech disorders* (4th ed.). Elsevier.

Durfee, A. Z., Sheppard, S. M., Meier, E., Bunker, L., Cui, E., Crainiceanu, C., & Hillis, A. E. (2021). Explicit training to improve affective prosody recognition in adults with acute right hemisphere stroke. *Brain Sciences, 11*(5), 667. https://doi.org/10.3390/brainsci11050667

Freed, D. (2020). *Motor speech disorders: Diagnosis and treatment* (3rd ed.). Plural Publishing.

Fridricksson, J., & Hillis, A. E. (2021). Current approaches to the treatment of post-stroke aphasia. *Journal of Stroke, 23*(2), 183–201.

Hegde, M. N. (1998). *Treatment procedures in communicative disorders* (3rd ed.). Pro-Ed.

Hegde, M. N. (2006). *Treatment protocols for language disorders in children, Vol. II: Social communication.* Plural Publishing.

Hegde, M. N. (2007). *Treatment protocols for stuttering.* Plural Publishing.

Hegde, M. N. (2018). *Hegde's pocketguide to treatment in speech-language pathology* (4th ed.). Plural Publishing.

Hegde, M. N. (2024). *A coursebook on aphasia and other neurogenic language disorders* (5th ed.). Plural Publishing.

Hegde, M. N., & Maul, C. A. (2006). *Language disorders in children: An evidence-based approach to assessment and treatment.* Allyn & Bacon.

Hegde, M. N., & Pomaville, F. (2022). *Assessment of communication disorders in children: Resources and protocols* (4th ed.). Plural Publishing.

Meulenbroek, P., Ness, B., Lemoncello, R., Byom, L., Macdonald, S., O'Neil-Pirozzi, T., & Sohlberg, M. M. (2019). Social communication following traumatic brain injury. Part 2: Identifying effective treatment ingredients. *International Journal of Speech-Language Pathology, 21*(2), 128–142. doi:10.1080/17549507.2019.1583281

Morris, L., Horne, M., McEvoy, P., & Williamson, T. (2018). Communication training interventions for family and professional carers of people living with dementia: A systematic review of effectiveness, acceptability and conceptual basis. *Aging and Mental Health, 22*(7), 863–880.

Pena-Brooks, A., & Hegde, M. N. (2023). *Assessment and treatment of speech sound disorders* (4th ed.). Pro-Ed.

Sapienza, C., & Hoffman, B. (2022). *Voice disorders* (4th ed.). Plural Publishing.

Vargas, J. S. (2020). *Behavior analysis for effective teaching.* Routledge.

Walker, J. D., & Barry, C. (2022). *Behavior management.* Plural Publishing.

Wilson, S. A., Byrne, P., Rodgers, S. E., & Maden, M. (2022). A systematic review of smartphone and tablet use by older adults with and without cognitive impairments. *Innovations in Aging, 6*(2), 1–19.

Evoked and Modeled Discrete Trial Baserate Recording Sheet Template

Name:	Date: Session #:	
Age:	Clinician:	
Disorder: Language	Target Behavior: Plural *s*	
	Trials	
Target Responses	Evoked Present a stimulus and ask a relevant question	Modeled Present a stimulus, ask the question, and model "Say, . . ."
1.		
2.		
3.		
4.		
5.		
6.		
7.		
8.		

continues

9.		
10.		
11.		
12.		
13.		
14.		
15.		
16.		
17.		
18.		
19.		
20.		
Total Percent Correct		

Record the responses as: + = Correct response; – = Incorrect response; 0 = no response.

First administer the evoked trials on all 20 stimuli and next administer the modeled trials. Do not alternate. Modify the form to suit your client's target (words, phrases, or sentences that help teach speech sounds, grammatical morphemes, sentence structures, and so forth). Do not reinforce or correct verbally.

Evoked and Modeled Discrete Trial Baserate Recording Sheet (Example)

Name:	Date:	Session #:
Age:	Clinician:	
Disorder: Language	Target Behavior: Plural *s*	

Target Responses	Trials	
	Evoked Present the stimulus and ask "What are these?"	**Modeled** Present the stimulus, ask the question, and model "Say, . . ."
1. Cups	–	+
2. Boots	–	–
3. Hats	–	+
4. Plates	–	–
5. Bats	+	+
6. Ducks	–	–
7. Ships	–	+
8. Cats	+	+

continues

9. Boats	–	–
10 Rabbits	–	–
11. Coats	–	+
12. Nuts	0	–
13. Goats	–	–
14. Plants	–	–
15. Blocks	+	+
16. Lamps	0	0
17. Rats	–	–
18. Ants	–	+
19. Trucks	+	+
20. Pots	–	–
Total Percent Correct	20%	45%

Record the responses as: + = Correct response; – = Incorrect response; 0 = no response.

First administer the evoked trials on all 20 stimuli and next administer the modeled trials. Do not alternate. Modify the form to suit your client's target (words, phrases, or sentences that help teach speech sounds, grammatical morphemes, sentence structures, and so forth). Do not reinforce or correct verbally.

Template: Treatment Recording Sheet

Name:	Date:		Session #: 4
Age:	Clinician:		
Disorder:	Target Behavior:		
Criterion:	Reinforcement:		

Target Responses	Blocks of 10 Training Trials									
	1	2	3	4	5	6	7	8	9	10
1.										
2.										

continues

3.								
4.								
5.								
6.								

Note: + = Correct response; – = Incorrect response; 0 = no responses; m = Modeled trial; e = Evoked trial.

This treatment data recording sheet for discrete trials allows for recording responses given for six target responses in a given session.

Treatment Recording Sheet (Example)

Name:	Date:	Session #: 4
Age:	Clinician: Linda Verbose	
Disorder: Language	Target Behavior: Plural *s* in words	
Criterion: 10 consecutively correct, evoked responses in words	Reinforcement: FR2 Verbal plus tokens	

Target Responses	Blocks of 10 Training Trials									
	1	2	3	4	5	6	7	8	9	10
1. Cups	m −	+	+	−	+	+	+	−	+	−
	+	+	+	−	+	+	+	+	+	e −
	−	m +	+	+	+	+	e +	−	+	+
	−	+	−	+	+	+	−	+	+	+
	+	+	+	+	+	+	+			
2. Boots	m +	+	+	+	+	e −	+	+	−	+

continues

	−	+	−	+	+	+	+	−	+	+
	+	+	+	+	+	+	+	+		
3. Hats	m +	−	+	+	−	+	+	+	+	+
	e −	+	+	+	−	+	+	+	+	+
	+	+	+	+	+					
4. Plates	m −	+	+	+	+	+	+	+	−	+
	+	+	−	+	+	+	+	+	+	+
	+	+	+							
5. Bats	m +	−	=	+	+	+	+	e +	+	+
	−	+	+	+	+	+	+	+	+	+
	+									
6. Ducks	m +	+	+	+	+	e +	−	+	+	+
	−	+	+	+	+	+	+	+	+	+
	+									

Note: + = Correct response; − = Incorrect or no response; m = Modeled trial; e = Evoked trial.

Illustration of an initial training sequence for six language exemplars. Note that each exemplar of the target behavior was taught first with modeling and then with evoked trials to a training criterion of 10 consecutively correct, evoked responses.

Intermixed Probe Recording Sheet (Example)

Name: Tommy Logos	Date: 2-15-97 Session #: 8	
Age: 6 years	Clinician: Linda Verbose	
Disorder: Language	Target Behavior: Plural *s* in words	
Criterion: 90% correct responses given to untrained stimuli	Reinforcement: Contingent on correct responses given to trained stimuli only	
Target Responses	**Stimuli**	**Score**
1. Cups	Trained	+
2. Ships	Untrained	+
3. Boots	Trained	+
4. Cats	Untrained	+
5. Hats	Trained	+
6. Boats	Untrained	+
7. Plates	Trained	+
8. Rabbits	Untrained	+
9. Bats	Trained	+
10. Coats	Untrained	+

continues

11. Ducks	Trained	+
12. Nuts	Untrained	+
13. Cups	Trained	+
14. Goats	Untrained	+
15. Boots	Trained	+
16. Plants	Untrained	+
17. Hats	Trained	+
18. Blocks	Untrained	+
19. Plates	Trained	+
20. Lamps	Untrained	−
21. Bats	Trained	+
22. Rats	Untrained	+
23. Ducks	Trained	+
24. Ants	Untrained	+
25. Cups	Trained	+
26. Trucks	Untrained	+
27. Boots	Trained	+
28. Pots	Untrained	+

Correct probe response rate: 93% (13 of the 14 probe responses were correct).

Note: The trained and untrained items were alternated. The trained items were used repeatedly. The responses given only to the trained items were reinforced. The percent correct probe rate is based only on the number of correct and incorrect responses given to the 14 probe stimuli.

APPENDIX $8-F$

Pure Probe Recording Sheet (Example)

Name:	Date: Session #:	
Age:	Clinician:	
Disorder: Speech and Language	Target Behavior: Plural *s* in words or the final /s/ in words	
Criterion: 90% correct responses given to untrained stimuli	Reinforcement: Contingent on correct responses given to trained stimuli only	
Untrained Target Responses	**Stimuli**	**Score**
2. Ships	Untrained	+
3. Boots	Untrained	+
4. Cats	Untrained	+
5. Hats	Untrained	+
6. Boats	Untrained	+
7. Plates	Untrained	+

continues

8. Rabbits	Untrained	−
9. Bats	Untrained	+
10. Coats	Untrained	+
11. Ducks	Untrained	+
12. Nuts	Untrained	+
13. Cups	Untrained	+
14. Goats	Untrained	+

Note that the example provided could work for probing both the plural grammatical morpheme *s* or production of /s/ in word final positions. Present only the untrained stimuli on a pure probe. In this example, 20 stimuli were baserated and six were trained to a training criterion of 90% correct. The remaining 14 untrained stimuli were presented on the pure probe. No reinforcers or verbal corrections were offered. The data show 92% correct probe responses (13 out of 14 correct).

Quantitative Summary of Conversational Skills

Duration of conversation: _____   Total Number of words spoken: _____

Sample setting: ☐ Clinic ☐ Home ☐ Other (specify): _____

Session Type: ☐ Baserate ☐ Treatment ☐ Probe

Topic initiation: # of topics initiated: ___   ☐ Appropriate ☐ Inappropriate

Topic maintenance: Average duration: ___   ☐ Appropriate ☐ Inappropriate

Turn-Taking: # of turns taken: ___   ☐ Appropriate ☐ Inappropriate

Request for clarification: # of requests: ___   ☐ Appropriate ☐ Inappropriate

Response to request for clarification: ___   ☐ Appropriate ☐ Inappropriate

Eye Contact: ☐ Appropriate   ☐ Lacking   ☐ Lacking, but cultural

Comments:

Clinician's signature and date:

Supervisor's signature and date:

CHAPTER **9**

Reducing Communication Disorders and Behaviors That Interfere With Treatment

Student Learning Outcomes

After reading this chapter, student clinicians are expected to:

- Describe the procedures to decrease communication disorders
- Describe behaviors that interfere with treatment and suggest their potential maintaining causes
- Specify why is it necessary to understand and use the strategies of decreasing undesirable behaviors in communication treatment sessions
- Define, compare, and contrast the direct and indirect strategies for decreasing undesirable behaviors
- Summarize the steps they would take in designing an effective response reduction strategy

In treatment sessions, clinicians teach, shape, increase, and strengthen desirable communication skills with the help of the core treatment techniques described in the previous chapter. But the clinicians also need to reduce two kinds of responses with different techniques.

First, the clinician needs to reduce the incorrect or inappropriate speech-language responses themselves. Speech sound errors, misuse of grammatical features, agrammatic speech, irrelevant speech, undesirable vocal qualities, dysprosody, stuttering and cluttering, hyper but meaningless fluency, and misnaming objects or persons are just a few examples of incorrect speech-language responses ("symptoms") that need to be reduced. They are the communication disorders that should be reduced with specific techniques while increasing desirable communication targets with the core treatment procedures described in the previous chapter.

Second, the clinician needs to reduce inappropriate and uncooperative general behaviors that interfere with communication treatment. Such behaviors can be serious enough to prevent speech-language pathologists (SLPs) from doing their job: treating communication disorders. SLPs may wish that they did not have to deal with this behavioral problem and that they could get on with their business of treating communication disorders. Unfortunately, SLPs face problem behaviors that prevent treatment work in their sessions as often as behavioral psychologists do in their sessions. SLPs cannot always send their clients to other professionals to "fix" the behavior problems and send the individuals back to them so they can treat communication disorders. Even if the SLPs could do that, the client who returns to speech-language intervention holding *a good behavior certificate* is likely to exhibit the same interfering behaviors because of lack of generalization. Therefore, SLPs themselves first need to reduce behaviors that make their treatment difficult, if not impossible, to implement. Unfortunately, speech-language pathology has paid little or no attention to this problem. Therefore, SLPs have turned to applied behavior analysis for solutions. Inevitably, this chapter draws procedures from applied behavior analysis.

This chapter is about reducing communication disorders (inappropriate speech and language responses) as well as general problem behaviors that interfere with communication treatment. Although student clinicians may readily recognize speech-language impairments that need to be treated, they may not be fully familiar with the general problematic behaviors that interfere with treatment. A child who erupts in crying or begins to crawl under the table may throw a beginning student clinician off guard. Student clinicians should expect and be prepared to handle problem behaviors that make treatment of communication problems difficult, if not impossible. The next section gives an overview of such problem behaviors.

Behaviors That Interfere With Treatment

Children, more often than adults, exhibit treatment-interfering behaviors in speech and language treatment sessions. Adults, too, however, may exhibit some of the interfering behaviors, as noted in the following list. Unless interfering behaviors are reduced, you are not likely to make much headway in treatment sessions. Therefore, among others, plan on reducing the following *undesirable general behaviors* to increase the efficiency of speech-language intervention:

1. **Inattention**. Many children, as well as individuals of all ages who have sustained traumatic brain injury (TBI) and adults with right hemisphere disorder (RHD), tend to exhibit inattention and distractibility, which interfere with treatment.

2. **Indifferent and unmotivated**. Lack of interest in, and motivation for, treatment is more frequent in adults than in children. Uninterested children are more likely to exhibit other kinds of interfering behaviors (e.g., out-of-seat and uncooperative). Indifferent and unmotivated clients exhibit a general unresponsivity to the clinician's demands and requests.

3. **Crying, fussing, clinging to the caregiver, and other emotional responses**. These are among the strong disrupters of treatment offered to children. Initially and until you learn to control them, such behaviors may emotionally upset you.

4. **Out-of-seat and other uncooperative behaviors**. Children who begin to move around in the therapy room, crawl under the table, constantly grab things on the table, kick the table leg, make faces at the observation mirror, or simply wiggle around in their seats cannot focus on treatment targets.

5. **Distracting verbal behaviors**. Children who constantly ask, "Are we done yet?" and "You know what?" are trying to distract you from treatment they do not enjoy. Such distracting verbal behaviors, too, need to be eliminated or reduced.

6. **Absenteeism**. A larger problem is a no-show or frequent cancellation of treatment sessions. Obviously, clients who do not attend treatment sessions cannot be helped.

An occasional interfering behavior, such as wiggling in the chair, is not a serious problem. These may be controlled easily by repeating instructions and praising the child for quiet sitting. However, interfering behaviors that are exhibited at high frequency are a serious problem and need special procedures to reduce them.

Maintaining Causes of Undesirable Behaviors

Undesirable and interfering behaviors, just like the desirable ones, have their causes. Interfering behaviors may be more effectively reduced if their causes are understood. A functional analysis is an assessment of the causes of behaviors, both desirable and undesirable. A clinician's common-sense reason for such behaviors may or may not be valid.

Functional analysis of undesirable and interfering behaviors is a complex topic. To understand the procedures fully, you need to consult the original studies (Iwata & Dozier, 2008; Mayer et al., 2019; McKenna et al., 2016). Here, you will find a summary of the results of those studies.

Generally undesirable and treatment-interfering behaviors may have the following causes:

- **Positive reinforcement**, especially in the form of attention, is a powerful reinforcer that maintains many undesirable behaviors. A teacher who otherwise ignored a child may promptly attend to a child's misbehavior, thus inadvertently reinforcing the troublesome behavior. Experimentally, attention may be paid to, and then withdrawn from a behavior. If the behavior increased when attention is paid and decreased when it is withdrawn, attention is the maintaining cause of the behavior.

- **Negative reinforcement** maintains an undesirable behavior when that behavior terminates an aversive event. Some children try to leave their chair, cry, or become reticent when they find the treatment task difficult (aversive). Their uncooperative or interfering behaviors terminate the aversive treatment trials and therefore are negatively reinforced. Presenting and then withdrawing more complex and difficult treatment tasks will confirm this.

- **Automatic reinforcement** is presumed when known positive or negative reinforcement do not seem to account for the undesirable behavior. Automatic reinforcement is often presumed in case of stereotypic or self-stimulatory behaviors that persons with autism and those with brain injury exhibit. Such behaviors are reinforced by the neural or sensory consequences they generate. Lack of stimulation and activity frequently are cited reasons for undesirable behaviors that are maintained by automatic reinforcement. Left alone, some children with autism rock themselves endlessly or hit themselves. If the behavior increases when the child is left in a stark room with no stimulation and opportunities for activities, and if the behavior decreases when stimulation and access to opportunities are provided, automatic reinforcement is confirmed. Parents of a boy with TBI might say that he "enjoys" hitting the table and making loud noise. The loud noise may be a sensory consequence that reinforces the unwanted behavior.

There are two kinds of response reduction strategies: direct and indirect. In **direct response reduction strategy**, you place a contingency on the behavior to be reduced. *Placing a contingency on a behavior* means that you take an immediate action (e.g., saying "No") followed by a wrong response during treatment. In the **indirect response reduction strategy**, you place no contingency on the undesirable behavior but place a positive contingency on the desirable behavior that increases. This increase causes an indirect effect of decreasing the undesirable behavior. In this strategy, a desirable behavior increases because of reinforcement and *replaces* the undesirable behavior, though nothing specific is done to it. Therefore, you should not say that you used reinforcement procedures to decrease behaviors. By definition, reinforcement procedures increase behaviors.

Direct Strategies for Decreasing Behaviors

In the direct strategies, you say or do something as soon as a wrong response occurs. In using this strategy, you may either present or withdraw a stimulus to reduce behaviors (Maag, 2018; Martin & Pear, 2016; Mayer et al., 2019; Vargas, 2020). There are specific procedures under these two categories.

Stimulus Presentation

Responses may be reduced by *presenting a stimulus immediately after a response is made*. Several response-contingent stimuli (stimuli delivered soon after a response is made) can reduce behaviors. All SLPs routinely use this procedure.

SLPs most frequently present verbal corrections. To reduce incorrect speech and language responses, clinicians typically say "No," "Wrong," and "Not correct." The clinician may shake her head in a disapproving manner or show other facial or hand gestures that suggest to the client that the response was not correct or acceptable. In all such cases, the clinician will have used stimulus presentation to reduce the incorrect response.

Verbal corrective stimuli (such as "No" or "Wrong") by themselves may not be effective in reducing all kinds of undesirable behavior. They may be especially ineffective in reducing disruptive behaviors (e.g., crying, leaving the chair, paying no attention). However, when combined with strong reinforcers for desirable behaviors that are shaped in carefully designed incremental steps, verbal stimuli may be sufficient to reduce incorrect speech and language responses. For instance, clinicians who say, "Not correct" for incorrect productions of phonemes also say, "Good job!" for correct productions that are shaped. Clients' errors persist when clinicians fail to give corrective feedback for incorrect responses.

How to Use Stimulus Presentation to Reduce Behaviors

1. **Present the verbal stimulus soon after the response is made.** To do this, you must make quick evaluations of the correctness of client responses.

2. **Present the verbal stimulus in a firm and objective manner.** Say "No" in such a manner as to suggest that you mean it. You should not sound unsure. The message, not necessarily the voice, must be clear and loud.

3. **Use an objective tone devoid of emotionality.** Do not use an angry or otherwise emotionally laden tone. Being a professional, you should not give an emotional reaction to an incorrect response.

4. **Vary the words you use.** Do not use the same "No" or "Wrong" throughout an entire session.

Reinforcer Withdrawal

Immediately after a response is made, *you may withdraw something that presumably maintains or increases that response.* While presenting stimuli that weaken a response (e.g., saying "Not correct" to a wrong response), you may also withdraw a reinforcer the client will have earned for the correct responses (e.g., taking a token away when a wrong response is made). In reducing undesirable speech and language responses or errors, at least two of the three reinforcer withdrawal procedures, reviewed next, may be more effective than verbal correction and other stimulus presentations.

There are three specific procedures of reinforcer withdrawal: *time-out, response cost,* and *extinction.* In all three, reinforcing events or consequences are withdrawn or made unavailable immediately following a wrong response or at the earliest sign of that response. Of the three, time-out and response cost may be used to reduce speech-language errors as well as most interfering behaviors. Extinction is not a method of choice to reduce speech and language errors. A combination of verbal correction for errors (e.g., speech sound errors) and shaping of correct responses is effective.

Time-Out

Time-out is a brief period of time during which all reinforcing events are suspended contingent on a response, and as a result there typically is a decrease in the rate of that response. Exclusion and non-exclusion are the two forms of time-out.

In **exclusion time-out**, the client is excluded from the current stream of activities that contain social and other kinds of reinforcers. For example, you might ask a child to sit in the corner the instant he or she exhibits an undesirable behavior. All activities are terminated; the child is told to sit quietly. In this case, the setting is changed from the regular seating place to the corner. Generally, exclusion time-out is not a useful strategy for reducing undesirable behaviors in communication treatment sessions.

In **nonexclusion time-out**, an undesirable behavior is followed immediately by cessation of all activity, but there is no physical movement and there is no change in the setting. For example, in stuttering treatment, you signal the client to stop talking for 5 s as soon as you observe a dysfluency or stutter. You avoid eye contact for the duration. At the end of the duration, you signal the person to resume talking (Hegde, 2007). In this case, it is presumed that talking is reinforcing, and interruption and silence are aversive events that reduce the behavior. Incidentally, the term pause-and-talk better describes what the clinician and clients do in administering time-out. Pause-and-talk is a preferred term when used in speech-language therapy sessions.

Many research studies have shown that time-out can reduce several forms of undesirable behavior (Maag, 2018; Vargas, 2020; Walker & Barry, 2024) as well as such specific communication disorders as stuttering (Hegde, 1998, 2018). Unfortunately, time-out is also most often misused. Careless use of time-out may have a paradoxical effect on behavior: the behavior to be reduced might increase in frequency. When correctly used, time-out should only decrease the undesirable behavior.

Advantages of Time-Out. Prudently and sparingly used, time-out has many advantages. Compared with several other response reduction procedures, time-out is only mildly aversive. It is relatively easy to learn and use. Brief time-out periods do not waste much teaching time. Therefore, consider using time-out to reduce undesirable behaviors in your client.

Note that time-out will not reduce all behaviors in all clients. When you observe no reduction or even a paradoxical increase in the undesirable behavior under time-out, you should find an alternative procedure to reduce that behavior.

How to Use Time-Out

1. **Avoid too brief or too long durations of time-out**. Durations that are too long may be ineffective because they may allow opportunities for other behaviors and take valuable time away from treatment. An appropriate duration depends on the nature of the behavior to be reduced. In reducing stuttering, for example, 5 to 10-s durations may be effective; longer durations are unnecessary; fewer than 3 s may be ineffective. In controlling more global uncooperative, destructive, or inattentive behaviors, longer durations may be necessary.

2. **Try to avoid exclusion time-out, as it is the least desirable procedure**. Do not use it unless you have tried nonexclusion time-out, extinction, response cost, and other procedures first and have found them ineffective.

3. **Signal the beginning of the nonexclusion time-out with a stimulus**. For example, you may raise your index finger to signal to a person who stutters that a 5-s time-out has begun and that speech must be terminated. In exclusion time-out, a young child may be guided physically to a time-out area without any signal. But in all cases, either a verbal statement or a nonhuman sound such as a buzzer should announce the end of the time-out period.

4. **Avoid physical contact in administering exclusion time-out**. If the child complies with your instruction to go to the time-out area, do not use physical contact. Ask the child to go to the designated area and stay there until the end of the time-out period. Physically guide the child to the area only when the child does not comply.

5. **Use time-out on a continuous schedule**. Impose time-out on every instance of an undesirable behavior. Do not use an intermittent schedule, especially in the beginning of the response reduction program. Intermittent scheduling may be useful in later stages of training when the undesirable behavior is of low frequency and you wish to keep it that way or reduce it further.

6. **Eliminate unintended positive reinforcement that may be associated with time-out**. Time-out may provide unintended positive or negative reinforcement. If so, the undesirable behavior

may paradoxically increase. When you use exclusion time-out, the area to which you send the child to spend the time-out should not contain reinforcing objects, people, or events. For instance, do not ask the child to sit in a hallway full of people and events. Failure to follow this rule is the main reason why sending a child to his or her own room for misbehaving usually is not only ineffective, but also reinforcing; the undesirable behavior may actually increase. Typically, a child's room may be a reinforcer treasure trove.

7. **Release the client from time-out only when the undesirable behavior has been stopped.** If the child continues to fuss in the corner, extend the time-out until the child becomes calm. However, release the child promptly when the undesirable behavior stops.

8. **Enrich the treatment situation with powerful and varied reinforcers.** Time-out is more effective when the return to the teaching station is highly reinforcing and the time-out situation is dreary and unreinforcing. You will be in serious trouble if the situations are reversed.

Response Cost

A procedure of withdrawing a conditioned reinforcer contingent on the behavior to be reduced is **response cost**. Tokens are the most frequently used conditioned reinforcers. Each undesirable response results in loss of a token. In young children (perhaps under 10 years of age), response cost is effective in decreasing and eventually eliminating stuttering and reducing speech sound errors in children with articulation problems (Hegde, 2007, 2018). Children earn a token for every fluent utterance or any other correct speech-language responses and lose one for every stutter or other kinds of errors.

Time-out and response cost are similar in that both deprive the client of some reinforcers. But their procedures are different. In time-out, you arrange a brief duration of no reinforcement of any kind; during this time, there is no responding; the person may even be moved to another scene that lacks reinforcers. In response cost, you take away a specific, tangible, reinforcer the client has earned or has been given for desirable responses; there is no particular interruption of responses; the client does not move physically; and it is not a duration of time devoid of reinforcers.

Response cost is implemented most effectively and efficiently in a *token system*. **Tokens** are presented for the desirable behaviors and withdrawn when the undesirable behavior occurs. At the end of a treatment session, the remaining tokens are exchanged for a **backup reinforcer**, usually a small gift in the case of children. The procedure is most effective if the child is allowed to choose a backup reinforcer from a reinforcer menu at the beginning of the session. The reinforcer in this case is client-specific and personally meaningful.

The response cost procedure may be used individually or in small groups. When used with groups, any individual's undesirable behavior will cost the group a token. The group earns tokens only when all members exhibit the desirable behavior. This variation has been used in classroom management in schools (Vargas, 2020; Walker & Barry, 2022).

Like all other response-reduction procedures, response cost may be ineffective or may increase the rate of undesirable response under certain conditions. But a correct use of the procedure helps avoid such unwanted consequences.

Advantages of Response Cost. Along with time-out, response cost is a widely researched method of reducing undesirable behaviors, including stuttering in young children (Hegde, 2007; Maag, 2018). It is effective, socially acceptable, and less aversive than some of the other methods of behavior reduction.

How to Use Response Cost

1. **Give more tokens than you take back.** To this end, simplify the target response and shape it, if necessary. The child should experience more success (reinforcers) than failures (token loss). At the end of the session, the child should be left with some tokens to be exchanged for backup reinforcers. The child should never experience *token bankruptcy* or *client indebtedness*, which would also mean you cannot offer the backup reinforcer. The child should always get the backup reinforcer.

2. **Withdraw tokens promptly.** There should be no delay between the undesirable response and token withdrawal.

3. **Increase the number of tokens withdrawn per response only if necessary.** Do this when a single or fewer token withdrawals

are not effective. But do not decrease the number of tokens withdrawn, because it will be ineffective.

4. **Control potential emotional responses**. Any emotional response will be evident on the first token withdrawal. If this happens, reverse the roles for a few minutes. Let the child be the clinician who withdraws tokens for your wrong responses. For example, assume that the child who stutters gets suddenly upset when you withdraw the first token contingent on stuttering. You can then say, "Hey you know what! I too have bumpy speech sometimes! You want to take a token away from me?" The child is usually delighted to do this. Keep a few tokens for yourself, exhibit a few dysfluencies, and ask the child to withdraw one for each of your dysfluencies. Clinical observations suggest that this is effective in eliminating emotional responses (Hegde, 2007). When you return to the procedure, the child is likely to accept it.

As with any response-reduction procedure, watch for excessive and uncontrollable emotional responses and paradoxical increase in undesirable behaviors. Always be prepared to use another response-reduction procedure.

Extinction

The procedure of simply withholding reinforcers of a behavior is called **extinction**. Note that extinction is not a punishment procedure. Because of lack of reinforcement, extinction weakens and eliminates the behavior.

Extinction is a *do-nothing procedure*. When nobody does anything to sustain a behavior, it will weaken and eventually disappear. It weakens a response by removing reinforcing consequences. Children's *uncooperative behaviors* are prime targets for extinction. Such treatment-interfering behaviors as crying, fussing, frequent verbal requests to go to the bathroom or see the parent waiting outside, irrelevant talking (the "you know what?" type of interruptions), and many other similar behaviors are maintained by clinician's unintended positive reinforcement, typically attention.

The reinforcement may be positive or negative. The clinician may pick up and console a crying child to terminate crying. The action will terminate crying but will also positively reinforce it. The next session will begin with a crying child. Another child may repeatedly request permission to go to the bathroom. The clinician who complies each time will have negatively reinforced the child. By leaving the treatment room, the child will have terminated unwanted (aversive) treatment. This is negative reinforcement.

Note that if the child simply begins to leave the treatment room, you cannot just ignore the behavior. You need to prevent escape, thus depriving the child of negative reinforcement. *Prevention of escape* is described as **escape extinction**. This procedure implies that extinction is not always a passive or indirect procedure.

Advantages of Extinction. Used correctly, extinction is an effective method of reducing undesirable behaviors. Consider it for reducing crying, undesirable verbal interruptions, inappropriate requests to leave the treatment room, and similar problem behaviors.

How to Use Extinction

1. **Discuss the problem and the extinction procedure with the parents**. Some parents may be alarmed to see you sitting still when their 3-year-old child is loudly and tearfully crying and screaming "Mommy!" If they understand what you are doing and why, they may tolerate the procedure. The slow process of extinction is unpleasant for the child, the clinician, and anyone who watches it. It is distressing to the parents.

2. **Remove positive reinforcers inherent to your actions promptly and fully**. Withdraw all attention from undesirable behavior. Avoid eye contact; sit motionless. Be firm, wait it out; do not change anything. For example, once you initiate extinction for crying behavior, do not lecture, do not admonish, do not cajole, do not try to charm the child, do not try to talk the child out of crying, do not reorganize the materials on the table. Sit still and do not look at the child.

3. **Remove positive reinforcers that are unrelated to your actions**. If the child on the floor begins to play with a toy, look at pictures, examine your bag, and so forth, remove the objects promptly and then sit motionless.

4. **Remove negative reinforcers as promptly and fully as possible**. Prevent the child from leaving the seat and walking around or out of the treatment room. Do not stop treatment because

the child asks interrupting questions. Do not answer such questions as "Do you know what?" If you answer such questions, you will have positively reinforced such interruptive questioning and negatively reinforced the escape behavior that terminates your teaching.

5. **Do not terminate the extinction procedure when you see an extinction burst, which is a temporary increase in the response frequency when extinction is initiated.** Extinction burst often scares the clinician, who quickly turns attention to the client. Do not do this. Continue to withhold reinforcers by sitting motionless, and the behavior will eventually subside.

6. **Reinforce desirable behaviors promptly and lavishly.** For example, the instant the child stops crying or fussing, you should smile, hug the child, wipe the tears, praise, give a token, and reinforce the child in other ways. Make the desirable behavior pay off better for the child than the undesirable behavior.

A Word of Caution. *Behaviors that are reinforced automatically and those that are destructive or aggressive are not candidates for extinction.* You cannot ignore a self-stimulatory behavior (e.g., rocking by a child with autism), self-injurious behavior (e.g., self-biting by a child with autism), or an aggressive or destructive behavior (e.g., hitting others, destroying property) and expect the behavior to diminish. Such behaviors are automatically reinforced by their sensory consequences. Aggressive and destructive behaviors carry their own reinforcers: injury to others and destruction of property will reinforce the troublesome behaviors. Do not use extinction to reduce these behaviors because it will be ineffective and dangerous to the child and others. Such behaviors should first be stopped physically, and exclusion time-out along with such procedures as differential reinforcement, described later, are safer alternatives.

Indirect Strategies for Decreasing Behaviors

In **indirect strategies**, desirable behaviors replace the undesirable behaviors (Maag, 2018; Martin & Pear, 2016; Mayer et al., 2019; Vargas, 2020). It contrasts with the direct strategy in which you do something (e.g., verbal correction) when the undesirable behavior occurs. In the indirect strategy, you do nothing specific to the behavior to be reduced. Instead, you reinforce a desirable behavior, which will have an indirect effect of reducing the undesirable.

Reinforcing carefully selected desirable behaviors will weaken corresponding undesirable behaviors. But as noted before, you should never make the mistake of saying, "I use reinforcement to decrease undesirable behaviors." Reinforcement can only increase behaviors. *When you use reinforcing procedures, reduction in another behavior is a by-product.* Undesirable behaviors decrease only because other behaviors increase. Therefore, you might say, "I use reinforcement to increase desirable behaviors so that the undesirable counterparts decrease."

The use of reinforcement to increase some behaviors while other behaviors decrease as a result is known as **differential reinforcement**. Although some behaviors increase because of the reinforcement, others decrease as a by-product. This is the meaning of *differential reinforcement.*

There are several differential reinforcement procedures. The following four are clinically useful: *differential reinforcement of other behavior (DRO), differential reinforcement of incompatible behavior (DRI), differential reinforcement of alternative behavior (DRA), and differential reinforcement of low rates of responding (DRL).* These procedures increase certain behaviors and thereby decrease certain other behaviors.

Reinforce Any Other Desirable Behavior

In this procedure, known as DRO, you *reinforce a person for exhibiting any desirable behavior but not the specified undesirable behavior.* For example, you may reinforce a child for not wiggling in the chair for 2 min. If the child does not wiggle for that entire duration, you may give the child a token. Gradually, you can increase the duration for which the child should refrain from the undesirable behavior. A child who frequently interrupts you during treatment may be asked not to do it for a period of several minutes. The child is then reinforced for compliance. A verbally aggressive child may be told that he or she will receive a token if aggressive verbalizations stop for a certain duration.

The examples of DRO show that what is reinforced is left open. The procedure does not specify a particular desirable behavior to earn reinforcers; it requires the child to omit the undesirable behavior. A hyperactive child, for example, may sit quietly for the specified duration to earn reinforcers. But the child may also read, color, work on mathematical problems, or put puzzles together to earn the reinforcer. You reinforce these and many other forms of acceptable behaviors, none specified ahead of time.

Reinforce an Incompatible Behavior

In this procedure, known as DRI, you *reinforce behaviors that are topographically incompatible with the undesirable behavior.* A child who is verbally abusive may be reinforced for nonabusive and socially acceptable verbal expressions. A child who snatches toys from other children may be reinforced for giving his or her toy to playmates.

Note that the described abusive actions are *incompatible* with socially acceptable actions in that both cannot be produced at the same time. Snatching and sharing or wandering around and sitting quietly cannot occur simultaneously. Therefore, when the desirable behavior is increased with reinforcement, the incompatible undesirable behavior should decrease. To use DRI, you must find a response that cannot coexist with the undesirable behavior and target that for reinforcement.

Reinforce an Alternative Behavior

In this procedure, known as DRA, you *specify and reinforce a behavior that is an alternative to the undesirable behavior.* In DRA, the desirable behavior is an alternative to, but not incompatible with, the undesirable behavior. For example, a child who lacks academic or social skills may exhibit disruptive behaviors. In this case, you may target specific reading or writing skills and adaptive social skills that the child will enjoy more than the disruptive behaviors. Technically, this means that you teach a desirable behavior that is *functionally equivalent* to the behavior to be reduced (Iwata & Dozier, 2008). If it looks like the child is crawling under the table to get your attention, then provide lavish attention to quiet sitting in the chair; if that troublesome behavior seems to be due to a difficult treatment task, simplify and shape it. Teach mands to minimally verbal children who fuss. Children who can successfully request what they need are less likely to adopt unwanted strategies to get them.

One potential problem with the DRA procedure is that because the desirable behavior is not incompatible with the undesirable behavior, both may be exhibited. While learning better academic and social skills, the child may continue to disrupt, although this is less likely. If it does happen, teach behaviors that are incompatible with the undesirable behavior. You may reinforce the child to sit quietly for periods of time, which would be incompatible with disruptive behavior.

Reinforce Progressively Lower Rates of the Undesirable Behavior

In this procedure, known as DRL, *you reinforce the child when the frequency of undesirable behavior is below the baseline level.* In DRL, you shape the undesirable response down until it is eliminated or reduced to a manageable level. The effect of the procedure is gradual. For example, a child might ask, "Are we done yet?" once every 2 to 3 min in treatment sessions. You can then set a criterion of no more than two interruptions in a 10-min interval. Normally, the child would have interrupted some three to five times during this interval. You can reinforce the child, if during the previous 10 min, the child had interrupted you only two times or less. In using this procedure, you should not reinforce the child soon after an interruption.

In all of the differential reinforcement procedures, you make sure that you do not reinforce undesirable behaviors. A common theme of these procedures is that (a) the client gains access to reinforcing affairs through desirable behaviors; (b) the undesirable behaviors do not get reinforced anymore; (c) consequently, the undesirable behaviors do not serve the client as they did before; and, therefore, (d) the desirable behaviors replace the undesirable behaviors.

Other Indirect Procedures

Two other indirect procedures that may be used include behavioral momentum and the presentation of a sudden, surprising stimulus. These techniques can be effective with many children who are noncompliant (and may exhibit other undesirable behaviors) or who are unlikely to produce the target behaviors with modeling and shaping.

Behavioral momentum is a procedure in which the physical force or velocity of one or more behaviors in progress causes another behavior that is not typically exhibited (Baldwin & Baldwin, 2000; Cowan et al., 2017). In using this procedure, you first repeatedly ask the client to do what that person is likely to do; as soon as this behavior occurs in rapid succession, you suddenly ask the client to perform an unlikely action. The unlikely action may be performed because of the force (momentum) of the previous, readily exhibited (high-probability) behavior.

This method may be used to reduce noncompliant behaviors. For example, assume that a girl does not comply with your request to look at the stimulus picture used in training words but she readily claps her hands when asked to. Then, you could ask her to clap three or four times in rapid succession and immediately ask her to look at the picture. She may then immediately look at the picture. If so, reinforce it lavishly. In this case, you decreased noncompliance behavior by behavioral momentum.

Surprising stimulus presentation also can terminate or prevent an undesirable behavior. A sudden loud noise (but not too loud as to be dangerous) can terminate an ongoing undesirable behavior. You may also *prevent* an imminent undesirable behavior by presenting a sudden and surprising stimulus. For example, a child's imminent crying may be prevented if you suddenly and dramatically pull out a clown or an animated toy just before the crying is about to erupt. You suddenly may turn on the radio, get up from the chair, pull something from a box, or behave in some dramatic fashion. Stimuli that appear so suddenly and dramatically tend to inhibit certain undesirable behaviors.

To prevent undesirable behaviors by sudden stimulus presentation, you must watch the client very closely to detect the *earliest signs* of troublesome behavior. The surprising stimulus or action must be presented before the response onset; if not, you may reinforce the undesirable response.

How to Design an Effective Response Reduction Strategy

Instead of using an isolated procedure in reducing or increasing behaviors, you must design a comprehensive program of behavior management involving both response strengthening and weakening consequences. A combined procedure that simultaneously shapes and reinforces a desirable behavior while withdrawing reinforcers from the undesirable behaviors and presenting them with other response reduction consequences will be the most effective (Hegde, 1998, 2018; Martin & Pear, 2016; Mayer et al., 2019).

Designing and implementing an effective response reduction strategy takes careful planning to avoid any negative consequences for the client and the caregivers. First try to use a differential reinforcement of desirable behaviors that might concomitantly reduce the undesirable behavior. Use a direct response reduction procedure (e.g., time-out or response cost) when indirect strategies are ineffective. Extinction is appropriate if the behavior suits it.

Verbal correction, however, is ubiquitous in intervention sessions. Clients do need the information that their responses are wrong, and they not only tolerate it, but also expect it. Response cost, time-out, and differential reinforcement have been shown to be effective in reducing many types of undesirable behaviors. Therefore, the clinician should not hesitate to use them prudently and properly.

Take the following steps in designing an effective response reduction strategy involving multiple contingencies or procedures:

1. **Define clearly and narrowly both the behavior to be increased and the behavior to be decreased**. For instance, *increasing correct production of /s/* is a better definition than *improved articulatory skills; decreasing out-of-seat behavior to fewer than two occasions per session* is better than *minimizing uncooperative behaviors*. Similarly,

production of pronouns he *and* she *in response to pictures with 95% accuracy* is a better definition than *increasing grammatical ability*; *decreasing the frequency of interrupting questions or comments to no more than three per session* is more precise than *eliminating irrelevant verbalizations*. Again, *naming 10 pictures of family members with 90% accuracy* is a more accurate description than *improving naming ability*. Generally, avoid the term *ability* in your description of target behaviors; instead, specify an observable action. Use response reduction procedures only when you have such clearly defined behaviors on which you can place differential (increasing and decreasing) response contingencies.

2. **Use extinction first if it is appropriate for the behavior to be reduced.** If the troublesome behavior is infrequent and innocuous, continue to reinforce the desirable behavior and ignore the undesirable behavior. For example, if wiggling in the chair is infrequent and does not interrupt the session, ignore it. Use another response reduction procedures only when extinction proves ineffective. However, if the behavior escalates, introduce a more active response reduction procedure (e.g., response cost, time-out, or one of the differential reinforcement methods).

3. **Use procedures that increase the chances of success and thus help prevent undesirable responses.** Recall that persistent failures at treatment tasks may induce unwanted behaviors. Shape and model the correct response so that the client experiences success from the beginning. Do not persist with difficult treatment trials; simplify the target skill and shape the more complex skill. Prompt the correct response when the client hesitates, signaling an imminent wrong response; this may prevent the wrong response and the need to provide verbal correction. Clients who are successful in learning the target skills are less likely to exhibit undesirable behaviors.

4. **Use one of the differential reinforcement procedures to increase desirable behaviors while decreasing undesirable behaviors.** Because the emphasis in differential reinforcement procedures is strengthening positive behaviors, the session will also remain largely positive for the client. Reinforce any form of cooperative behavior to reduce incompatible uncooperative behavior; replace inattention by attention; crying by smiling.

5. **Use varied consequences to reduce a response.** Do not use one type of response consequence constantly unless the reduction rate

is satisfactory. For example, in the same treatment sessions, alternate the use of verbal "no," "wrong," "incorrect," "not quite," and so forth. Also consider response cost, time-out, and other response reduction consequences as needed. Similarly, use varied reinforcers to increase the desirable behavior that will replace the undesirable behavior. Verbal praise, tokens backed with varied reinforcers, frequent feedback on response accuracy, opportunities for exhibiting high-probability behaviors—all may be used in a single session.

6. **Capitalize on an unwanted but high-frequency response to reinforce correct responses**. For example, a child may frequently leave the seat, go to the chalkboard, and scribble on it. Instead of trying to suppress this interfering behavior with a verbal "no," a lecture, and such other ineffective means, you can make short durations of drawing or writing on the chalkboard contingent on sitting for a few minutes and giving correct responses. You will then have turned an annoying, interfering behavior into a reinforcer of desirable target behaviors. This is similar to high-probability behavior reinforcing low-probability behavior.

7. **Use behavioral momentum to decrease certain undesirable behaviors**. Repeatedly and rapidly evoke a likely response, reinforce it, and immediately demand the production of the unlikely target response. Reinforce its occurrence as well.

8. **Use a strong, sudden, and surprising stimulus to terminate or prevent an undesirable behavior**. Present the surprising stimulus (such as pulling a clown out of a bag) as soon as you anticipate its occurrence.

9. **Use a continuous schedule**. Apply the selected response reduction procedure for every instance of an undesirable behavior. Whether it is response cost, time-out, or verbal stimuli, apply it continuously until it is no longer needed.

10. **Present or withdraw consequences immediately**. Do not hesitate, wait, or be slow in responding to the undesirable response.

11. **Do not allow escape from the response-reduction procedure**. A crying child being ignored (extinction) should not get out of the treatment room only to be consoled and reinforced by the parent waiting outside. Similarly, clients under other response-reduction procedures should not be allowed to leave the treatment scene. If they are, the clients will escape from treatment, get negative reinforcement, and continue to exhibit the undesirable behavior.

12. **Apply the response-reduction procedure at the earliest sign of the undesirable response**. Do not wait until the undesirable response is completed to apply the procedure. For instance, to reduce a child's behavior of leaving the chair, do not wait to say "No" until after the child has left the chair and is on the floor. The best time to say "No" (assuming it will be effective) is when you see the slightest movement of the child that suggests an imminent response. In using time-out for stuttering, you should not wait until an instance of stuttering has run its course. Instead, you must watch for the earliest signs of stuttering and apply the procedure.

13. **Dissociate response-reduction procedures from those that reinforce responses**. Do not deliver reinforcers along with or in proximity with response-reduction procedures. If you do, you will have reinforced the undesirable behavior. Some clinicians say "Wrong," but immediately smile, touch, or hug the child. Such reactions negate the effects of verbal correction and may reinforce the undesirable response.

14. **Minimize the duration of response-reduction procedures**. Time-out should be brief. No response-reduction procedure should be applied for too long. If it looks like you have to, you are not using an effective treatment procedure. Maybe you have a wrong or extremely difficult target for the child; maybe you do not have effective reinforcers to increase the desirable behavior; perhaps you are not administering treatment contingencies properly; most likely you are not gradually shaping the target behavior. Analyze your procedures to make them more effective. If you cannot figure it out, talk to your supervisor, but do not continue with the ineffective response-reduction procedure.

15. **Remove reinforcers that maintain undesirable behaviors**. If you see the child constantly reaching for your bag on the table, do not continue to reprimand the child; instead, remove the bag and keep it out of the child's reach and sight. See what reinforces the undesirable behavior. If it is something that can be eliminated, do so immediately.

16. **Expose the client to more reinforcing consequences than to response-reduction consequences**. Overall, treatment sessions should be much more reinforcing (fun) than aversive to the child. You should be giving more tokens than you withdraw; you should be praising the child more frequently than you give corrective feedback. Of course, to do this, you should be using procedures that effectively shape the target behaviors.

Reducing behaviors that make communication treatment difficult, if not impossible, is a responsibility of all SLPs. The preference, however, is to use procedures that positively reinforce other desirable behaviors that replace or eliminate interfering behaviors. Therefore, the emphasis should be on positive reinforcement procedures. Other than the ubiquitous verbal correction, which is essential for reducing the incorrect speech-language responses, treatment should be designed to avoid or minimize the use of response-reduction procedures. All response reduction procedures should be used correctly, sparingly, and only as long as needed.

⑦ Questions for Self-Assessment

1. Distinguish between the direct and indirect strategies of reducing behaviors that interfere with treatment. Give examples of each strategy.

2. The 4-year-old girl client you are working with began to cry incessantly when the mother left her in the treatment room for the first session. You picked her up, consoled her, shown pictures in the picture book, gave her toys to play with for a while, and pleaded with her to stop crying. She stopped crying but began to cry at the beginning of the next two sessions. What did you do wrong, and what would you do next to eliminate crying?

3. Compare time-out and response-cost procedures. For what disorders and age groups would you use them? Point out the strengths and limitations of each procedure.

4. You just started speech sound training with a 5-year-old boy. As soon as you begin a treatment trial by showing a picture and asking him to imitate a fricative sound in two-word phrases, he leaves the chair and crawls under the table. What might be reinforcing this undesirable behavior and what strategy would you use to eliminate it?

5. Define, compare, and contrast the strategies of teaching *incompatible* versus *alternative* behaviors to reduce the frequency of undesirable behaviors that keeps interfering with your treatment of communication disorders. Illustrate how the two strategies are used, giving an example of an undesirable behavior for each.

References

Baldwin, J. D., & Baldwin, J. I. (2000). *Behavior principles in everyday life* (4th ed.). Prentice-Hall.

Cowan, R. J., Abel, L., & Candel, L. (2017). A meta-analysis of single-subject research on behavioral momentum to enhance success in students with autism. *Journal of Autism and Developmental Disorders, 47*(5), 1464–1477.

Hegde, M. N. (1998). *Treatment procedures in communicative disorders* (3rd ed.). Pro-Ed.

Hegde, M. N. (2007). *Treatment protocols for stuttering.* Plural Publishing.

Hegde, M. N. (2018). *Hegde's pocketguide to treatment in speech-language pathology* (4th ed.). Plural Publishing.

Iwata, B. A., & Dozier, C. L. (2008). Clinical application of functional analysis methodology. *Behavior Analysis and Practice, 1*(1), 3–9.

Maag, J. W. (2018). *Behavior management: From theoretical implications to practical applications* (3rd ed.). Cengage.

Martin, G., & Pear, J. (2016). *Behavior modification: What it is and how to do it.* Routledge.

Mason, S. A., & Iwata, B. A. (1990). Artifactual effects of sensory-integrative therapy on self-injurious behaviors. *Journal of Applied Behavior Analysis, 23*, 361–370.

Mayer, G. R., Sulzer-Azaroff, B., & Wallace, M. (2019). *Behavior analysis for lasting change* (3rd ed.). Sloan Publishing.

McKenna, J. W., Fowler, A., & Adamson, R. (2016). A systematic review of function-based behavior interventions for students with and at risk for emotional and behavioral disorders. *Behavior Modification, 40*(5), 678–712.

Vargas, J. (2020). *Behavior analysis for effective teaching* (3rd ed.). Routledge.

Walker, J. D., & Barry, C. (2024). *Behavior management: Systems, classrooms, and individuals.* Plural Publishing.

CHAPTER **10**

Generalization and Maintenance of Target Behaviors

> ## Student Learning Outcomes
>
> After reading this chapter, student clinicians are expected to:
>
> - Distinguish generalization from maintenance of target behaviors
> - Specify the reasons for failed maintenance of treated behaviors
> - Describe and be prepared to use the 14 steps of promoting generalization and maintenance of target behaviors
> - Summarize the follow-up assessment procedures and suggest a follow-up schedule for their clients

Intervention does not end when the clients begin to reliably produce the target behaviors in clinical sessions. From a basic level of teaching speech sounds, words, grammatical morphemes, fluent speech, desirable voice characteristics, and others, you may shift training to more complex levels, terminating in conversational speech, narration, and discourse. If the target behaviors meet your defined mastery criteria (e.g., 90% accuracy), you may think that the treatment is completed and the client is ready for dismissal. But the client is not yet ready for dismissal.

There are two other treatment-related activities you need to complete before dismissing the client. First, you should demonstrate that the treated skills *generalize* to novel (untreated) verbal contexts, physical situations, and conversational partners. Second, you need to take steps to increase the chances of long-term *maintenance* of clinically established communication skills. Within-clinic generalization is easier to achieve than long-term maintenance in natural settings. Therefore, clinicians should pay at least as much attention to maintenance strategies as they do to establishing target responses.

Generalization of Target Behaviors

Generalization is the production of clinically established skills in untrained verbal contexts, in nonclinical physical environments, and while interacting with persons unrelated to treatment. Generalization is new learning based on old or recent learning. Untrained verbal and physical contexts include all naturalistic situations where individuals verbally interact with other individuals. Clinicians depend on generalization because it is not possible to teach all the varied verbal responses with all their complexity. Fortunately, there is no need to teach an infinite variety of verbal skills because teaching some will result in the generalized production of similar responses in novel contexts. Generalization is the mechanism of treatment economy.

Successful and effective treatment, unfortunately, does not guarantee generalization. *Generalization should be a part of the overall treatment strategy.* With well-planned training, target responses may generalize to untrained verbal contexts, new physical environments, and unfamiliar conversational partners. For instance, a person with aphasia who has re-learned to name objects shown in treatment sessions may begin to name new objects not involved in teaching. A child with speech sound disorder who just learned to produce the /s/ in selected words may produce the sound correctly in new, untrained words, phrases, and sentences. This is *response generalization*. Clinically, educationally, or incidentally (naturally) acquired skills may be produced in new physical environments (homes and other social situations). This is *setting generalization*. Newly learned verbal skills may be produced while interacting with both familiar and unfamiliar persons in their natural social contexts. This is *communication partner generalization*. These forms of generalization are the most valuable outcome of treatment.

Generalization is measured through various kinds of probes, as described in Chapter 8. Initially and for a short duration, treated skills may generalize without explicit reinforcement. You may recall from Chapter 8 that you do not reinforce responses given to probe (untrained) stimuli. However, if not supported by naturally occurring reinforcing consequences, generalized responses decline and eventually may get degraded or even extinguished (Regnier et al., 2022). Gradual decline in clinically established and initially generalized fluency, voice characteristics, and language skills in both adults and children in their natural environments has been a serious concern to clinicians. Generalization is a desirable outcome of treatment but is not an end in itself. Maintenance, not just the initial and unreinforced generalized responses, is the final goal of clinical intervention. Maintenance, however, is built upon the foundation of generalization (Jokel, 2022; Stokes & Osnes, 1989/2016; Swan et al., 2016). No maintenance program can be initiated when the target skills do not generalize to natural settings.

Because generalization is a prerequisite to maintenance, procedures designed to promote generalization are also those that are essential to promote maintenance. Procedures that induce robust generalization contribute to maintenance. Both generalization and maintenance should be considerations in treatment planning, not as afterthoughts (Tolan, 2014). Therefore, this chapter describes a set of unified procedures to promote both generalization and maintenance. Nonetheless, you may notice that certain procedures are emphasized as primarily maintenance strategies.

Maintenance of Target Behaviors

Unless the clinically established communicative behaviors are sustained over time in conversational speech produced in the natural environment, treatment has not benefited the client. Communication skills that generate favorable consequences to the speakers are likely to be maintained. If clients reliably produce the newly taught behaviors in the clinic but not at home, school, work, and other social settings, then the clinicians must have people in those settings do some of the things they themselves did to establish those behaviors.

Maintenance of treatment gains is largely the responsibility of typical conversational partners in everyday situations; clinicians are not permanent features of their clients' everyday living environments. Thus, modifying the social interaction patterns between the clients and their conversational partners in such a way as to support the clinically established communication skills is the **maintenance strategy** (Hegde, 2018; Regnier et al., 2022; Tolan, 2014). The key players in the maintenance strategy are the clients and people who interact with them.

Why Treatment Gains Are Not Maintained

Lack of maintenance of learned behaviors is a basic problem of all kinds of learning: naturalistic, educational, and clinical. Healthy and desirable behaviors acquired more naturally than in the clinics are also vulnerable to extinction. For example, sustained effort is needed to maintain physical exercise regimes, healthy diets, cessation of smoking, or regular studying of textbooks.

Treatment gains dissipate over time in the natural setting for several reasons (Falcomata & Wacker, 2013; Regnier et al., 2022; Saini et al., 2018; Stokes & Osnes, 1989/2016; Swan et al., 2016). First, and perhaps the most important, is that the natural settings (which include the familiar physical stimuli and the typical conversation partners) may fail to support the clinically established behaviors. Instead of noticing, praising, and otherwise reinforcing newly learned communication skills, people may ignore them, though covertly happy that the client did exhibit them. Clinicians may have noticed parents who exchange happy glances when their child who used to stutter speaks fluently after treatment but may fail to praise the child for fluency.

Second, the natural settings have always been where the communication disorders and deficits were sustained prior to treatment. Therefore, the setting is an array of stimuli and response consequences that have evoked and sustained the disorders and deficits and may continue to do so. For example, you may have taught a nonverbal child certain words that the child reliably produces in the clinic. But at home, the child may continue to point to things he or she wants, and the parents continue to give what the child pointed to. As a result, the nonverbal pointing continues to be reinforced, and the newly established words are not produced or maintained at home.

Third, the people in the client's life may not demand the clinically established skills from the client. As in the previous example, parents may not ask the client to produce words, fluent speech, soft voice, correct naming, and so forth. A demand to produce the newly learned skills also sets the stage for those skills. It is not just an ordinary demand or command. It includes such supports as modeling and prompting that increase the chance of the speech-language skills being produced.

Fourth, the structure and function of clinical treatment environments and the natural settings greatly differ. The treatment sessions are structured, formal, and include explicit stimuli, modeling, prompting, reinforcement, and verbal correction. The same factors are loose, variable, and incidental in the natural environment. When the two conditions are different, generalization is less likely, discrimination, opposite of generalization, is more likely. When there is no generalized responding, persons in the client's natural environment may not know what to do.

Fifth, some clinically established target behaviors may require additional effort to produce and sustain, compared to their baserate disorders and deficits. Slower rate of speech to avoid stuttering or cluttering is an example. The speech rate that is typical of the person who stuttered or cluttered is easier to sustain than a slower rate. When the speech rate returns to the pretreatment level, stuttering and cluttering also return. For a person with voice disorder (vocal hoarseness), it is easier to cheer boisterously rather than softly. Loud cheering is also socially reinforced, while soft and subtle appreciation is ignored or even punished ("not enthusiastic about the home team?").

A maintenance program should address these and other variables that negatively affect response maintenance over time and across situations. Most of those variables should be considered in treatment planning itself.

Generalization and Maintenance Procedures

If the crucial treatment variables are ubiquitous in natural settings, treated communication skills will be maintained. Generalization may be bypassed. However, people's patterns of interactions do not always support desirable behaviors, including communication skills, as noted.

Generalization and maintenance are neither afterthoughts nor just an outcome hoped for (Stokes & Baer, 1977). The two require careful planning from the beginning of intervention. Therefore, to promote generalization and maintenance of treated communication skills, take the following steps.

Step 1. Select Functional Target Behaviors

Functional communication targets are personally and socially meaningful, produced in natural settings, and effective in social interactions. They are likely to be generalized to, and reinforced in, natural settings. Consequently, they serve as foundation for maintenance strategies. Instead of trying to teach grammatically correct complex or compound sentences to a minimally verbal child, a person with Broca's aphasia, a person with severe apraxia of speech, or a client with severe dysarthria, teach them simple requests and everyday speech elements that are more *functional* for them. Functional skills serve the needs of the person with communication limitations. Consequently, such skills generalize more readily and are maintained over time because they are always reinforced.

Typically and historically, clinicians have selected impaired, lost, absent, or inappropriately produced speech-language skills for treatment. This is the traditional **remediation approach**. However, SLPs treating persons with neurodegenerative diseases that result in dementia of various types have reported that remediated deficient skills may not be maintained over time. Therefore, several investigators have suggested **prophylaxis treatment targets**, which are *unimpaired skills* that the individuals practice daily at home to slow down their decline (Jokel et al., 2014; Meyer et al., 2018). Treatment of intact skills is also called **maintenance-based treatment**, but the term is used in a special sense: it the is the maintenance of repeatedly practiced intact skills, not the maintenance of typical treatment-reinstated impaired skills (Flurie et al., 2020). A review of studies suggested that regularly practiced *intact* core words are better maintained than the impaired and treated words (Jokel et al., 2014). Therefore, to promote better maintenance, you may consider intact functional skills for repeated home practice for individuals with neurogenerative diseases.

Selection of target skills should be a joint effort involving the clinician, the client, and the caregivers. Clients and their caregivers should suggest target behaviors, approve those the clinician suggests, and together they should expand the skill repertoire. This strategy is likely to promote the client's communicative effectiveness, help improve the quality of life, and support generalization and maintenance.

Step 2. Select Familiar Treatment Stimuli

Treatment stimuli should be familiar to the client. If possible, select stimuli form the client's home environment. Parents of young children can bring toys and other materials from home to speech sound and language treatment sessions. Family members, especially the spouses of adult clients, may bring relevant photographs of persons whose names are treatment targets for persons with aphasia. When the response-evoking stimuli are common to both the clinic and home, the two settings are more similar than different, and hence generalization of target skills is more likely.

Step 3. Teach Multiple Exemplars

Teach speech sound, grammatical morphemes, sentence structures, naming skills, prosodic features and almost all skills with multiple exemplars. In Chapter 8, baserating with 20 stimulus items for most speech and language skills was recommended. After establishing the baserates, teach multiple exemplars that are sufficient to produce generalization that may contribute to maintenance.

Step 4. Give Sufficient Treatment

Insufficient treatment does not strengthen the target behaviors, does not generalize to other responses, settings, and persons, and consequently, the maintenance strategy cannot be implemented. To avoid this problem, **do not prematurely dismiss your clients**. Do not assume that the target responses are stabilized because they have met the training or probe criteria. A child who correctly produces phonemes in words may still need help in producing them in conversational speech. A man who has learned to maintain an appropriate vocal pitch in the clinic may still be speaking with his unacceptably high pitch elsewhere. A woman with aphasia may say a few words in the clinic but may not remember any of them after the treatment sessions. In all such cases, treatment should be continued until the target behaviors are stabilized in conversation and with minimum and natural (social) reinforcers.

Step 5. Reinforce Target Responses in Conversational Speech

Target behaviors **reinforced in conversational speech** are better generalized and maintained than those that do not reach that level of training. Phonemes trained only at the word and phrase levels may not be produced in natural settings where the speech is connected and continuous. Certain other target behaviors—for example, fluency, voice qualities, naming—trained only at the word level may be ineffective when the client speaks continuously in natural settings. Therefore, the target behaviors must always be reinforced in conversational speech in the final stages of treatment.

As early as possible, move treatment to conversational speech level. Whether you are working with clients with speech sound disorders, language problems, voice disorders, stuttering, apraxia of speech, dysarthria, or aphasia, move through the simpler levels of words and phrases as rapidly as the client's performance supports. Spend more clinical time monitoring and reinforcing the target behaviors in conversational speech than in words or phrases.

Step 6. Thin Out the Reinforcement

Reinforcement is sparse and incidental in natural settings. Verbal praise is not constant in social contexts, but it is in the initial treatment sessions. Once the behaviors are established, start using an **intermittent reinforcement schedule** in which you do not reinforce every response but only certain responses. Paradoxically, a behavior reinforced continuously (Fixed ratio 1, FR1) does not resist extinction as much as the one reinforced intermittently (e.g., an FR5, every fifth response is reinforced). The longer a behavior resists extinction, the greater the chance that it will be reinforced in natural settings and maintained over time. Therefore, after having established the target behaviors initially through continuous reinforcement, begin to reduce the amount of reinforcement. Shift the schedule to progressively thinner (higher) ones. Reinforce every other response (FR2), every third (FR3), or every fourth (FR 4) response.

Lower the ratio if the response frequency declines. In the final stages of treatment, when you monitor the target responses in conversational speech, reinforce only sporadically and only with natural social reinforcers (e.g., nodding, smiling, maintaining eye contact, agreeing with the client's statements).

Step 7. Use Social and Conditioned Generalized Reinforcers

Social reinforcers are those that are more prevalent in natural settings. Therefore, even when you have to use primary (food and drink) and tangible (small gifts for children), pair them with what is more common in natural settings: social reinforcers (e.g., verbal praise, smiling, nodding, agreement). Do not dispense tokens without social reinforcers. If the same kinds of reinforcers are encountered in the clinic and natural settings, the responses are more likely to be maintained.

In addition to social reinforcers, use **conditioned generalized reinforcers**, such as tokens that are backed up with a variety of reinforcers to increase the chances of similar reinforcers being encountered in natural settings. Also, the family members may be able to implement a similar token system at home to sustain the skills. The job of the client's family members will be easier if they can use a clinically established (and effective) system of reinforcement.

Step 8. Expand the Range of Discriminative Stimuli

A **discriminative stimulus** is a stimulus in whose presence a response has been reinforced. As a result, the response is likely in the presence of that stimulus. Any stimulus may acquire the power to evoke a response because of its systematic association with reinforcement.

The discriminative stimulus will not continue to evoke the response for very long if the response is not reinforced. However, an initial, **generalized response** in the presence of a discriminative stimulus gives the opportunity to reinforce that response to sustain it.

The most important discriminative stimuli are persons, physical stimuli, and physical settings. The clinician is the first discriminative stimulus for the target response. By systematically reinforcing the target response, the clinician makes the response more likely in her presence and in her clinical setting.

Some dramatic occurrences illustrate the power of the clinician and the clinical setting in evoking target responses. For instance, parents often are amazed at the amount of fluency their children who stutter exhibit in front of the clinician and in the treatment room. Anywhere else, however, the children may stutter just as much as they did before treatment. The child who reliably produces words in the treatment room may continue to gesture at home. A woman's hoarseness may all but disappear when she walks into the treatment room. But just as dramatically, her typical hoarse voice may reappear as she leaves the clinic. This disappearance and reappearance of problem behaviors are due to the discriminative stimulus value of the clinician and the treatment room and lack of discriminative stimuli in nonclinical settings.

The task is to expand the range of stimuli that reliably evoke the clinically established skills in the natural environment. When associated with reinforcement, other people and other settings begin to evoke target behaviors. To accomplish this, do the following:

- **Ask the client's family members to sit in the treatment room**. Because the family members will then be associated with treatment and reinforcement, they are likely to evoke treated skills at home. Initially, the family members may only observe, but eventually learn to evoke and reinforce the client as described later. In the latter stages of treatment, ask your friends or others who are strangers to the client to observe treatment sessions. Discuss this with parents and clients before you invite other persons to sessions because it raises the issue of confidentiality. You need the permission of adult clients and parents or guardians of minors.

- **Move treatment to outside the treatment room**. The restricted treatment room is useful and necessary to establish target behaviors because it provides a controlled environment free of distractions. But the room is so different from a client's everyday environment that the client's learning is restricted to its confines. Therefore, when the client begins to produce the target behaviors in conversational speech, move treatment out of the treatment room. Use the following guidelines:

  1. **Hold informal treatment sessions outside the clinic**. Take a walk with the client outside the clinic. Converse with the client and monitor the target behaviors in conversational speech. Move back into the clinic if the correct responses decline.

2. **Move to progressively different situations.** If the client sustains responses in the first nonclinical situation, then move to other situations.

3. **In the beginning, take the client to less-threatening situations.** Let the client talk to you in the new environment while you monitor and reinforce the target responses. Subsequently, let the client talk to strangers.

4. **Let the client rehearse what he or she will tell a stranger in a new setting.** For example, you might have a client who stutters talk to a bookstore clerk. Have the client rehearse what he or she plans to ask the clerk slowly and fluently.

5. **The first few times, stay close to the client.** To prompt the correct response, give a subtle signal such as touching the client's shoulder as he or she begins to speak. In the case of a person who stutters, for example, the touch may mean that the speech rate should be reduced.

6. **Take note of correct and incorrect productions.** Give subtle and quick reinforcement because the strangers will not reinforce the client. Because of your reinforcement, the new situations and persons may become discriminative stimuli for the target responses.

7. **Gradually increase the distance between you and your client.** As the client begins to talk to strangers, slowly move away from him or her.

8. **Take the client to progressively more difficult situations.** As the target responses are maintained in each new situation, take the client to shopping centers, restaurants, bookstores, toy stores, and other relevant places and have the client talk to people there. Reinforce the client in all situations for maintaining the target skills.

Step 9. Teach Others to Evoke and Support Target Behaviors

This step is the heart of maintenance strategy. It must be implemented whether there is initial generalization or not. Treatment will have been **extended to the natural environment** if the significant others in the client's life know (a) the exact target behaviors, (b) how to evoke them, and (c) how to enhance them. The target behaviors then have the greatest probability of being maintained.

Take the following steps in teaching others to evoke and support target behaviors:

1. **Describe and demonstrate the target behaviors to others.** When you invite the family members and others to observe the

treatment sessions, describe the target behaviors being taught. Tell them precisely what the client is expected to do. Do not use jargon. Give simple and direct descriptions. For example, while treating a child with English morphological deficiencies, say, "I want Johnny to add the plural s at the end of plural words. He says, *two book*, but we want him to say *two books* when he sees two of them." As another example, "We are teaching your wife to initiate speech softly, easily, and in a relaxed manner. Like this" [demonstrate].

2. **Demonstrate how to evoke target behaviors**. Let family members watch you evoke the target behaviors so they understand how to model the target behaviors for the client. Train the parents, spouses, and siblings to prompt or suggest the target behavior when the client fails to produce it at home. For instance, train the family members of a child with a language or a speech sound disorder to correctly model words, phrases, and sentences that you are teaching.

3. **Teach family members the subtle ways of prompting target behaviors**. When the parents begin their work at home, the need to model extensively will be minimum. The parents most likely need to prompt the target responses, however. When prompts do not work, the parents need to model.

   Teach parents to give subtle prompts when a failure to produce the target behavior seems imminent. Ask the caregivers to avoid loud and obvious signals the clients will not accept. In the presence of guests and visitors, ask the family members to prompt in a subtle manner that the others present may not notice. A subtle and brief hand gesture or even a movement of a finger may be all that is needed to slow down the rate of speech, reduce the vocal pitch, increase vocal intensity, and decrease hoarseness of voice. They can devise similar gestures to remind the client to open his or her mouth to increase oral resonance or to assume a certain articulatory posture. A person sitting next to the client at the dining table may touch the client to prompt the production of a target response. For each specific target response, devise such a specific, brief signal.

   In training the family members to provide such prompts, demonstrate selected unobtrusive signals and teach the client to reliably respond to them in the clinic. Then ask the parents to give those signals frequently at home. Some clients may need a more pronounced stimulus in the beginning. If so, in progressive steps, reduce that obvious stimulus to a brief signal that only the family and the client will know has transpired.

During treatment sessions, give the same signal you ask the family members to use at home. When you take the client out of the treatment room to natural settings, experiment with different types of signals and isolate the signal that works best for the client. Ask the parents to use the same signal at home.

4. **Teach family members to create opportunities for the client to produce the target behaviors.** Often, clients who have communication problems are reluctant to talk, even after their problems have been mostly remediated. Persons who stutter or those with hearing loss may talk less in groups just as they did before treatment, although they are now expected to produce their newly acquired skills of fluency or oral language. Treated persons with aphasia also may be reluctant to talk in front of other persons. A child who has just learned to say some words may not speak them. Having gotten used to the client's role as a silent partner, the family and friends may not ask the person with a communicative disability to take part in conversation. Therefore, train family members and other persons to include the client in verbal exchanges. If the family members previously spoke for the client, ask them not to do that. For instance, the child who has learned to make requests should be asked to make relevant requests. The wife of a person who stutters should stop ordering for him at restaurants.

5. **Teach how to reinforce target behaviors.** The client's family, teachers, friends, or colleagues should know how to reinforce the target behaviors produced at home and in other situations. Point out to parents and others the importance of immediate reinforcement and demonstrate how to provide it. Also tell them it is equally important to stop the client at the earliest sign of a wrong response. Ask them not to wait until a lengthy but wrong response is completed. Show how you do this.

Like prompts that help evoke responses in natural settings, reinforcers also should be delivered in a subtle manner. Most clients do not want to be reinforced in front of other persons. A man who stutters does not want his wife to say, "You are very fluent, honey!" in front of formal dinner guests. But reinforcing a person for speaking fluently in such formal occasions is important. Therefore, a special signal that is not a prompt, but a reinforcement, may be given discreetly. Signals that prompt behaviors are given when the behavior is imminent and signals that suggest approval and praise (reinforcement) are given soon after the target behaviors are produced. If such signals are used often in the company of strangers and acquaintances, and backed up by verbal praise as soon as possible, the signals may act as discriminative stimuli.

Do not ask parents and others to reinforce continuously. By the time maintenance strategies have begun at home, the client will have been reinforced in the clinic on a fairly large intermittent schedule. Therefore, infrequent reinforcement might be effective. Ask family members to increase the frequency of reinforcement only when the correct responses do not seem to be nearly as high as they were in the treatment sessions.

6. **Teach how to provide corrective feedback, but only minimally**. Generally, train parents and others to praise more often than to correct. When wrong responses are produced, it is better to give a swift prompt than to give a punishing signal. For example, to slow down the speech rate of a person who stutters or clutters, it is better to prompt rather than whisper "no!" A hand gesture to slow down is more neutral than such verbal punishers and may be more effective. Therefore, train family members and others to prompt correct responses when incorrect responses seem imminent.

7. **Train family members to stop reinforcing inappropriate behaviors**. Family members may continue to reinforce incorrect or inappropriate behaviors. As noted before, a previously nonverbal child may continue to get reinforced for gestures at home. Train parents and others to withhold reinforcers for gestures, verbal errors, and other nonverbal behaviors when it is clear that the child can produce words. Let them make reinforcement contingent on newly learned desirable behaviors.

8. **Assess whether family members are doing the right things**. Make sure others are prompting and reinforcing the target behaviors. Ask them to audio- or video-record a sample conversation and bring it to you. Ask for such recorded evidence periodically so you may give the family members feedback on their performance. You should catch any mistakes the family members are making to give them corrective instructions. By this, you will also have collected data on response maintenance at home.

Telepractice may afford an excellent opportunity to supervise and modify home treatment programs the family members implement. You can observe, supervise, and make online corrections or reinforce the family members' implementation of recommended procedures.

9. **Train family members to conduct formal treatment sessions at home**. Although you will most often train parents to promote maintenance of target behaviors, you may sometimes ask family to conduct formal treatment sessions at home. For example, while working with small children and infants, you often have to train parents to conduct some portion of treatment at home. Infant language stimulation, early intervention for stuttering and speech sound disorders, and intervention for vocal abuse in young children may require a substantial amount of parental work.

   If parents and spouses can be trained to hold brief and parallel training sessions at home, responses may be stabilized at home sooner than otherwise expected. Parents and spouses who also are therapists (even in an informal or limited sense) will better promote response maintenance. If parents and spouses cannot do this, a few minutes of brief informal sessions at home are highly desirable. When family members agree to do this, ask them to set aside a time for speech work at home. Request them to record a representative session they hold and submit it to you for your review and feedback. As noted, a better method might be to hold periodic online telepractice sessions to modify the work of the family members.

   Training significant persons in a client's life is perhaps the most challenging and yet the most necessary task in promoting maintenance. You will have to constantly think of new ways of meeting this challenge.

10. **Keep in touch with family members**. Maintain frequent telephone contacts to answer family members' questions and to offer suggestions based on submitted data or online observation of sessions. If necessary, be prepared to visit the home and observe the parents. At this time, demonstrate new procedures. Ask your supervisor about the rules you should follow in making home visits.

Step 10. Teach the Client Self-Control

Self-control is monitoring and changing one's own behavior. People modify their behaviors with varying degrees of success. But clients who learn to control their clinically established skills will have become their own therapists to some extent. They will be less dependent on family and friends to help sustain their speech and language skills. Therefore, teaching self-control is an important task in promoting response maintenance. Several tasks promote self-control and self-monitoring of skills.

1. **Teach clients to judge the accuracy of their behaviors**. Ask the child in speech sound or language intervention to say whether his or her productions were correct or not. With just a few training trials, most children learn to make this judgment. Children who are taught to make those judgments frequently begin to monitor their behaviors more closely. They stop as soon as they begin to misarticulate a sound or miss a grammatic morpheme. Adults with dysarthria and apraxia of speech may also be encouraged to self-judge the accuracy of their speech production.

   Ask the persons getting treatment for stuttering to judge the occurrence of stutterings, abrupt onset of phonation, a faster than required rate of speech, muscular tension while speaking, and most other target responses. Likewise, ask them to judge the occurrence of smooth phonation, desired rate, relaxed articulation, and so forth. Speakers who stutter and who appreciate the contrast between their stuttered speech and target fluency skills will begin to monitor their speech production. They are likely to stop at the very beginning of a stutter. With further training in self-monitoring, they may stop as soon as they feel tension in their speech musculature and start with greater relaxation. Adults with dysarthria and apraxia of speech who learn to judge the accuracy of their speech production may also catch themselves at the beginning of wrong responses and correct themselves. Persons with aphasia may stop as soon as they start to name a picture with the wrong initial phoneme. When clients use such tactics, you can reduce the amount of reinforcement or corrective feedback and help sustain the skills in nonclinical environments.

2. **Train clients in target behavior counting and recording**. Ask clients who become proficient in recognizing their own correct and incorrect responses to record their behaviors along with you. Ask them to make a tally mark on a sheet of paper every time they stutter or produce a fluent utterance, articulate a phoneme incorrectly or correctly, produce a desirable or undesirable vocal characteristic, name the stimulus item correctly or incorrectly, and so forth. Also ask them to tally their correct responses. Many children are eager to do it. Some children may be asked to count their correct and incorrect behaviors by placing different colored plastic chips in two cups placed in front of them.

When your clients learn to measure their correct and incorrect behaviors in the clinic, ask them to bring data on their performance outside the clinic. Measuring their behaviors at home and other situations will help them monitor their target responses more closely. Individuals who stutter may be asked to record the frequency of their dysfluencies in situations when audio-recording their speech is not practical. Adult voice clients also may record the frequency of occurrence of hoarseness or hard glottal attacks and so forth. Small, handheld counters can be used to record the frequency of behaviors. Persons with aphasia can record the frequency of their correct naming at home.

3. **Teach clients to implant signals and reminders in everyday situations**. For instance, clients who stutter or have high-pitched voices may draw arrows pointing downward on small pieces of paper and paste them on telephone receivers, office desks, and other places where they need reminders to reduce the rate of speech or the pitch of their voice.

   Signals implanted in natural environments have been successful in helping persons with dementia and other neurodegenerative diseases to maintain certain skills for longer durations than without such signals. Written or iconic reminders of appointments and specific daily activities (e.g., the time to exercise, eat lunch or dinner, bathe, or watch TV) can prompt the person to perform the action. Smartphones and tablets also may be used to remind clients of scheduled appointments and activities.

Step 11. Teach the Client to Prime Others to Reinforce

Priming is prompting others to reinforce one's own behavior; in this procedure, clients draw attention to their own behavior so as to get reinforced. A common problem with clients' family members is that they may not notice the production of improved communicative behaviors or may take them for granted. They may think that their only job is to stop undesirable behaviors. They may not realize that it is more important to encourage the desirable behavior. For instance, parents who are asked to monitor their child's correct and incorrect productions of target phonemes may notice incorrect production more often than correct productions. The child then hears more critical words than encouraging words. To counter this unhelpful tendency:

1. **Train the family to prompt and reinforce as often as they can and correct as minimally as possible**. Train them to keep the reinforcement: verbal correction ratio clearly in favor of reinforcement.

2. **Teach clients to prime (prompt) others to reinforce them**. To receive reinforcements in natural settings, clients must be taught to point out their own productions of desirable and newly acquired behaviors. People prime others for reinforcement all the time. The tactic is used when others tend to ignore good behaviors, or too busy to notice, or take good behaviors for granted. Whenever we show off our good behaviors or point out something we did well, we prime others for reinforcement.

Teaching reinforcement priming to clients should go hand-in-hand with teaching family members to reinforce immediately. Tell the family and teachers in a school that you want the client to draw attention. Otherwise, they may think the client is showing off. A girl may let her parents, siblings, playmates, and teachers know that she correctly produced a phoneme throughout a segment of conversation. Soon after fluently ordering food in a restaurant, a man who stutters may draw his wife's attention to his successful but previously troublesome performance. A woman with hoarseness may tell her listeners that she has been speaking very softly and smoothly in an otherwise loud family discussion. A man with aphasia may draw his friend's attention to correct naming of persons or objects.

Vocal emphasis on a target language feature may be another way of drawing attention to it. A boy who has learned to produce the regular plural morpheme slightly emphasizes it in his words, phrases, and sentences. This vocal emphasis may force attention of a parent who may otherwise ignore the production.

Train clients to ask their friends and family to signal with a subtle hint that an undesirable response has occurred. A woman with vocal pitch breaks may request her roommate to signal with her finger that pitch breaks occurred. A man who stutters may ask his wife to stop him whenever he stutters or speaks rapidly.

Step 12. Train Clients to Use Electronic Devices for Home Practice

Research the available tablet-, computer-, and smartphone-based applications the client with specific disorders can use to practice target skills at home. When combined with self-monitoring of skills, electronic devices with specific applications make it possible to practice oral and written communication skills every day or as frequently as possible. Daily practice of target skills is an excellent maintenance strategy.

Persons with chronic aphasia and dementia have benefited from regular home practice. The practice may be done with or without such electronic devices as tablets and computers (Henry et al., 2019; Jokel et al., 2014; Kurland et al., 2018). For instance, persons with aphasia or dementia may repeatedly name objects and photographs of persons to retain the naming skills. Children with speech sound disorders may practice the correct production of speech sounds at home; video clips of modeled correct productions of speech sounds may be loaded to the device for the child to practice. Children with language disorders, too can practice at home while watching similar video clips of specific language targets.

Step 13. Use Telepractice to Monitor and Promote Maintenance

Use the telepractice sessions to monitor the client's maintenance of clinically established skills. The skills may have been established in face-to-face clinical sessions or in prior telepractice sessions (Theodoros et al., 2016). In either case, telepractice sessions on a reduced schedule, such as once a week, may be an efficient method to monitor the target skill productions at home. Brief samples of speech and language produced at home with typical conversational partners may help assess the maintenance of speech, language, fluency, and voice characteristics.

If the skills have declined, the prior telepractice treatment sessions may be offered as booster treatment. If necessary, the client may return to the clinic for face-to-face therapy. See the special issue of *Language, Speech, and Hearing Services in Schools, Volume 53,* Issue 2 devoted to telepractice in speech-language pathology, especially in the school setting.

Step 14. Give Booster Treatment

Booster treatment is treatment reinstated for a client sometime after dismissal because of lack of response maintenance. Research supports booster treatment as a strategy for maintenance of treatment gains (Jokel, 2022; Tolan, 2014). Some clinicians assert that treatment is not successful unless clients are permanently cured so that they never need our services for the rest of their lives. Any relapse of stuttering in a treated person often is sharply pointed out by critics who claim there is no successful treatment for stuttering. Relapse of a successfully treated disorder is not necessarily a negative reflection on the previous success. No successful medical treatment comes with a guarantee that the patient will not catch the same disease again. Similarly, successful treatment of stuttering or any other communicative disorder does not come with a guarantee that clients will be free from the disorder for the rest of their lives. Such a guarantee is not a precondition to judge the effectiveness of a treatment procedure. Nor is it ethical to offer such a guarantee to the client.

Clinicians may reduce or eliminate a disorder, but they cannot always eliminate the biological or environmental conditions that cause disorders. Relapse of a communicative disorder after successful treatment suggests that the treated person again faced the conditions that created the disorder in the first place. We may not fully understand those conditions, or if we did, we may have no control over some or all of them. This is a matter for further research.

Meanwhile, the clinician can take pride when a disorder is treated successfully, knowing well that there is likelihood of relapse. But a careful clinician takes the following steps to reduce the chances of relapse:

1. **Educate the clients about potential relapse**. Let them know that relapse is a possibility and that they may need additional treatment sometime in the future. Assure them that when the problem emerges again, it can be handled successfully. Caution them, though, that they should contact you at the earliest sign of relapse. They should promptly alert their clinicians of a slight increase in dysfluencies, hoarseness or harshness of voice, undesirable pitch, increased difficulty remembering events, reduced speech intelligibility, deteriorated language skills, and so forth. The sooner the process of relapse is caught, the faster the progress in resumed (booster) treatment.

2. **Schedule booster treatment as quickly as possible**. The need for booster treatment shows that we have many problems to solve in the maintenance of treatment gains. But until research solves them, you need to have a schedule for booster treatment for every client who needs it. The need may be most acute in achieving maintenance of treatment effects in clients with stuttering, voice disorders, aphasia, and most neurodegenerative diseases that impair communication (e.g., varieties of dementia, including primary progressive aphasia). These and other disorders may relapse not because the original therapy was useless, but because the clients did not receive booster treatment.

3. **Offer the same or another effective treatment**. Offer the *same treatment* that was initially successful. Include in booster treatment the technical improvements made during the intervening time. If a newer and more powerful treatment has been developed since dismissal, offer it.

4. **Keep the duration of booster treatment brief**. In most cases, a few sessions may be sufficient, especially if the client has returned in the early stage of relapse. If the relapse is substantial, prolong the booster treatment. To clients treated for stuttering, voice disorders,

or dementia, consider the need for repeated booster treatments spread over a few years. To gain cooperation from the discouraged clients, explain to them that a few repetitions of treatment are a method of fading out the treatment completely.

5. **Consider telepractice to offer booster treatment**. Telepractice may be an excellent format for booster treatment. Because of the prior face-to-face treatment, the client may find the telebooster format relatively easy to use, especially when the same treatment is offered. You may develop brief videos of treatment sessions the client can download and practice at home. The telepractice may be online or offline.

6. **Further strengthen the family's work with the client**. During booster treatment, *strengthen family members' skills* in monitoring the client's target behaviors. A client's target behaviors may have deteriorated mainly because the family members' monitoring of those behaviors faded.

Follow-Up Assessments

Follow-up is an assessment of response maintenance over time. It is a *conversational probe* of communicative behaviors, sampling especially the target behaviors that were clinically established. Students in clinical practicum often do not work long enough with the same clients to make follow-up assessments. Each semester of clinical practice, you may be assigned different clients. Nonetheless, you must know the follow-up assessment procedures. You will be making those assessments during your professional practice.

Adhere to the follow-up schedule of your practicum sites. Typically, the first follow-up assessment is scheduled *3 months* after a client is dismissed from services. Assuming that the client has maintained the communicative behaviors, the next assessment may be scheduled after 6 months. If the behaviors are maintained, subsequent assessments may be scheduled in yearly intervals. A 3 to 4-*year follow-up* is needed for speakers who received treatment for their stuttering. A similar schedule may be needed for voice clients. Children who receive treatment for speech sound disorders probably do not need such a lengthy follow-up. If correct production of speech sounds is maintained for a year or so, misarticulations typically do not relapse. Persons with dysarthria or apraxia of speech, often adults, may show deterioration in their clinically established speech production skills. For individuals with aphasia or progressive neurological and physical diseases, the follow-up assessment schedule is based on the client's health and progress in speech or language treatment. Timely follow-up assessments help determine the *need for booster treatment*, as described previously.

In a typical follow-up, do the following:

1. **Take an extended conversational speech sample**. Make it as naturalistic as possible. Also get a nonclinical sample. Take the client out for a walk and engage in conversation and audio-record it. Do not depend solely on standardized tests because most do not sample extended conversations. To sample the treated language features adequately, contrive the conversation or direct it in some specific manner to have the client produce those features. Visit the companion website for Obtaining and Analyzing Conversational Speech Samples and the Language Sample Checklist.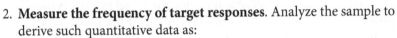

2. **Measure the frequency of target responses**. Analyze the sample to derive such quantitative data as:

   - Percentage of dysfluency or stuttering, as defined and measured

   - Percentage of correct production of treated phonemes

   - Percentage of correct production of grammatical morphemes, syntactic structures, topic initiation, conversational repair, and other language features that were taught

   - Number of words in sentences

   - Percentage of speech time a particular voice quality was maintained

   - Frequency of pitch breaks per minute of continuous speech

   - Percentage of words in which inappropriate nasal resonance was heard

   - Percentage of spoken words that were intelligible

   - Number of words or syllables spoken per minute

   - Durations of inappropriate prosodic features in conversational speech

   - Percentage of correct naming responses

   - Percentage of words spoken with adequate loudness as judged

   - Durations for which a conversational topic was maintained

   - Frequency with which conversational topics were abruptly changed

3. **Arrange for booster treatment if data warrant.** If the follow-up assessment data show a decline in the target behaviors from the time of dismissal, offer treatment to increase and strengthen communication skills so that maintenance is promoted. Consider in-the-clinic as well as telepractice sessions.

4. **Establish a new schedule of follow-up after booster treatment.** Perhaps the client may need to be assessed in 3 to 6 months. Ask the client and the family to contact you for a consultation as soon as they notice a response deterioration.

Much clinical research needs to be done on generalization and maintenance of treatment gains in natural settings. If you approach the problem from the standpoint of extending treatment to nonclinical settings, you may have notable success in getting the target behaviors stabilized and possibly sustained in natural settings. A sound maintenance strategy will include treatment planned and implemented to promote generalization and maintenance, scheduled follow-up sessions, booster treatment offered when warranted, and continuously refining family members' intervention techniques at home.

⟨?⟩ Questions for Self-Assessment

1. Distinguish between generalization and maintenance of treated target behaviors. Which one of the two, if it occurs first, is beneficial to promote the other? Explain why and give clinical examples.

2. What are the main reasons why treatment gains are not maintained in the clients' natural environment?

3. Describe how telepractice may be used in promoting generalization and maintenance of treated communication skills.

4. Describe how you would train family members to promote the maintenance of clinically established communication skills. Be specific about the actions the family members are expected to take.

5. Name the technical term for the following clinical actions and briefly describe why they are done:

   a) Teaching basic requests in words or phrases, pointing, and gestures, instead of grammatically complete utterances: _____
   _____.

b) Teaching clients in therapy sessions to chart their correct and incorrect responses: _____
_____.

c) Using a fixed ratio of 5 (FR5, every fifth response is reinforced)
_____.

d) Teaching clients to draw attention to their own clinically acquired skills. _____.

References

Falcomata, T. S., & Wacker, D. P. (2013). On the use of strategies for programming generalization during functional communication training: A review of the literature. *Journal of Developmental and Physical Disabilities, 25*, 5–15.

Flurie, M., Ungrady, M., & Reilly, J. (2020). Evaluating a maintenance-based treatment approach to preventing lexical dropout in progressive anomia. *Journal of Speech, Language, Hearing Research, 63*, 4082–4095.

Hegde, M. N. (1998). *Treatment procedures in communicative disorders* (3rd ed.). Pro-Ed.

Hegde, M. N. (2018). *Hegde's pocketguide to treatment in speech-language pathology* (4th ed.). Plural Publishing.

Henry, M. L., Hubbard, H. I., Grasso, S. M., Dial, H. R., Beeson, P. M., Miller, B., & Gomo-Tempini, M. L. (2019). Treatment for word retrieval in semantic and logopenic variants of primary progressive aphasia: Immediate and long-term outcomes. *Journal of Speech, Language, Hearing Research, 62*, 2723–2749.

Jokel, R. (2022). Maintenance and generalization of lexical items in primary progressive aphasia: Reflections from the roundtable discussion at the 2021 Clinical Aphasiology Conference. *American Journal of Speech-Language Pathology, 31*, 2395–2403.

Jokel, R., Graham, N. L., Rochon, E., & Leonard, C. (2014). Word retrieval therapies in primary progressive aphasia. *Aphasiology, 28*(8), 1038–1068.

Kurland, J., Liu, A., & Stokes, P. (2018). Effects of a tablet-based home practice program with telepractice on treatment outcomes in chronic aphasia. *Journal of Speech, Language, and Hearing Research, 61*(5), 1140–1156.

Meyer, A. M., Tippett, D. C., Turner, R. S., & Friedman, R. B. (2018). Prophylaxis and remediation of anomia in the semantic and logopenic variants of primary progressive aphasia. *Neuropsychological Rehabilitation, 28*(3), 352–368.

Regnier, S. D., Traxler, H. K., Devoto, A., & DeFulio, A. (2022). A systematic review of treatment maintenance strategies in token economies: Implications for contingency management. *Perspectives on Behavior Science, 45*, 819–861.

Saini, V., Sullivan, W. E., Baxter, E. L., DeRosa, N. M., & Roane, H. S. (2018). Renewal during functional communication training. *Journal of Applied Behavior Analysis, 51*, 603–616.

Stokes, T. F., & Baer, D. M. (1977). An implicit technology of generalization. *Journal of Applied Behavior Analysis,10*, 349–367.

Stokes, T. F., & Osnes, P. G. (1989/2016). An operant pursuit of generalization: Republished article. *Behavior Therapy, 47*, 720–732. (Original work published 1989).

Swan, A., Carper, M. M., & Kendall, P. C. (2016). In pursuit of generalization: An updated review. *Behavior Therapy, 47,* 733–746.

Theodoros, D. G., Hill, A. J., & Russell, T. G. (2016). Clinical and quality of life outcomes of speech treatment for Parkinson's disease delivered to the home via telerehabilitation: A noninferiority randomized clinical trial. *American Journal of Speech-Language Pathology, 25,* 214–232.

Tolan, P. M. (2014). More than afterthoughts and details: Maintenance and booster effects as critical elements of intervention research. *Journal of Abnormal Child Psychology, 42*(3), 399–402.

GLOSSARY

Alternative assessment—Procedures to assess communication disorders that do not rely heavily on standardized tests; considered more appropriate for ethnoculturally diverse individuals; see also *Authentic, Dynamic, Client-specific, Criterion-referenced,* and *Integrated assessments.*

American Speech-Language-Hearing Association (ASHA)—The national professional organization representing speech-language pathologists and audiologists.

Antecedents—Events that occur before responses; clinically, all kinds of treatment stimuli, including pictures and clinician's modeling.

Assessment—Clinical procedures implemented to understand a client's communicative problem and his or her personal and family history, along with existing and non-existing communicative skills; includes measurement of communicative skills and related behaviors.

Authentic assessment—Approach that measures naturalistic and meaningful communication in real-life settings using speech and language samples from the client's functional environments during daily routines and activities.

Automatic reinforcers—Reinforcing sensory consequences of responses.

Aversive stimuli—Events that people work hard to avoid or move away from.

Avoidance—A behavior that prevents the occurrence of an aversive event and hence gets reinforced.

Avoidance conditioning—Teaching behaviors that terminate, reduce, or avoid aversive events.

Backup reinforcers—Events, objects, and opportunities that clients gain access to by exchanging tokens they have earned in treatment sessions.

Baselines—Pretreatment target skill measures that help demonstrate improvement under treatment; the same as baserates.

Bedside evaluation—A quick and subjective evaluation of a patient; in speech-language pathology, it is often an evaluation of a patient's swallowing, memory, orientation, and so forth.

Behavioral momentum—Rapidly evoking a high-probability response and immediately commanding a low-probability response to reduce noncompliance or to increase the low-probability behaviors.

Benchmarks—Used synonymously with objectives to outline steps and outcomes necessary to obtain a long-term goal.

Block scheduling—A service scheduling method found in public schools; students in specific schools receive services for only a predetermined period of time (e.g., only for 6 weeks, 4 to 5 days each week); clinicians then move on to serve children in another block; contrasted with *intermittent scheduling*.

Booster treatment—Treatment given any time after the client was dismissed from the original treatment to help maintain the treatment gains.

Cardiologist—A physician with specialized training in cardiovascular diseases.

Certificate of Clinical Competence (CCC)—Awarded by the American Speech-Language-Hearing Association to speech-language pathologists and audiologists who have met certain standards.

Client-specific approach—A method of selecting target behaviors that are relevant and useful for the individual client; contrasted with normative approach.

Clinical fellowship—A period of paid or voluntary professional work done beyond the master's degree under supervision; required by ASHA to award its Certificate of Clinical Competence.

Cluttering—A disorder of fluency characterized by an excessively fast rate of speech negatively affecting speech intelligibility.

Collaborative instruction model—A model in which the speech-language pathologist and classroom teacher coordinate their lessons and work together to provide students with appropriate learning opportunities.

Conditioned generalized reinforcers—Tokens, money, and such other reinforcers that are effective in a wide range of conditions because their effects do not depend on a specific state of need (as food does).

Conditioned reinforcers—Social consequences that reinforce behaviors because of past learning experiences; the same as secondary reinforcers.

Consecutive interpreting—An individual talks and pauses, and then the interpreter translates.

Consultative model—The speech-language pathologist works with the client's family, teachers, or other professionals to address the needs of the client.

Contingency—An interdependent relation between events that help teach and sustain skills; the dependent relation between stimuli, responses, and their consequences.

Contingency priming—Prompting others to reinforce one's own behaviors.

Continuing education units (CEUs)—ASHA and licensing agency requirements that stipulate a certain number of annual hours of attendance at approved educational experiences (e.g., lectures, courses, conferences, seminars) to keep current in the profession.

Continuous schedule—A schedule in which all responses are reinforced.

Control group—The group that does not receive treatment in a treatment evaluation study that uses the group research design.

Controlled evidence—Data that show that a particular treatment, not some other factor, was responsible for the positive changes in the client's behavior.

Corrective feedback—Response-contingent presentation or withdrawal of a stimulus that reduces the frequency of that response.

Council for Clinical Certification (CFCC)—Sets the standards for and awards the Certificate of Clinical Competence.

Council on Academic Accreditation in Audiology and Speech-Language Pathology (CAA)—Accredits university training programs that meet ASHA standards.

Credential—A document that indicates that certain competencies have been met and authorizes the individual holding the credential to provide services according to its parameters.

Criterion-referenced assessment—An alternative assessment procedure in which a client's skills are judged against a criterion of performance (e.g., 80% accuracy).

Diagnosis—A determination of the nature of a disorder and its causes, if possible.

Diagnostic report—Provides comprehensive information on a client's pretreatment status.

Dietitian—A professional with training in nutrition and diet.

Differential reinforcement—Use of reinforcement techniques to increase certain behaviors, while at the same time certain other behaviors decrease as a side effect.

Differential reinforcement of alternative behavior (DRA)—Reinforcing a specified desirable behavior that serves the same function as the one to be reduced.

Differential reinforcement of incompatible behavior (DRI)—Reinforcing a desirable behavior that is not compatible with an undesirable behavior targeted for reduction.

Differential reinforcement of low rates of responding (DRL)—Reinforcing progressively lower frequencies of an undesirable behavior to shape it down.

Differential reinforcement of other behavior (DRO)—Reinforcing many unspecified but desirable behaviors while not reinforcing a specified but undesirable behavior targeted for reduction.

Direct response-reduction strategy—Reducing behaviors by placing a contingency on them. Contrasted with *indirect response-reduction strategy*.

Discharge report—A report written at the time clients are dismissed from treatment.

Discrete trials—Successive opportunities for producing responses that are clearly separated by brief durations of time.

Discrimination—A behavioral process of establishing different (and appropriate) responses to different stimuli.

Dynamic assessment—Assessment approach that involves both the assessment of a client's skills as well as intervention intervals to identify if and how improvement is achieved during a short interval of intervention.

Dysarthrias—Motor speech disorders caused by damage to the central or peripheral nervous system that affect (among other systems) speech-related muscles.

Dysphagia—Swallowing disorders due to various diseases that affect the swallowing mechanism.

Effectiveness (of treatment)—Assurance that treatment, not some other factor, was responsible for the positive changes documented in a treatment research study.

Electronic data interchange (EDI)—Any electronic transaction that happens between a provider and an agency such as a hospital or third-party payer.

Escape—A behavior that reduces or terminates an aversive event (such as moving away from a dangerous situation) and hence becomes more frequent under similar circumstances. See also *avoidance*.

Escape extinction—Blocking an escape response (such as a child's attempt at leaving the treatment room) to prevent negative reinforcement for it.

Ethnocultural generality—Applicability of treatment procedures across clients of varied ethnocultural backgrounds.

Ethnographic interview—An interview that is directed by the responses a family member provides and that focuses on the client and his or her interactions within the family.

Evoked trial—A structured opportunity to produce a response when the clinician does not model but asks questions or provides other more naturalistic stimuli.

Exclusion time-out—Response-contingent exclusion of a person from a reinforcing environment; the typical effect is response reduction. See also *nonexclusion time-out* and *time-out*.

Exemplar—A response that illustrates a target behavior; all individual target responses the clinician teaches a client.

Experiment—A controlled condition in which a treatment is applied, withheld, reapplied, and so forth to show that the treatment is effective.

Experimental group—The group that receives treatment and hence shows changes. See also *control group*.

Extinction—The procedure of terminating reinforcers for responses to be reduced; the same as ignoring.

Fading—A method of reducing the controlling power of a stimulus while still maintaining the response.

Family Educational Rights and Privacy Act of 1974 (FERPA)—A federal law that protects confidentiality of student education records.

Fixed interval (FI) schedule—An intermittent schedule of reinforcement in which an invariable time duration separates opportunities to earn reinforcers.

Fixed ratio (FR) schedule—An intermittent schedule of reinforcement in which a certain number of responses are required to earn a reinforcer.

Follow-up—Probe or assessment of response maintenance subsequent to dismissal from treatment.

Free and appropriate public education (FAPE)—As outlined in the *Individuals with Disabilities Education Act* (IDEA), public education agencies are required to provide special education and related services that are free of cost, meet the standards of the state educational agency, and are provided in accordance with the *Individualized education program* (IEP).

Functional independence measures (FIMs)—Patient objectives used in medical settings, written with the emphasis on a patient's ability to perform functional tasks (e.g., tell when he or she is ill) with as little assistance as possible.

Functional outcome—Generalized, broader, and socially and personally meaningful effects of treatment; an overall improvement in communication between clients, their families, and their caregivers.

Generality (of treatment)—The applicability of a treatment procedure in a wide range of situations involving other clients and clinicians.

Generalization—Production of clinically established responses evoked by untrained stimuli in the clinical and naturalistic environments with no or typical social reinforcers.

Group design strategy—Methods in which treatment effects are demonstrated by treating individuals in one group and not treating individuals in another group. See also *single-subject strategy*.

Health Insurance Portability and Accountability Act (HIPAA)—A law passed by the U.S. Congress in 1996 to improve the effectiveness and efficiency of health care and protect client confidentiality.

Heterogeneous grouping—A practice used in the schools of grouping together students who exhibit different disorders.

High-probability behaviors—Frequently exhibited behaviors that reinforce less frequently exhibited behaviors.

Homogeneous grouping—A method used in the schools of grouping together students with similar disorders.

Imitation—Learning in which responses take the same form as their stimuli; modeling provides the stimuli.

Implied consent—Approval given without a specific statement of authorization. For example, it may not be necessary for a secretary to obtain written authorization before accessing a client's record, because reviewing client records is typically a part of a secretary's duties.

Improvement—Documented positive changes in a client's behavior under treatment; no guarantee that the treatment was effective.

Incompatible behaviors—Behaviors that cannot be produced simultaneously.

Indirect response-reduction strategy—Reducing certain behaviors by increasing other behaviors; indirect because no contingency is placed on behaviors to be decreased.

Individualized education program (IEP)—Mandated by IDEA, this is a legally binding educational program for students ages 3 to 22 who are determined to have a disability by meeting the federal and state requirements for special education.

Individualized family service plans (IFSPs)—Mandated by IDEA, this is a legally binding educational program for students ages birth through 2 who are determined to be eligible for the plan by meeting federal and state requirements.

Individuals with Disabilities Education Act (IDEA)—Federal law that ensures that children with a disability are provided with a free and appropriate public education that addresses each child's unique needs.

Informative feedback—Information on the performance levels that reinforce behaviors.

Inherent consent in the private interests of the client—Permission to release information assumed when release of information is in the best interest of the client.

Initial response—The first, simplified component of a target response used in shaping.

Instructions—Verbal stimuli that gain control over other persons' actions.

Integrated assessment—Assessment approach that incorporates the advantageous components of the traditional and various alternative assessment methods into one comprehensive assessment procedure.

Interdisciplinary team—A team of different specialists who conduct an assessment independently, but the report is written by all members of the team.

Interfering behaviors—Behaviors that interrupt the treatment process.

Intermediate responses—Responses other than the initial and final that are used in shaping.

Intermittent reinforcement—Reinforcing only some responses or responses produced with some delay between reinforcers.

Intermittent scheduling—A method of scheduling services in public schools; services are offered each week to all students in all schools; contrasted with *block scheduling*.

Intermixed probes—Procedures of assessing generalized production by alternating trained and untrained stimulus items. See also *probes* and *pure probes*.

Interpreters—Those who translate spoken language into signs, gestures, and other forms of nonverbal communication as well as do the opposite.

Isolation time-out—Response-contingent removal of a person from a reinforcing environment and placing him or her in a nonreinforcing environment; the typical effect is the reduction in that response.

Joint Commission on Accreditation of Healthcare Organizations (JCAHO)—A regulatory agency that sets standards for patient care and accredits many hospitals.

Knowledge and Skill Acquisition (KASA) Form—A format approved and required by ASHA to document students' progress in meeting its academic and clinical requirements to enter the profession of speech-language pathology or audiology.

Laryngectomee—Individuals who have had their larynx surgically removed, often because of diseases such as cancer.

Laryngectomy—The surgical procedure of removing the diseased or badly damaged larynx.

Least restrictive environment (LRE)—The more typical educational environment of children without disabilities; as outlined in IDEA, children with disabilities should be educated with children without disabilities.

Lesson plans—Written statements used in school settings to describe treatment planned for one or a few sessions.

License—A state-issued document that allows a qualified person to offer clinical (or other kinds of) services to the public. Unlike ASHA's *Certificate of Clinical Competence*, a license has the authority of a state law.

Maintenance strategy—Extension of treatment to natural settings to help sustain treatment gains over time and across situations.

Manual guidance—Physical guidance provided to shape a response.

Minimal competency core—Typical speech-language skills of children at specified age levels, often described for diverse children.

Mode (of responses)—Manner or method of a response; imitation, oral reading, and conversational speech are different response modes.

Modeled trial—An opportunity to imitate a target response when the clinician models it.

Modeling—The clinician's production of the target response the client is expected to learn; used to teach imitation.

Multidisciplinary team—A group of professionals (and family members) who work together within their respective scopes of practice to determine and provide optimal patient management.

Multi-tiered system of supports (MTSS)—A tiered level of intervention targeting multiple domains (academic, behavioral, social-emotional) to meet the needs of students in a public school setting.

Natural environment—The typical, nonclinical places where people live and interact with others; a term the federal government uses to describe a typical location where children without disabilities can be found (and educated).

Negative reinforcers—Aversive events that are removed, reduced, postponed, or prevented; responses that do these increases in frequency. See also *reinforcers* and *positive reinforcers*.

Neurologist—A physician with specialized training in function and disorders of the nervous system.

Nonexclusion time-out—Response contingent arrangement of a brief duration of time in which all interaction is terminated; the typical effect is response education. See also *exclusion time-out* and *time-out*.

Normative strategy—A method of selecting target behaviors for clients based on age-based norms.

Norms—Averaged (mean) performance of a typical group of persons on a selected test or measure.

Omission training—Reinforcing a person for not exhibiting a certain behavior and reinforcing some other behavior; the same as *Differential reinforcement of other behavior* (DRO).

Operational definitions—Scientific definitions that describe how what is defined is measured.

Orofacial examination—An assessment of the structural and functional integrity of orofacial structures; also known as oral-peripheral examination.

Orthodontist—A dentist with specialized training in dental occlusion.

Otolaryngologist—A physician specializing in evaluation and treatment of disorders of the ear, nose, and throat.

Partial modeling—Withdrawing modeling in gradual steps.

Pediatrician—A physician specializing in the medical care of children.

Physiatrist—A physician trained in rehabilitative medicine.

Population—A relatively large number of individuals with defined characteristics from which a sample is drawn for scientific study. See also *sample*.

Positive reinforcers—Events that, when presented immediately after a response is made, increase the future probability of that response. See also *reinforcers* and *negative reinforcers*.

Post-reinforcement pause—A period of no response after one receives a reinforcer.

Posttests—Measures of behaviors established after completing an experimental teaching program. See also *pretests*.

Preferred practice—Desirable professional activities and practices; often recommended by such professional organizations as ASHA.

Premorbid—A client's state before an incident resulting in a disorder.

Pretests—Measures of behaviors established before starting an experimental teaching program. See also *posttests*.

Primary reinforcers—Unconditioned reinforcers (e.g., food) whose effects do not depend on past learning.

Probes—Procedures to assess generalized production of responses. See also *intermixed probes* and *pure probes*.

Procedures (of treatment)—Technical operations the clinician performs to effect changes in the client behaviors; behaviors of clinicians.

Professional liability—Legal and ethical vulnerability to charges of malpractice; often covered by an insurance policy.

Progress report—A written summary of a client's treatment and its results.

Prompts—Special stimuli that increase the probability of a response; prompts may be verbal or nonverbal.

Prophylaxis treatment targets. Unimpaired (intact) skills that are targeted for daily practice to slow their deterioration in persons with dementia.

Protected health information (PHI)—A term used to describe any health information that is created or received by the health care provider and can or does identify the individual.

Pure probes—Procedures for assessing generalized production with only untrained stimulus items. See also *probes* and *intermixed probes*.

Random assignment—A method of assigning randomly selected subjects to either the experimental or the control group without bias.

Random procedure—A method of selecting subjects from a large population without bias; all subjects in the population have the same chance of being selected.

Reinforce—Strengthen, increase.

Reinforcement—A method of selecting and strengthening behaviors of individuals by arranging consequences under specific stimulus conditions.

Reinforcement withdrawal—Taking reinforcers away to decrease a response (e.g., *response cost* and *time-out*).

Reinforcers—Events that follow behaviors and thereby increase the future probability of those behaviors. See also *positive* and *negative reinforcers*.

Related services—Certain special education services, including speech-language pathology, audiology, psychological, occupational, physical, interpreting, and nursing services.

Reliability—Consistency with which the same event is repeatedly measured.

Replication—Conducting repeated research to show that a given procedure works with different clients, in different settings, and when used by different clinicians.

Response class—A group of responses created by the same or similar contingencies; functionally but not necessarily structurally similar responses.

Response cost—Response-contingent withdrawal of reinforcers that decreases those responses.

Response to intervention (RtI)—A multi-tiered, systematic, data-driven intervention system in the public school setting that falls within the *Multi-tiered system of supports* (MTSS) model.

Sample—A smaller number of individuals selected from a larger population. See also *population*.

Satiation—Temporary termination of a drive or need because it has been satisfied.

Schedules of reinforcement—Different patterns of reinforcement that generate different patterns of responses.

Scope of practice—Professional activities that are approved by virtue of training, awarded license, or earned certification and credentials. Professionals cannot perform activities that are outside the scope of practice.

Secondary reinforcers—Conditioned reinforcers whose effects depend on past learning (e.g., verbal praise).

Self-control—Behaviors that monitor other behaviors of the same person.

Shaping—A method of teaching nonexistent responses that are not imitated. The responses are simplified and taught in an ascending sequence. Also known as successive approximations.

Simultaneous interpreting—The interpreter translates as the individual talks.

Single-subject strategy—Methods of demonstrating treatment effects by showing contrasts between conditions of no treatment, treatment, withdrawal of treatment, and other control procedures when all subjects are treated. See also *group design strategy*.

SOAP notes—Brief progress notes frequently written in hospitals; acronym for subjective, objective, assessment, plan.

Social reinforcers—A variety of conditioned reinforcers that include verbal praise.

Speech-language pathology aides—Individuals with a bachelor's degree, often in speech-language pathology who assist speech-language pathologists (SLPs) in some public schools.

Speech-language pathology assistants (SLPAs)—Those who have an associate degree and restricted coursework and practical experience in speech-language pathology and perform services assigned and supervised by a certified and licensed speech-language pathologist.

Stuttering—A disorder of fluency characterized by excessive amounts of dysfluencies or excessive duration of dysfluencies, both often associated with such additional features as muscular tension, avoidance of speaking situation, and negative emotions associated with speech and speaking situations.

Swallowing disorders—The same as *dysphagia*.

Target behavior—Behavior a client is taught.

Telepractice—Clinical practice from remote sites using the Internet and special computer applications.

Terminal response—The final response targeted in shaping.

Time-out (TO)—A brief period of time when reinforcers are terminated for a response, typically causing its decrease. See also *exclusion time-out* and *nonexclusion time-out*.

Tokens—Objects that are earned during treatment and exchanged later for backup reinforcers.

Topography—The form or shape of behaviors; how behaviors sound, feel, or appear.

Transdisciplinary team—A team of different professionals who observe and assess individuals together.

Translators—Those who transform spoken or written material from one language into another.

Transliterators—Those who mouth the spoken words or sign words in the same order as spoken for the benefit of Deaf persons.

Treatment—In communicative disorders, it is the management of contingent relations between antecedents, responses, and consequences; it is a rearrangement of communicative relationships between a speaker and his or her listener.

Treatment plan—A report that describes short and long-term goals and the procedures used to obtain those goals.

Trial—A structured opportunity to produce a response.

Universal health care precautions—Common procedures that help prevent or minimize the changes of potential infections while working with patients and clients.

Validity—The degree to which a measuring instrument measures what it purports to measure.

Variable interval (VI) schedule—An intermittent reinforcement schedule in which the time duration between reinforcers is varied around an average.

Variable ratio (VR) schedule—An intermittent reinforcement schedule in which the number of responses needed to earn a reinforcer is varied around an average.

Verbal stimulus generalization—Production of unreinforced responses when untrained verbal stimuli are presented.

Videofluorographic evaluation—An objective procedure in which the client's swallowing mechanism is recorded on a video.

INDEX

Benchmarks, in IEP goals, 193
Bias, writing without, 182–185, 201
Bilingual
  children, 163
  speech-language pathologists,
    163–164
Biofeedback, 310
Blood, health precautions for, 84,
  114–115
Board of Ethics, ASHA, 92, 102–103
Board of Examiners in Speech-
  Language Pathology and
  Audiology, 10
Board-certified behavior analyst
  (BCBA), 77
Booster treatment, 187, 378–382

C
Case history, 149
  counting clock hours spent on
    taking, 33
  in diagnostic report writing,
    158–159
  form for, 150
  in integrated assessment, 167
  sources of, 28
Case law, 59
Caseload vs. workload, 55, 57
Centers for Disease Control and
  Prevention (CDC), 113–114
Cerebral palsy, 57, 67, 220, 241, 314
Certificate of Clinical Competence.
  (CCC), 13, 94, 206
  and clinical supervisors in
    schools, 50
  eligibility for, 13
Child abuse, suspected, 108–111
  emotional maltreatment signs of, 111
  general signs of, 109
  neglect signs of, 110
  parent or caregiver signs of, 111
  physical abuse signs of, 110
  reporting to the supervisor, 111
  sexual abuse signs of, 110
Client bill of rights, 117–118

Client confidentiality, 97–100, 105
  in FERPA, 36
  guidelines to ensure, 98–100
  in HIPAA, 36, 98
  internet communication and, 100
  protected health information and,
    106
Client files, content and maintenance,
  205–206
Client management skills, 128–129
Client-specific approach to target
  selection, 221
Client-specific assessments, 166
Clinic policies and procedures,
  135–136
Clinic supplies, materials, and
  equipment, 83–85
Clinical certification by ASHA, 13–18
  clinical fellowship year, completion
    for, 15–16
  degree requirement for, 14
  passing the Praxis examination for, 15
  maintenance requirement of, 17–18
  required knowledge for, 14–15
Clinical decisions
  criteria for advancing treatment,
    316–20
  supervisor approval of, 103
Clinical Fellowship, 15–16
Clinical internships, 75–76
Clinical interview, 149–150
Clinical observation, 22–26
  clock hour requirements of, 22
  questions to answer after, 23–24
  reports, 26
  responsibilities of student observers
    in, 24–26
  supervision requirements of, 23
Clinical practicum, 4–42
  administrative procedures for, 82–83
  clinical observation in, 22–26
  clock hours required, 27,
  common sites for, 46–47
  at hospitals, 60–64
  internships, 75–76